THE PRESIDENT'S CALL

Pitt Series in Policy and
Institutional Studies

Bert A. Rockman, *Editor*

THE
PRESIDENT'S
CALL

◦〜◦

*Executive Leadership
from FDR to George Bush*

Judith E. Michaels

*For Ed —
With all
good wishes —
Judith,
Mays 2008*

UNIVERSITY OF PITTSBURGH PRESS

Published by the University of Pittsburgh Press, Pittsburgh, Pa.
15261
Copyright © 1997, University of Pittsburgh Press
All rights reserved
Manufactured in the United States of America
Printed on acid-free paper
10 9 8 7 6 5 4 3 2 1

Library of Congress Cataloging-in-Publication Data

Michaels, Judith E., 1948–
        The president's call : executive leadership from FDR to George
Bush / Judith E. Michaels.
            p.   cm. — (Pitt series in policy and institutional studies)
        Includes bibliographical references (p.   ) and index.
        ISBN 0-8229-3977-0 (cloth : acid-free paper). —
ISBN 0-8229-5628-4 (pbk. : acid-free paper)
        1. United States—Officials and employees—Selection and appoint-
ment—History—20th century. 2. Government executives—Selection
and appointment—United States—History—20th century. 3. Presidents—United States—History—20th century. 4. United States—
Politics and government—1933–1945. 5. United States—Politics and
government—1945–1989. 6. United States—government—1989–1993.
I. Title.   II. Series.
JK731.M53   1997   97-4562
352.3′9′0973—dc21

A CIP catalog record for this book is available from the
British Library.

Contents

Tables

Acknowledgments

The number of Senate-confirmed political appointees (PASs) who took the time to complete the Bush PAS Survey, sent notes of apology if they were late in returning it, called me for clarification, or signed their names indicating a willingness to be interviewed (35 percent of the respondents) was most heartening. Clearly, this project could not have been completed without their cooperation and I extend to them my most sincere thanks.

I am especially indebted to the PASs who allowed themselves to be interviewed in connection with this research. They each gave me as much as an hour and a half of uninterrupted time and were, to a person, gracious, attentive, and forthcoming. Some requested anonymity or asked that parts of the interview be kept off the record, but most felt able to be open and were willing to be quoted by name. Those who did not want direct attribution often provided very useful insights into "behind the scenes" politics.

That all these PASs, at the highest levels of government and living under the stress of incredible responsibilities and time pressures, were so candid and accessible was, to me, a reassuring indication of the health of our nation's system of governance. They made a significant contribution to this study and are listed by name, title, executive level, and agency in appendix 5.

Thanks are due also to the many persons (careerists, congressional staff, appointees, and others) in various agencies who assisted in this study, from its initial conception to survey design, pretest, and postsurvey interviews. They provided context and background, as well as many useful ideas for the PAS Survey and follow-up interview questions. These individuals are listed in appendices 3, 4, and 6.

Individuals such as James Pfiffner at George Mason University, Gail Johnson at Old Dominion University, John Trattner at the Council on Excellence and Government, and Mark Abramson at Leadership Inc. were also helpful in the early stages. I especially thank the draft reviewers, Jim Pfiffner and Carolyn Ban, at the University of Pittsburgh, who offered perceptive and very helpful criticism that did much to shape the final form of this book. To Jim, gracious and insightful, I owe particular thanks.

The General Accounting Office, through its Doctoral Research Fellowship, made possible the survey and access to the political labyrinth that is Washington, as well as the year I spent in residence there. Thanks to its fellowship staff director, Ken Hunter, and to Bernie Ungar and his Group within GAO's General Government Division, especially Dick Caradine, Helen Fauntleroy, Bill Trancucci, and, in the Design Methodology Technical Assistance Group, Rudy Chatlos and Marge Schauer, who worked with me to create the survey instrument. Thanks also to George Quinn and DeLois Richardson, who did the typing and data input for the survey.

Special appreciation is due Roger Sperry and the National Academy of Public Administration. They graciously allowed me to adapt many of the questions from their 1984 study of presidential appointees and were a valuable source of information in the survey's initial phases. Thanks also to Julie Dolan for her work on the index for this book.

This book is based on my doctoral dissertation at the University of Delaware, College of Urban Affairs and Public Policy. My dissertation committee members, Jeffrey Raffel, Timothy Barnekov, and Deborah Auger were very supportive, asked good, if not always easy, questions, and made practical suggestions along the way. For these contributions, I am most appreciative. To my committee chair and advisor, Mark Huddleston, I owe special acknowledgment for his stamina, confidence in me, friendship, openness, and wise counsel. He was a steady source of encouragement and support, a true mentor and intellectual colleague. I remain in his debt.

THE PRESIDENT'S CALL

1

Introduction

Presidents, more than anyone else, are judged by the company they keep. The appointees who head and administer the executive branch's cabinet agencies exist not only to carry out the policy of the occupant of the White House, they also reflect back distinction or disgrace on that occupant. An incompetent or unqualified secretary of the Department of Energy, for example, or a corrupt secretary of the Department of Housing and Urban Development exposes the whole administration to intense scrutiny from an insatiable press and ridicule from television and radio talk show hosts. A poor appointee anywhere in the bureaucratic hierarchy can cast a shadow over the entire presidency. Conversely, creative and politically astute cabinet secretaries reflect a president in clear charge of the nation; they inspire confidence in the entire administration.

Presidents' choices tell the country who and what its leader is, and speak volumes about his or her character, credibility, and suitability for the job. Therefore, *who* these choices are is of great moment in any president's administration and consequently to the nation it serves. This book examines the Senate-confirmed presidential appointees (PASs) of one cohort of appointees, that of the George Bush administration. It does so within the larger context of the institution of presidential appointments in the modern era to analyze what his choices disclose about this president, his administration, and the institution. Of particular interest is how Bush's PASs compare with those of his predecessor, Ronald Reagan.

1

Political appointees head a federal workforce of some two million people in the civilian labor force, of whom only 537 (the president, vice president, and members of Congress) are chosen by election. The rest serve by virtue of civil service or political appointment and are divided into three branches and two camps that, at the highest levels of government bureaucracy, can be competitive as often as complementary. The larger camp is composed of career employees in the civil service or other comparable categories. The smaller camp is composed of nearly four thousand full-time and sixteen hundred part-time appointees, persons appointed by the president or his surrogates to oversee the career workforce.

These political appointees, the focus of this book, are commonly called "in-and-outers," "short-timers," or "short-termers." They come and go with the current administration and as an institution are deeply rooted in the nation's history:

> From the earliest days of the United States as a nation, the highest-ranking administrators of the federal government have been drawn largely from a category of people known in federal parlance as "in-and-outers," individuals for whom government service is neither a profession nor a career. No other nation relies so heavily on noncareer personnel for the management of its government. In its breadth and importance, the in-and-outer system of leadership is uniquely American. (Mackenzie 1987, xiii)

Political appointments and appointees have been a source of controversy in American government since nearly the founding of the Republic. Numerous issues have arisen and continue to arise about this in-and-outer, or short-termer, system and the political leaders it produces to serve in the federal government. Ongoing questions pertain to: their number and placement; their qualifications; their relations with the White House, the Congress, high-level political executives in other executive agencies, and senior career executives; their tenure in office; and the appointment and confirmation process by which they come to hold office.

While the development of the civil service merit system in the late nineteenth century established a career counterbalance to political appointments, the growing number of appointees and their infiltration into the bureaucracy not only continued, it accelerated and deepened, particularly with the advent of the modern presidency in the administration of Franklin Delano Roosevelt.[1] Political appointees of all types proliferated with the expansion of government wrought by FDR's New Deal (see table 1.1 for outline of PAS structure).

Immediately below the PASs in the political food chain are the members of the Senior Executive Service (SES), the top-level bureaucrats whose ranks are 10 percent (non-Senate-confirmed) political appointees and 90 percent careerists. The civil service with grades fifteen and below comprises the bulk of the career bureaucracy below the SES, but within the civil service there is a special class of political appointees, the Schedule Cs, who are appointed to ranks nine through fifteen and fill whatever activity their political superiors devise, from chauffeur to personal secretary or assistant. They occupy positions of a confidential, non–policy-making nature.

Concomitant with the growth and filtration of appointees down the ranks of the bureaucracy, questions arose about the quality and qualifications of the president's people. Part of the difficulty in addressing these is-

Table 1.1. PAS Executive Level Positions

Executive Level	Position
EL 1	Cabinet secretaries, agency chiefs, and a few others, such as the director of the Office of Management and Budget and the U.S. trade representative
EL 2	Deputy directors of cabinet agencies, heads of major noncabinet bureaus, such as NASA, the Office of Personnel Management, the FBI, the Federal Emergency Management Administration, the chair of the Federal Reserve Board, members of some independent regulatory commissions (IRCs), and heads of some offices in the Executive Office of the President, such as the Office of Technology Policy and the Council of Economic Advisers
EL 3	Agency undersecretaries, members of IRCs whose chairs are 2s, and heads of other agencies, such as the Federal Maritime Commission, the Interstate Commerce Commission, the Federal Trade Commission, the General Services Administration, and the Peace Corps
EL 4	Assistant secretaries and administrators of major units in the cabinet agencies, inspectors general, general counsels, deputy directors whose boss is a 3 or commissioners whose chair is a 3, and heads of specialized agencies such as the Federal Labor Relations Board, the U.S. Commission on Civil Rights, the Selective Service Administration, and the Panama Canal Commission
EL 5	Deputies to 4s, directors of smaller agencies or large departments, such as the Asian Development Bank and the Smithsonian Astrophysical Observatory, assistant secretaries, and general counsels in the smaller agencies

sues is what might be termed a knowledge gap about the appointees themselves. Who are they? From whence do they come? Why do they choose to respond to their president's call to serve in what can be a demanding and thankless task?

Meanwhile, a certain conventional wisdom has developed that posits the typical appointee as a "political hack," someone who has a political job for which even the most charitable person would not consider him or her qualified. Usually, persons so labeled are large contributors to or loyal workers in the party, such as fourth-level campaign workers (or their sons and daughters), who are placed in a top-level position in the administration. Additionally, they are thought to possess limited knowledge of or commitment to government and to be self-aggrandizing, agenda-driven ideologues, more committed to their own goals than to the competent administration of their agency. This "wisdom" regarding political appointees has been sliding on a mostly downhill trajectory since FDR's administration, coinciding with government's growth and with the increased number and deeper placement of political appointees that has accompanied the modern presidency.

While appointees have been used for more obviously political strategies since FDR's New Deal, it took Ronald Reagan to mobilize political appointees into a full-blown frontal assault force on the very government they served, that government on which Reagan blamed many of the country's problems. His "bureaucrat bashing" was the rallying cry of many of his political appointees who were appointed, in significant cases, to dismantle the very programs they were named to head. Further, the near-religious fervor with which the Reaganites embraced the business lobby and sought to "get government off its back" led the president to appoint regulators from the industries they were charged to regulate, particularly at the Environmental Protection Agency (EPA) and the Department of Housing and Urban Development (HUD). Reagan's people might fairly be termed emotional (as well as virtual) short-termers because so many were actively hostile to that which they served. Simply put, their hearts were not in it.

According to many, the defining characteristics of the Reagan political appointees were personal loyalty to the president, passing a political litmus test on abortion (against), and sizeable contributions to the Republican party. Prominent features demonstrated by members of this group included little or no previous government experience, frequent turnover, the dominance of an aggressive political agenda over general administrative concern or competence, conflict of interest, and often aggressive, sometimes personal hostility toward the careerists in the bureaucracy. Finally, Reagan's appointees included a large number of political appointees eventually under criminal indictment, some of whom were convicted and served time in prison. It all added up to the "sleaze factor."

These characteristics fed the conventional wisdom about political appointees and led to a certain disdain for them that was confirmed by the postadministration revelations of high-level wrongdoing by several Reagan appointees long after he left office. Specifically, the scandals in Reagan's Department of Housing and Urban Development and unresolved questions about the role of President Reagan and then–Vice President Bush in the Iran-Contra arms deal continued to tarnish the integrity and plague the credibility of the Reagan and Bush administrations.

With the election of George Bush in 1988, there were hopes that the credibility of political appointees would be elevated beyond that of "rich party hacks being rewarded for loyalty," as cocktail chatter and political punditry would have it. In contrast to Reagan, Bush stressed the value of public service and public servants, attempting to restore respect for both. He also moved to screen political appointees more carefully in order to assure both competence and absence of scandal. The watchword of this guarded administration, according to inside observers, was "make no mistakes."

To what extent, then, was George Bush successful in reversing the downward trend of the conventional wisdom by upgrading the image of high-level political (presidential) appointees? Were his appointees emotional as well as virtual short-termers, or did they have a larger commitment to government and its smooth running? Further, what is the future of the institution of PASs in the modern era?

To answer these questions a survey of the full-time Bush PASs in the executive branch was conducted. Sponsored by the General Accounting Office, the Bush PAS Survey was mailed to the entire universe of PASs at their homes late in the administration.[2] There was one follow-up mailing. The overall response rate was 38.4 percent, with some 35 percent of the respondents volunteering for follow-up interviews. Some twenty-eight PASs were then interviewed in their offices in one-on-one confidential interviews that lasted from an hour to an hour and a half. Intended to add color and flesh to the Bush PAS Survey, the interviews helped round out the picture of this group and contributed additional data to the study. Twenty-three congressional staff, careerists, and former PASs were also interviewed to help complete the picture.

Beyond an examination of the institution of presidential appointments, this book presents a composite picture of the Bush PASs themselves. It delineates four major areas of inquiry that are grounded in the empirical study of and personal interviews with the PASs: PASs' personal identity; their professional backgrounds and qualifications; intrabureaucratic issues and interbureaucratic issues.

PASs' Identity

In analyzing the Bush presidential appointees, the first issue is that of identity. Simply put, who were the people at the highest levels of government? How did they attain their positions? What were their general political leanings and party affiliations? What was their gender and racial/ethnic mix? What kinds of sacrifices did they make to accept a PAS position? What kinds of rewards did they reap?

The most recent comprehensive study of PAS executives was conducted during the second Reagan administration by the National Academy of Political Administration in 1985. It surveyed PASs who had served as far back as 1964 but encompassed relatively few current PAS appointees. Therefore, a picture of PAS executives through the Bush administration is lacking. This work fills the information gap by providing an analysis of the Bush administration's PAS workforce.

PASs' Professional Background and Qualifications

The second issue is the qualifications of the PASs. What kinds of professional background and experience did the Bush appointees offer? What was their knowledge of government and its workings? As mentioned, the conventional wisdom emanating from the Reagan era was that appointees had limited knowledge of and experience in government.[3] The temporary and short-term nature of political appointments means that those with few qualifications and little experience in government of necessity spend most of their limited time in office learning the ropes, "two years of on-the-job training," as one PAS termed it. Then they (theoretically) move on to more lucrative jobs outside government, using their government service as a useful line on their resume and their government contacts as a bargaining chip with prospective employers. To what extent was this true of the Bush appointees? Were they also emotional short-termers, or did they have a more long-term commitment to government service? Where would they go after their current PAS service?

Intrabureaucratic Issues

The third issue examined here is the relationship between political and career executives. What were PASs' sense of job satisfaction and feelings about working in government and their relations with career executives? The general consensus is that there is a long history of poor relations between political and career executives in the federal service, fueled by politicians' hostility toward "the entrenched bureaucracy." This history found its modest genesis in the modern activist presidency of Franklin Delano Roosevelt, took a great leap forward under Dwight D. Eisenhower, and stalled until Nixon revitalized it. From Nixon, the old hostility accelerated to its apex in the administration of Ronald Reagan, when poor political-career relations were cemented in his bureaucrat-bashing, "government-is-the-problem" mantra.

The Bush administration claimed that its political-career relations were much improved over those of the Reagan era. To what extent, then, was the time-tested, Reagan-perfected, bureaucrat-bashing mentality characteristic of the Bush appointees? How did the Bush PASs feel about and relate to the career executives with whom they worked? Were they more interested in managing their agencies well or in promoting a particular political agenda? To what extent was their self-reported priority of sound agency management affirmed by the careerists?

A related area of inquiry is PAS job satisfaction. What kinds of satisfaction did PASs derive from their job? In other words, were the Republicans, traditionally antigovernment, actually *enjoying* the business of running the government after twelve years of controlling the executive branch? Further, how did PASs assess their own level of work-related stress?

Interbureaucratic Issues

A final question concerns the reputed insularity of these political policy actors. How did PASs' operate within the larger political context? Did federal statecraft in the Reagan-Bush era still constitute a government of strangers, each isolated in her or his own village/agency, as Heclo asserted? Or did the long Republican dominance of the executive branch lead instead to a government of colleagues with a shared sense of purpose? Did facing the Democratic-controlled Congress and negotiating the bureaucratic labyrinth that is Washington create solidarity among the PASs?

This book moves from the general to the specific to address these four issues. Chapter 2 establishes the overall political and bureaucratic context in which high-level federal political appointees work. It sets the stage for analysis of interbureaucratic issues by discussing the constitutional separation of powers, the politics/administration dichotomy, and the administrative state. The chapter then examines the development and use of the logical extension of the administrative state, the administrative presidency, as practiced by Richard Nixon and Ronald Reagan, its most dedicated practitioners.

Chapter 3 discusses the fruits of this style of presidential leadership, the centralized presidency and politicization of the bureaucracy. It uses as examples the politicization of the budget and personnel processes in the Office of Management and Budget and in the Office of Personnel Management.

Chapter 4 discusses the approach toward appointments used by presidents in the modern era, the growing number of political appointments, and the larger ramifications of this spoils system.

Chapter 5 discusses qualifications issues via the appointment and confirmation process. It analyzes the benefits and risks of this appointment, or short-termer, system, as well as issues of tenure, PASs' general qualifications, and the costs and benefits of PAS success.

Chapter 6 examines intrabureaucratic issues primarily from the PAS perspective, with particular focus on political-career relations. It looks at the different roles assigned each group and how the inevitable conflict between them is played out, as well as ways in which the politicization of the personnel process affects their relationships. It then surveys various models of political-career relations, from the metaphors of war to the metaphors of appeasement, and concludes with the importance of realistic, pragmatic association between the two camps of federal executives.

Chapter 7 discusses the results of the Bush PAS Survey in terms of identity and qualifications. It presents the composite personal and demographic picture of the PASs with data about their age, gender, race, educational background, executive level, salary, and political party affiliation. It also provides the composite professional picture of those in the Bush PAS workforce, examining their background and qualifications and the sectors in which they have worked (public, private, or nonprofit), their previous level of responsibility for personnel and budget, and their commitment to government service.

Additionally, Chapter 7 compares the Bush and Reagan PASs and revisits the conventional wisdom about political appointees and the extent to which George Bush was successful in upgrading the public image of presidential appointees.

Chapter 8 addresses the intrabureaucratic issues. It analyzes the Bush PASs' relations with their political colleagues and career subordinates within their own agency, examining in particular issues of job satisfaction and stress (both agency and personal). It also defines George Bush's model of political-career relations as a public service model grounded in competent comity.

Chapter 9 examines the larger context of interbureaucratic relations, beginning with PASs' relations with the White House and the Congress. It then examines ways the Bush PASs related to one another within and across executive agencies. It revisits the theory of village-like isolation of PASs and how this was overcome in twelve years of Republican lease on the White House.

Chapter 10 offers advice to future PASs from the Bush PASs, conclusions from this study, and implications for the ongoing institution of presidential appointments in the federal government. It also suggests areas of future study regarding the appointment system and its products, the PASs.

The appendices discuss the methodologies employed in the study of the Bush PASs and reprint the Bush PAS Survey with the raw response data. They also detail the name, title, executive level or designation, and agency of those interviewed in conjunction with this project and the questions addressed in the confidential interviews with the PASs and others.

2

⚭

Presidential Appointees in the Modern Era: Political and Bureaucratic Context

Franklin Delano Roosevelt inaugurated the modern presidency that heralded an unbroken trend toward centralization of the institution of the presidency. This centralization featured control over a growing government bureaucracy exercised by an expanding White House bureaucracy. Increasing demands on modern government produced the administrative state and an expanded federal bureaucracy in both the political and career camps to meet those demands.

Beyond merely moving in tandem with the growth of government, the presidency in this era has evolved into an administrative force of its own whose directors seek greater control over government's bureaucracy for increased command of both budget and policy. The centralized presidency that resulted from this political growth has both positive and negative ramifications for the efficient and effective governance of the nation.

Focused on interbureaucratic issues, this chapter sets out the background political and bureaucratic contexts in which modern governance occurs. It discusses the role of the Congress in the bureaucratic dance, the constitutional separation of powers, the politics/administration dichotomy, and the administrative state. It looks at the benefits and costs of the administrative presidency, particularly as practiced by Richard Nixon and Ronald Reagan (its prime exemplars), and the ongoing trend toward centralizing and bureaucratizing the presidency.

Relations Between the Executive and Legislative Branches

Just as the nation's history impacts the role of the bureaucracy, relations between the executive agencies and the Congress are not unaffected by that same history. As some have noted, the Revolutionary War, with its battle cry of "No taxation without representation!" was, in essence, a revolt against the executive, as embodied in George III's colonial officers. The new nation's constitution reflected this anti-executive bias in the pride of place it gave to the Congress, the closest thing to the Continental Congress. The legislative branch was allotted far more attention as to its powers, rules, and duties than was the executive branch.

Furthermore, the Constitution was "conspicuously mute" on the subject of administration of the government's bureaucracy:

> The Constitution makes no mention of "administration" or "management" and refers sparingly to "executing the laws." . . . The Constitutional Framers were not necessarily against strong, efficient management, although suspicion of British executive excesses still ran strong. [However,] the role of administration was perceived differently at a time when members of Congress outnumbered the entire executive branch workforce in Washington. Constitutional machinery was designed for its time, before the onslaught of modernizing and bureaucratizing forces. (Garnett 1987, 35–36)

Prior to the adoption of the Constitution, the Continental Congress carried total responsibility for executive, judicial, and legislative functions for the new union. That pattern was carried into the creation of the first five federal departments: in 1789 the Congress stipulated in great detail the functions of each agency and the positions and salaries therein. From the beginning, then, Congress has been involved in the implementation, as well as the formulation, of public policy (NAPA 1992, 20).

This history means that the Congress today continues to feel a responsibility to ensure the proper functioning of the executive agencies, particularly the Treasury Department, to which it has long-standing ties, thanks to its responsibility for the purse. The Constitution established a "system of separate institutions sharing powers—a design intended to prevent tyranny, protect liberty, and promote good government" (ibid., 21).

There can, of course, be no absolute separation of powers because the executive branch and the Congress overlap in function and responsibility. As discussed above, the paired doctrines of the separation of powers and the system of checks and balances are the key principles in the ongoing debate between the executive and the legislative branches. Congress is accused of micromanagement (what one observer defines as "mucking with the petty details of policy execution") by the very branch over which it is called to exercise vigilant oversight (ibid., 24).

There are, certainly, historical reasons for legislative-executive conflict. While Congress granted broad discretionary powers to the executive agencies in order to increase their flexibility, an unintended consequence of that grant was that successive presidents could bend the laws to serve their values and policy goals through their control of the bureaucracy. These discretionary powers allow

> presidents to make dramatic changes in public policy when they take office without having to undertake the difficult task of persuading Congress to repeal or amend existing statutes. President Reagan demonstrated the importance of this power in 1987 when he promulgated new and much more restrictive rules governing federal funding for family planning clinics so as to prevent information on abortion from being dispensed at these offices. (Rourke 1991b, 125)

"Put another way, politics, policymaking, and policy implementation have become inseparable" in the collapse of the separation of powers (NAPA 1988, 2). This guarantees that the president and the Congress will be locked in a power struggle that is both deep-seated and perpetual.

A 1992 NAPA case study of congressional interventions indicates the conundrum in which Congress finds itself when it seeks to do the work of the bureaucracy without access to its resources. Congress goes this route when it

> perceives it has little choice but to do so because executive branch difficulties—delays, cost inefficiency, program breakdown, executive refusal to adhere to congressional directives, even outright management failures and deceit—all but impel it to intervene at the administrative level. [However], Congress does not have and cannot create the resources to intervene effectively as an administrative manager across the enormous range of governmental programs. Yet increased congressional interventions are unavoidable unless the executive branch: 1. fulfills its responsibilities with renewed determination, vigor, and management skill consistent with congressional mandates and 2. reorganizes and upgrades its managerial systems accordingly. (NAPA 1992, 9)

While the NAPA study finds that "direct congressional intervention in policy administration is a forceful lever for change yielding significant results," there are costs to such a strategy. Congress, by paying too much attention to administrative and implementational detail, undercuts its own capacity for effective oversight. Bureaucratic accountability then suffers as an overburdened Congress focuses on details rather than on broad policy issues (ibid., 6, 9).

Because presidents and their appointees operate in a limited time frame they are more inclined to take short cuts (of sometimes dubious legality, or even outright illegality, e.g., Watergate, Irangate) and less inclined to develop norms of cooperation. However, if they follow their short-term interests in the name of policy advancement, they are more likely to provoke congressional retaliation, as transpired in the Nixon era. What happens then, of course, is that presidents have incentives to take more short cuts or violate laws to circumvent congressional response, as occurred in the Reagan administration's Iran-Contra scandal, a prime example of policy desires driven by a short time frame overcoming institutional integrity.

Because the bureaucracy and the Congress have no choice but somehow to work together, NAPA calls for a long-term commitment to reforming the relations between these two branches of government: a new era of bridge-building between the two sides of divided government to reduce tensions and improve the operation of government.

Some also look to the development of new norms of cooperative behavior as a way to move the American system of governance beyond paralyzing competition. In order to avoid congressional and judicial backlash they urge presidents to cast their command and control net more narrowly in order to "influence a government that they only partially head and which has an executive apparatus that is not under their exclusive control" (Aberbach and Rockman 1988, 611).

Bureaucratic Legitimacy, the Separation of Powers, the Politics/Administration Dichotomy, and the Administrative State

The issues surrounding the roles and relations of the PASs within the bureaucracy are many, varied, and complex. They spring in part from the ambiguous role of the bureaucracy itself and, in part, from the de jure and de facto aspects of its context. On the one hand, the bureaucracy is not identified, per se, in the Constitution of the United States, and so lacks the automatic de jure legitimacy of the legislative, executive, and judicial branches. On the other hand, history has played a key role as the bureaucracy has grown and developed, along with the nation, to meet the increasing demands placed on the government by the citizenry. Its very existence and size, not to mention its essential place in modern government, give the bureaucracy a de facto, if sometimes begrudged, legitimacy.

In fact, the omnipresence and power of the bureaucracy in American life provides grounds for more-than-grudging acceptance of the legitimacy of the nation's permanent government:

> Knowingly or not, Americans are governed by a modern administrative state which has developed alongside and within constitutional democracy. People's lives, fortunes, and futures are today decided by both the Constitution and an administrative state. Grafting this "unwritten constitution" into our written document (remember, the U.S. Constitution says nothing about bureaucracy, budgets, personnel rule, civil service, or legislative oversight, and it does not use even the term, "executive branch") was a substantial accomplishment, perhaps matching some of the brilliant achievements of the Philadelphia Convention in 1787. (Stillman 1987, 6)

The constitutional separation of powers comes from the founders' desire "to create a system that would give each branch a motive and a means for preventing abuses or misguided action by another. This would prevent the 'accumulation of all powers, legislative, executive, and judiciary, in the same hands'" (Rosenbloom 1983, 224).

This separation fostered the development of the theory of the politics/administration dichotomy when, late in the nineteenth century, with Congress ascendant and problems with the patronage system readily apparent, a growing reform movement sought to end corruption by strengthening the executive. Another group of reformers sought to strengthen the legislative branch to the same end. The politics/administration dichotomy, with its simplistic "division . . . between deciding and executing," provided the answer to the constitutional "ambivalence in the status and direction of American public administration" and united the two groups of reformers in a compromise position. "The dichotomy in its less rigid form appeared as an innovative and promising development. Even a crude version could provide some support for the emergence of the administrative state" (O'Toole 1987, 18).

The Pendleton Act of 1883 created the civil service and enshrined competition-based merit in the American personnel system. It also strengthened the separation of powers and furthered the development of the administrative state through its implicit support for the politics/administration dichotomy. The act's commission mechanism insulated "the civil service and various aspects of its administration from the overtly political actors in government; the Pendleton Act erected a kind of politics/administration border" (ibid.). It also distinguished positions related to government careers from strictly political appointments. It allowed the Congress and the executive to take a step back from the treacherous shoals of patronage and at the same time created "'the first institutional recognition of the president' as 'the active head of the administrative system.' The Pendleton Act was a momentous innovation in the American system of governance because it simultaneously strengthened executive leadership, legitimized neutral competence as the goal of the civil service, and gave a boost to the separation of powers" (O'Toole 1987, 19–20).

The Hatch Acts of 1939 and 1940 served to augment the original Pendleton Act's goal of creating a neutral civil service by prohibiting permanent federal employees from engaging in certain partisan activities, such as running for party office, some campaign activities, and fund-raising. They also insulated them from political pressure by forbidding political superiors to "entice or coerce partisan support from the bureaucracy." While maligned and altered several times since their inception and in large measure repealed in 1994, the acts "represent quite clearly an American effort to accommodate the neutrality goal, embraced by the politics/administration dichotomy, in a system of party competition, fragmentation, and separation of powers" (ibid., 22).

However, the separation of powers also created a "tendency toward inaction," because the checks and balances designed to keep the three branches of government coequal "also serve(d) as a check on popular political passions," making the government responsive to issues of broad agreement among the electorate, but only in the long run (Rosenbloom 1983, 224). In the short run, this form of government tends toward "inertia and inflexibility." To counter this tendency, the nation has gradually developed a more flexible "administrative state" to respond as needs arise and circumstances change. An unintended consequence of this is that the powers have become more merged than separated in an institutional bureaucracy that "makes rules (legislation), implements these rules (an executive function), and adjudicates questions concerning their application and execution (a judicial function). [Thus is seen] the collapsing of the separation of powers" (ibid., 224–25).

With the collapse of the separation of powers has come the virtual collapse of the formal politics/administration dichotomy. O'Toole's perceptive insight is that "focusing on the separation of powers in the national government's structure neglects the important reality of sharing" of powers that goes on between the executive and legislative branches. The existence and operation of numerous regulatory agencies demonstrate the reality of powers shared on the current governance landscape (O'Toole 1987, 23).

Exercising Power in the Administrative Presidency

Lacking unambiguous constitutional authority to manage the administrative state, what resources are at a president's command to do so? Advocates of the strong presidency lament the president's lack of real command power to master the "unruly beast" that is his or her own bureaucracy: "The most difficult task most presidents face is trying to sell their programs—not to Congress but to the bureaucracy. This is the case even when an agency is headed by an official selected by the president" (Waterman 1989, 20).

There are, however, three well-worn strategies—legislative, judicial, and administrative—that presidents can use to promote their policy objectives both inside and outside their administration. A legislative strategy focuses on passage of favorable legislation and involves close work with congressional leaders. A judicial strategy focuses on the selection of judges who are supportive of administration goals, and it seeks heightened court activity on behalf of policy goals. An administrative strategy looks to political appointees to shape the bureaucracy so that policy goals are paramount (Nathan 1986, 125).

Richard Nathan was once in Richard Nixon's employ and, by his own admission, "no shy flower" when it came to advocating a strong president. He represents those who think it "appropriate and, in fact, desirable in our governmental system for political appointees to be involved in administrative processes." Because the agencies they head are legally empowered to create, implement, and adjudicate regulation, the PASs have significant power to set direction and tone for their agency. The responsive competence embodied in the president's own appointees is expected to dominate and lead the careerists' neutral competence to govern in accord with the president's agenda (Nathan 1985, 376–77).[1]

Nixon is widely credited with originating what Nathan christened "the administrative presidency," though FDR, Eisenhower, and Kennedy had all used it to some extent, devising new programs and agencies to bypass the existing administrative structures. President Eisenhower's 1953 creation of Schedule C political appointments allowed higher-level appointees to place partisans deep in the agencies as secretaries, confidential assistants, even chauffeurs, as low as General Schedule (GS) grade 9. Jimmy Carter's civil service reforms of 1978 created the Senior Executive Service, composed of noncareer partisans (10 percent) and supergrade (GS 16 to 18 or equivalent) careerists (90 percent) significantly accountable to political supervision. With these and other innovations, presidents hoped to find more political responsiveness in new people and agencies loyal to them and their policy ideas.

In the modern era, this substitution of "responsive competence" for "neutral competence" becomes even more pronounced in a time of divided government, in which one or both houses of the Congress and the White House are in the hands of different parties. Divided government has become the modus vivendi of American government; consequently, one should expect more use of the administrative presidency as presidents seek to achieve through administrative means what they cannot through legislative.[2]

The administrative presidency puts the career bureaucracy in a difficult position. Careerists must be both neutral and competent, serving the policy goals of the current president yet maintaining sufficient professional proficiency and credibility to work effectively and efficiently in their agency. Their success at the former, however, makes them suspect the next time the White House changes parties (or even presidents within the same party).

As the administrative strategy developed over time, so did an array of tools with which to implement it and to elicit responsive competence from the bureaucracy. These tools are the powers to: appoint and remove surrogates, control budgets, reorganize agencies and government, delegate program authority to the states, mandate central clearance from the White House for agency actions, and order cost-benefit analysis before decisions are made (Waterman 1989, 185–86).

While confrontation can be an effective tactic, prudent exercise of the administrative tools can best be of use to presidents if they understand the limits of their power and are careful not to invite unintended or poorly planned confrontation. These tools can also be used in tandem, as, for example, when loyal appointees support Office of Management and Budget (OMB)-mandated budget reductions in their own agencies, in which case, surrogates, central clearance, and budget control are all utilized.

The improvident use of these tools, however, can weaken the presidency more than strengthen it. These tools are also based on the questionable assumption that presidents *can* control the bureaucracy, an assumption that may not give sufficient credit to the tenacity of the bureaucracy itself, the dynamism of the political system, and the other major player in that system, the Congress. Congress initially delegates many of the tools to the president through confirmation of appointees, enactment of enabling legislation, and appropriation of operating budget, and so shares authority over their use. Other key players in this policy drama are the courts, the cabinet, the PASs, the career bureaucrats, the media, the general public, and interest groups (ibid.).

Because presidents' power is so widely shared, confrontation is a tactic best used sparingly; theirs is the power to persuade more than to command. Presidents must adopt a political approach, even within their own bureaucracy. They "must bargain and compromise. . . . This is so because presidents share authority with their subordinates within the Executive Branch; they do not control them. The best way is to work with the bureaucracy and not against it" (ibid., 169–70).

Presidents can strengthen their hand through clarity of presidential intent and the appointment of competent loyalists, clear transmittal of presidential orders to the agencies, and personal presidential interest and involvement in key issues and areas. Other means are lines of authority that give subordinates the power to accomplish presidential policy desires, respect for the power of other policy actors in the field, and care not to overstep presidential bounds (ibid., 190–92).

Any of these tactics, no matter how ably applied, can backfire unexpectedly in what Pfiffner calls the "central paradoxes" of the managerial or administrative presidency. For example, while one administrative strategy is to flood the bureaucracy with loyal supporters, that strategy can have unintended consequences and dangers; the greatest threats to the reputations and political interests of recent presidents have come from "over-enthusiastic loyalists [seeking to do their boss's will regardless of the consequences] rather than from political 'enemies'" (Pfiffner 1991, 4).

The Iran-Contra arms-for-hostages deal is a case in point. As this convoluted tale slowly unwound, White House aides Oliver North, John Poindexter, and Robert McFarlane claimed to have acted independently of presidential directive. However, their close association with the president meant that, even though they fell on their swords for their leader, as loyal aides are expected to do, they could in no way shield President Reagan and then–Vice President Bush from at least indirect responsibility for the scandal.[3]

While the president should designate a chief of staff to handle routine matters, he himself "must be involved sufficiently to ensure that his interests are being well served. The president must probe enough to guard against the overzealous subordinate who is willing to bend the laws or the

Constitution in what is thought to be the president's interest. No one should be allowed to think that the buck stops short of the president" (Pfiffner 1991, 15).

Because government is so large and complex, the best way for a president to "control" the executive branch is to manage it indirectly, to delegate most issues that are not clearly presidential to department and agency heads. Presidents should lean on their cabinet secretaries; direct presidential involvement should be very selective.

Similarly with respect to political personnel: the president should play a positive role in setting the tone for recruiting political appointees, but he should delegate the selection of most subcabinet appointees to department and agency heads. Personal or ideological loyalties to the president do not in themselves guarantee the effective implementation of presidential priorities because, as noted, there are so many other actors and intervening factors (Pfiffner 1991, 4).

Overzealous subordinates in the agencies can work against the president's best interests, as did Elizabeth Tamposi and John Berry when they conducted an inappropriate, if not illegal, search of the passport files of Candidate Clinton and his mother during the presidential campaign of 1992. Though they vowed they were acting independently of White House control, their claims were met with nearly universal skepticism that reflected badly on their boss, President and Candidate George Bush.

However much a president may seek to control the administration, countervailing forces mitigate that control: infighting among White House staffers and their attempts at excessive control, as mentioned above, work against the administrative presidency in the long run. And

> even loyal ideologues with presidentially informed policy agendas and a modicum of experience and savvy find their ability to influence the bureaucracy contingent on such key factors as: 1. perceptions of how strongly the president is concerned with their efforts; 2. how well-honed their managerial skills are; 3. how relevant their prior policy experience is to the task at hand; 4. how suitable their personalities are to relevant bureaupolitical environments; 5. whether opportunities to accomplish change emerge; and 6. how predisposed they are to alter core agency activities (processes and bureaucratic routines) rather than discrete tasks. (Durant 1991, 463)

Additionally, recruitment of highly qualified political appointees suffers in the administrative strategy, as does PASs' willingness or ability to carry out the president's agenda. The lower into the bureaucracy political appointees are placed, the less attractive are those jobs to potential PASs with appropriate experience and qualifications. As a result, these positions tend to be filled by "younger, less experienced, less knowledgeable 'ticketpunching' appointees . . . who embrace or become dependent on entrenched bureaucratic cultures, routines, and dominant coalitions" (ibid.).

With respect to the permanent bureaucracy; the career bureaucracy is often seen by new presidents as an obstacle to the achievement of presidential priorities. FDR, for example, had inherited a civil service, twelve years in the employ of Republican presidents, that was termed by one observer as "merely a mass of Republican political appointees frozen into position by act of Congress" (Hess 1988, 23). This problem transcended party lines. In 1954 Eisenhower issued the Willis Directive, setting the stage for further centralization in Nixon's White House and central clearance in Reagan's. It placed

> a special assistant in each department and agency to control vacancies in both the higher competitive [career] and political posts by reporting [vacancies] to the Republican National Committee. . . , [which] was to be given time to recommend candidates with satisfactory political clearances. The secretiveness surrounding the plan and the uncertainty of its application gave the impression—probably a correct one—that this was a thinly veiled raid on the federal service. (Light 1995, 46)

Presidents continue to be vexed by their assumptions about the careerists who served their predecessors. Nevertheless, cooperation with the career service is essential to accomplishing presidential goals; enlisting the bureaucracy's enthusiastic support can enhance the probability of presidential success (Pfiffner 1991, 4).

As the mixed blessings of an administrative presidency were most definitively exercised and honed by Richard Nixon and Ronald Reagan, their administrations are examined in this chapter in some detail. George Bush's administration receives initial observation here, to be followed by in-depth analysis in later chapters.

Greta Garbo in the White House:[4] Richard Nixon's Administrative Presidency

Richard Nixon's administrative strategy involved the exercise of government by executive action, relying heavily on the power vested in the hands of the PASs who headed the executive agencies (Rourke 1991a,

114). He made extensive use of the tools of appointment, budget, and re-organization powers.

Preparing the way for Ronald Reagan, Nixon's administrative strategy also involved claims of executive authority, as in his attempts at budget impoundment to achieve policy goals, and a general "go it alone" attitude vis-à-vis the Congress. So-called executive privilege was used extensively by Nixon to shield his office from congressional inquiry. He set the White House over and against not only the Congress, but also against the rest of the executive branch, making broad use of the president's appointment powers to procure heads of domestic civilian agencies who were opposed to the basic mission and goal of the agencies they administered (ibid., 114–15).

Not unlike President Eisenhower, Richard Nixon came into the White House with the conservative's bias against big government and its bureaucracy, suspicious of a career civil service that had spent the past eight years working at the behest of Democratic social policies (Aberbach 1976, 466–67). According to Nathan,

> The plan for an "administrative presidency" helps to explain Nixon's en-tire domestic policy. The roots of this plan were in the experience of his first term. The president and John D. Ehrlichman, his chief domestic ad-visor, came to the conclusion sometime in late 1971 or early 1972 that, in most areas of domestic affairs, *operations constitute policy*. Much of the day-to-day management of domestic programs—regulation writing, grant approval, personnel development, agency organization and reorga-nization, program oversight, and budget apportionment—can involve high-level policymaking. Getting control over these processes was the aim of the President's strategy; and judged against the lack of legislative success on domestic issues in the first term, there are grounds for con-cluding that this was a rational objective. (Nathan 1975, 70)

While the regulatory agencies and smaller administrative units gen-erally were spared a direct attack, "the (Nixon) administrative presidency focused on the big-spending cabinet agencies, especially Health, Educa-tion, and Welfare, Housing and Urban Development, Labor, Transporta-tion, and Interior." Thus, Nixon's New Federalism was considered by many to be nothing more than an "elaborate rationale for paring down so-cial spending" (ibid., 26, vii–viii).

"Nixon and his White House loyalists increasingly saw themselves as pursued by three demons: the press, Congress, and the federal bureau-cracy." To counter the press, his staff developed innovative techniques for managing the news. He was the first president to put political people in charge of agencies' public affairs departments. Under the tutelage of media wizard and political image-maker Roger Ailes, Nixon cut back the number of press conferences, holding only twenty-eight his entire first term. He also staged White House briefings and a series of prime-time television appearances; fourteen in his first nineteen months in office, as compared to Kennedy's four (Hess 1988, 122).

To deal with the Congress, he attacked the Senate as being anti-Southern for its rejection of two of his Supreme Court nominees, G. Harrold Carlswell and Clement Haynsworth. He then basically ignored the Congress and concentrated on his administrative strategy (ibid., 123). As Nathan describes it,

> The "traditional legislative strategy" of governing was abandoned and a "fundamentally different approach" was adopted. The new strategy . . . would be designed "to *take over* the bureaucracy and *take on* Congress." This would be accomplished . . . by placing Nixon's "own trusted appointees in positions to manage directly key elements of the bureaucracy. . . . The new appointees would be the President's men. The bureaucracy would report to them; they would be held accountable." (Cole and Caputo 1979, 400–01)

The first step was to remove the independent power base of cabinet officials. In the process, the cabinet itself receded into grayness. With the full deployment of the Nixon strategy,

> No longer would the cabinet be composed of men with national standing in their own right. . . . The president's men—trusted lieutenants, tied closely to Richard Nixon and without national reputations of their own— were to be placed in direct charge of the major program bureaucracies of domestic government. (Nathan 1975, 7–8)

Nixon's administrative strategy beyond the cabinet was two-pronged: it involved taking more control over both subcabinet political appointments and the career civil service. Initially, the White House had given cabinet members responsibility for selection of their subordinates, telling them they should choose subordinates on the basis of ability first and loyalty second. However, this changed in late 1970 when Frederick V. Malek, former deputy undersecretary of HEW, joined the administration as associate director of OMB. His "forte at HEW had been the removal and Siberian placement of troublesome officials" and their replacement by more compliant ones. His function at the White House was no different. Under his direction "the White House role in the selection and approval of key agency officials would be much stronger. . . . By the end of Richard Nixon's first term, the original strong cabinet model had been fully displaced" (ibid., 50–51).

Control extended to performance in new ways, as well. Malek took to visiting agencies to assess personally how PASs were doing. He had "points of contact" within many of the agencies to deal with recruiting and serve as liaisons with his office. "Later, to further solidify his grip on the bureaucracy, Nixon loyalists were strategically planted in departments and agencies as overseers of administration policy" (Bonafede 1987a, 40–41).

At the same time the White House was moving to exert more control over political appointments in the agencies, OMB was being strengthened and politicized, and Ehrlichman's White House counterbureaucracy for domestic affairs was being established. The White House intended to get deeply into the operational workings of the agencies. One result of this centralizing strategy was an overload at the White House. To deal with it, Nixon turned increasingly to his chief of staff, H.R. Haldeman, who operated in the hierarchical manner that further contributed to the president's isolation.

Then, immediately after his reelection, Nixon turned on his own cabinet. In what Hess calls "perhaps the most remarkable statement ever made by a president who has just been re-elected," Nixon declared that he had lost confidence in the people he had called to serve him and that a major overhaul of the government was imminent. "Having realized the failure of his counter-bureaucracy, he nonetheless did not blame himself or his practice of isolation and remote-control government, but instead chose a strategy of massive restructuring and personnel shuffling" (Hess 1988, 126).

First, he demanded the pro forma resignation of his entire cabinet. Next, just before Christmas 1972, Nixon "announced 57 resignations and 87 other personnel decisions." As a "technique for prolonging the vitality of political appointees," the reorganization might have made some sense, but many agencies suffered from the loss or transfer of appointees, some of whom had only recently come on board, only to be moved elsewhere. Cabinet tenure also suffered. "From 1933 to 1965 the median length of service for cabinet officials was 40 months; during Nixon's presidency it dropped to 18" (ibid., 126–27). Thus began a trend from which cabinet tenure never recovered.

At the same time he fired his cabinet, Nixon unveiled a new and-grandiose "supercabinet" structure. It basically consisted of two tiers of policy makers perched at the peak of the White House: on the upper tiers were five presidential assistants, each with a special area of responsibility, and below them three cabinet secretaries who were made responsible for coordinating interagency affairs and given the additional title of counselor. (Bonafede 1987a, 41–42)

However, the brouhaha over the Watergate break-in and cover-up and the resignations of Haldeman and Ehrlichman on April 30, 1973, effectively derailed the supercabinet plan (ibid.).

Deeply conflicted regarding the federal bureaucracy, the Nixon White House thought it a principal and often hostile obstacle and at the same time a "potentially powerful political resource" (Cole and Caputo 1979, 400). But unlike the Eisenhower administration, which came into office blaming the bureaucracy for "the mess in Washington" but eventually developed a suitable working relationship with it, the Nixon administration never did reach an accommodation with the bureaucracy. On the contrary, Nixon's distrust "hardened to the point where unprecedented reorganizational steps were planned for the second term to take control of the machinery of domestic government" (Nathan 1975, 82).

Fred Malek was a crucial ingredient in this hardening process. His dislike of the federal bureaucracy was phrased with notable lack of restraint:

> Because of the rape of the career civil service left by the Kennedy and Johnson administrations . . . this administration has been left a legacy of finding disloyalty and obstruction at high levels while those incumbents rest comfortably on career civil service status. Political disloyalty and insimpatico relationships with the administration, unfortunately, are not grounds for the removal or suspension of an employee. (Aberbach 1991, 226)

While Watergate undercut Nixon's dreams of controlling the bureaucracy, his efforts were not in vain. Gaining early training in bureaucrat bashing under Fred Malek was E. Pendleton James, later to head Ronald Reagan's preinaugural talent search and become his assistant for personnel. Malek's credo, "You cannot achieve management, policy, or program control unless you have established political control" would live on in the Reagan administrations. "The Nixon experience, then, was more than just a historical aberration. It was a school for many who followed; its lessons were assimilated and applied with telling effect in the Reagan period" (Aberbach 1991, 225).

Thanks to Malek, Nixon was largely successful in his attempts to exercise political control over the civil service personnel system. The majority of the careerists had come in during the Democratic years when many domestic social programs were expanding and defense allocations decreasing. Nixon's New Federalism was designed to reduce the power of the federal bureaucracy and its careerists, bypassing them and sending funds directly to the states.

> The tensions between the White House and the bureaucracy were intensified as many of Nixon's new federalism proposals called for a reduction in the number of categorical grants, the consolidation of various departments and agencies, and the elimination of federal bureaucratic discretion in various grant-in-aid programs. . . . [Thus,] many of Nixon's domestic programs could be interpreted as posing direct threats to the careers [and power bases] of many federal executives. (Cole and Caputo 1979, 400)

Cole and Caputo's 1979 study of supergrade political and career officials traces how this administrative strategy created a "fundamental shift in bureaucratic-presidential relations" to redirect the loyalties of the senior-level bureaucracy (Cole and Caputo 1979, 401). Malek's specialty, direct attack on the career bureaucracy, shines here in its own way: if no vacancies were identifiable, the PAS should create them. The so-called Malek Manual provided specific guidelines for how to do it:

> "There are several techniques which can be designed, carefully, to skirt around the [difficult problem of firing established career executives]. You simply call an individual in and tell him he is no longer wanted . . . you expect him to immediately relinquish his duties. There should be no witnesses in the room at the time."

If this "frontal assault" (the manual's own terminology) were not successful, the manual went on to suggest transferring unwanted personnel to regional offices, described by the manual as "dumping grounds." "If you have an employee," the manual advised, "who was born and raised in New England and is currently serving in your Boston regional office, and his record shows reluctance to move far from that location, a transfer accompanied by a promotion to an existing or newly created position in Dallas might just fill the bill." If the transfer technique failed, the manual recommended other "special assignments" as well as other techniques. But the point was clear: where no positions at the senior career levels were open, political executives were instructed in the art of creat-

ing such openings by encouraging the firing or transferring of personnel.
(Ibid., 403)

For those troublesome careerists who simply would not go away, a
technique was devised that offered flash but no substance, a "new activity technique designed to provide a single barrel into which you can dump
a large number of widely located bad apples." The manual suggested the
creation of a new unit or program:

> "By carefully looking at the personnel jacket of your selected employee-
> victims, you can easily design an organization chart for the project that
> would create positions to which these employee-victims can be trans-
> ferred that meet the necessary job description requirements, offer promo-
> tional opportunities in grade, and by having the project report directly
> into the Secretary's office provide for promotions in status." The only
> thing missing is impact. (Light 1995, 53)

The White House also "facilitated" the personnel process by suggest-
ing acceptable senior career people for vacancies in the agencies. When
combined with its removal and replacement scheme, the White House
hoped this strategy would "circumvent the 'normal' civil service process
and . . . achieve a high degree of managerial control over the federal bureaucracy" (Cole and Caputo 1979, 403). Another technique was to simply move the careerists down the food chain by adding new partisans,
SESs, or Schedule Cs above them. While Malek's machinations did long-
term damage to the concept of neutral competence, they also added to the
overall "thickening" of government by interposing additional layers of
political appointees between the top careerists and the top politicians.

While absolute control of the bureaucracy is unlikely, given the total
number of vacancies available in any given presidential term, Nixon's
strategy was remarkably successful in changing the face of the federal bureaucracy. Although some Democrats were appointed to high-level political and career positions, they were far outnumbered by Republicans.

> Republican career executives were about 3 times as likely to be promoted
> to senior positions in the social service agencies during the Nixon years
> and more than 1.5 times as likely to be promoted to senior positions in
> all other departments and agencies. . . . Proportionally more Republicans
> were selected for more career executive positions during the Nixon years
> than before and, through this process, the White House was beginning to
> achieve partisan equality in the key social service agencies. Additionally,
> by the selection of Independents who voted Republican or by influencing

some Independents to lean in a Republican direction (or through some combination of these), the administrative presidency was to achieve among Independent bureaucrats a level of support for the Republican party much greater than before. (Ibid., 407–08)

Reagan was to be even more aggressive in promoting Republican partisans, as discussed below.

This study carries key implications for partisans of the strong presidency: bureaucrats identifying themselves as Independent tend to favor presidential programs. This is a particularly important finding, as studies have found 36 percent to 44 percent of the senior careerists identifying themselves as Independent. Therefore, "Independents and party identifiers combined assure either a Republican or a Democratic president substantial support at the senior career levels of the federal bureaucracy" (ibid., 412).

Additionally, "the 'pull' of the presidency [is] strong" regardless of party identification. By 1976, substantial proportions of Democrats also identified with Nixon's programs. Thus, "bureaucratic accommodation" will lend presidents considerable success, even among bureaucrats of the opposing party, despite the relatively few vacancies at their disposal in any given administration (ibid., 412). This "cycle of accommodation" is discussed in more detail in chapter 6.

Quoting Aberbach and Rockman, Cole and Caputo conclude:

"The framers of the Constitution, having given us little guidance (in the area of bureaucratic control and responsibility), have left these problems as part of their enduring legacy." Yet, lacking constitutional directives we find that political realities provide considerable relief. The influence of the president is so strong as to sway even protected career service personnel. While maintaining its formal independence (and perhaps even basic philosophic differences), the bureaucracy still responds to specific presidential initiatives. To this extent a certain degree of presidential control is accomplished even in the absence of a clear constitutional directive. (ibid., 412–13)

Political Costs of Nixon's Administrative Strategy

The successes of Nixon's administrative strategy were not unalloyed, of course. During his first term it became obvious that Ehrlichman's counterbureaucracy strategy was a failure. According to Nathan,

as the White House became more and more involved in routine administrative matters, the time and energy it had to devote to truly important policy issues was correspondingly reduced. This concern with routine matters acted like a mosquito bite; the more you scratched it, the more it itched. Senior White House staffers could not keep up with what their subordinates were doing. Moreover, the supply of talented aides for the White House who understand the substance of domestic policy is limited. The Republican party's most able and experienced substantive experts generally preferred the more prestigious and visible posts. As the White House staff grew, its general caliber declined. (Nathan 1975, 51–52)

Thus, one political cost of this counterbureaucracy strategy was that as those at the top tried to control more details, they controlled less policy. Operational details tended to drive out policy making as minor issues began to take up a disproportionate percentage of top officials' time and energy. The resulting flow of small matters upward left careerists with more actual policy power because they were the ones left with more thinking time and creative energy (ibid., 52).

Nixon's administration fell victim to the built-in attraction of depending on the White House staff at the expense of the bureaucracy or even the organizations with a lower level of responsiveness, such as OMB. This invariably led to a more centralized and bureaucratized presidency. As mentioned, the overload at the White House led Nixon to lean more on Haldeman who arrogated more power to himself. What Campbell labels Nixon's neuroses

combined with Haldeman's imperiousness to breed unprecedented degrees of White House isolation, backstabbing, paralysis, and paranoia. The resulting liberties taken with the rule of law, especially in the Watergate breakin and its attempted cover-up, convinced most observers that the hierarchical White House with a strong chief of staff presented real dangers for continued democratic rule. (Campbell 1991, 188)

There is a fine irony in all this: Nixon eventually abandoned the counterbureaucracy approach because, rather than weakening the bureaucracy, it tended to strengthen it. A certain chaos had settled in on the executive branch as a result of this centralizing strategy:

the lines of authority became blurred, decisions were delayed or never made, and increasingly the result was that career officials in the domestic program bureaucracies were in the catbird seat. . . . The responsible cabinet appointees were out of touch, too busy, or too harried by the White House to find out [what was happening]. Not only were domestic affairs not handled well under this type of a system, but tensions arose as junior White House staffers second-guessed presidential appointees on matters that the latter thought were of relatively lesser consequence and that they should have been trusted to handle themselves or to delegate. (Nathan, 52–53)

An unintended consequence and additional irony of this strategy was that the White House and Executive Office staffs, in contrast to the original plan, grew in size and power early in the Nixon administration. The result was that by the end of its third year the cost of the Executive Office staff had doubled since the Johnson years. Nixon, "'distrustful of bureaucracy, . . . built a kind of defense against it—and in doing so he . . . built his own bureaucracy'" (ibid., 45).

There were other costs to Nixon's administrative presidency. For one, it roused the Congress to action. In response to his budget impoundment actions, the Congress acted to protect its role in the governing process by passing the Budget Impoundment and Control Act in 1974. This act sought to restore congressional oversight of federal expenditures by, among other actions, forbidding backdoor spending of funds by agencies without advance allocations. It also prohibited executive impoundment of congressionally mandated funds for programs the president sought to kill administratively when he could not do it legislatively (Warren 1988, 183).

The impoundment strategy also provoked the first rumblings of impeachment of the president and put the Congress on general alert:

> In part at least because of its conviction that presidents were ignoring or usurping legislative authority by governing in a unilateral way through the administrative presidency, the Congress has reacted against this presidential strategy. In recent years, the Congress has both strengthened its own surveillance of the executive branch and sought to subject the decisions and actions of executive officials to closer scrutiny by outside forces. (Rourke 1991a, 116)

These outside forces include the courts. The Democratic-controlled Congress, distrustful of executive agencies headed by the Republican White House, made it easier for the agencies to be taken to court through its writing of legislation and encouragement of watchdog public interest groups. The courts have thus become involved in the bureaucracy through judicial review, subsequently limiting administrative discretion in carrying out agency mission (ibid., 117).[5]

Congressional retaliation also resulted in the enactment of the War Powers Act that sought to limit the president's power to wage undeclared wars and in revisions to the Freedom of Information Act to provide greater access to government materials. Congress also made alterations to the Privacy Act, giving individuals access to files the government might be keeping on them, and to the Hughes-Ryan Amendment, which required the president to notify the Congress of covert operations abroad. Regardless of the long-term efficacy of these acts, they signaled the power of the Congress to block or blunt presidential administrative aspirations.

Ronald Reagan's Administrative Presidency

Although most presidents in the modern era employed the administrative presidency to some extent, President Reagan was President Nixon's true heir in that respect. Proclaiming a counterrevolution to the past fifty years of social and political affairs, Reagan rode into office on a wave of popular discontent. He intended to reverse the nation's course held since FDR's New Deal and to undo the Great Society programs of LBJ. "Government is not the solution to our problem," said the new president in his inaugural address, "government is the problem."

Reagan's administration placed strategic emphasis on political control of the bureaucracy. In fact, he so successfully exploited the powers vested in political appointees by the Civil Service Reform Act (CSRA) of 1978 that

> One informed observer "concluded that the CSRA has been "a disaster for merit". . . , that traditional merit values have been undermined. . . . Under Reagan, responsibility of the personnel system to the political system is largely defined as responsiveness to ideological executive control. That contrasts with the traditionally neutral civil service responsibility to statutory provisions in a constitutional system of separation of powers and a rule of law. (Newland 1983, 15)

Unlike Nixon, who determined the need for an administrative strategy by the end of his first term, Reagan coupled his legislative strategy with an administrative strategy almost from the beginning. His legislative strategy initially met with sweeping success with passage of the budget act in 1981, but stalled thereafter. As that happened, he stepped up his administrative strategy in the second and third years of his first term. Those years also saw an increase in use of the judicial strategy as the administration assumed a more aggressive stance in court cases (Nathan 1986, 128–35). The Reagan (and later Bush) Justice Department became a frequent complainant against the extension of civil rights and regulatory control of industry, particularly in regard to the banking and airline industries and in health, safety, and environmental issues. Also, by the end of his two terms Reagan had appointed four Supreme Court justices and over half of the federal judiciary, filling those positions with predominantly young judges who passed his political litmus test.

Nixon's "executive privilege" was perfected to a fine art by Reagan, who made joint appointments of individuals to both PAS and PA (appointments in the Executive Office of the President [EOP] that do not require Senate confirmation) positions. When called upon to testify before Congress, these PAS/PA appointees would simply don their PA hat and refuse to testify, citing this executive privilege. As had Nixon before him, Reagan set the White House over and against not only the Congress, but also against his own bureaucracy, appointing chiefs of domestic civilian bureaus who were hostile to the basic mission and goal of their agency (Rourke 1991a, 114–15). One commentator, Harold Raines, described the "Reagan appointments strategy in the *New York Times* in 1981 as 'a revolution of attitudes involving the appointment of officials who in previous administrations might have been ruled out by a concern over possible lack of qualifications or conflict of interest or open hostility to the mission of the agencies they now lead'" (Aberbach 1991, 227).

The breadth and depth of Reagan's approach made Nixon's administrative strategy look amateurish by comparison, as Reagan made use of all the strategic tools of the administrative presidency—appointment, removal, budget, reorganization, delegation to the states, central clearance, and cost-benefit analysis.

Facing a Democratic House and, after 1986, a Democratic Senate as well, the Reagan administration increasingly looked to the PASs and their powers to advance its policy objectives. According to Salamon and Abramson,

> The predominant characteristic of the Reagan approach to personnel selection was its emphasis on centralized, unrelenting White House control of the appointment process. The control was achieved through a variety of means: starting the personnel search early; giving the personnel chief access to the president; discouraging independent "head hunting" on the part of cabinet secretaries; making a heavy commitment of senior White

House staff time to the selection process; and reserving for the White House all final decisions even on subcabinet selections. Also, the Reagan personnel selection process subjected candidates to an unprecedented effort to "align presidential appointment decisions with presidential policy objectives." Appointees were carefully screened for policy and political background, legislative ties, ethics, and general compatibility with the core team—with sign-offs required from key people in each area. (Salamon and Abramson 1984, 46)

Central clearance as a philosophy of management in the Reagan White House meant that control and ideological purity were the dominant themes, particularly for appointments to subcabinet positions. While earlier administrations had reviewed approximately 10 percent of the appointments, Reagan's team oversaw the entire slate of some three thousand positions (Smith 1988, 302). They focused heavily on the second- and third-tier positions, "insist[ing] on the litmus of Reaganite conservative ideology, [and] push[ing] names from Reagan's conservative movement onto cabinet secretaries" for these positions. The resulting long delay in filling positions "left agencies decapitated and thus even more susceptible to White House control" (ibid., 302–03). According to political theorist Paul Light, the White House appointed lower-level appointees who

> would cut their [political] boss's throat to please the president, . . . They are an entirely different breed of appointee than in the Carter, Nixon, and Ford administrations. They are ideologically committed. There is no allegiance to the department, but to the Oval Office or the conservative cause. No administration has penetrated so deeply [into the bureaucracy]. (Ibid., 302–03)

Reagan's people were remarkably successful in "purging the federal government of moderate appointees" (Aberbach 1991, 230), recruiting more Republicans and more conservatives to his administration. Some 93 percent of his appointees and 40 percent of his senior careerists were Republicans, in contrast to Nixon's 66 percent and 17 percent, respectively. While 19 percent of Nixon's partisans and 13 percent of his careerists opposed an active role of government in the economy, 72 percent and 47 percent, respectively, of Reagan's harbored the same beliefs. And, building further on Nixon's teachings to strengthen political leverage, Reagan repoliticized the deputy assistant secretary (DAS) layer by converting them back into political appointments (Light 1995, 56–57).

While the traditional approach of new administrations is to claim to seek qualified persons for the top positions, actual practice often produces only lip service to quality. As political pressures are applied, they produce

> the need to reward specific constituencies and contributors, the success of some cabinet appointees in negotiating the right to control the appointment of subordinates, and the wish to have appointees who will be dedicated to the president and to his political philosophy. The usual result is cadres of appointees who exhibit divided loyalties and uncertain reliability. Anticipating this result, presidents are reluctant to delegate or decentralize control over policy to political appointees or even to view the use of their appointment power as more than peripheral to the achievement of their policy goals. (Lynn 1985, 339)

The Reagan administration, however, veered from this well-trod path to seek out and use surrogates to drive administration policy goals aggressively in the face of expected opposition from a government assumed to be in enemy hands. Consequently, "the primary qualification for appointment—overshadowing managerial competence and experience or familiarity with issues—appeared to be the extent to which an appointee shared the president's values and would be reliable and persistent both in transfusing these values into agency practices and in executing central directives bound to be unpopular in his or her agency" (ibid., 340).

Loyalty to Reagan and his philosophy became the unifying force for his appointees, his front line in attacking the bureaucracy. Beyond merely seeking to tame the bureaucracy, Reagan used his appointees

> as agent provocateurs, enforcers, and proconsuls in the agencies. Intimidation and the threat of reductions in force (RIFs) and budget cuts undeniably caught the attention of bureaucrats. . . . (A)ppointees became [the] agent of an effort led by OMB Director David Stockman to force retrenchment on the federal bureaucracy, and . . . were associated with implementing deregulation in line with guidance from Bush's Task Force on Regulatory Relief. (Ibid., 360)

The Reagan personnel operation started in April 1980, a full seven months before his election. By late summer Pendleton James had an office up and running. He claimed five criteria for political appointments: "'compatibility with the President's philosophy, integrity, toughness, competence, and being a team player.' [However, above competence or expertise], loyalty as ideological consistency was applied far more extensively as the test for appointment in the Reagan administration than in any other presidency in at least a half century" (Newland 1983, 3)

However, the Far Right was not satisfied by the resultant choices and the week of the inauguration saw heavy criticism of both the process and the appointees. In response, "presidential appointments moved more to the ideological right, and ultra-conservatives were selected for some targeted positions." Even those moves were not enough to satisfy New Right critics, however (ibid.).

White House attempts to influence the PASs did not end with their confirmation:

> Cabinet appointees met frequently with the president-elect to establish a bond that Reagan hoped would prevent them from "going native" later on. Lower-level appointees were thoroughly socialized about agency programs and operations before assuming their position; and they were socialized by Reagan aides and the conservative task forces, not by the career agency personnel whose corrupting influences were to be minimized. (Moe 1991, 151)

There is general agreement on the success of this approach: Reagan's subcabinet choices "tended to be even stronger ideologues than their cabinet superiors" (Nathan 1986, 130), exhibiting "an uncommon degree of ideological consistency and intensity" (Salamon and Abramson 1984, 46). The advantage of this strategy was that the subcabinet officers operated outside the "glare of the media spotlight in Washington" and were thus able to change agency policy to reflect "pure Reagan conservative ideology [more] than the views of their generally more conciliatory cabinet chiefs." Like Nixon, Reagan focused on the big-ticket agencies that administered social programs of which he disapproved—Health and Human Services, Labor, and Education (Nathan 1986, 131).

Reagan made significant changes in the bureaucracy through adroit use of these second- and third-tier PASs who in their agencies used administrative strategies to write, change, or delay regulations, deploy personnel, and rearrange budgets. There is a clear advantage of such a distancing tactic—the cabinet officials who shared Reagan's conservative ideology were the ones most likely to be pressured from office, with Reagan taking some heat for their activities (e.g., James Watt and Anne Burford Gorsuch) (ibid., 131). With subcabinet officials carrying out his orders, however, Reagan and his cabinet lieutenants were able to stay a step away from the action and therefore be insulated from blame. Nothing stuck to him; thus was born, in Representative Patricia Schroeder's memorable phrase, "The Teflon President."

Ronald Reagan and the Career Bureaucracy

Reaching below the PAS positions, Reagan also exerted considerable control over the SES noncareer positions. By law, the president is allowed to fill up to 10 percent of all permanent Senior Executive Service positions with noncareer appointees. In any one agency, the noncareer SES can reach 25 percent as long as the overall governmentwide balance of 10 percent holds. Another 5 percent can be noncareer in transition times. However, if significant numbers of career positions are left unfilled (often an appointee's call) and the allocated noncareer positions are filled, the noncareer positions can easily and legally exceed 10 percent of the total SES workforce. This is exactly what happened in the Reagan administration. A passive appointment, or more accurately, nonappointment strategy was utilized. In this variant of the administrative strategy, career positions were left vacant while noncareer positions were aggressively filled.

Additionally, taking his cue from Jimmy Carter, Reagan interpreted the 10 percent limit on noncareer SES appointments to apply to *allocated* rather than filled positions. Since at any given time, there are generally more than one thousand unfilled positions, that gives the administration one hundred noncareer appointments in the bureaucracy it would not have otherwise. The result was that by September 1983, political appointees constituted over 10 percent of the government's executive population for the first time (Salamon and Abramson 1984, 46).

Table 2.1. Growth in Political Appointments in the Reagan-Bush Era

Selected Agencies	1981	1991
Commerce	146	204
Education	85	137
Agriculture	128	180
Justice	71	122
Treasury	48	97
Energy	99	145
State	88	130
Defense	118	156
General Services Administration	20	51
Labor	74	105
Environmental Protection	30	51
Health and Human Services	139	156
Interior	77	92
Total governmentwide	2,022	2,436

Source: Washington Post, June 1, 1993.

The Reagan-Bush era carried on and burnished Nixon's politicization of the bureaucracy[6] as appointees flooded into targeted agencies in what Senator John Glenn called "creeping politicization." From 1981 to 1991 overall political appointments grew by more than 20 percent (see table 2.1).

The administrative presidency as practiced by Reagan was more subtle than that of Nixon. Using a legislative strategy for cover, battles in the Congress over budget and taxes effectively served as a diversion from the real battle that was taking place in the bureaucracy. There, "an ideologically oriented team of subcabinet officials moved into place and began implementing the Reagan agenda by administrative means, particularly in the regulatory arena" (ibid., 47).

While the Reagan administration was increasing the number of political appointees, it was also enacting severe reductions-in-force in domestic agencies targeted for major alterations in program priorities. And, not coincidentally, the two phenomena occurred at the same agencies and at the same time the Office of Personnel Management (OPM) was increasing political leverage over careerists, giving PASs and noncareer SESs more power to relocate careerists or downgrade their responsibilities (Goldenberg 1985, 396). "Under Reagan, most key administrative positions [were] staffed on the basis of partisan and personal loyalties, and career professionals [were] largely excluded from many leadership networks and responsibilities" (Newland 1983, 2).

Following Nixon's lead, Reagan's administrative strategy advanced beyond this somewhat passive strategy to an active one, vis-à-vis the careerists:

> Reagan ultimately went ahead to make explicit political use of the Senior Executive Service, usually by removing career officials from important slots and filling them with partisans. He also used reductions in force as a legal means of eliminating whole bureaucratic units staffed by careerists. This was done systematically, in the interests of presidential control and successful pursuit of the Reagan agenda. As a strategy for infiltrating the bureaucracy, it went way beyond anything Nixon had attempted. Yet it met with no opposition. (Moe 1991, 151)

Meanwhile, the numbers of limited-term political executive and Schedule C positions had also grown, more so at some agencies than at others. Like Eisenhower, who in 1953 created the political Schedule C positions to move partisans into the lower reaches of the bureaucracy, Reagan also used these positions to place loyalists where he hoped they could actually run the agencies. "The effect of this is that by August 1983 the number of Schedule C appointments exceeded the total number of Carter's Schedule Cs during his four-year term" (Salamon and Abramson 1984, 46).

This administrative presidency ploy meant not just the strategic placement of ideological soul mates but encouragement for them to advance policy objectives through use of their administrative power. Using this gambit, the PASs killed pending regulations left over from the final days of the Carter administration and slowed the issuance of new ones through executive orders and OMB procedures. They initiated "severe budget cuts, staff reductions, and a general easing of regulatory vigor," which led to reduced regulatory enforcement actions in many areas. They also "reinterpreted the conduct of agency business in accord with the administration's philosophy . . . of cooperation with business rather than confrontation in achieving regulatory compliance" (ibid., 47).

What was the ultimate result of the administrative presidency as practiced by the Reagan Republicans? Heclo describes the American system resulting from the Republican's version of the administrative presidency as being "hollow at the center" (Ingraham and Ban 1988, 12). Mark Goldstein, a staff member of the Senate Governmental Affairs Committee, in a personal interview extended Heclo's theory to the government as a whole: "hollow government" was the result of twelve years of Republican administration. Government after the Republicans had neither the resources nor the management expertise to accomplish the tasks it had been given. The government had been hollowed out—the shell remained but the inside was empty.

Political-career relations reached new lows during the Reagan years. The high turnover rate of political appointees was second only to presidential hostility as a reason for this nadir. In one study, the career executives

> reported an average tenure by their superiors of 12 months. Some noted that appointees who stayed longer than eight months were considered "old timers". . . . Obviously, when political tenure is so short, building a relationship of trust and respect is unlikely. One respondent, who in six years has worked for six different political managers, noted "nobody cared about good management, and even if they did, they were not here long enough to do anything about it." Said another, "Five years [into the Reagan presidency] we are still circling one another in this agency, and there is still a we-they mentality." (Ingraham and Ban 1986, 155)

The Reagan administration's approach had other negative impacts on political-career relations. Because it placed an overriding emphasis on political responsiveness, it created problems for careerists in that it "neither valued nor tolerated more traditional public management perspectives," their area of expertise. This, in turn, poisoned the atmosphere, creating "an environment of hostility and lack of trust in some agencies." Further, Reagan's appointees managed to move career managers "out of the decisionmaking loop" in some agencies, making them, "in a very basic sense . . . superfluous to decisionmaking" (ibid., 158).

The politicization and centralization of power within the White House during Reagan's activist presidency was a "continuation and acceleration of the developmental logic apparent in the Kennedy, Johnson, and Nixon years." But more than that, Reagan's success at strengthening the institutional presidency meant that he built "a set of administrative arrangements that by past standards proved coherent, well integrated, and eminently workable." These arrangements would also provide a model for future presidents (Moe 1991, 153, 157).

> Not surprisingly, the Reagan administration is typically viewed as anti-bureaucracy. Nathan (1983), Newland (1983), Ingraham (1987), Kirschten (1983), Rosen (1981), Carroll et al. (1985), and Pfiffner (1985) have noted the anti-bureaucratic rhetoric and tone of the administration. Rubin (1985), Waterman (1989), and Harris and Milkis (1989) have studied administration treatment of specific regulatory and social welfare organizations and found that the Reagan appointees did in fact seem more intent on limiting organization missions than enhancing efficiency. (Maranto 1993, 683)

However, this view must be placed in context. It is clear that organizations whose goals were in conflict with administration ideals (such as social welfare and regulatory agencies) indeed experienced antibureaucratic administration. However, organizations with "ideologically neutral missions" experienced less tension, and relations in the defense bureaucracies were positively harmonious. "In short, the Reagan administration cannot be considered anti-bureaucracy as such; rather, it opposed bureaucracies with liberal missions and embraced those with conservative missions," such as the defense organizations (ibid., 696).

This administrative presidency also built on the changes of the Nixon years, transforming the nature of the bureaucracy itself. Selective promotion in the upper civil service grades, beginning with Nixon and picking up speed over the long Reagan years, along with changing ideas in society, worked to create a bureaucracy far more conservative than that of the late 1960s and early 1970s. This helped to reduce further internal agency tension by creating a bureaucracy predisposed to be in tune with a conservative administration (ibid., 696).

As Aberbach observed,

> Reagan left Bush a bureaucracy that was at least somewhat more Republican and noticeably more conservative than had probably been the case in recent history . . . And [as noted above] he left a record that indicated how to structure the appointments process to find and place committed conservatives in appointive positions and how to use the new civil service law to influence the positioning of key top civil servants. (Aberbach 1991, 231–32)

Reagan's approach to the Democratic Congress was marked by adversarial stridency from the beginning.

> Congress was largely viewed as an obstacle to be got around rather than as a partner in government. To help in overcoming congressional opposition to his policies, Reagan was able to use his prestige with the American public to influence the actions of those he dealt with "inside the Beltway." But he often went further and appealed directly to the American people to show their support for his policies by lobbying their representatives on his behalf. In competition with Congress, this strategy of "going public," made the best possible use of the president's own gifts. (King and Alston 1991, 275)

Reagan enlarged the role of the institutional presidency, keeping it center stage in American political consciousness. In doing so, he moved beyond traditional conservative notions of a presidency that merely responds to overtures from the Congress or other entities. He instead embraced the style, if not the content, of the activist presidency of FDR, even to the point of evoking FDR's memory in his speeches. As it was observed, Reagan adopted the approach of Wilson and Roosevelt in order to pursue the objectives of Coolidge and Harding (Salamon and Lund 1985, 22).

Some found positive elements in Reagan's administrative presidency:

> it has created an elaborate new system for tracking budgetary decision-making in Congress so that the administration can participate in the process more effectively. It has also extended the procedures for Execu-

tive Office scrutiny of regulations begun under presidents Gerald R. Ford and Jimmy Carter, and it has taken steps to strengthen financial controls in the executive branch. It has also furthered the review of federal credit activities and accelerated the move to establish a regular credit budget. In addition, its "Cabinet Councils" have improved internal executive branch communication. Beyond that, the administration has given greater salience to the potential role that both private-sector institutions and state and local governments can play in dealing with public problems. (Ibid., 23)

However, as with Nixon, these advances came at a price.

Political Costs of Reagan's Administrative Strategy

There are strengths to the Reagan approach to political appointments: "loyalty to the president, a clearance process that touches all bases, and clear White House control of appointments in the administration." However, there are weaknesses as well, related to

> slowness due to the elaborate clearance procedures, the narrowness of the pool of potential candidates (due to ideological criteria and bias against previous experience), and the large volume that must be handled by the White House personnel office since clearances extended to the lowest levels. (Pfiffner 1987a, 73–74)

Other factors slowed the Reagan appointment process, as well. Primary energy went to the legislative strategy group that was successfully moving the economic policy program through the Congress. "The disclosure requirements of the 1978 Ethics Act had to be applied for the first time [and] the Presidential Personnel Office was deficient in staff and operations" (Newland 1983, 4).

Pressure from the Republican right wing also slowed the Reagan screening and appointment process, as mentioned. It charged that many of the candidates had not supported Reagan soon enough and were "retreads" from previous Republican administrations (Pfiffner 1987a, 73).

> The ideological battles over appointments and the elaborate clearance procedures resulted in significant delays in staffing the administration. Despite claims that the administration was making major appointments faster than Presidents Carter or Kennedy, the National Journal reported that after 10 weeks Reagan had submitted to the Senate 95, as compared to Carter's 142 nominations. Time calculated that, as of the first week in May, of the top 400 officials, only 55 percent had been announced, 35 per-

cent formally nominated, and 21 percent actually confirmed. (Ibid., 73–74)

Another result of the Reagan ideological litmus test was that significant numbers of the appointees had no previous government experience. Of those confirmed as of late June 1981, "59% (76 of 112) of subcabinet appointees lacked prior government experience, as did 78% (18 of 23) of those in independent agencies and 100% (seven of seven) of those in independent regulatory agencies" (Newland 1983, 3). The Bush appointees stood in marked contrast to those of the first Reagan administration, as will be discussed in later chapters.[7]

Reagan's administrative strategy fell apart late in his first term as abuses by some of his appointees started to come to light. Excessive loyalty to the president, single-minded focus on his agenda, and standard-issue corruption had led some of the president's men and women outside the law. In Ronald Reagan's eight years in office, more than one hundred officials were accused of illegal or unethical conduct.[8] As one reporter put it, in terms of sheer criminality, the Reagan administration, mainly because of Iran-Contra, took the prize for ethics violations. The guilty verdicts of John Poindexter, national security adviser, and Oliver North, White House aide, were overturned only on procedural grounds; Caspar Weinberger was indicted but spared trial in that scandal by a pardon from President Bush.[9]

Other violations abounded. For example, Paul Thayer, deputy defense secretary, pleaded guilty to obstructing justice and giving false testimony in an insider-trading case. Rita Lavelle, EPA toxic waste cleanup chief, was convicted of lying to Congress, as was Michael Deaver, White House deputy chief of staff. Questionable or illegal financial dealings led to trouble for others: both of Reagan's attorneys general, William French Smith and Edwin Meese, faced ethics investigations, as did the CIA's director, William Casey, and chief spy, Max Hugel. Deborah Gore Dean, top aide to HUD Secretary Samuel Pierce, and two of her assistants were convicted of corruption. The secretary himself escaped indictment but not suspicion. In a plea bargain case that eventually saw a twenty-five-count indictment reduced to a one-count misdemeanor of perjury, a sympathetic judge decided to give former Interior Secretary James Watt "a break" and sentenced him to only six months of probation, a $5,000 fine, and five hundred hours of community service for his scheme to defraud HUD by funneling millions of dollars in low-income housing funds to his friends and then lying about it to Congress and a federal grand jury. The heads of numerous agencies were involved in ethical breaches: Food and Drug Administration, Federal Emergency Management Agency, Occupational

Safety and Health Administration, Maritime Administration, Legal Services Corporation, Veterans Administration, Federal Home Loan Bank Board, and Synthetic Fuels Corporation.[10]

There were personnel as well as agency casualties of Reagan's administrative strategy. For one reason or another, Labor Secretary Raymond Donovan, EPA head Anne Burford Gorsuch, and John P. Horton, also of EPA, White House aides Robert McFarlane, Michael Deaver, David Stockman, and others were ousted or resigned under fire. "Ten senior officials at EPA resigned or were fired and seven at HUD quit under pressure. Nine independent counsels conducted inquiries during the Reagan years."[11] Long past Reagan's presidency, investigations continued into the various HUD and Interior scandals. Nevertheless, as countless commentators noted, the genial, aw-shucks, Teflon president escaped unsullied as many aides fell in disrepute or political controversy around him.

While there were numerous accomplishments of the Reagan administration, the final assessment of its effect on government must be more negative than positive:

> Overall . . . the Reagan Administration has weakened more than strengthened the more permanent institutions of presidential management, has undermined the morale of the civil service, has taken a narrow auditing approach to improving management in the executive branch, has done little to encourage competent professionals to serve in the federal government, and has overlooked opportunities to strengthen existing partnership arrangements between the federal government and other institutions at the state and local level and in the private sector. . . . Pressure has been placed on the bureaucracy to cut costs, but far less has been done to improve program effectiveness. In fact, some of the basic information resources needed to gauge program effects have been sharply cut back. (Salamon and Lund 1985, 23)

George Bush's Administrative Strategy: A Tory at the Helm

Lacking what he called "the vision thing," i.e., an overriding ideological impetus, such as that driving Nixon and Reagan, George Bush was, perhaps, less likely to turn to an administrative strategy.

Nonetheless, he did employ some of its aspects, particularly in his use of appointees and in the regulatory realm. In terms of his appointees, according to Chase Untermeyer, Bush's Presidential Personnel Office (PPO) director, the new president "'wanted to make clear this was a new administration, not Ronald Reagan's third term, but George Bush's first'" (Aberbach 1991, 239). While it was said that Bush initially kept at least 50 percent of Reagan's appointees, many of these appointees were originally his people within the Reagan administration. Apparently, Bush had been successful in getting Reagan to appoint many of his campaign workers to administration positions, particularly in the second Reagan administration.

When George Bush came into office there was a rather determined effort to relocate those former non-Bush Reagan appointees who did stay on in the administration. With "Old faces in new places, new faces in old places" as the working motto of the PPO, the remaining Reagan appointees were shifted around to other agencies. One PAS in the Bush PAS interviews mentioned that he was the only Reagan PAS to be left in his incumbent position in the new Bush administration.

Those Independent Regulatory Commission (IRC) members who chaired their agency under Reagan (and who, by statute, Bush could not dismiss or reassign) were removed from the chair and generally ignored, according to one IRC PAS interviewee; there were to be no Reagan people left heading Bush administration agencies. The Bush administration was successful in this effort, leaving many Reagan people feeling somewhat abused or at least misused, according to this PAS who characterized Bush and his people as "rude and crude."

Another of Bush's administrative strategies was in the regulatory, or rather, deregulatory realm. He first moved to delay implementation of regulations and to eviscerate the agencies' independent power to promulgate regulations not mandated by Congress. In his State of the Union address in 1992 he issued and later extended an executive order mandating a moratorium on all new agency regulations.

He then moved to strengthen the Competitiveness Council, headed by Vice President Dan Quayle. This council had the power to supersede regulations promulgated by any of the executive agencies if it felt they would be bad for American businesses. With such a broad mandate there was plenty of room for conflict between the White House and the agencies and, of course, between the White House and the Congress. The EPA, for example, was a highly visible target of the Competitiveness Council's fire. In fact, as of the fall of 1992, the council or OMB had held up some seventy-six regulations the agency proposed, some in violation of deadlines established by the Congress. Thanks to the council's decrees, the EPA had missed forty-six deadlines in the Clean Air Act by October 1992. As one careerist observed, "The climate at the White House has been to do nothing. It stops regulators. It makes regulators question every step they take. It's chilled their work." It also led to numerous lawsuits against the EPA for violating the law by not creating regulations to implement laws passed by the Congress.

While this council existed in a previous incarnation in Reagan's administration under then–Vice President Bush, it had a much lower profile as the Task Force on Regulation. President Bush, as committed to deregulation as Reagan and spurred on by Vice President Quayle, elevated its status and power. However, when the council flexed its muscles to undercut the authority of the agencies to implement legislation, it drew heavy fire from the Democratic Congress who eliminated funding for the council in the summer of 1992 (and President Clinton abolished the council in the second week of his administration).

Bush's approach to the Congress was markedly different from that of his predecessor. While Ronald Reagan faced off with a "Make my day" sneer, Bush initially held out a hand of comity, calling for dialogue and communication with the Democratic Congress. As he said in his inaugural address, "We need compromise; we've had dissension. We need harmony; we've had a chorus of discordant voices. . . . To my friends—and yes, I do mean friends—in the loyal opposition and yes, I do mean loyal—I put out my hand. I'm putting out my hand to you, Mr. Speaker. I'm putting out my hand to you, Mr. Majority Leader. For this is the thing: this is the age of the offered hand."

The Congress took Bush at his word in the early days of the administration:

> During the early period of Bush's presidency, negotiation between the White House and Capitol Hill produced progress and substantial agreement on clean air legislation, aid to the Nicaraguan contras, and the bailing out of stricken savings-and-loan associations. Such was the cooperative spirit that was now abroad that, reviewing his first six months in office, a *Time* cover story [August 21, 1989] dubbed Bush "Mr. Consensus," concluding that "after eight years of the Reagan revolution, Bush's modest pragmatism seem[ed] more welcome than unwavering single-mindedness." (King and Alston 1991, 276)

George Bush's willingness to work with rather than against the Congress was a refreshing change for the Congress and for the country. It could hardly have been otherwise, however, given the factors facing the new president: the Reagan Revolution had pretty well run its course and was out of gas, the huge deficit Reagan bequeathed his successor precluded any new policy initiatives, and the Democrats still controlled the Congress (Pfiffner 1990, 70). Further, Bush's personality and the lack of depth of his election victory made his a presidency of consolidation.

Bush's election victory, while certainly his, owed a great deal to his predecessor's popularity and to Bush's clear promise not to deviate from Reagan's path. His lack of independence was based on his trouble with "the vision thing" and his modest rhetorical skills. Lacking the actor's gift of infusing what message he had with urgent sincerity, he stuck with the tried and true and promised basically a third term of the Reagan-Bush era, more than a first term of the Bush era. Further, he was not able and he did not even try to claim a clear popular mandate since the Congress was firmly in the hands of the Democrats and his party had lost seats in both houses with him at the helm. In fact, although he had won forty states, he had actually run behind the winners in 379 of the 435 congressional districts. The incoming Republicans felt they owed him little, the veterans had nothing to fear from him—his coattails were neither wide nor long (Edwards 1991, 130).

The huge budget deficit that was Reagan's legacy to Bush and the country further constrained Bush's ability to implement a vision, had he had one. Even if he had been so inclined, there would have been no great policy initiatives because there was no great source of funds to execute them. Bush was able to show some of his "kinder and gentler" side, however, in his appointments. While Reagan used his appointments to attack the federal government, often appointing bureau chiefs who were opposed to their bureau's mission, Bush changed symbols and opted for "the politics of social harmony," in Rockman's phrase, appointing "firefighters rather than flamethrowers," establishment types, not revolutionaries. For example, EPA chief William Reilly, well respected in the environmental communities, was appointed to show that the president cared about the environment (regardless of the little power actually given Reilly in the administration—this was, after all, the politics of symbolism). Early judicial appointments, though partisan, did not see the severe ideological trial that they faced in the Reagan administration (or would later in Bush's) (Rockman 1991, 11–12).

George Bush's personality bears some analysis, given his difference from his predecessor and how personal style influences public action. In contrast to the very popular president whose gift for verbal persuasion was world renowned ("The Great Communicator," as Reagan was called), George Bush suffered public problems with syntax, simple sentence construction, and a frequent inability to carry a consistent thought through a complete sentence, let alone an entire paragraph. Further, Bush did not carry the personal conviction of Reagan's radicalism. He was, in Bert Rockman's estimation, an old-fashioned Tory, one for whom great, moving rhetoric is unnatural, even a bit unseemly, one for whom compromise is a modus vivendi, not a four-letter word, one whose best work is done behind closed doors with other members of one's circle of peers, whether allies or foes, and one for whom the term *loyal opposition* is not an oxymoron. As was often noted, "Bush does not stir hearts. Nor does he stir sentiment of virtually any sort. As an individual, he contrasted markedly with Reagan in presenting self. Reagan stirred partisan hearts, but opposition fears. Bush does neither. Reagan could express radical ideas in dulcet tones. By contrast, Bush sounds flat and, when excited, even a bit tinny" (ibid., 6).

The election of 1988 saw no sweeping new ideas from the Bush camp. In fact, the campaign Bush waged was marked by the absence of energy and focus and by the disquieting appearance of a blatantly racist television ad that raised white fears of black crime (Lee Atwater's infamous Willie Horton ad) and cost Bush considerable credibility. Although victorious, he was in a politically weak position, facing a Democratic majority in the Congress that was battle-hardened and used to confrontation with the White House. Bush's personal style of compromise and conciliation was well suited to the situation he faced. Because he had no agenda to sell, there was little he needed from the Congress. With a minority of one-third plus one he had enough votes to sustain his vetoes. That is all he needed to maintain the status quo, which seemed to be *his* mandate (ibid., 10).

The "politics of social harmony is not driven by strong ideas, indeed, it is a politics that is virtually antithetical to powerful ideas." Thus, while Bush did not reverse any of Reagan's major policies, he usually did not pursue them with the fervor of the latter. As Rockman notes, "Like a well-honed bureaucrat, Bush has a high regard for the virtues of 'not doing'. . . . If Bush is a man of few ideas, correspondingly few are disastrously bad." He was a president who did well in good times but when situations called for mobilizing others, as in the budget deal of 1990, he was far less adept (ibid., 12–14).

While Reagan could glide quietly into his huge tax increase, for Bush it meant having to go back on his snarl of "read-my-lips-no-new-taxes" in order to cut a budget deal with the Congress. While he won the battle (the budget *was* passed), he lost the war (his reelection campaign). His success hurt him with Republicans far and wide who, rather than considering him a pragmatic statesman who did what he had to do, felt deeply and personally betrayed by his decision to raise taxes. It seriously alienated him from the Reaganites who still controlled the party and, increasingly, the Congress (e.g., House Minority Leader, self-proclaimed revolutionary, and Speaker-in-Waiting Newt Gingrich, never one to be mistaken for a Tory). The charge that Bush "tacked to the slightest breezes of political opportunism, rather than clinging to a clear and steadfast course," lingered with him throughout his administration. (In other instances, he won plaudits for bringing others along, as in the Persian Gulf War, but even there he was criticized for ending the war before it was won (i.e., before Saddam Hussein was destroyed) (ibid., 15).

Although there were some setbacks (e.g., the failed nomination of John Tower for Defense, a less-than-robust nominee, William Lucas, for assistant attorney general for civil rights, and the Exxon oil spill in Alaska that raised questions about Bush's claims to be the "environmental president"), he managed to put off dealing with the deficit, and events in the larger world conspired to make him look good in his early administration (ibid., 14–15).

> The breakup of the Soviet empire, the cozy relationship with Mikhail Gorbachev, the Soviet withdrawal from Afghanistan, arms and troop cutbacks, the end of the cold war and the triumph of democracy and capitalism, the end of civil strife in Nicaragua and the surprising election of the U.S.-backed opposition there—all these played to what Bush saw as his great strength and his image as a judicious and prudent policymaker.
>
> "Bush's temperament as an old-fashioned Tory (adjusted to American conditions) and the favorable-events stream were conjoined. As Bush read it, the obvious prescription was to 'do nothing, but do it well.' Old-fashioned Tories are, by definition, not in the vanguard for or against anything, but they are not necessarily in the rearguard either. When the nature of change becomes virtually self-revelatory is the time when conservatives of Bush's stripe find it useful to change course. The obvious eventually concentrates the mind of even the most skeptical, and Bush's beliefs, such as they are, are generally organized around whatever conventional wisdom is prevalent. But old-fashioned Tories are mainly empiricists, less likely to lead fashion than follow it. When fashion changed, Bush's posture also changed. Being more addicted to cold-war orthodoxies when he began his administration than Ronald Reagan was when he ended his, Bush's reaction to the powerful events around him was slow and cautious until it became clear that the old orthodoxy was crumbling. Once the obvious became obvious, the Bush administration moved accordingly, if unradically." (Ibid., 15)

In mid-1990 Bush abandoned his "read my lips" posture and as mentioned negotiated a budget deal cum tax increase with the Democrats in hopes of avoiding a recession that could hurt his reelection chances. Rather than proclaim that as a statesman he had to act for the good of the party and beyond narrow ideology and thus he went for the budget deal, he laid low and seemed to be hiding from the responsibility, which, of course landed squarely on his shoulders. After all his schoolyard brag- gadocio ("read my hips" in his jogging shorts), he looked as though he had caved in, rather than as though he had made a difficult but courageous de- cision, the kind citizens elect their leaders to make. He lost all around with Republicans in the Congress, with the Reaganite true believers, and with the populace at large, whether it supported a tax increase or not, be- cause he had gone back on the pledge he had so often and adamantly made, and on the strength of which many had voted for him.

> In both the budget episode and the Persian Gulf crisis, it is apparent that Bush works best as a low-key version of Lyndon Johnson—cutting deals with other leaders. His is the insider game. His weakness is in sensing outside perspectives and in extending the ambit of discussion and debate. This is not because, like Reagan, Bush has strong passions about the sub- stance, but because his style of operation is fundamentally boardroom politics and brokerage among "proper gentlemen," as traditional Tories conceive it. "Proper gentlemen" do not include Saddam Hussein, and cer- tainly not Newt Gingrich. Boardrooms, as well, are notorious for erring on the side of exclusivity. (Ibid., 18)

Bush's manners seem to be those of the manner to which he was born: be modest about yourself and considerate to others (ibid., 27). Only occa- sionally did hot flashes of testosterone break through his gentility, as when he boasted that he had "kicked ass" in a debate with vice presiden- tial candidate Geraldine Ferraro in 1984. In that same season the wealthy and patrician Barbara Bush, with a carefully cultivated image of grand- motherly warmth with her faux pearls and mismatched tennis shoes, slipped and let it be known that she considered the working-class Ferraro "that rich rhymes-with-witch."

In terms of his decision-making style, Rockman finds Bush to be of two irreconcilable minds, one characterized by risk aversion, caution, and prudence, the other by an impulsiveness in which he is "occasionally given to barroom language in lieu of the gentility in which he was raised. From time to time, he seems to feel the necessity to proclaim his man- hood by 'kicking ass'" (ibid., 29).

And so, on the one side, he carefully chose a David Souter, a gray suit without a paper trail whose nomination to the Supreme Court would not cause controversy, and on the other he ran racist campaign advertise- ments (Willie Horton), attacked Geraldine Ferraro, invaded Panama, and charged off to war in the Persian Gulf, playing "madcap golf" (eighteen holes in an hour and a half) as he went (ibid., 30).

Bush's random impulsiveness alarmed and shocked Republican elders on occasion, such as when he chose the barely known, untested, and not highly regarded Dan Quayle as his running mate, seemingly displaying an almost juvenile willfulness in the face of opposition from the party regulars. Then he nominated John Tower for Defense against their advice and stuck with him through a losing confirmation battle. Similarly, he ignored the advice of James Baker and others who urged him to adopt the triumvirate model of senior aides, rather than the strong chief-of-staff model that had proven so disastrous for Nixon with Haldeman and Ehrlichman and for Reagan with Don Regan in his first term. Instead, Bush chose John Sununu as his chief of staff, who operated in a hierarchical manner to similar negative results. While Sununu ostensibly ran an open and informal shop, characterized by face-to-face meetings and informal conversations rather than memoranda, his hierarchical style peeked through as he "placed himself as the final judge of whether aides could proceed with what they proposed or Sununu should first consult with the president." Indeed, aides with opposing viewpoints could be easily shut out of the policy process with no direct access to the president (Campbell 1991, 199).

Sununu's problems stemmed in part from his hierarchical style and in part from his insistence on a streamlined staff, another dimension of his overbearing style, a small staff being easier to control. Several trial balloons landed with the thud of lead: the early attempt to levy a tax on deposits in bank accounts in an attempt to stave off the crisis in the savings and loan industry caused a hail of protest and a hasty retreat; a barnstorming trip to mark the first one hundred days of the administration created no storm; the proposed reduction in the capital gains tax rate caused tumult among Republicans on the Hill. Other issues, such as Medicare catastrophic coverage, funding of abortions, and clean air legislation, caused him grief; all these events and issues were marked by inadequate staff work and hasty mop-up operations of damage control within the president's own party (ibid., 200–01).

In the fall of 1989, a strong secrecy motif emerged in the administration. For example, Bush did not tell his defense secretary, Richard Cheney, or CIA director, William H. Webster, about the planned Malta Summit between Bush and Mikhail Gorbachev. In December 1989 protests about inconsistencies in his China policy stemming from a visit to China by foreign adviser Brent Scowcroft, and Deputy Secretary of State Lawrence S.

Eagleberger, led to the embarrassing admission that Bush had secretly
sent the pair to Beijing one month after the massacre in Tienanmen
Square. The national security process [came up short in the] October 1989
attempted coup against Manuel Antonio Noriega of Panama when the
chair of the Joint Chiefs of Staff, General Colin Powell, was kept out of
the loop. Some suggest that Powell's "pique (at this turn of events) tipped
the scales toward an invasion that caught many insiders by surprise."

In the wake of these revelations during fall 1989, articles about
Bush's penchant for secrecy and distrust of open discussion—even within
the administration—of key foreign policies began to supplant those pur-
veying the previous conventional wisdom. This had breezily argued that
Bush held foreign policy so closely to his chest only because he preferred
to serve as his own secretary of state. One Republican knowledgeable
about both the Reagan and Bush administrations suggested that the president's secrecy amounted to an obsession that distorted other values: "A
lot of the way the White House operates is based on the leaks thing . . . I
think you know how obsessed George Bush is about leaks. What you
don't know is the fullness of the obsession. It's right up there as one of his
core values. You know, service, family, religion, leaks." (Ibid., 201–08)

One recurring theme of the administrative strategy is the centralization of power in the EOP at the expense of the cabinet. George Bush's administrative strategy was no exception to the rule. According to Campbell, the Bush White House more often than Reagan's bypassed the
cabinet council system in resolving key issues. It did the same with the
interagency process when it would not yield what the prime shakers in
the White House sought. "A former Reagan official who worked closely
with Bush asserted that his secretiveness stemmed from his impatience
with the messiness of democratic processes: '[the president] thinks our
system—with an excess of Congress and Press involvement—has made it
impossible to do what is right'" (ibid., 208).

Thus, OMB chief Richard Darman was able to establish himself as
the champion of cutting spending, holding back the demands of the agencies. Sununu established himself as the champion of conservative and
business causes: he was unusually successful at supplanting Treasury Secretary Nicholas Brady during the negotiations over the deficit (ibid., 211).

One final word about presidential personality is in order. A key aspect
of any president's public persona is the image his First Lady projects.
Rockman notes that the First Ladies Bush and Reagan were the opposites
of their husbands (Rockman 1991, 9). Barbara Bush was the warm and
supportive wife who played the part of the country's favorite grand-

mother, disclaiming any policy interest or role, talking about hearth and home, and displaying her large and happy family before the American public. Even Millie Bush, the family dog, having authored her own book (ghosted by Barbara Bush), was part of the four-year family photo opportunity that marked Bush's term.

In contrast, Nancy Reagan was widely feared in the White House for her behind-the-scenes power to dispatch aides who displeased her or threatened her husband's image and to protect those whom she favored. In her fierce defense of her husband and what she perceived to be his best interests and his place in history, she modified his more radical positions on issues such as abortion and relations with the Soviet Union (Campbell 1991, 192); she also consulted astrologers to plan her husband's schedule. A former actor like her husband, Nancy Reagan carried an innate bandbox fashion sense and was seen by many insiders as petty, tyrannical, vengeful, and extravagant. Both Reagans had been divorced and rarely attended church. The children of the president who so effectively preached family values, promoted prayer in the public schools, and was the hero of the Christian Right were in various stages of alienation from their parents— the Reagans had never even seen one of their grandchildren until he was nearly eighteen months old. The Reagan dogs rarely entered the public consciousness.

Conclusion

As observed above, the personality and style of the president significantly influence his approach to the presidency, whether he emerges as a paranoid schemer who suggests vandalizing his own party's headquarters to frame the Democrats, as did Nixon,[12] or as a Tory who claims office by virtue of his personal and political lineage. The administrative presidency has held particular attraction for presidents of the modern era who practiced it with varying degrees of success in an attempt to break gridlock and have their way with public policy. However, it is clear that the separation of powers, the politics-administration dichotomy, and the administrative presidency weigh heavily on the ability of government to function efficiently and effectively. Responsibility for the gridlock that many deplore must in some measure be laid at the door of the Constitution, with its mandated separation of powers. While some collaboration between the executive and legislative branches is, to a certain extent and fortunately, unavoidable, jealously guarded prerogatives resulting from the separation of powers incline both sides more toward competition than cooperation.

The venerable politics/administration dichotomy shares culpability for gridlock because its insistence on a wall of separation between policy-making political overlords and careerist spear-carriers continues to limit the contribution of just those individuals who "know how to put their hands on the right switches." Because careerists are not always able or willing to dance to the tune of those who mandate policy without having responsibility for its implementation, the dichotomy, while honored more in articulation than in action, also encourages the bureaucrat bashing that both disheartens careerists and lowers respect for the public service.

The administrative state, led by the administrative presidency, rounds out this troika of gridlock as it aspires to set in concrete the theories of the politics-administration dichotomy. In pursuing tight control of the executive branch agencies through politicization and centralization, the administrative state instead creates less control, more confusion, and ineffective government. Presidents are motivated to rely on the administrative state when they have a weak hand vis-à-vis the bureaucracy, a shaky mandate, or a strong vision they want to promote in a hurry. Yet, imprudent exercise of the tools of the administrative strategy can cause shipwreck rather than smooth sailing, as Richard Nixon, in particular, discovered. The following chapter explores in some detail the use of persons and the federal bureaucracy in the administrative strategy.

3

⚬✠⚬

Politicization and Depoliticization in the Nation's Pressure Cooker: Using the Bureaucracy to Secure the President's Agenda

Presidents have engaged in various strategies to gain control of the bureaucracy. The most popular are politicization, which involves use of appointees to exercise a heavy hand in the agencies, depoliticization, in which agency heads exert more independence from direct White House oversight, and centralization, which concentrates power in the Executive Office of the President (EOP) at the expense of the cabinet secretaries. The advantages and disadvantages of these strategies are the subject of this chapter.

Politicization: Presidentializing the Bureaucracy

Presidentializing the bureaucracy, or politicization, is a strategy for increasing presidential control of the executive branch through use of appointees as surrogates to implement policy goals. It can also involve increasing the number, power, and infiltration of appointees, especially in the lower levels of the bureaucracy, and increasing White House control and direction of the agencies.

Politicization is viewed differently by the two camps of executives, political and career. As one careerist explained the PAS perspective, "Political appointees want change, and they want it now. They've only got eighteen months or so and they want it to happen on their watch." They think politicization is the way to accomplish it.

Partisans of political leadership (and these almost always include the incumbent set of leaders) are doers, not doubters. They want tools, not obstacles. To the extent that doubts exist about the willingness of career administrators to carry out faithfully the policy directions of the political leadership, career administrators are viewed by political actors as impediments rather than implements. Partisans of politics, consequently, typically look to enhance procedures for control and supervision of the permanent administrative apparatus and, when deemed necessary, to politicize it. (Aberbach and Rockman 1988, 606)

Partisans of political leadership often use the concept and language of mandate, with the logic that presidential election confers automatic rights of sole determination of policy direction. This rationale is favored by theorists such as Nathan, Lowi, Rosen, Lynch, and Moe. Increasingly, those advocating strong presidential control want complete command of civil servants, as well. "As ex-White House aide (and not just coincidentally also ex-convict) John Ehrlichman so starkly put it . . . : 'When we say jump, the answer should be, how high?'" (Aberbach and Rockman 1988, 607).

Others, however, point to this nation's system of divided authority, checks and balances, in which other entities, such as the Congress and the judiciary, press legitimate claims to authority. They see a similar role for the career bureaucracy.

Partisans of the career or administrative perspective believe that a professional bureaucracy is necessary to achieve its goal of effective government. "Partisans of the career administration, on the other hand, view it as the ballast that maintains the ship of state in unsteady seas. Its resistor-like qualities to the super-charged enthusiasm of new political leaders are seen as a virtue, not a vice—a deterrent, in fact, to longer-run damage inflicted by political leaders on themselves as well as on the organizational fabric of government" (ibid., 606). Charges of career sabotage of changes in policy direction are not substantiated when good management practices are followed. In fact,

> good management, as reflected in open channels of communication, willingness to listen to advice, clear articulation of goals, and mutual respect . . . may also constitute good politics for department secretaries or their assistant secretaries. No evidence shows that good management is incompatible with effective politics unless the imposition of stringent command procedures is regarded as an integral part of a presidential administration's political style. The anti-bureaucratic styles of recent ad-

ministrations suggest that this symbolic component has become at least as important as achieving results. (Ibid., 609)

While politicization and centralization strategies have their place in the political landscape, their exact placement is a question of degree. Carried to extremes, they are schemes for sole presidential rule and are ultimately destructive to the effectiveness of the career bureaucracy on which government management turns. "The issue is not whether responsiveness should be promoted, but rather how reflexively and to whom." Attempts at presidential aggrandizement through politicization will only "rob government of its capability for reality testing, and it is without doubt a model for demoralization of the career service" (ibid., 609).

Furthermore, presidents and political administrators need career administrators to apply the brakes on occasion. Said one PAS:

One of the major functions . . . of the permanent apparatus is to serve presidents by helping them avoid stupid mistakes that threaten their political viability. The urge to command and to centralize often fails to recognize that political impulses should be subjected to tests of sobriety. Though there are a good many reasons to argue on behalf of the basic idea of "neutral competence" and against the politicization of all executive organizations, the most fundamental one that a president ought to consider is the avoidance of error and illegality that have wracked recent presidencies. (Ibid., 610)

Or, as he succinctly put it, "We do some stupid things. Trust the judgment of careerists in substantive issues . . . their program identification is very high but not partisan."

While some would argue that politicization of the federal bureaucracy is in the president's interest or in the public interest, neither rationale is likely to be true and, in fact, attempts at politicization invite retaliation by the Congress.

Nixon's fall from power was paved by the Watergate break-in, but it had as much to do with abuses of the executive as anything else. Even had Watergate not occurred, but with Congress remaining in the hands of the Democratic opposition, it is hard to imagine that the congressional hand would have been stayed for long. The revelations of 1986–87 involving the White House-NSC operation of arms shipments to Iran and laundered funds to the Nicaraguan contras also threatens to erode fatally the political standing and the policy credibility of the Reagan presidency. Operating through the back door and around the institutionalized apparatus of government can lead to decisions and illegalities that are truly presidency-threatening. It is hard to imagine that this is in a president's interests. (Ibid., 610)

The presidentialist literature, as represented by Nathan and Moe, urges reform of the political system to make it more amenable to presidential control through politicization of the bureaucracy and centralization of command in the executive. However, when presidents with short-term vision or goals make maximum use of these administrative tools, they are likely to provoke congressional retaliation and judicial stop signs in the long term.

If swift and sure congressional retaliation were a given in the game, presidents would learn to replace their competitive behavior with norms of cooperative behavior. However, there is scant hope for this eventuality because presidents have incentives to operate with a short time frame, rather than with a longer one, and Congress does not hold them accountable for the latter.

If presidents follow their short-term interests, they are likely to stimulate more and more restrictive congressional bonds on their behavior, thereby giving presidents incentives to engage in the types of behavior exemplified by the Iran-Contra Affair. Yet each individual president is likely to put his short-term interests above the institution's interests. As in many other aspects of American politics, Congress is key here. It will ultimately determine the kind of presidency we get. It must act expeditiously when presidents arrogate for their exclusive use constitutionally shared authority. Otherwise, presidents will take as theirs what Congress by its inaction bestows. (Ibid., 611)

Depoliticization and Debureaucratization: Push and Pull on Appointees

As Mosher observes, the claim that "the government of the United States is run not by career ministers but by amateurs" is something of an exaggeration.

A substantial part of the government is in fact run by career officials and under laws that permit little discretion; and a good many noncareer officials are in fact professionals, not amateurs. Yet the central fact remains:

a relatively small number of political appointees, whose tenure is typically temporary, are presumed to govern the activities of [the 4.25 million, excluding the 600,000 employees of the U.S. Postal system] mostly permanent federal employees in the civil service, the military services, and other career systems. The politically appointed and presumably responsive executives amount to less than one-tenth of one percent of total direct federal employment. (Mosher 1985, 405)

The institution of the federal bureaucracy exists in more-or-less creative tension with the institution of democracy in this country. While career executives might be seen to represent the former, political executives who serve at the pleasure of the democratically elected president represent the latter. It is the interaction of the career professionals with the democratic controls of the political appointees that keeps the political dynamic alive.

There is a careful sense of interplay and interdependence between these two institutions of bureaucracy and democracy as represented by their practitioners, the career and political executives. Bureaucracy thrives on the democratic values of openness, fairness, and achievement. Neutral competence is its highest standard. Democracy depends on the public service ethic and administrative expertise to bring to fruition its commitment to the common good through exercise of responsive competence.

Bureaucracy and democracy are two of the great political forces of the modern age. That [their] growth has been parallel seems paradoxical, as they appear wholly opposed in spirit; the former requires hierarchy, order, and technical expertise, the latter equality, freedom, and participation. While these conflicts should not be minimized, neither should they obscure the common heritage and continuing interdependence of these forces. Both bureaucracy and democracy, as Max Weber, the great German sociologist, observed, rest on the Enlightenment impulse to law and reason, on the rejection of traditional, ascriptively based systems of authority. And more to the point, neither force can survive and prosper without the other. Just as true bureaucracy thrives on the democratic values of achievement, fairness, and unfettered information, so is bureaucracy a fundamental requisite of modern democratic government. Absent the administrative capacity to give them substance, public policies in pursuit of the public good, as articulated by elected representatives, can be no more than feeble and sterile avowals of intent. (Huddleston 1987, 79)

However, neither bureaucracy nor democracy operates in a political vacuum; they both relate to and influence one another with sometimes adverse effects. Depoliticization and debureaucratization take place simultaneously in the government as a result of this reciprocal relationship and both constitute a danger to the higher federal service.

Depoliticization, or movement away from the president's policy agenda, happens when appointees seek to get deeply involved in the daily workings of their agency and to micromanage the work of the career people they supervise. The more involved they become, the more they take on the perspective of their agency and the less responsive they become to the president who appointed them.

Debureaucratization happens when the White House responds to political executives' distancing by trying to exert more control over the top career levels. The result is that the careerists then tend to identify more with the policies and purposes of the executive and to move away from the career standard of neutral competence.

This scenario has political and career executives taking on each other's characteristics and passing one another in the wrong directions. While its degree of accuracy may be a point of debate, the theory does raise important questions because the ability of the two groups to associate with one another with integrity and to work cooperatively relates directly to the quality of government the citizens receive.

The political agenda of the president and his appointees emerges as a key factor in the roles-and-relationships issue, as can be seen in the ferocity of the policy conflicts that occasionally surface between political and career executives. However, despite the rhetoric of the Reagan administration and with some glaring exceptions from that era (e.g., EPA, DOE, FDA, Interior, Labor), political appointees are not generally independent policy actors within the bureaucratic agencies of the federal government.

Even if appointees do come with an ideological axe to grind and a powerful president behind them, ideas cannot be put into practice immediately in democratic governments. It takes time to set the stage for policy changes. Presidents and their appointees can start the process but, given the limited tenure of PASs, in most cases they will not be around long enough to bring their heart's desire to fruition. As they know, to their sometimes considerable frustration, the career bureaucrats can simply outwait them.

It is more likely, however, that while political appointees often enter an agency with hostility and suspicion toward the career employees whom they must supervise, they eventually come to respect the careerists, their expertise, and their dedication to their work. They come to see them as colleagues who are a valuable resource for managing the affairs of state.

While there is a certain inevitability of politicization in the system, undue politicization is the real issue. As political control of administration is fundamental to a democracy, the question of greater significance is how much and what kind of politicization exists. It is a question that cannot be answered empirically because its answer is grounded in values. Asking this question about the degree and kind of political control, however, is an important component of the debate.

Bureaucratizing the Presidency:
Centralizing Power in the Executive Office, from FDR to George Bush

As discussed above, bureaucratizing the presidency, while highly refined by Nixon, did not originate with him. The genesis of the movement toward bureaucratizing the presidency or increasingly concentrating power in the White House staff is generally credited to the 1937 Brownlow Report's plea that "the President needs help" in running the government. Prior to FDR, cabinet officers carried the primary policy portfolios and presidents looked to executive assistants and personal service aides for other needs. The first sign of policy power leaking away from the cabinet came when Roosevelt turned to the Bureau of the Budget "to put the presidential stamp on the federal establishment [and] the modern, centralized apparatus of the White House began to take shape" (Smith 1988, 301).

Then, demands for an activist presidency provided the impetus for the expansion of the White House staff at the expense of both the permanent government and the president's cabinet. "As modern presidents mistrusted the permanent civil service to carry out their policies, they added staff to develop the reach and expertise to impose presidential will on the parochial interests of the departments" (ibid.).[1]

Aggrandizement of the EOP at the expense of the cabinet began in the Truman administration, when staff moved from being generalists to taking areas of specialization and assistants of their own, "precedents for the fiefdoms that later distinguished the White House. At the same time, two major units, the Council of Economic Advisers and the National Security Council, joined the White House complex, each giving the president a capacity for overseeing important government activities that was not totally dependent on the departments" (Hess 1988, 2–3). Truman generally used the cabinet as a board of directors until the Korean War, when the National Security Council became his chief policy advisor (ibid.).

Eisenhower turned back to the cabinet for policy advice and slowed "the assimilation of power [somewhat] . . . , still expecting cabinet officers to run their departments with a minimum of second-guessing from his staff." Meanwhile, the White House staff continued to expand under Eisenhower due to "the president's faith in [military-style] management (a staff secretariat, a cabinet secretariat, and so forth)" (Hess 1988, 83). In 1954 he established "a two-person cabinet secretariat [as well as] several subject-oriented interagency councils and committees that operated independently of one another" (Newland 1985, 138).

Kennedy cut back on Eisenhower's institutional machinery, but the demands of an activist liberal administration with its belief that "government should do more faster" soon meant more growth for the "president's personal staff, Executive Office units, and presidential councils; . . . agencies such as the Office of Economic Opportunity were placed directly under the presidential umbrella" (Hess 1988, 3). "The growth of the Kennedy White House was based on the president's belief that if a task was important enough, it was necessary to have someone at the White House with responsibility for prodding the bureaucracy. Roosevelt's favored technique was to spawn new agencies; Kennedy more often chose to add White House expediters" (ibid., 83).

With Nixon's suspicions being at what Hess termed a "pathological" level, he had little or no confidence in either the civil service or his own appointees to carry out his policies. His White House got involved in department operations to the point that EOP staff sometimes bypassed cabinet officers and issued instructions directly to lower-level appointees. While Nixon used cabinet-level bodies, councils, for various policy issues, "that policy management approach was soon discontinued as being too fragmented and time-consuming." In the reorganization that followed, more power accrued to the EOP under Ehrlichman's Domestic Council, which used interagency task forces as "vehicles for isolating cabinet officers from the president and from channels of direct EOP control of subordinate agency levels. A curious mixture of extreme centralization and fragmentation within the EOP developed" (Newland 1985, 139–40).

As discussed in chapter 2, Nixon and his top aides so abused the prerogatives of the office, particularly following the 1972 election victory, that many began to worry about the imperialization of the presidency. Their excesses led his immediate successors to reject the strong-chief-of-staff model in favor of the spokes-in-a-wheel model. This model features several senior advisors who operate somewhat independently in their own domain and have direct access to the president; the chief has more of a coordinating than a commanding role. This model lasted until the beginning of Reagan's second administration, when Donald Regan reasserted the strong-chief model to similarly negative effect (Campbell 1991, 188).

Gerald Ford quickly restored cabinet and agency involvement in policy development. While his domestic policy staff coordinated interagency task forces, agency heads or other appointees chaired them. Coordination and involvement of all policy actors was improved (Newland 1985, 140).

However, management went downhill in the Carter administration.

> Domestic policy under . . . Carter was characterized by incoherence and even disorder. Though boasting competent policy staff in Stuart Eisenstadt and Jack Watson, and interagency task forces to facilitate EOP/agency interaction, cabinet departments were endlessly involved in policy formulation—and in disputes. In part, the Carter problem was caused by some trivialization of the policy staff role. Carter pulled back at midterm from his initial heavy involvement of the cabinet, and his Domestic Policy Staff became increasingly used for casework and for short-term political and legislative activities at the expense of policy development and synthesis. . . . A clear Carter difficulty was weak EOP leadership outside the Domestic Policy Staff. . . . The agencies included some strong domestic policy figures, . . . but generally the administration was a collection of disparate elements that never jelled. (Ibid., 140–41)

Further, partisan staffing took a great leap forward under Carter, both in the staffing of the EOP and in that of the top level of the administrative and program management of the agencies. This was accomplished with the passage of the Civil Service Reform Act of 1978 that created the Senior Executive Service. This "resulted in deinstitutionalization at the top of the career civil service, opening the way legally for further partisan politicization not only in the EOP but at key operating levels throughout government" (ibid., 141).

Additionally, Carter's administration saw a denigration of expertise, per se, and a resurgence of neo-Jacksonianism, "the notion that in this democracy any citizen [could] do any public job. Anybody chosen for whatever reason unrelated to management experience or talent, [could] run any government agency" (Sundquist 1979, 4).

Jimmy Carter's outsider status, while largely responsible for his election, also meant that his grasp of the nature and needs of his new office was unsophisticated and provincial. His knowledge of political and administrative personnel in Washington was likewise limited. So he used his experience as governor of Georgia to map out a plan for organizing and staffing his office "as though Washington were Atlanta, writ large" (ibid., 4). This was not at all unusual, for

> all presidents, even those with long experience in Washington, have surrounded themselves with home-state personnel to some degree. Truman had his Missouri "cronies," Kennedy his "Irish Mafia" from Massachusetts, Nixon his southern Californians. Yet Carter seems to have carried home-state cronyism beyond the point of any other recent president. The result was an inner circle that, far from compensating for Carter's personal weaknesses, compounded them to a singular degree. Except for the fortunate influence of Vice President Mondale—the only outsider who seems to have become a generalist adviser—the inner circle was ill-equipped for the crucial task of broadening Carter's own perspective, of educating him in the problems and outlooks of other regions and in the ways of the Congress and of the labyrinthine executive branch over which he now presided. (Ibid., 4)

However, the early days of Carter's administration saw an intentional downgrading of the EOP to balance what was widely understood as its excess power under Nixon. At the same time, Carter emphasized "cabinet government" as distinct from "White House government" and expended considerable care and energy in selecting his team. A thorough nationwide talent search resulted in a cabinet of women and men of "experience and proven competence. . . . [Though] most of the Cabinet members had made no reputation as managers at all, . . . by the standard of any recent presidency [the] twelve rank high—not a hack among them" (ibid., 5).

> Carter's notion of a non-ideological process that would create the best of all possible policies required, above all, the best of all possible people—experienced, intelligent, open-minded. His instructions, therefore, were for the transition staff to identify the most qualified people available, which resulted in a confused and redundant talent search that generated 125,000 resumes, not including 16,000 suggestions from Congress. Because he thought experience and considerations of affirmative action more important than . . . political philosophy, the administration he cobbled together showed a wide range of opinion that ultimately caused turmoil. (Hess 1988, 154)

By the summer of 1979, Carter was facing growing lines at gas stations, soaring inflation, and conflicts within his administration. He retired to Camp David to regroup. He restructured his office and installed Hamilton Jordan as the formal chief of staff. Loyalty rather than competence became the main criteria for evaluating department heads. Cabinet heads were instructed to complete "evaluation sheets on subcabinet officers, which Jordan later used to target about 50 for replacement." Carter demanded pro forma resignations from his entire cabinet and then fired five cabinet officers. This move, eerily reminiscent of Nixon's identical action in 1972, was to similar negative effect, as "the departing secretaries were generally considered among the most effective, making it seem as if Carter were blaming the cabinet for his own short-comings." As one observer uncharitably noted, "They're cutting down the biggest trees and keeping the monkeys" (ibid., 160).

Reagan followed a different, more focused, path than Carter. As discussed in chapter 2, he

> was not interested in diversity and had two good reasons for seeking a cadre of distilled conservatives. The success of his hands-off management style would depend on trusted subordinates in tune with his policies. And his presidency was to be geared toward policy implementation instead of policy development, since the policies were to be those that he had spent two decades promoting. Diverse opinions would only get in the way. Personnel Director [Pendleton] James scrutinized resumes to find loyal and ideologically pure applicants—expertise was a secondary consideration. (Ibid., 154)

There was a delicious irony to the Carter and Reagan appointments: "For two presidents who arrived in Washington speaking the language of insurgency, vowing to challenge the power of the Washington establishment, Carter and Reagan ended up appointing supremely conventional cabinets" (ibid., 155).

Reagan, like Truman, initially treated his cabinet as members of a board of directors of a corporation, which was fine with them, "since virtually all were successful businessmen, many of them epitomizing Reagan's ideal of a self-made man" (ibid., 161). Having made heavy use of his cabinet while governor of California, he was comfortable with his cabinet members as policy-level colleagues (Campbell 1991, 189). From the start, Reagan established a bond with his appointees so they would identify with him rather than with their agency. He made it clear that they were his representatives to the agencies and not vice versa.

Reagan's long-term commitment to a particular agenda produced an initial emphasis on collegiality among his cabinet and with the EOP, using the same approach as Ford and Carter of a coordinating rather than a dictating chief of staff. However, when Don Regan took over in 1984, that approach was quickly dismissed in a return to hierarchical organization; the EOP gained power at the expense of the cabinet as, "in the interests of agenda enforcement, teamwork was sought and, with conspicuous exceptions, significantly achieved. . . . [I]n the design of the official policy management apparatus, efforts [were] made to create coordinated but differentiated networking structures and processes" (Newland 1985, 142).

Regan resigned in the midst of the Iran-Contra scandal in early 1987 and Reagan, with more felicitous results, returned to the directing rather than dictating model under first Howard Baker and then Ken Duberstein (Campbell 1991, 188).

The early part of the Bush administration saw a change from the strict EOP control of the cabinet and agencies practiced in the Reagan White House, a downgrading of White House staff power in favor of cabinet leadership. Initially, George Bush was more likely to surround himself with technically competent staffers who would not seek to manage him too tightly or to dominate the cabinet. He was also more likely than Reagan to deal with his cabinet secretaries directly and individually, rather than using his staff as intermediaries, although he tended to use his monthly cabinet meetings for briefings rather than for policy deliberation (Pfiffner 1990, 67). "The use of the full cabinet as a deliberative body had greatly diminished since its effective use by President Eisenhower. This was due to its increased size (with 14 cabinet departments in 1989), but more importantly to the cross cutting nature of most presidential policy issues and the president's need for advice from a broader perspective than that of the individual department heads" (ibid., 67).

Taking sixty-five days to complete his cabinet, George Bush appointed highly experienced people with a cumulative one hundred years of government experience. He told them he wanted them to "think big" and "challenge the system." Roger Porter, Bush's assistant to the president for economic and domestic policy, had advanced the cabinet council in Gerald Ford's administration and had helped implement it in Ronald Reagan's. His influence was clearly seen in the system of three councils used by Reagan and continued by Bush (the councils were Economic Policy, Domestic Policy, and National Security) (ibid., 67).

Porter's influence was also present through the "multiple advocacy" he promoted "as a model for advising the president." To accommodate the president's "preference for oral briefings White House aides set up 'scheduled train wrecks,' policy free-for-alls in which administration officials would engage in policy disagreements and answer questions from the president." He told them he wanted frank and open discussion and advocacy for particular positions, but when a decision was made they were expected to support it. Those closest to the president were given significant latitude in policy development in the early months of the administration, to the extent that some secretaries initiated policy without prior White House approval. This administration was characterized by the president's team values and the familiarity of colleagues who had long worked together, many of them (e.g., Brent Scowcroft, Richard Cheney, and James Baker) veterans of the Reagan administrations (ibid., 67).

> By the summer of 1989 it appeared that President Bush might have formed the most influential cabinet since President Eisenhower in terms of the willingness of the president to give cabinet secretaries the latitude within which to operate in their jurisdictions. It is ironic that President Bush, one of the few recent presidents who did not talk about "cabinet government," may have come closest to implementing it. (Ibid., 67)

The relative power of the EOP and the cabinet would change over the course of the administration, as discussed in later chapters. For now, two examples of EOP muscle flexing give evidence of the reversion of power to that office. Both occurred in the pretesting stage of the General Accounting Office (GAO)–sponsored Bush PAS Survey for this book. In April 1992, when the deputy secretary of the Department of Housing and Urban Development casually mentioned to the White House political staff that he was going to pretest the survey, they told him he could not do so. Somewhat baffled, he backed out of the pretest, saying, "I don't have any problem with it, I'm happy to do it—but I work for them." He referred the author to a member of the Office of the White House Counsel for further discussion. (In the Department of Veterans Affairs, however, the assistant deputy secretary discussed participation with the secretary who gave him the go-ahead, and the assistant deputy secretary then pretested the survey.)

The second example of centralized White House control occurred when the head of the Presidential Personnel Office (PPO), Constance Horner, directed the head of OPM, Constance Berry Newman, not to cooperate with the PAS study by withholding a mailing list of PAS executives. The mailing list for the survey was subsequently sought through other, more laborious, expensive, and ultimately fruitless means. Then, after a delay of some two months, the White House mysteriously agreed to cooperate with the GAO to the extent that it would mail the surveys to the PASs. Citing the Privacy Act, however, it refused to let any GAO staff even see (let alone have) the list of political executives to whom it was sending the survey.[2]

Four features characterize the modern presidency, according to Hess. First, tremendous growth has occurred in the size of the White House staff. In the fifty years from Roosevelt to Reagan, it grew from thirty-seven to more than nine hundred individuals, the Executive Office of the President from zero to thousands (Hess 1988, 5). Exact numbers, however, are very difficult to obtain because the White House does not make public the numbers of employees from the various agencies who are detailed to the White House and work for it alone or on a shared-time basis. A recent study by the GAO found 116 detailees in three of the fourteen offices of the EOP it studied (the White House Office, the Office of Policy Development, and the Office of the Vice President). An additional twenty-eight persons, called nondetailees, who seemed to have no formal status, were also found to work in these three offices (see chapter 4 for details on the White House staff).[3]

A second feature of the modern presidency is that blaming the permanent government for the problems of the country has led to the proliferation of special and functional offices in the White House itself by presidents who do not trust the bureaucracy to carry out their policies (ibid., 5).

A third feature is that "the rising influence of White House staff members on the president and the corresponding decline in cabinet influence has meant a serious separation of policy formulation from policy implementation." This shift of balance may also have an effect on the type and feasibility of proposed policy as White House aides, being more isolated from the pressures of implementation, have fewer bureaucratic restraints and reality testers than cabinet officers (ibid., 5).

Fourth, White House aides have "increasingly become special pleaders. . . . When Truman gave an aide responsibility for minority affairs" he established the precedent whereby an increasing number of groups felt the need for an inside person looking out for their interests in the White House. This further moved the action away from the agencies to the EOP to the point "where once the White House had been a mediator of interests, it now had become a collection of interests" (ibid., 6).

These features have led to what is termed "the bureaucratization of the presidency" and mean that "ultimately the modern presidency has moved toward creating all policy at the White House, overseeing the operations of government from the White House, using White House staff to operate programs of high presidential priority, and representing in the White House all interests that are demographically separable" (ibid., 6).

Difficulties controlling the executive agencies and keeping PASs in line with White House policy drive presidents to seek to concentrate more power in the hands of their White House staff. However, centralization can backfire and damage the president, as happened in the Iran-Contra scandal when White House tracks were everywhere in abundance.

> In this case, as in others, policies that are secretly devised in the White House bypass an important error-correction mechanism—criticism from well-informed departmental [career] officials. And policies executed with dispatch may only be ill-considered schemes that could not survive prolonged examination and debate. So they are high-risk undertakings from which a president may extract great benefit but [that] may also have disastrous consequences. (Rourke 1991b, 132)

Bureaucratizing the presidency, then, can be a risky strategy. Presidentializing the bureaucracy, or following a decentralization strategy, as discussed above, is a safer way for presidents to "imprint their own preferences on their administration's record in office." Its clear advantage is that "it helps distance the president from the political damage caused by failure in making or executing policy that inevitably occurs in every administration. On such occasions it is far better for the president if an agency outside the White House has hands-on responsibility for policy decisions in the area where a mishap has taken place" (ibid., 133).

For example, because the 1986 *Challenger* disaster was safely located in NASA (presidentialized and decentralized), the White House managed to quiet speculation that the launch was timed and perhaps rushed for presidential advantage in the congressional elections. In contrast, as discussed earlier, because the Iran-Contra affair was managed from the White House (bureaucratized and centralized), Reagan could not escape at least some responsibility for it. As Rourke observes, "it is not easy to remove the president's fingerprints from a policy disaster when it is engineered by his immediate circle of White House advisers and assistants" (ibid., 133).

Ups and Downs of the Centralized Presidency

There are questions and problems with this strategy of centralization, such as the extent to which the EOP staff can act on its own initiative to carry out what it perceives to be presidential policy. "Presidents can become captured by the strongest personality in their White House. Bob

Haldeman had this effect on Nixon, as did Donald Regan on Reagan" (Campbell 1991, 216). Beyond drawing power away from the cabinet, centralization has the potential to "become an irrational force in executive policymaking, capable of inflicting far more damage on the president's and the nation's welfare than any of the executive agencies whose errors it has been charged with preventing" (Rourke 1991b, 134). As in the Watergate and Iran-Contra scandals, centralization, simply put, can spell the potential for huge disaster with no one else to blame.

Another problem is the extent to which the shift of power to the White House staff has undermined the value of expertise and the career bureaucracy.

> the administration can become so absorbed with retention of its approval ratings that it stops looking after the long-range interests of the United States. The systematic discounting of the advice of career civil servants and the reflex to accuse dissenting cabinet secretaries of having "gone native" serve as the principal symptoms of this condition. The Reagan administration displayed this syndrome to an unparalleled degree. We need only point to the still unresolved deficit issue and its many consequences for economic, social, and foreign policy to highlight the dysfunctions of White Houses governed by polls. (Campbell 1991, 216)

This is discussed further in chapter 5. There is also a significant potential for overload on the White House as it seeks to micromanage issues and the agencies, massage the Congress, direct spin control, and plot the political course. The White House could easily collapse under the weight of its own self-imposed overload, a problem that plagued the Carter White House (ibid., 216).

Additionally, tight control may work against the mission of some agencies, threatening their perceived integrity. As Rourke points out, "Agencies such as the Fed and independent regulatory agencies (IRCs) such as the TVA have found their effectiveness and credibility enhanced by their independence" (Rourke 1991b, 134).

Given the problems and dangers of centralizing the presidency and the advantages of a certain degree of administrative freedom, centralization is a strategy presidents would do well to employ only sparingly.

The centralized presidency can work if the president is in tune with public opinion, if lines of communication to the cabinet remain open, and if the president does not become a prisoner of his own inner circle of advisors (Hess 1988). Lyndon Johnson effectively managed a centralized presidency until massive popular resistance to the war in Vietnam drove him into isolation and what many considered paranoia. Nixon, on the other hand, early on violated all of the guidelines for a successful centralized presidency. Nixon, "the first activist conservative president [actually] . . . sought isolation." Suspicious of both his cabinet members and government bureaucracy, "he structured his staff to limit his association to those with whom he felt most comfortable. . . . In the end this Greta Garbo conception of the presidency was unsuited to democratic leadership" (ibid., 3–4).

Nixon was the first president, but not the last, to suffer the self-inflicted wounds of the isolated and overly centralized presidency. To some degree, those who followed him have had the same set of issues with which to deal, particularly with regard to political appointments.

In contrast to Waterman and Nathan who argue for a strong presidency, Hess argues for a president who is the "chief political officer" rather than the "chief manager" of the federal bureaucracy. As he notes, there is no constitutional support for this chief manager function; the role of program manager is given directly to the various agency heads by the Congress. As discussed previously, the president simply needs the bureaucracy to run the country. "This attempt [at centralized White House control] can never succeed. Even an overblown White House staff is simply too inadequate a fulcrum for moving the weight of the executive branch, which employs more than 5 million people and spends over a trillion dollars annually" (ibid., 6).

Hess believes the president's major responsibility is to set national policies and priorities through the budget and legislative proposals and to guarantee the nation's security. When presidents overstep that function they "undermine confidence in the presidency by burdening the White House staff beyond its capacity to effect change and deliver services" (ibid., 7). Additionally, the inevitable tensions between the career bureaucrats and the EOP staff "are heightened when the competing White House bureaucracy is staffed with inexperienced outsiders with little knowledge of the federal government" (Seidman and Gilmour 1986, 77).

Carter and Reagan further exacerbated those tensions by bringing novice supporters from their home state to Washington, rather than relying on those who already knew the system. The personal loyalty that outside supporters bring, while making the president feel more at ease, tends to create a closed system of go-it-alone independence that isolates the president, à la Nixon and Reagan. With them it created "a presidential court with all the trappings and intrigues associated with an ancient monarchy." Not a Republican failing alone, this tendency toward a closed system fed George Reedy's characterization of Johnson's court late in his administration as a "mass of intrigue, posturing, strutting, cringing and pious commitment to irrelevant windbaggery" (quoted in Seidman and Gilmour 1986, 77).

Because White House staff possess no power in their own right and serve only at the pleasure of the president, competition and turf battles are a constant feature of court life as aides jockey with one another, other units within the EOP, and agency heads for information and access to the president's ear (Seidman and Gilmour 1986, 77). The many dangers and shortcomings of the centralized presidency argue against excessive bureaucratization of the presidency, but, as developments in two key agencies, the Office of Management and Budget (OMB) and the Office of Personnel Management (OPM), demonstrate, it continues to be a favored presidential strategy.

OMB: The Metamorphosis of BOB, the Politicization of the Budget Function

Politicization (the replacement of careerists with politicals and the resultant agency movement away from neutral competence and toward political responsiveness) has been particularly vigorous at two central executive agencies, the Office of Management and Budget (OMB) and the Office of Personnel Management (OPM). The budget function began its slide toward politicization, however gently, under Truman, when the Bureau of the Budget (BOB) took on more responsibility and power to provide staff and services for presidential assistants. Thus was blurred "the theoretical line between the institutional and personal presidencies that separated the Executive Office from the White House" (Hess 1988, 2–3).

However, BOB, from the director on down, was totally staffed by careerists for the twenty years of Democratic governance that ended with Eisenhower's inauguration. His suspicions of an entrenched bureaucracy loyal to Democratic philosophy minimally furthered politicization of the budget function. But, while Eisenhower initiated cabinet-oriented innovations, "BOB's neutral policy role survived with orthodox integrity," at least for a while (Newland 1985, 138). BOB started to lose ground, however, as Kennedy

> reduced cabinet meetings to a bare minimum and trimmed [the] national security affairs machinery. He appointed political task forces prior to and after his election to develop policy topics or fields. By late December 1960 Kennedy had eleven such groups in foreign affairs and eight in domestic policy. . . . Policy staff functions were increasingly separated out of the

BOB, partisan politicization increased, . . . and policy influence began to slip away from the BOB. (Ibid., 138)

BOB's role as a source of impartial, nonpartisan advice diminished further under Johnson, who used more policy task forces than Kennedy, many of which functioned predominantly off the record. BOB's fate was sealed under Johnson when he gave coordination of Great Society policy to two of his aides, Joseph Califano and Larry Levinson, with power to detail BOB personnel for policy roles (ibid., 138). Johnson's action indicates considerable thought and intent, as his memoirs suggest:

> Previously the standard method of developing legislative programs had consisted of adopting proposals suggested by the departments and agencies of the government. The Bureau of the Budget and to a lesser degree the White House staff would analyze the suggested measures and submit them to the President. From this process derived the programs that an administration presented to the Congress. I had watched this process for years, and I was convinced that it did not encourage enough fresh or creative ideas. The bureaucracy of the government is too preoccupied with day-to-day operations, and there is a strong bureaucratic inertia dedicated to preserving the status quo. As a result, only the most powerful ideas can survive. Moreover, the cumbersome organization of government is simply not equipped to solve complex problems that cut across departmental jurisdictions. (Qtd. in ibid., 139)

His new strategy was designed to do more and to do it more quickly. While BOB's civil service workers were committed to giving budget-pruning advice and serving the institution of the presidency with neutral competence throughout Johnson's administration, Nixon introduced a new layer of political control into the agency—the program associate directors (PADs). These PADs quickly assumed great power in nearly every agency. They currently head the permanent examining divisions and are responsible for line operations, unlike the former political assistants who served as staff aides to the director on ad hoc assignments. This means that the budget-making process resides in the hands of political appointees, which further politicizes the entire budgeting process (Heclo 1977, 80).

EOP's grasp caught up with its reach during Nixon's administrative reorganization under Ehrlichman, and BOB's credibility gasped its final breath in 1970 when it became the Office of Management and Budget, "deeply layered with partisan officials, and . . . often in competition with other EOP political offices." Nixon had gone so far as to move the OMB director's office into the White House West Wing, giving him the status of presidential assistant. Its directors, George Schultz and Roy Ash, shifted from the "neutral competence" of their former role to active involvement in policy decisions (Newland 1985, 139–40).

Soon the OMB director became a key policy player. "Because no president can spend more than a fraction of his own time on management, he must depend in this aspect of his job on the skills and stature of a managerial alter ego. The Director of the Budget, since that office was created, has been the nearest thing to such a person" (Sundquist 1979, 5).

While Ford tried to depoliticize the office somewhat, Carter repoliticized OMB, thanks to his interest in budget details and in OMB's executive branch reorganization, and his close personal association with his budget director, Bert Lance. Consequently, OMB fared no better under Carter:

> Every chief executive before Carter at least searched carefully for a director with the special talents and interests required to enable him to master the details of government and to act for the president in monitoring the implementation of governmental programs. Jimmy Carter did not. In appointing Bert Lance, he gave priority to considerations other than capacity for management and became the first president to bring the directorship of OMB within the ambit of home-state cronyism. Then Lance himself, instead of applying himself to learning the job of Management and Budget, became best known as the president's emissary to the business community. [Lance likewise surrounded himself with political appointees several levels down who were equally unschooled and unconcerned with knowledge of the federal government, budget or management.] . . . Of the top 10 political appointees in OMB, only one had worked in the executive branch of the federal government. (Ibid., 5)

Reagan raised the stakes by adding more political appointees to OMB, further politicizing the budget function. OMB also suffered self-inflicted wounds in Reagan's first term. Under Budget Director David Stockman, OMB cut back 20 percent of some ten thousand federal regulations and involved the office in lobbying Congress for the passage of the budget for the first time. "As it became more and more embroiled in partisan politics its credibility as the source of objective numbers plummeted" (Hess 1988, 163).

Stockman, widely termed brilliant, eventually admitted in an interview with the *Atlantic Monthly* (August 1981) that even he never really believed the numbers and budgetary projections his office was publishing.

This led to even further diminution of OMB, already weakened after a decade of growing politicization. As Newland explains it: "Politicization of the OMB since the 1960s is not a matter of partisan use of reliable expert information; it is a deterioration of capacity to produce believable information due to displacement of professional expertise by political partisans at levels below the director. Reagan, with his inexperienced partisan appointees, has given a far greater unprofessional cast to OMB than Carter" (Newland 1983, 12).

Bush's OMB saw no gain in credibility. OMB Director Richard Darman, widely feared for his (domestic) agency budget cutting prowess, was intensely disliked by the right wing for his leadership in convincing the president to break the "read my lips, no new taxes" mantra that had helped get him elected.

Further, some of the Bush PASs expressed concerns about OMB career staff and the power they exerted. Said one:

> Careerists play a negative role regarding PASs' ability to effect change—the career bureaucracy is the maintainer of the status quo. At OMB and my agency careerists are very entrenched, control the budget process and administration offices—it goes down to GS-12. My agency deals with GSs 12 and 13 at OMB who oversee PAS testimony. PASs have to stand up to OMB careerists. Political people at OMB don't usually get involved but PASs have to escalate the conflict so politicals at OMB *do* get involved—when they do, they support the PASs in the agency.

Other PASs talked about the power the OMB politicals wielded in the bureaucracy. When Nixon tried the administrative strategy of cutting off the air supply (i.e., money) of disfavored agencies with budget impoundments, he was sharply cut down by the Congress. His Republican successors tried a more subtle strategy. They simply asked Congress for less money for the agency in the federal budget. This was tried with the Interstate Commerce Commission but the Democratic ICC commissioners were able to persuade the Congress to save much of their budget. Legal Services was another favorite Republican target, as was the Environmental Protection Agency.

The Vulnerability of the Personnel Function: Politicization and Depoliticization at OPM

The trend has been for heads of the central agencies, such as OMB, to become personal advisors to the president. As discussed, since 1971 OMB has been seen far more as a political ally of the president, taking on the

Congress and the other agencies to promote presidential policy, than it has been seen as a source of independent, neutral budget counsel.

Likewise, another major central agency, the Office of Personnel Management (OPM), also experienced increased politicization during the Reagan era. OPM oversees the administration of the civil service system and the SES. According to one critic, it easily fell victim to the reforms of the Civil Service Reform Act of 1978 (CSRA), which served to "facilitate presidential political domination of the federal government's personnel management" (ibid., 15).

> The OPM director (Donald Devine) was selected on ideological criteria; his personal aides were selected on similar grounds, most initially from associates in Maryland politics. Other key OPM positions, starting with the general counsel and executive personnel management, have been staffed largely on the basis of political considerations, with little evidence of related experience, specialized expertise, or professional interests related to the position filled. . . . [An intensive effort to place political appointees at OPM] means that remaining senior career personnel in OPM's headquarters have felt largely excluded from significant involvement in matters related to policy. By December 1982, only two senior career OPM managers remained in headquarters functions previously performed by them. In short, CSRA has been highly successful in facilitating partisan presidential control of personnel: Ideological politics and politicians now clearly control OPM and effectively dominate the federal government's personnel system. (Ibid., 15–16)

Regardless of perspective on the benefits or deficits of the CSRA, there is no denying the political impact it had on the personnel function. While the number of political appointees in OPM increased from twelve to thirty-four in Reagan's first term, its overall workforce was reduced by nearly 20 percent (followed later by deeper cuts); thus further damaging morale, credibility, and operations (Cigler 1990, 644).

According to many, participation in political campaigns appeared to be the primary qualification of many appointees at OPM in the first Reagan term. In fact, one appointee (OPM's Devine) left his post to manage a Maryland Republican senatorial campaign and then returned to his old position, which had been held for him, in clear violation of the spirit of the Hatch Act, which forbade most partisan political activity by federal employees (Mosher 1985, 409).

Devine eventually placed more than forty political appointees in OPM (Newland 1983, 15). In addition to increasing their number at the headquarters, he positioned a political "regional watchdog" in each regional office to keep an eye on the career regional director. Considered by many to be "an abusive interlude" in OPM's evolving tradition, congressional hostility to his excesses derailed his nomination to a second term. Since Devine's four-year term had already expired before his second was confirmed by the Senate, he tried to run the agency through his deputy, the acting director, during his confirmation for a second term. In the process he sealed his own fate: Reagan was forced to withdraw his name. He nominated the deputy instead. However, Devine's antics had so enraged the Senate that she, too, had to be withdrawn from consideration as OPM chief.

The placement of partisan appointees with a control agenda in so many key places in OPM's structure meant that little in the way of staff development was done until late in the Reagan era. According to Mosher, "The OPM has done little or nothing to improve development and training programs, to improve labor-management relations, to improve morale—now probably at its lowest point since the era of Joseph McCarthy in the early 1950s—or to encourage personnel research" (Mosher 1985, 409).

Things took a turn for the better for OPM with the nomination of Constance Horner as chief in 1986. Having served in political positions at OMB and ACTION prior to her elevation to OPM head, she moved quickly to depoliticize the agency and the personnel function. Horner's reorganization replaced the political appointees with careerists in nearly all the line positions, as well as in the regional offices, and brought in more experienced line managers to "leaven the balance" with the appointees. This included ten to fifteen SESs from other agencies, who, having been on the receiving end of OPM actions, had a better sense of what the agencies could do and how OPM could be useful to them. Stressing the importance of good political-career relations, Horner decreased the number of political SESs from forty to eight; Schedule C appointments also dropped significantly.

Additionally, staff development, training, and personnel planning took on major importance in the revitalized OPM under the succeeding director, Bush appointee Constance Berry Newman. Governmentwide, new personnel policy initiatives and regulations, orientation for new employees, training needs assessments, and executive development became priorities for the agency.

Meanwhile, the career camp of the bureaucracy had undergone major changes of its own, largely along lines of politicization. The Civil Service Reform Act of 1978 was the primary vehicle for this transformation. The

CSRA grew out of a combination of several factors, in part in reaction to Nixon's misuse of the civil service system. "The Act of 1978 was born with a split personality. On the one hand, it was the culmination of several generations of effort by good government types to produce a high-level role for senior civil servants. On the other hand, the Act was responding to a more recent surge of anti-Washington, government-is-the-problem sentiment." [4]

In any case, the CSRA was political in its original intent. Replacing the old Civil Service Commission, it separated the personnel function into two parts, political and nonpolitical (career), both designed to be responsive to the president. OPM deals with career positions within the civil service merit system; the Merit Systems Protection Board and the Federal Labor Relations Board review and evaluate personnel matters to safeguard against excessive politicization or presidential abuse.

The Senior Executive Service was designed specifically to be both political and responsive to the president. Career executives entering the SES lost the protections of the merit system but gained greater benefits and flexibility. The SES is discussed at some length in chapter 6, but at this point suffice it to say that by the summer of 1992, after a tumultuous infancy, the SES was healthier and in its adolescence enjoyed a higher morale than ever in its previous eleven years of existence, thanks to a long-delayed pay raise and the attitude of President Bush toward the public service. He had made a point of making his first public address as president to the SES and was much more positive and cooperative with it than either Carter or Reagan had been. His OPM chief, Newman, maintained Horner's stance of depoliticization and positive political-career relations. The SES under Bush was considered politically responsive but not overly politicized. Successive OPM chiefs learned from the mistakes of the first Reagan administration: there has not been a pattern of punitive action in the SES since Reagan's second administration.

Until late in his reelection campaign, Bush, the lifelong public servant, was considered a friend of public service. Then, with his standing in the polls slipping, he turned to the well-worn path of bureaucrat bashing and suggested a 5 percent salary cut for the SES. In a very short time he destroyed most of the goodwill and credibility he had so carefully established with the SES. He would not regain it before he left office. Had he been reelected, Bush would have faced a surly and resentful career executive workforce. As one well-placed SES careerist put it,

> Bush did long-term damage because the history is so bad regarding executive pay. He took us back to the previous time when salary was so low for so long; people had people working under them who made the same

pay they did. He was turning things backward. These people are angry and they have long memories. They won't forget. While there won't be any sabotage, they will be very wary if there's a second Bush administration.

Conclusion

Centralization, with varying degrees of intention, has been the dominant theme of the past few decades. It is a risky presidential strategy because when lightning strikes, as in the Iran-Contra scandal, the perpetrators are seen to be acting in the interests of the White House. Managed carefully and with moderation, centralization can yield positive results for agenda-oriented presidents. However, that same agenda, if followed too enthusiastically, can lead to overcentralization, abuse of power, loss of credibility, and backlash.

Depoliticization, or PAS movement away from presidential policy, carries risks for any chief of state intent on reshaping the bureaucracy quickly. However, if presidents turn to politicization as a solution they create other problems for themselves. While they may profitably employ politicization in the short run, situations such as those at OMB and OPM lend credence to arguments that politicization "will prove unsatisfying and unworkable in the long run because the complexity of the administrative process requires that the roles of career and political appointees be interwoven—a partnership must exist between the two cadres to assure sensible policy formulation and effective policy implementation" (Levine 1986, 201).

It is also clear from the above discussion how vulnerable government agencies are to politicization. Clearly, there is nothing save good sense to stop future presidents from repoliticizing OPM again. Recent presidents have shown no inclination to depoliticize OMB, despite its obvious lack of credibility. President Bill Clinton, in his State of the Union economic address, in an off-the-cuff remark, inadvertently underscored the political nature of OMB's numbers: he used the budget projections of the Congressional Budget Office, rather than those of Bush's leftover OMB, to plan his budget. As he pointedly told the chuckling Congress, "Don't laugh, these are your numbers."

Decentralization works to the president's advantage when lightning strikes, as it did in the *Challenger* disaster, when the Bush White House was able to claim innocence and be somewhat believed. With competent, honest, and loyal appointees in charge of the bureaus, decentralization seems the safest course for any president intent on a second term and a securely honorable place in history.

4

⊙〰⊙

Appointments and Appointees in a Politicized Atmosphere: Distinguishing People from Voters

How do presidents choose the company they keep? What qualifies a person to be a presidential appointee? How do appointees affect the governmental apparatus? What effect does the growth of appointees in the modern era have on the bureaucracy? To answer these questions it is instructive to look to the larger issues in the recent past because this history, while evolving with each administration, tends toward repetition. Consequently, this chapter analyzes the legitimacy and power of political appointees, their selection and confirmation in the modern era, and the effects of increased numbers of appointees and their deeper infiltration into the bureaucracy. It also examines personal and political qualities that create competence and the costs and benefits of the short-term personnel system in the dance of bureaucracy. The chapter concludes with an overview of five recent studies of the public service and its improvement.

What legitimizes the existence of political appointees in the federal bureaucracy? How do they justify their exercise of authority over career bureaucrats in the system? While neither they nor their career counterparts are specifically mentioned in the Constitution of the United States, article 2, section 2 gives the president the authority to make appointments to the federal bureaucracy. As that article states:

> [The president] shall nominate and by and with the advice and consent of the Senate, shall appoint Ambassadors, other public Ministers and Consuls, Judges of the Supreme Court, and all other officers of the United

States, whose appointments are not herein otherwise provided for, and which shall be established by law: but the Congress may by law vest the appointment of such inferior officers, as they think proper, in the President alone, in the courts of law, or in the heads of departments.

History has also given the nation additional statutes regarding its bureaucracy. The political context of those later statutes created a federal personnel and organizational structure of some complexity and confusion:

> In examining the table of organization for the federal government, it is not uncommon to find a bureau the chief of which is appointed by the president juxtaposed to another bureau of similar size and responsibility where the chief is appointed by a department head. Nor is it uncommon to find a pair of similar offices, both filled by presidential appointment but only one of which requires confirmation by the Senate. (Macy et al. 1983, 4)

While later reforms standardized most of the position titles, resulting in relative uniformity across the agencies, considerable complexity still exists. The designation of executive level (EL) remains the clearest indication of place at the top of the political federal hierarchy.

As the constitutional language makes clear, the appointment process is a shared and two-step process: the president nominates and the Senate confirms PAS executives. However, there is relatively little to counter the aspirations of the president, as the Senate, while a significant partner with the president in the appointment process, has often been a silent one. In general, it withholds its consent "only in those rare cases when serious questions have arisen about the competence, integrity, policy views, or freedom from bias of a particular candidate for appointment" (ibid., 5).

From the beginning of the Republic, presidents, having few alternate sources and limited time and staff resources, relied on political allies close to them, such as members of Congress, personal acquaintances, or party leaders for suggestions for appointments.

> Not surprisingly, this made for some odd bedfellows. Presidents in the 19th and 20th centuries often presided over cabinets and administrations in which comity and cooperation were scarce commodities. Because the selection of their appointees had followed from no consensual definition of a presidential philosophy or approach to government management, appointees were often ill-suited to that task. And because they realized that

their appointments had resulted not from the personal preferences of the president himself but rather from the recommendations of party leaders, their loyalty to the president's objectives and their responsiveness to his orders were anything but ensured. Appointment decisions vibrated to the rhythms of political exigency; administrative considerations rarely intervened. (Bonafede 1987a, 35)

Until Roosevelt's "vision and political practicality" produced reforms that would restructure the presidency itself, the political parties, "the dominant force in American politics," controlled the distribution of political patronage positions. However, as discussed above, the Rooseveltian reforms accelerated a trend toward a centralized presidency that has led to the administrative presidency in its various contemporary manifestations (ibid., 35).

This centralizing trend is buttressed by the political and governmental developments of the past several decades, according to Bonafede (ibid., 32). Among them are: 1. The power of the national parties as broker and conduit for patronage declined. This was largely due to an emphasis on grassroots politics and political reforms that increased the role of state primaries at the expense of the parties. Presidents, no longer obligated to the parties for their election, had less need to extend patronage to them.

2. The emergence of political action committees and changes in election finance laws reduced somewhat the influence of major contributors, many of whom in earlier days had been repaid with prestigious presidential appointments. 3. The movement toward a centralized, strong presidency worked against the competing powers of the Congress and the bureaucracy.

4. The rapid growth of government created jobs that of necessity accompanied that growth. 5. The need for substantive knowledge and managerial competence escalated as domestic and international issues, such as arms control, tax reform, federal deficits, and trade imbalances, grew and became more complex.

As discussed above, the 1937 Brownlow Report sparked what Bonafede refers to as "evolutionary changes" toward a centralized presidency. From it, the Executive Office of the President (EOP) was created, the Bureau of the Budget was integrated into the president's domain, and the president's personal staff was substantially increased. This was the genesis of the bureaucratization of the presidency. It was given further credibility by the proposals of the Hoover Commissions of 1949 and 1955 to extend the president's control over the executive branch through a strengthened White House staff and cabinet. According to presidential advisor Fred Malek, these changes strengthened PASs' power such that

> the degree to which they succeed will have a powerful influence on the
> effectiveness of government and consequently on the quality of life in the
> United States. . . . In today's government, the Cabinet and White House
> staff exert powerful influence on the direction of an administration and
> most decisions that are credited to a president are actually made at the
> staff level with only pro forma approval from the president. The people
> around the chief executive are the ones who actually run the agencies,
> sift through the issues, identify the problems and present analyses and
> recommendations for the chief's decision. It is they who give shape to the
> administration's governing strategy and transform vague party platforms
> into hard policies and legislative proposals. This does not mean that the
> president is only an automaton, but one should never underestimate the
> power of those around him. (Bonafede 1987a, 32–33)

Pfiffner argues that this is, indeed, how it should be. The president
should not try to manage much *directly*, but must set the general tone
and focus and count on surrogates to handle the details, striking the right
balance between management and political leadership.

> From a broader perspective, presidential control of the government means
> realizing that the president leads better by persuasion than by command.
> Our fragmented separation-of-powers system will not allow the type of
> tight presidential control over the government that some presidents seem
> to want. Effective presidential control derives from the realization that
> real power in the U.S. political system grows out of political consensus
> forged by true political leadership, not stratagem or management tech-
> niques. (Pfiffner 1991, 16)

The lack of continuity from one administration to the next characterized all presidencies in the past half-century until the succession of
George Bush. Bonafede notes the volatility of modern politics, which has
served to weaken the appointments process:

> Not since Herbert Hoover in 1928 had a president succeeded an immedi-
> ate predecessor of his own party who had completed a regular term of of-
> fice. Truman, Johnson, and Ford entered in the White House through the
> deaths or resignation of their predecessors; Roosevelt, Eisenhower,
> Kennedy, Nixon, Carter, and Reagan each succeeded a president of the op-
> posing party. Consequently, each . . . has come into office with a distinct

handicap. Those who ascended to the presidency because of the inter-
rupted terms of their predecessors were compelled to accept, at least in
the beginning, inherited political appointees.

Those who succeeded presidents of the opposing party felt obliged to
build their own organizational and operational structure distinctive from
that of the previous administration. A mutually cooperative transition
could possibly have averted errors of the past and ensured a legacy of
proved techniques and practices, but mutually cooperative transitions
have not been commonplace in modern government. (Ibid., 54–55)

The quality of the selection process for political appointees is a source
of much debate and study, as is the quality of its product, the appointees,
themselves. Selection holds a central place in the functioning of government. The country needs an "appointment process that is able consistently to identify and recruit government leaders with expertise, integrity,
creativity, and political sensitivity. . . . We cannot have good government
in the United States without good people making and implementing the
important decisions" (Macy et al. 1983, 3).

In the dance of bureaucracy, selection is key to the appointee partner,
much more so than to the career partner. This is because the majority of
appointees emerge with the advent of a new administration (most are chosen within the first few months), receive only cursory pre-appointment
examination, stay for a relatively short time, and soon leave government
or recycle into another agency. The career executives, on the other hand,
spend years preparing for their positions, undergo periodic review and
evaluation, and will generally be in place long after the appointees are
part of agency history.

"Nine Enemies and One Ingrate": Presidential Approaches
to Political Appointments

In the modern milieu of expanded government size and jurisdiction,
the responsibility of the president to name political appointees has also
grown. It is not a task he can delegate to others and still expect felicitous
results from, because "presidential involvement and identification with
the appointments process is indispensable in attracting qualified people
who combine professional competence and political compatibility"
(Bonafede 1987a, 55). Yet, the past several decades have seen a generally
growing antipathy toward the federal bureaucracy, viewing it as the
nemesis on which to blame the nation's problems. Eisenhower was deter-

mined to clean up "that mess in Washington" and "Kennedy was intent on imposing presidential control over 'the feudal barons of the permanent government, entrenched in their domains and fortified by their sense of proprietorship.' Nixon referred to the federal bureaucracy as 'a faceless machine.' Carter gained the presidency as a crusader against Washington, and Reagan insisted that Washington was the problem, not the solution" (ibid., 55).

Theoretically, presidents have far-reaching power to appoint individuals to deal with "the problem" of the federal bureaucracy. But while they are aware of the political capital to be gained from the judicious appointment of several thousand persons, for the most part, time and interest force them to focus chiefly on the high-level positions: "Carter candidly confessed, 'The constant pressure of making lesser appointments was a real headache.' Nixon dealt with lower-ranking appointments exclusively through memoranda, and Reagan passively [went] through the motions of rubber-stamping them" (ibid., 55).

Traditionally, political appointments were filled in this country using the method known affectionately (by some) as "BOGSAT, a bunch of guys sitting around a table asking each other 'Whom do you know?'" (Macy et al. 1983, 27). However, the personnel system has, of necessity, grown in the past several decades with each administration adding incrementally to it.

> Truman was the first to set up a personnel section in the White House independent of the party and separate from patronage demands. Eisenhower established the office of special assistant to the president for personnel management and was the first to require FBI clearance for prospective nominees. Kennedy's personnel staff developed a national network of sources and initiated an outreach recruiting operation and eventually compiled a list of potential appointees.
>
> Lyndon Johnson extended the work of his predecessors by institutionalizing modern personnel techniques, introducing the use of computers, and demonstrating the benefits of presidential participation in the system. Nixon aides further professionalized the process through the use of personnel recruitment specialists and sophisticated managerial practices. Ford formally created the White House personnel office and emphasized ethical considerations in the appointments process. Carter formed a nonpartisan nomination commission in a move toward the merit selection of federal judges. Under Reagan, the circle of White House aides involved in the process was expanded, and tighter control was exercised over a broad array of appointments. (Bonafede 1987a, 56–57)

The overall result of these changes, as discussed in chapter 3, was greater centralization of the personnel selection process in the White House, the emergence of the EOP as a command and control center, and the conversion of the appointment power into an instrument of control for the president (ibid., 56–57).

As the personnel selection function expanded, its staff size kept pace with its growing importance:

> The recruiting that Dan Fenn was doing [for Kennedy] with three people, Frederic Malek was doing [for Nixon] with 25 to 30 and William Walker with 37 or 38. In 1981 Pendelton James had 100 people on his staff to recruit for the Reagan administration. The rank and access to the president of the chief personnel person [had] also increased, with James holding the title of assistant to the president (Executive Level II) and having an office in the West Wing of the White House. (Pfiffner 1987a, 69)

Nevertheless, the personnel function is still undervalued and no president has fully used this tool so readily at his disposal:

> The personnel office is accorded middle-level status. It lacks institutional stability; the process varies from one presidency to another, and it even varies in the zeal and orderliness with which it is conducted within the same administration. Each incoming administration, distrustful of past personnel procedures, feels compelled to reinvent its own system. Few presidents have been willing to lend their prestige to the office. (Bonafede 1987a, 57)

No matter how efficient and proficient the personnel office, then, it will not work to the president's best advantage if he or she does not lend it presidential prestige and communicate staffing priorities clearly to it.

But the freshly minted president may not be in a position to communicate her or his policy desires. New presidents are never prepared for their job.

> If he is like most of his predecessors, he probably has a background as a legislator or a governor. If the nation has recently fought in a popular war, he may be a military man. It is possible that he has served as vice president. The odds, however, are great that he has not held an executive position in the federal government. . . . One consequence is that a new president will make some of his most important decisions at a time when he is least capable of deciding wisely. (Hess 1988, 12)

The president will bring with her or him a core of faithful followers who also most likely have had more experience in politics, that is, in running for office, than in governing. And, while the policy commitments of a candidate are known through campaign speeches, they are, of necessity, vague and generalized and can "in no sense be considered a presidential program—a program has a price tag and relates to available resources" (ibid., 13). As a consequence, valuable "honeymoon" time is lost because the president is least likely to have a coherent program just when the Congress is most likely to accept one.

> On the morning after his victory a president-elect is consumed with thoughts of choosing his cabinet and other matters of the transition. No shadow cabinet waits in the wings, and he suddenly discovers how few people he knows who are qualified to assume major posts in government. "People, people, people!" John Kennedy exclaimed three weeks after his election. "I don't know any *people*. I only know voters." (Ibid., 13)

Presidents in the modern era have approached personnel in ways characteristic of each. Roosevelt was "disdainful of formal chain-of-command structures, and he insisted on personally controlling the reins of the executive branch, including the personnel process. [His] 'staffing practices were primarily a haphazard blend of fortuity, friendship, obligation and pressure' . . . : 'there was neither a well-defined purpose nor an underlying principle' that guided Roosevelt" (Bonafede 1987a, 34).

Harry Truman continued the Rooseveltian reforms by creating the first personnel office in the White House that was separate from the party organization. Headed by Donald Dawson, it "functioned primarily as a clearinghouse of names of candidates and political referrals." Later, the office created a file of "prospective nonpatronage appointees, including some civil servants already in the government, and attempted to bring a sense of order to the process but did little evaluating or active recruiting" (ibid., 35).

President Eisenhower's reluctance to deal with personnel matters was well known. However, from his military background he adapted the command structure to the EOP and established a secretariat, naming Sherman Adams as chief of staff. Even before the 1952 election, Eisenhower's supporters hired a consulting firm "to study the appointment process, the nature of the positions available and lists of potential candidates . . . and interviewed candidates for the cabinet—mostly businessmen who met their political and executive standards" (ibid., 35–36).

Presidents and their appointments secretaries from Kennedy onward have sought to professionalize the appointments process in order to broaden the base from which personnel were chosen, as well as to assess the skill level of appointees. Kennedy's personnel people were the first to establish a "contact network," an up-to-date talent bank of potential appointees from which he could draw. This gave him a recruiting capability independent of the political patronage system pressed on him by his party, Congress, and special interests. Unfortunately, the system never worked as well as it might have, due to Kennedy's inconsistency in using it (Macy et al. 1983, 30).

The Kennedy people paid scant attention to appointments until after the election and then did not really concentrate on them until midway through 1961, when Dan Fenn was brought in to head personnel.

> Kennedy, like FDR, was uninterested in organizational charts or procedural methods, and his interest in personnel appointments was selective and sporadic. He was more concerned about individual quality and hopefully sought "new faces". . . . Kennedy was avidly involved in the selection of his cabinet and other high-ranking officials during the transition, but his interest waned with time, as other matters of state occupied him—a not unusual presidential trait. (Bonafede 1987a, 36)

Lyndon Johnson, not wanting to risk political suicide by appearing disloyal to the slain president who preceded him, asked all of JFK's appointees to remain in the cabinet and, in all, filled fewer than fifty major Senate-confirmed (PAS) positions during the transition year, most of them in the independent regulatory commissions (IRCs) and the Defense Department. Not only was he seeking to reassure the country and help heal the shock of the assassination, but he would have had trouble getting individuals to accept short-term positions with an election not far away. Also, some of JFK's appointees were already Johnson's trusted friends or long-term allies. Still, in his administration, seventeen of the twenty-five persons holding cabinet posts were originally chosen by Kennedy (Schott and Hamilton 1983, 10–11, 35).

After election in his own right, Johnson took a greater interest in the appointment process and used it to better advantage than did Kennedy. With his support the talent bank was expanded with new emphasis on professionalism, administrative efficiency, and specialization within the White House Personnel Office.

> Johnson's interest in personnel, his search for "the best and the brightest" and his control over the process became almost legendary. He had a special interest in bringing in bright people under forty who had been at the

top of their class, who were Phi Beta Kappa or had been Rhodes scholars
. . . had been in the Peace Corps and/or were women and minorities. . . .
He felt that government was no better than the people you had around
you. He even, on occasion, inquired about Schedule C positions. On
major appointments he consulted with advisors both inside and outside
of government, such as Clark Clifford, Abe Fortas, CBS president Frank
Stanton, Joe Califano, Horace Busby, Bill Moyers, Harry McPherson and
Jack Valenti. (Bonafede 1987a, 38)

Johnson's people under John Macy brought the computer age to the
appointments process. By the end of his administration they had expanded the talent bank to thirty thousand names, all cross-referenced by
skills and background characteristics (Macy et al. 1983, 32).

Johnson ran parallel appointment systems. One operated under Macy,
who headed both the political hiring and the merit-based Civil Service
Commission and remained in both positions at Johnson's insistence.[1]
Macy's operation was housed in the Executive Office Building rather than
in the White House. The fact that he was not part of the White House
staff gave him and his office some neutrality and credibility in the appointments process (Schott and Hamilton 1983, 16).

Macy looked for professionalism and merit and at first had Johnson's
full support.

Previous experience in governmental affairs was an important criterion in
Johnson's mind . . . 50% came to PAS positions from service elsewhere in
the federal government . . . ; he demonstrated a proclivity to appoint individuals of established competence rather than take a chance on persons
from outside the governmental establishment. . . . When Johnson did
reach beyond those with governmental experience to bring in appointees
from the private sector as in the case of John Connor at Commerce, the
appointment occasionally did not pan out as well as he had hoped. (Ibid.,
204)

A second personnel process operated out of the White House. It was
"based on a shifting constellation of personal relationships among Johnson, his White House aides, and his numerous confidants outside the executive branch and often outside government as well." It was run first by
Jack Valenti and later by Marvin Watson (ibid., 18).

The above innovations aside, Johnson's administrative personnel
strategy was clearly modest, relative to what was to follow in Nixon's administration.

Johnson seems rarely to have thought about appointments in the abstract. Engaged in the active, daily business of making decisions, he appears to have considered cabinet appointments as means to ends. The ends were the policy directions in which he wished to move. The particular cabinet members selected were those he felt most suited personally and politically to move their departments closer to his goals. Most of those men already in office appeared well suited to provide the necessary leadership. (Ibid., 59)

Party service or even affiliation did not particularly interest Johnson. For example, he did not inquire as to John Gardner's party and only found out he was a Republican after his nomination was announced. The survey of Johnson's political executives "indicated less partisanship among them than among the appointees of previous Democratic administrations" (ibid., 204).

What did matter to Johnson was loyalty to him and his policies. Early on, the primary criterion was the candidate's allegiance to Johnson, as opposed to loyalty to Robert F. Kennedy, JFK's and then Johnson's attorney general. After 1964 the litmus test was fidelity to the Great Society programs and the activist role of the federal government in various policy areas; then it was personal loyalty to Johnson vis-à-vis his critics. Finally, the criterion was the candidate's support of the war in Vietnam (ibid., 204).

As popular discontent with the war grew, recruitment became more difficult; many potential candidates simply did not want to be associated with the war and the administration waging it. After Johnson announced in March 1968 that he would not run for reelection, recruitment from outside government became even more difficult and there was then a tendency to promote from within, to take the closest and most trusted people, or to fill positions on an acting basis (ibid., 31–33).

Nevertheless, Johnson's desire to be remembered as a great domestic president, though foiled by the war, can be seen in the quality and caliber of his appointments. Indeed, his

"system" worked well. Almost without exception, the individuals selected to PAS positions in the Johnson administration were of very high caliber, experienced, and qualified. The Johnson executive group stands up well in comparison with those of Franklin Roosevelt and John Kennedy—although, as we have noted, most of Johnson's cabinet members were originally drafted by Kennedy. . . . the end result of the appointments process he developed was a cadre of exceptionally talented in-

dividuals [committed to] social reform and a mechanism for the amelio-
ration of social ills. There were, finally, also persons of substantial character and high ethical standards who led an administration remarkably
free of the scandal, personal pettiness, and adventurism which, unfortunately, came to characterize the presidency that was to follow. (Ibid., 209)

Nixon's personnel staff, determined to establish its own recruiting
operation, spurned any guidance from LBJ's outgoing administration.
Lack of institutional memory meant that they had to start from scratch
and, being fragmented and disorganized, they did not do well, according
to Macy et al. (1983).

An early and fundamental problem was the president's personal indifference to and dissociation from the selection process. In this regard, he
and Lyndon Johnson were polar opposites. Nixon rarely suggested possible candidates for vacant positions, consistently delegated final selection
authority to his chief of staff, and almost never took the time to meet
with his nominees before their names were sent to the Senate (Mackenzie 1981, 44). According to some of his personal aides, Nixon possessed a
"consuming desire" to master the government and its servants. It is
ironic that Nixon's administration, so intent on controlling the government, was

> so poorly organized to do it. . . . Indeed, in some ways the personnel op-
> eration interfered with, rather than facilitated, the accomplishment of
> that objective. By keeping his distance from both the selection process
> and the nominees it produced, Nixon constrained the ability of his per-
> sonnel staff to clarify the criteria he deemed most important and lost the
> opportunity to imbue his new appointees with his own order of priorities
> and objectives. In the long run, this course of action weakened his ad-
> ministration's efforts to "get control of the government." (Ibid., 45)

The result of Nixon's delegation of authority was that the White
House lost much of the initiative and had great difficulty centralizing appointments in a way that supported administration policy objectives.

> The combination of an inexperienced personnel staff, ambiguous selec-
> tion criteria, presidential noninvolvement, conflicts with the depart-
> ments, and an opposition Congress constituted a nest of trouble for the
> White House personnel operation. It was soon acknowledged both inside
> and outside the White House that the personnel function was dysfunc-
> tional. (Ibid., 46)

Nixon created another problem for himself when, early in his first administration, he gave cabinet secretaries authority for subcabinet appointments and told them to fill positions "on the basis of ability first and loyalty second. This was a significant, if impulsive, delegation of personnel selection that members of the cabinet would not soon or easily surrender." Nixon recognized his error almost immediately. On leaving that fateful cabinet meeting at which he gave his secretaries carte blanche appointing authority, he told an aide, "I just made a big mistake;" but by then it was too late (ibid., 45).

It was soon apparent that this cabinet-style government would not work. In 1970 Nixon brought in Fred Malek to restructure the process, which he did, using techniques from the preceding administrations: centralization of the appointment process in the White House, clearer specification of selection criteria, a more explicit clearance process, and a much more aggressive recruitment effort, with a significantly heightened level of intensity.

Malek took tight control over all major appointments, including those of subcabinet officials and staff assistants to top PASs, as discussed in chapter 2. By the end of Nixon's first term the strong cabinet model was no more.

Pursuing Nixon's goal of controlling the government, the White House Personnel Office (WHPO) expanded in size and attempted to influence both noncareer and career positions further down in the bureaucracy. As discussed in chapter 3, it applied political criteria and found ways to skirt the merit system. It is from this era that the White House "enemies list," illegal controls over careers, and Watergate emanated. For all its efforts, however, it did not produce the desired effect of controlling the bureaucracy or producing better relations with the Congress (ibid., 54).

The political reaction to the White House Personnel Operation and the Watergate fiasco caused the fall of the presidential appointments system in the shambles of the Nixon administration. It would have to be reinvented in a different form by Gerald Ford (Macy et al. 1983, 35).

Ford, the first president to assume office without being elected to either that office or the vice presidency, did so at a unique and critical period in the nation's history. "A United States president had resigned in disgrace, the Watergate scandal had drawn the curtain on a seamy side of political life, and the public's confidence in its governing institutions had been severely shaken. The new president's paramount goal was to lead the country out of its 'long national nightmare' and restore public trust" (Bonafede 1987a, 42).

Initially, Ford moved cautiously, much as Johnson had, following

JFK's assassination. Seeking to ensure stability and continuity, he did not purge his ranks of Nixon appointees. "He didn't want people to think all of Nixon's appointees were "bad guys" and he was throwing them to the wolves" (ibid., 42). And, given his lame duck status, with two years left in an office to which he had not been elected and for which he was not going to run, heading a public service tarnished by Watergate, Ford's administration was hardly attractive to potential appointee candidates.

Nonetheless, Ford was an active participant in the appointments process. His chief of staff, Donald Rumsfeld, exercised considerable control over appointments, but the final decision was the president's. Ford, without Rumsfeld's advice or sometimes despite his opposition,

> personally selected David Mathews as HEW secretary, decided that Kissinger should hold the single job of secretary of state and thus relieved him of his other position as White House national security adviser, and installed Vice President Nelson A. Rockefeller as operating director of the White House Domestic Council . . . , [and] fired defense secretary James R. Schlesinger because of his "aloof, frequently arrogant manner" and combative attitude. He then appointed Rumsfeld as defense secretary, replaced him with Cheney, named George Bush as CIA director, and elevated General Brent Scowcroft to NSC director. (Ibid., 43)

In these actions Ford bypassed the newly renamed Presidential Personnel Office (PPO) that focused on subcabinet and other presidential appointments. The PPO, meanwhile, had taken the symbolic step of moving away from using the professional recruiters employed by Malek to using knowledgeable Washington generalists in an effort to shift the focus from pure politics to good government in the wake of Watergate. William Walker, the PPO director, had regular access to Ford, though, and a good working relationship with him (ibid., 43).

There was, however, a certain ambiguity in Ford's administrative style: "while endorsing cabinet government, he would express hostility toward the bureaucracy, claiming in a familiar litany, 'A government big enough to give you everything you want is a government big enough to take from you everything you have.' He further vowed to reduce the size of the permanent government and the White House staff, neither of which occurred during his term" (ibid., 44).

Early 1976 saw a shift in the political climate when Ford changed his mind and decided he would run for the office to which he had been elevated. Word soon went out that political considerations would be paramount in presidential appointments. The political nature of the appointments process accelerated as appointees left to return to the private sector, as is customary near the end of a presidential term. The Democrat-controlled Senate began flexing its muscles in regard to PAS replacements, delaying or denying some appointments, such as that of Joseph Coors of beer manufacturing fame, an ideological conservative, slated, but not fated, to be a director of the Corporation for Public Broadcasting (ibid., 44).

While Gerald Ford's personal interest in the appointment process helped restore some respect for public service and the executive personnel function, with the passage of the White House to Democratic control, Jimmy Carter's staff began again to reinvent the personnel wheel. He was the first president to begin planning for his administration before the general election. From the summer of 1976 onward his staff prepared for victory and transition and had TIP, the Talent Inventory Program, in place by election day. It was hailed as "the first step in a nationwide recruiting effort, which provided a comprehensive inventory of potential appointees and indicated the kinds of positions for which their qualifications recommended them" (Macy et al. 1983, 37).

However, infighting among the Carter staff over the nonpolitical nature of the program wasted the advance work done on it. Moreover, in Carter's administration, decisions were effectively decentralized, resulting in broad inconsistencies in the character and quality of his appointments; they ranged from "good old boy" hiring to stringent requirements for qualifications. As Carter's energies were diverted to other matters and the system was trying both to invent itself and to function at the same time, appointments soon bogged down (ibid., 37).

Carter allowed cabinet officers nearly free rein to choose their subordinates:

> In many—perhaps most—respects, this was an improvement. To the extent such discretion was granted, cabinet members were not saddled with incompatible associates thrust upon them by the White House. Nor did patronage considerations dictate the appointment of poorly-qualified persons, as had been know to happen in the past. Nevertheless, the results in terms of managerial capacity were bound to be spotty. [Cronyism often showed up in the choices secretaries made for their deputies.] . . . Scanning the list of deputy secretaries, one finds fewer than half with previous experience in federal government administration—and some of these for only two or three years—but several others had been managers in private industry or in state government. All of them brought important qualifications to the job, but managerial deputies were not recruited as a

matter of course; if they were found at all, it was the product of the chance good judgement of the cabinet member. (Sundquist 1979, 6)

However, Carter largely created his own problems with his approach to the cabinet, giving his officers Nixonian carte blanche to choose their subordinates and likewise to manage their departments. Carter "proudly boasted, 'There will never be an instance while I am President where the members of the White House staff dominate or act in a superior position to the members of the cabinet'" (Bonafede 1987a, 46).

As happened to Nixon, this laissez-faire approach soon backfired. According to one White House aide, running battles between cabinet and White House staff over staff appointments, policy, media communication, etc., "ran the gamut from an unwillingness to cooperate to outright defiance. Carter was very supportive of the cabinet; he thought the White House staff was overreacting, and he'd give departmental appointees the benefit of the doubt" (ibid., 46). Carter only changed this position after intense pressure from the Congress.

Over time, fears of disloyalty eventually led to a White House directive to cabinet officers to institute

"[p]ersonal and professional evaluations" of all presidential appointees. . . . Inevitably, Carter's frustration in dealing with recalcitrant cabinet-level appointees led to a dramatic shake-up; in mid-July 1979, [he announced the departure of several key cabinet members]. The cabinet exorcism, widely criticized for the graceless way in which it was handled, was conducted without the involvement of the personnel office. (Ibid., 47)

A new personnel director, Arnie Miller, had reorganized the office in 1978 and helped restore White House control and professionalism to the appointments process. "But it came too late—the Iranian seizure of the American hostages had effectively sealed Carter's political fate" (ibid., 47).

Like Carter, Ronald Reagan began planning for his administration far in advance. He was more successful at embodying his policy focus in his appointments because his personnel staff maintained a consistent focus through the first eighteen months of his term and Reagan himself sustained a personal interest and the appearance of active participation in it (Macy et al. 1983, 39).

Reagan's investment in the appointment process was carried by his White House staff under Personnel Director E. Pendleton James who, having cut his political eye teeth under Fred Malek in Nixon's administration, took a page from the Nixon playbook and was determined to keep appointments under tight control. To that end, Reagan, James, and Reagan's "kitchen cabinet," his close friends and political associates,

> insisted on a narrow definition of loyalty to the president and had cabinet members agree to accept White House selection of their subordinates. Loyalty to the president was assured by examining the background and attitudes of potential nominees. Heavy weight was given to support for Reagan in previous campaigns and Republican primaries. There was also a relatively narrow set of ideological values concerning the role of the federal government, the military, and social issues that could be applied to prospective candidates. This rigorous ideological screening ensured that appointees would put loyalty to the president and his policies above the tugs of Congress, interest groups, and the bureaucracy. Reagan's clearly defined ideology made this type of screening possible in ways that would not have worked in the administrations of previous presidents, such as Kennedy, Nixon, Ford, or Carter, who had much broader sets of values. (Pfiffner 1987a, 72)

Despite the stringent litmus test applied to appointees, the New Right venomously attacked the White House, claiming it had been "denied a fair share of the spoils and that the policy jobs went to moderates and so-called pragmatists" (Bonafede 1987a, 50).

Like Carter before him and George Bush and Bill Clinton after him, Reagan was criticized for the length of time it took to fill his positions. Reagan's personnel director declared that "each week he received 900 resumes, 1,100 telephone calls, and about 350 pieces of mail from Congress bearing job recommendations and endorsements. 'It's like a stockbrokerage. You're dealing jobs, people, phone calls, pressure all day long'" (ibid., 51).

In the early Bush administration the Reaganite system of control was kept in place but not aggressively pursued. Some secretaries (notably James Baker, Nicholas Brady, and Robert Mosbacher) were given greater latitude in selecting their staff and, in general, mutual accommodation was the more likely practice. Bush's personnel chief, Chase Untermeyer, asserted the guiding principle that "No department or agency chief will have an appointee forced down his or her throat, that is, imposed by the White House. Conversely, every decision is a presidential decision" (Pfiffner 1990, 69).

The internal clearance process in the new administration was simple compared to Reagan's, whose system had numerous veto points. The cabinet secretary and Untermeyer would agree on a person and forward the nominee to Chief of Staff John Sununu, who would pass it on to the president, where in all likelihood, it would be approved (ibid., 69). Late in the term when reelection panic had set in, however, that pattern changed and there was more scrutiny for political correctness.

As had become the tradition, most political paybacks were in the Schedule C positions. The administration let it be known that approximately half of those positions (some 700–800 jobs) were to be held for campaign workers and key supporters. The president's nephew, Scott Bush, headed the "Special Schedule C Project," sending lists of people to the agencies with a strong recommendation for their placement (though these appointments legally belong to the agency heads). This early placement of partisans caused some administrative problems for the agencies when they had to absorb large numbers of appointees before their sub-cabinet appointments were made (ibid., 69).

George Bush chose not to take a page from Ronald Reagan's playbook in terms of his pre-election appointments strategy. The results were hardly felicitous. In late 1987 Untermeyer began a transition planning process but Bush insisted that it be low key, due to his shaky footing in the Republican primary campaigns. Even later in his campaign, having survived the primaries, he feared distracting the campaign and would not allow the existence of anything that even looked like a real transition office; according to Untermeyer, Bush forbade him to "set up an office, establish mail handling operations, create computer programs, or even recruit his own staff, much less do any actual personnel planning. Bush also insisted that the small operation be entirely separate from the campaign and from the Office of the Vice President" (ibid., 65).

The result of this delay was that the Presidential Personnel Office, first under Chase Untermeyer and then under Constance Horner, was even slower to fill his top spots than was Reagan's, leaving many empty for long periods. By mid-March eight departments and agencies had only one Bush appointee in place.

By April 1 only 28 policy-level appointments had been confirmed by the Senate, 22 had been nominated and were awaiting confirmation, and 97 had undergone initial background checks. On 10 August, 156 of 394 of the top executive branch positions had been filled . . . but there were no nominations for 160 of the positions. Even if the 60 nominees who were awaiting Senate confirmation at that time were counted as on board, the absence of over 40 percent of policy level executives half way through the administration's first year could not help but to hamper leadership of the executive branch. (Ibid., 69)[2]

It is clear that appointments are taking longer in the late modern era. According to C. Calvin Mackenzie, "Kennedy took an average of 2.38 months; Nixon 3.3 months, Carter, 4.55 months, Reagan, 5.3 months; and Bush, 8.13 months" to make their PAS appointments. A full year after Bush's inauguration, only 49 percent of his appointees were in place.[3] Bush White House personnel staff attributed the delay in nominations to the careful search undertaken for each position and the detailed background check required of each nominee (the legacy of the Nixon and Reagan years). Delay in the Bush administration's appointments is discussed in more detail in a later section.

Limitations on Presidential Appointing Authority

Presidents do not enjoy unrestricted power in making PAS appointments, of course. External factors limit their ability to appoint those whom they believe would best carry out their agenda. "Presidents often are forced to use their appointing authority not so much to advance their own policy goals as to satisfy the claims of potential allies. Groups within their own political coalition commonly believe that they are entitled to high-level representation in an administration they helped put into office" (Rourke 1991b, 127). Additionally, "firmly tying the appointment power to presidential leadership is easier said than done," because the president does not enjoy absolute control over the process. There are other players and factors to be considered.

> First, the president does not command the complete loyalty of his own appointees. . . . Most political appointees are acutely aware of both the identity of their political patrons and the reasons they were chosen. . . . their natural reaction is to retain a lingering sense of gratitude and allegiance to the person or group who sponsored their appointment. Or if they were chosen for some obvious reason—to appeal to moderate Republicans, to represent big labor, to mollify feminists—that reason often remains a principal guide to their subsequent decisions and actions. (Mackenzie 1981, 249)

The White House, being at "the confluence of diverse political forces" and unable to act unilaterally in its personnel system, is subject to intense pressures from other players in the political game, such as

Congress, organized special interests, party leaders' prominent friends, and supporters of the president—and at times even foreign governments. Not without justification, President Taft lamented, "Every time I make an appointment I create nine enemies and one ingrate." Competition can be fierce, leaving a field of bruised egos. Frequently, administration officials promote their own favorite candidates. . . . [According to Macy], "There is more personal patronage than political patronage in every administration—it's people you know." (Bonafede 1987a, 33)

Money, "the mother's milk of politics," has often helped smooth the way for a presidential appointment, or so it would seem. What commentator Bill Moyers refers to as the "money-policy connection" was at work in Bush's 1992 State of the Union address when he pledged to "modify the passive loss rule for active real estate developers." This amounted to "a giant tax break for . . . the wealthy folks who helped put Mr. Bush in the White House by giving big money to political action committees that promoted Mr. Bush's candidacy. . . . Anywhere but in Washington, they'd call it bribery. . . . Moyers calls it 'legalized corruption,' part of our 'mercenary culture where the vote doesn't matter as much as the dollar.'"[4] Moyers calls the tax break

> a straightforward quid pro quo. Before public financing became available for his presidential campaign in 1988, Bush operatives put together the Bush Team 100, a group of 249 people who contributed $100,000 or more to political action committees that indirectly helped Bush. [Many] were later named ambassadors to foreign nations. And many others were real estate men, including Alfred Taubman and Donald Trump, who now benefit from the change in the "passive loss rule." Their $100,000 contributions turned out to be shrewd investments.[5]

Eventually, eight persons who had contributed at least $100,000 to the National Republican Party's 1988 campaign for the White House were awarded ambassadorships. Three other such nominees were denied this prize, however, by a wary Senate Judiciary Committee, prodded by Senator Paul Sarbanes.

There is an ironic twist to presidential appointments in that those individuals chosen for political positions who come solely from the White House are viewed with suspicion by all the other policy actors (Congress, the bureaucracy, interest groups, etc.). Their effectiveness in carrying out administration policy within their agencies is compromised by their status as White House emissaries. If seen as "carrying the President's flag and acting as his eyes and ears, [the PAS] may well be shut out of just the decision-making processes he was sent to infiltrate." The other PASs and both the career and noncareer SES executives of the agency are much more likely to work well with a newcomer if they are consulted ahead of time on the appointment than if they feel that person is foisted on them by a suspicious White House. Consequently, those most loyal to the White House and owing their position solely to it are the least likely to be effective in impacting the bureaucracy (Mackenzie 1981, 249).

The debate over the degree of presidential control in appointments has gone on since the advent of the modern presidency. One side supports White House control in order to foster loyalty to the president. The other endorses cabinet control to facilitate better working relationships within agencies.[6] However, this is a somewhat moot debate if seen in black and white terms. One solution is a double veto, or put more positively, mutual accommodation, to satisfy both sets of authority needs;

> a delicate negotiation between White House personnel officer and cabinet official that leaves neither totally dissatisfied if they cannot agree wholeheartedly. Most important is that all participants understand the rules. New cabinet officers must know how their top aides will be selected. Failing to set things straight at the beginning, a problem in the Carter administration, inevitably leads to friction. But no matter how sophisticated the apparatus, presidential appointments will always be subject to the intractable tension between loyalty and expertise. A new president must somehow balance the deserving claims of campaign and party faithful with the need for quality and experience. Sometimes they happily coincide. Often they do not. (Hess 1988, 201)

A second effect of the diffuse nature of the appointment process is that it contributes to what Heclo has labeled "a government of strangers." Because administrations are put together hurriedly after an election, the PASs are

> drawn from no common source, and their political bonds, even in the best of circumstances are tenuous. They lack the unity that might be provided by a programmatic political party, by a set of consistent and clear selection criteria, or by any other coherent frame of reference. Instead, the tendency is to choose each member individually, often at different times, usually for different reasons, and frequently with different sponsors or supporters. The ad hoc nature of the contemporary appointment process guarantees this result. Just as each selection decision rotates on its own

axis, so each appointee arrives with his own kit bag of abilities, attitudes, loyalties, and commitments. (Mackenzie 1981, 249–50)

This, however, was Mackenzie writing in 1981, at the dawn of what was to be the unprecedented tour de force of ideological purity and unity known as the "Reagan Revolution." Now, more than a decade later, one can observe the changed nature of political appointments, which actually began with the election of the outsider Jimmy Carter. While in the past the national parties had been the main source of pressure for presidential appointments, the power of the parties declined as that of interest groups grew. This means that contemporary appointment pressure

is more likely to spring from the coalition of groups that have now re-placed party organizations as the chief political allies on whom presiden-tial candidates must rely during their long pilgrimage to the White House. Jimmy Carter ran without the blessing of major segments of his own political party, and he was most beholden to outside groups, like the National Education Association (NEA), that provided the organizational muscle for his presidential campaign, particularly during the primary sea-son. Not surprisingly, a number of former leaders of such groups subse-quently showed up in the Carter administration. (Rourke 1991b, 127)

Similar pressures materialized in Reagan's appointments. "Many of Ronald Reagan's early appointments reflected the fact that his election in 1980 was as much the triumph of a rising conservative political philoso-phy as it was the victory of a political party." As discussed above, Rea-gan's personnel director, Pendelton James, came under fierce attack from conservatives even during the inauguration week for bringing in too many Nixon and Eisenhower "retreads" or others who had not supported Rea-gan early enough or strongly enough. He was thus forced to send more ap-pointments their way to appease the conservatives (ibid., 127). The same pressures later beset President Bush.

These New Right PASs served with varying degrees of success. Some became good soldiers of administration policy. "Others, however, proved to be stormy petrels—more attached to their own creed than to the goals of the president, or perhaps, as in the case of the 'Right to Life' movement, bent on actually achieving goals to which the Reagan White House—at least in its early years—was prepared only to give lip service" (ibid., 127).

Partisan considerations aside, there are some positions the president is not free to fill solely on political grounds. Scientific, medical, and technological positions require someone of recognized competence in those fields with partisan acceptance coming in second. It "is not altogether impossible for presidents to identify candidates who are politically in tune with administration policies and also have the necessary scientific qualifications in the eyes of their professional peers. A good fit, however, is often hard to find" (ibid., 128).

Another limitation on the president's appointing power is the prospect of the Senate confirmation process and a public grilling in the Senate and the press. Though the Senate rarely rejects a presidential nomination, the process itself may make a president or candidate reconsider an appointment. As one PAS noted, a nominee who values her or his privacy doesn't want to find herself or himself on the front page of the *Washington Post* for something innocuous outside of the governmental pressure cooker but easily made to look suspicious in Washington's supercharged political atmosphere.

As discussed above, presidents also have to decide how much appointing power they share with their cabinet officers. "Presidents like Nixon and Carter, who delegated the power to make subcabinet selections to their cabinet, subsequently regretted that decision" (ibid., 128). However, some secretaries (e.g., Jim Baker at Bush's State Department) come on board with the explicit understanding that they will choose their own top people in a take-it-or-leave-it deal. Also, presidents do not want to be too closely involved in the appointment of lower-level appointees for time reasons and to avoid the pressures for patronage, as well as to avoid responsibility when things go badly with appointees or agencies (e.g., Watergate, Iran-Contra, and the *Challenger* disaster) (ibid., 128).

Another limiting factor is that the later it gets in the president's term, the harder it is to attract competent individuals as they start to look for the proverbial greener pastures in the private sector, particularly if the president is not running for reelection or if his chances of winning seem slim. At this point careerists are often appointed to positions they would not have been considered politically qualified for earlier. In these cases and in some others, "the goal of an appointment is not so much to secure the loyalty of an executive agency to the president's goals as it is to symbolize the president's own loyalty to the goals and programs of the agency" (ibid., 129).

These "appointments that a president has no choice but to make" included FBI Director J. Edgar Hoover and Chairman of the Federal Reserve Board Paul Volcker. Hoover was reappointed to his position by presidents of both parties "to demonstrate . . . both their dedication to tough law enforcement and their fervent opposition to subversive activities in the

United States." It is also widely assumed that Hoover had amassed so much influence and damaging information through his largely unrestrained power of investigation that no president dared replace him. Fed Chair Volcker was reappointed by Reagan to reassure the financial community of Reagan's commitment to fighting inflation. "As one Reagan aide put it, 'We didn't reappoint Volcker. . . . The markets reappointed Volcker'" (ibid., 129).

Clearly, then, presidents operate within a complex web of both competing and interlocking interests and agendas in exercising their personnel prerogatives.

Executive-Legislative Tensions in the Short-Termer System: Appointment Time Lines

Executive-legislative tensions are a given in American politics because of the way powers and authority are apportioned in the Constitution.

> This separation and sharing of power between Congress and the President has made for a turbulent and divisive relationship. One effect is that those political appointees chosen by the President to head the executive agencies frequently find themselves in an ambiguous situation: They are accountable to the Congress for their authority, funds, and performance, but they are also accountable to the President who appointed them, who sets the general policy framework in which they must work, and who is responsible for seeing that the laws are faithfully executed. (NAPA 1980, 31)

It is ironic that the most careful presidential preparation is often coupled with the least timely appointments. As discussed above, this is due to a confluence of factors: the expansion of government in the modern era has meant many more positions to fill, and the political parties no longer act as clearing houses for patronage requests (these often go directly to the White House). Another factor contributing to delay is the ongoing need to scrutinize and make careful decisions. The post-Watergate emphasis on ethical and conflict-of-interest considerations, while providing benefits, has also introduced a new and complicating factor into the appointment process, "raising the stakes, and in some cases the financial costs," of government service (Macy et al. 1983, 40).

Generally, it is to the advantage of the president to fill positions as quickly as possible.

During a transition of the presidency, the permanent career bureaucracy continues to operate the government. But the machinery of government is in neutral. Routine operation will go on without many problems, but new directions in policy making will not be undertaken. Leadership is required that can only be provided by the appointees of a new president, and the longer the bureaucracy drifts, the longer it will be before the new president's priorities and policies can be implemented. (Pfiffner 1987a, 62)

In some cases a strategic inaction is employed. For example, it was generally understood that Reagan's anger at Health and Human Services (HHS) Secretary Margaret Heckler was the cause of the lack of appointments to fill vacancies there. It was his way of punishing her but it also hurt the agency, which may not have been coincidental, given his antipathy toward its mission.

Each side, executive and legislative, blames the other for the long delays that often accompany presidential nominations. The Senate appointed a Task Force on Confirmation Delay to study the appointments and confirmation process and make recommendations to ameliorate the situation. Its report, issued in early 1992, charged the White House with responsibility for most of the delay, noting that while the Senate takes, on average, forty-eight days to consider a nominee, the White House takes nearly three hundred days, on average, to announce an appointment and submit information papers to the Senate. Even something as simple and direct as delivering the nominee's paperwork to the committee takes from one to two months after the nomination is announced by the White House. Additionally, as the report noted, many posts simply sit vacant. "Currently, almost one of every six federal judgeships is vacant. Yet for 91 of these 135 posts, the president has failed to submit any nominee to the Senate" (U.S. Congress, Senate, 1992).

The *Report* called on the White House to consult more with senators prior to nominating key PASs and to restore to the Judiciary Affairs Committee full access to FBI investigative reports on the nominees. Previously allowed, this had been denied since October 1991 due to presidential anger over leaks during the Supreme Court confirmation hearings of Clarence Thomas. A standoff ensued when, in retaliation, the Judiciary Committee had, with bipartisan unanimity, refused to consider any confirmations not already in its pipeline. Subsequent to the report's issuance, however, the White House restored full access to the FBI reports nearly in accord with the previous agreement with the committee. The impasse passed. The other Senate committees dealing with confirmations continued, as before, to receive only summary memoranda of the FBI report.

The *Task Force Report* also called on the White House as well as the Senate to streamline its paperwork by adopting one standard form for all nominees, using specific addenda as appropriate. Currently, each Senate committee may have its own form but the body as a whole requires only one form to be completed for the nominee under its scrutiny. The executive branch often demands the same basic information on three different forms from each nominee. The *Report* also called for a more thorough FBI background report to save later investigation by the FBI or the committees (which do their own investigating, often more thorough than the FBI's). It also stressed the need to stop leaks of confidential information to protect the privacy of individuals under consideration (U.S. Congress, Senate, 1992).

The Senate, despite a few well-publicized battles with the White House over nominations (e.g., Clarence Thomas, Robert Gates, Robert Bork, John Tower), is markedly compliant in most of its confirmation decisions; it confirms some 97 percent of the White House's nominees. One committee, the Judiciary Affairs Committee, serves as an example. Judiciary processes about one hundred nominees a year, forty federal judges and sixty U.S. marshals and attorneys (the latter are executive branch, not judicial appointments, but have significant independent powers). Judicial branch appointees enjoy lifetime tenure. As the White House has to fill as many slots as possible before the clock runs out (read: the presidential term expires), there is a strong incentive to go for quantity over quality; consequently, this particular committee examines candidates closely.

However, even for judicial appointments, as one Senate staffer noted, "The process is remarkably nonpartisan. The number of partisan confirmation fights is unbelievably small. When persons are not confirmed it is almost always a joint decision between [Democrat] Biden, the chair, and Thurmond" (the ranking Republican committee member). Of those not confirmed, the smallest percent (1 percent) are denied.

Not all nominees reach the hearing stage, of course. In about 5 percent of the cases the chair simply refuses to schedule a hearing, allowing the nominee to "languish until he or she withdraws" or simply declining to consider a candidate until the president gives up and withdraws the name. This is due to low quality, lack of qualifications, or damaging information uncovered about the candidate that the White House did not know about or let slide, hoping it would not be discovered. Sometimes the president, responding to pressure from an interest group, submits a candidate who clearly is not qualified, leaving it for the committee to take the heat for rejecting her or him.

Nevertheless, between 1987 and early 1992, Judiciary held 212 hearings for judicial appointments. Headed by a Democrat and with a Democratic majority, the committee confirmed 99 percent of those who appeared before it; that is, 209 Republican candidates of a Republican president for lifelong jobs, hardly evidence of Senate independence or obduracy.

The Spoils System at Work in Political Appointments:
The Stockbrokerage Dealing Jobs

The president has appointing authority for some 3,925 civilian positions. These include the Schedule C, SES, PAS, and PA positions; the latter two are most crucial to presidential control of the executive branch. Patronage pressures are inevitable and particularly strong on new administrations; they come from various sources. One source is the Congress whose members have constituents, staff members, or policy advocates they want placed in the executive branch. Sometimes it is a loyal representative or senator, herself or himself recently defeated, retired, or simply desiring a change.

A more pressing source of patronage pressure is the successful campaign itself. Campaign workers expect a "fair share" of the spoils of victory. Presidents Nixon, Carter, Reagan, and Bush were all attacked for not appointing enough workers and party faithful.

> In the Reagan administration Lyn Nofziger represented those campaign workers who wanted jobs in the administration and felt that the White House was placing too many "retreads" from the Nixon and Ford administrations. According to Nofziger, "We have told members of the Cabinet we expected them to help us place people who are competent. . . . As far as I'm concerned, anyone who supported Reagan is competent." (Pfiffner 1987a, 67)

George Bush faced patronage pressure from within and without. Because his administration was a "friendly takeover" and seen by many, including at times Bush himself, as simply an extension of the Reagan presidency, a Republican third term, those Reagan appointees in place who had supported Bush expected to stay in office, at least somewhere in the new administration—they were in no hurry to leave. And, because there had not been a party turnover there was no rush to move them out, as there would have been otherwise.

Despite administration statements that turnover of some 80 to 90 percent was expected, the Bush people were not initially noticeably successful in eradicating every trace of Reagan. By the summer of the first year, approximately 35 percent of the subcabinet appointees were Reagan holdovers, though not necessarily holding the same position (Pfiffner 1990, 68). However, a year later only 22 percent remained (Aberbach 1991, 239).

Another important source of patronage pressure is the other appointees themselves. Robert Mosbacher, secretary of commerce, for example, publicly complained that not enough fund raisers were getting jobs in the administration, even though as many as 50 percent of them did. There was also a "must list" of fifty major donors who wanted jobs for themselves or their relatives; more than a dozen significant donors were appointed to major ambassadorial posts early in the administration (Pfiffner 1990, 68).

Conservative think tanks and the Far Right continued their importuning of the White House—the Heritage Foundation sent over a ten-foot stack of 2,500 resumes. The flood of resumes to the White House from all sources eventually numbered 70,000 (45,000 after duplicates were culled). As one administration official said, choosing among them was like "trying to take a sip from a fire hydrant" (ibid., 68). The sheer numbers are enough to stagger any personnel office, let alone one not firmly established and well positioned within an administration.

Models of Political Appointments:
Political Pay-Offs, Shadow Governments, and Counter-Staffing

In their study of noncareer SES executives in the Reagan administration, Ban and Ingraham discuss three models for political appointments and the relationships with careerists to which they lend themselves. Their analysis applies in large measure to PAS executives as well. One is the political payoff model, in which the appointment is made to please or appease a constituency group, party power base, large donor, or individual crucial to the success of the presidential campaign. Appointees occupying these positions are "particularly hard to control, since they are likely to define their role in terms of representing the interests to whom they owe their position, and to have strong ties to the 'iron triangle' [an agency, congressional oversight committee, and special interest groups] in their field." If they share similar values and priorities with their career staff their relationship is likely to be very good (Ban and Ingraham 1990, 109–10).

The shadow government model involves what Heclo terms "political careerists," who may be congressional staff members, academics, career civil servants, and those employed in think tanks or consulting firms who are tapped for temporary government service (this model dominates only at the Department of Defense). They are "people who build their careers around problems of public policy and do so outside the confines of the formal civil service personnel system." As professionals, they are more likely to treat careerists as knowledgeable colleagues and to know most effectively how to employ their expertise (ibid., 110).

The third version, the counter-staffing model, is employed when an appointee is put into an agency who is opposed to its direction or mission or who is

> deeply committed to the administration's ideology or policies. Their mission is to "turn things around." Such appointees may have considerable prior substantive experience, often challenging the previous policies in the field (e.g., James Watt). More often, however, they lack substantive experience and this is seen as a strength, rather than a weakness, since they will be less likely to have strong ties to the existing interests in the area. . . . These appointees are least likely to have had prior public-sector experience. (Ibid., 110)

As might be expected, these appointees are most likely to be suspicious of careerists' motives and capabilities and to assume them to be in the enemy camp and opposed to the kind of radical change the PASs demand, particularly if the White House has just changed parties.

Ban and Ingraham conclude that the majority of the Reagan noncareer SES executives they interviewed

> conformed closely to the counter-staffing model . . . , particularly at OPM and HUD. Most had neither prior substantive experience relevant to their current positions nor prior governmental experience. Their personal motivation for taking a political appointment was usually a strong commitment to the president's policies and programs. . . . Several also saw a political appointment as a smart career move; as one put it, "I didn't have executive experience and wanted it." Interestingly, almost all of those fitting the counter-staffing model actively sought political appointment. (Ibid., 111)

There is a close correlation between the entry patterns of the noncareer SES executives and the PASs. The latter are also perceived as being "highly committed to the Reagan ideology and as having less previous governmental experience than appointees of earlier administrations, and

viewing a political appointment as a ticket to the greater financial rewards available in the private sector" (ibid., 111).

The hoary short-termer personnel system traditionally "creates what
is basically an accidental collection of individuals with little past commitment to political leadership and few enduring stakes in government's
own capabilities and performance" (Heclo 1977, 154). In contrast, the
Reagan appointees were determined to change government and to do so
as quickly as possible, given their limited tenure.

> Many clearly entered government because of their strong commitment to
> Reagan and to his political agenda. While some of our interviewees were
> uncomfortable with the label "ideologue," almost all expressed clear
> knowledge of, and support for, the Reagan agenda. The core of that polit-
> ical agenda was limited government, particularly in domestic agencies,
> and a strong defense posture. [They] lent support to the view of Newland
> (1983) that "(p)ublic administration under President Reagan . . . (was), to
> a significant extent, ideological political administration." (Ban and Ingra-
> ham 1990, 115–17)

George Bush's appointees, as discussed below, were of a different stripe.
While generally less radical and with a revolution to extend rather than
create, they were more likely to value government and good management,
per se.

Risks Attendant to Appointments

Presidents face not only limitations on their appointing authority, but
risks in its use. One risk is that through an appointment, the president
may actually lose, rather than gain, control over the executive branch. Because a president cannot manage his entire government from the White
House, he must in large measure work through his cabinet, yet the truism holds that "the president and the cabinet are natural enemies," with
competing power bases and avenues of support. "Presidents thus make
their appointment decisions the way investors make their choices in the
stock market—with anticipation and trepidation, never being altogether
certain whether they will be helped or hurt by the people they elevate to
high government office" (Rourke 1991b, 124–25).

Operating in a zero-sum power game, the more appointment power a
president gives to his cabinet, the less loyalty he commands from his appointees' appointees. They are, understandably, most loyal to the person
to whom they owe their position, in this case the cabinet secretary.

When PASs prove "disloyal" by, for instance, publicly disagreeing with administration policy, or perhaps not supporting it strongly enough, the White House can demand the resignation of the PAS in what is essentially a political firing of a political appointee. However, to do so makes the administration look bad, or at least less than competent.[7]

> Removal can be politically costly. It may disturb groups that identify with the departing official and send a strong signal to the public of an administration in disarray. At the very least, it is an admission of a presidential mistake. Moreover, [there can be international repercussions. W]hen President Carter undertook his celebrated cabinet purge in 1979, he triggered widespread alarm in Europe as well as the United States as to the stability of his own government. (Rourke 1991b, 124)

PASs do have a defense against the charge of disloyalty, even if they are powerless to retain their positions through its use. That is that as political appointees, they serve solely at the pleasure of their political boss, the ultimate boss being the president. However,

> it is difficult, if not impossible, to be loyal to the president's objectives when these goals are so often ambiguous, poorly communicated, or subject to rapid change. Executive officials often complained that the policies of the Carter White House had these characteristics. Moreover, a president may well have a covert agenda—especially in foreign affairs—that differs radically from what White House pronouncements might suggest. (Ibid., 130)

While appointees can be fired, they can hardly be blamed for acting on their own initiative when agency decisions have to be made in the vacuum of White House indecision or inaction.

Disloyalty is not the only grounds for removal. Appointees can be fired or pressured to resign for illegal activities (à la Oliver North), to assume the blame for higher-ups (à la Robert McFarlane), or simply if they prove to be a political embarrassment or liability (à la Chief of Staff John Sununu, forced from office for a combination of arrogance and billing the government for the pursuit of his philatelic interests and other hobbies. . . . Famous for his utter boredom with budget matters, [he often put] his feet on the table and [read] stamp catalogues during budget meetings with the Hill.")[8]

Even when presidents appoint persons whom they believe will carry out their policy goals, there is a tendency for appointees' loyalty to shift to their agency or their agency's constituencies, "marrying the natives" as it is derisively called by White House aides, when appointees take on the perspective of their agency. Reagan made conscious efforts to counter these tendencies toward co-optation by encouraging his appointees

> to distance themselves from their own agencies' personnel during the transition period. They were also exposed to task force reports and briefings on the policies of their agencies by conservative organizations like the Heritage Foundation. This strategy was designed to inoculate them with conservative antibodies that would provide protection from the liberal viruses to which the administration expected appointees to be exposed once they began to have close contact with civil servants. (Ibid., 130)

Reagan also employed the tactic of frequent reassignment of his appointees so they would not get too close to their agency and careerists. These strategies may have worked to alienate PASs somewhat from their agencies but it did not do much to warm them to White House overtures on how to run their agencies. And, in fact, the Reagan PASs "were highly critical of the way in which White House staff members tried to interfere with their work. It turned out that Reagan's executives were no less determined to maintain their managerial autonomy than their predecessors in previous administrations had been" (ibid., 130).

Nixon's White House failed in its attempts at control because they were based on the faulty and hubristic assumption that the White House really *could* control the government directly. The Reagan White House had to face the same reality. As discussed above, there are too many other competing players—the Congress, the party, special interests, other PASs, and the federal bureaucracy itself—for the White House to exert direct control. The more it tries to do so, the more opposition it engenders. The managerial presidency soon finds its reach exceeds its grasp.

Even an operation as sophisticated as Nixon's White House Personnel Office was unable to accomplish its goals of controlling the government and improving relations with the Congress. As one observer notes, "Systems do not manage; people manage." The WHPO, despite its strengths, "never fully overcame the absence of presidential involvement, the insensitivity of senior White House staff, the unrestrained antics of some of its aggressive implementers, or its flawed perception of White House capabilities for administrative personnel management. The system worked, but the grand design collapsed" (Mackenzie 1981, 56).

A president who wants to exert a significant degree of power is well advised to concentrate on the top tier of his or her administration, filling those positions with individuals who support the administration's policies and are capable of inspiring the same support from both political and career subordinates in their agency. Mutual accommodation or double veto of lower-level PASs will do much to promote the twin goals of smooth relations and policy loyalty.

And what of civil servants in this mix? As their role and relationship with political appointees and the risks they pose to administration policy are discussed in chapter 6, they are considered only briefly here.

Goldenberg considers four roles civil servants can take vis-à-vis their political superiors. They can be passive extensions of the president, active supporters of the president, brokers of conflicting interests, or protectors of the public interest. Generally speaking, Reagan managed to enhance the passive extension role. His emphasis on control meant that he received relatively little active support from the civil service but, as Goldenberg notes, "its absence was hardly noticed during 1981 when administration attention was focused on cutting budgets." The usual difficulties of bucking policy in any administration made the brokering and whistle-blowing roles as risky as usual for civil servants in the Reagan administration (Goldenberg 1985, 383–403). With less energy having to go for self-defense, careerists in the Bush administration were more likely to fall into the broker or public interest roles.

Political Appointments as a Growth Industry

The federal bureaucracy was originally composed of limited numbers of short-term unpaid volunteer appointees who were mostly wealthy, landowning, white male citizens. Today, the bureaucracy has evolved into a paid, lifelong career for nearly two million persons of both sexes and all races and socioeconomic standings. However, the now paid, short-term political administrators continue to play an important leadership role in the country's bureaucracy. The interaction of political appointees with the subordinate career bureaucracy undergoes continual development and refinement. Political appointees head the bureaucracy of government, yet their relatively short tenure puts them at a comparative disadvantage vis-à-vis the longer-tenured career executives, 70 percent of whom have been with their agency for ten years, 50 percent for fifteen years (Volcker 1989, 215).

From the founding of the Republic, inevitable problems of turf, expertise, neutral competence, and political responsiveness accompanied the development of the bureaucracy and its division into political and career components. The growth of the bureaucracy with the New Deal and its politicization in recent years have added other issues to the mix, such as the relative and absolute growth of political appointments, the placement of political appointees lower down in the governmental hierarchy, the mobility and morale of career executives, and the overall politicization of the public service. Other issues are the political and policy agendas of presidents in appointing executives and the PASs' degree of commitment to those agendas once they are in office.[9]

Political appointments in this country proliferated with no apparent foresight or planning. "There is no document of state, no great debate or major decision of public record available which uncovers the foundations of our current in-and-outer system. The assorted arrangements for appointing political executives grew little by little in no preconceived way and in no particular order throughout the nooks and crannies of the executive branch" (Heclo 1987, 196).

As civil service reform from the 1880s through the 1940s moved more and more positions out of the spoils (political) system and into the merit (career) system, no clear plan of action emerged to deal with the remaining political positions. According to Heclo, the subtleties of Progressive Reform thought were lost in the popularization of the "politics/administration dichotomy" that most vigorously stressed the growing country's need for a professional bureaucracy inoculated from the corruption rampant at the end of the nineteenth century. Experience had taught that "Washington was failing to perform the first task of a government: to create an orderly community. . . . Modern government was no longer the place for amateurs" (ibid., 198).

The Progressive reformers envisioned what might be termed a "politics/administration partnership," with

> political departmental secretaries with small staffs of personal aides . . .
> and one career officer playing the role of general manager of the department. . . . Political officials would represent the public view and play the
> deciding role over policy issues. Permanent career officials would represent the expert point of view, offering their advice as nonpartisan professionals and line supervisors over the day-to-day work of government.
> Contrary to the later caricatures by their critics, the more thoughtful of
> the reformers did not see politics, policy, and administration as separate
> realms carried on in isolation. The design was intended to achieve a more
> reliable way of ensuring a proper mixture of perspectives in the work of
> government. (Ibid., 198–99)

Clearly, the design was significantly altered during the course of its haphazard implementation. There are a number of reasons why political appointments grew in a direction not foreseen by the reformers: First, presidents and the Congress have taken the path of least resistance, not stopping to step back and assess the overall appointments structure. It was easier simply to let "the system based on happenstance" grow largely unchecked. Second, as more demands were made on government and it grew to meet them, more political appointees were added to meet the crisis-du-jour. Departments were rarely eliminated, however, so the overall number of appointees kept growing to supervise them (ibid., 201).

Third, there is an ongoing asymmetry between PASs and careerists, with several facets. The former can operate on an ad hoc basis irrespective of maintaining institutional ties or traditions while the latter depend on a web of tradition, mentoring, and institutional connections. There are also significant power differentials between the two groups. High-level careerists have no opportunity to add more careerists to their number to solidify their ranks. Meanwhile, political appointees who supervise a system that was previously wholly career-run can more easily "manage the workflow, bring in personal assistants, and disregard successors in such a way as to undermine any first-rate career operation. In the first case the effects on the personnel system are never felt in the long run, while in the second case they are felt only in the long run, when there is no one around to blame" (ibid., 201–02).

Consequently, a self-perpetuating dynamic is set off that eventually locates politically connected technocrats in PAS appointments, ironically created specifically for them. It happens in what Heclo calls a two-step dance: An interest develops, for whatever reason, in having a particular position filled by a partisan. A struggle ensues in which Congress stipulates requirements for that position and, making it subject to Senate confirmation, another short-termer position is born (ibid., 202).

A fourth reason for the growth in appointments is that diffusion of powers between the legislative and executive branches means that there is no one center of decision-making power. The operating assumption of the Progressive Reform movement that gave birth to the notion of "political neutrality depended on a different kind of democratic regime [than the American model], a regime of government and opposition." It assumed a very highly placed civil service, a parliamentary government along the lines of Britain, Europe, or Japan with an ongoing state or crown, a ruling or governing party, and an opposition party.

"Neutral competence" by those civil servants at the top meant "being committed to serving the party in power to the fullest of one's professional competence, and then doing the same for any successor govern-ment." The American system of separation of powers between the Con-gress and the executive, even if both are controlled by the same party, means that responsibility is diffused throughout the political system. If different parties control the two branches, the government is further di-vided and responsibility diffused even more (ibid., 203).

This uniquely American situation leaves

> senior [career] executive officials . . . in an inherently ambiguous position. They cannot simply serve one government of the day but instead must accommodate a number of different power centers. They cannot live in an insulated departmental setting but must be in constant liaison with the legislature. They cannot hide under a doctrine of neutrality between succeeding governments because microgovernments—the ruling coali-tions around first one issue and then another—are constantly being formed and re-formed simultaneously on many different fronts. These strictures apply not only to the head of a department and his or her per-sonal assistants but to all persons in responsible executive positions. (Ibid., 204)

The pressures on civil servants leave them walking a political tightrope strung between two jealous branches of government." It is little wonder, then, when they abandon neutral competence for technical competence and avoid any responsibility to offer political or policy advice (ibid., 204).

Political Appointee Numbers

The number of political appointees of all types has increased dramat-ically in the past few decades, from approximately twelve hundred in the late 1960s to nearly four thousand in the early 1990s. They have also moved from the top levels of the bureaucracy down lower into the ranks through Eisenhower's innovation of Schedule C in 1953. This creation al-lows the president to make appointments to relatively low-level (GS 9–15) assistant or secretarial positions so "his people" could serve the other political appointees in confidential or policy-making positions or keep an eye on the career staff.

It is difficult to give exact data on appointment numbers due to dif-fering definitions of which positions should be included in the count, due to hidden positions, and the cyclical nature of political appointments (lowest immediately following the inauguration of a new president and at the end of an administration, highest at the midpoint of the presidential term). Three different sources, two executive, one congressional, demonstrate this problem of ascertaining exact numbers of PASs.

The congressional version comes from *The United States Government Policy and Supporting Positions* (commonly called the *Plum Book*), published quadrennially in presidential election years by the Senate or by the House alternately. An invaluable resource, it catalogues by agency or department all the allocated executive and Schedule C positions throughout the government authorized as of the summer of the year just prior to the election. The 1992 version is instructive, seen next to the EOP and OPM lists (data from each office given personally to the author) (see table 4.1).

The Plum Book also lists 4,305 General SES positions (to which either a noncareer or a career appointment may be made). By this count, then, presidents have at least 4,795 positions (plus an indeterminate number in the General SES category) to fill by appointment. Further confusing the search for hard numbers, Pfiffner (1994, 123) lists a total of 5,823. (Of the Senate-confirmed there are 505 part-timers, 165 ambassadors, 187 U.S. attorneys and marshals, and 663 executives and IRCs. Of the nonconfirmed there are 24 executive branch officials, 438 White House officials, and 1,405 part-timers. There are 711 SESs and 1,725 Schedule Cs.)

While PAS positions are established by Congress, it is often difficult for those outside the executive branch to gather pertinent information to make an accurate and current count of the political appointees, as the above attempt at enumeration demonstrates. Also, the president can change the executive level of any PAS position, request that Congress create a new position, or delete or downgrade a position to SES status. (Schedule C positions are not statutory positions; they do not exist when

Table 4.1. Political Positions According to *The Plum Book*, EOP, and OPM

Position	Plum Book 1992	EOP 10/31/91	OPM 6/30/92
PAS (both part-and full-time)	1,163	903 (nonjudicial)	693
Noncareer SES	723	485 (mid-1989)	731
Schedule C	1,794	1,005 (mid-1989)	1,735
PA	561	225	
Statutory excepted	459		
SES limited or emergency	62		
Other	22		

vacant and they have to be requested by an agency or the White House in order to be recreated by OPM once their incumbent has left.)

Useful as the *Plum Book* is, it is not infallible. It lists far fewer staff available to the White House than actually work there (many are detailed from the agencies and thus hidden from accurate cost accounting) and, by a quick glance, is incorrect in its count in at least one agency, the Central Intelligence Agency, which is listed as having two PASs but which actually has three. It also fails to register the 903 judges appointed to the federal bench in the judicial branch.

> The inclusion of presidential staff, other White House staff, military, foreign service appointments and part-time appointments are points of continuing debate. Since 1978, the Senior Executive Service has added a new dimension to [the] total appointee count. . . . "hidden appointees," known only to White House personnel office staff [the detailees and nondetailees], who elude official counts. Despite these concerns, there is general agreement, among even the most conservative counters, that the total number of political appointees has increased in the last ten years. It is only the dimension of the increase that is in dispute [given the difficulty of finding agreement on whom to count]. (Ingraham 1987, 426–27)

The Executive Office of the President houses a unique genre of political appointees and is a far-flung operation that serves the president's needs on every front.[10] In addition to the president's personal office and physician, there are the chief of staff and deputy chief, personal assistant, press secretary, cabinet secretary, executive secretaries of cabinet councils, and assistants for national security affairs, domestic policy, legislative affairs, political affairs, and intergovernmental affairs. There is legal counsel, a director of communications, press secretary, public liaison staff, speech writers and researchers, the presidential personnel office, advance and ad hoc special assistance, and military office staff covering everything from Air Force One to Camp David to the Naval Imaging Command to the White House Garage. The EOP also includes the White House units of the Secret Service, the chief usher, and the operations office that handles everything from correspondence to telephones to records to visitors. The Office of Management and Budget (OMB), the Council of Economic Advisors (CEA), and the National Security Council (NSC) are also related to the EOP (Patterson 1988, 91).

Additionally, the Office of the Vice President, housed in the West Wing of the White House, has a full staff complement of some ninety, including a chief of staff and a deputy; personal, military, legislative affairs, and national security affairs assistants; counsel; speech writers; a press secretary; and advance and scheduling staff. The Office of the First Lady, housed in the East Wing, has a staff of approximately thirty, including a chief of staff, personal assistant, press and social secretaries, correspondence, scheduling and advance staff, and a graphics and calligraphy office (ibid., 91).

John Hart lists the total number of staff at the White House at 1,692 (not counting detailees) with a total budget of $172,596,000 (not counting special funds) for fiscal year 1994 (see table 4.2).

This count does not include the military office (1,300 full time, 2,500 part time), the Executive Residence staff (129), engineering and maintenance staff (190), the U.S. Secret Service assigned to the president and vice

Table 4.2. Executive Office of the President Budget and Personnel, FY 1994

Division	Budget ($)	Staff (as of 10/1/94)
Office of Management and Budget	56,539,000	572
White House Office	38,754,000	430
Office of Administration	25,010,000	189
Office of U.S. Trade Representative	20,600,000	191
Office of National Drug Control Policy	11,687,000	25
National Security Council	6,648,000	147
Office of Policy Development (includes National Economic Council, Domestic Policy Council, and Office of Environmental Policy)	5,122,000	50
Office of Science and Technology Policy	4,450,000	46
Council of Economic Advisers	3,420,000	35
Council on Environmental Quality	375,000	0
Total	172,596,000[a]	1,685

Source: John Hart, *The Presidential Branch: From Washington to Clinton,* 2d ed. (Chatham, N.J.: Chatham House, 1995), 46.

[a]Amount indicated as in original.

president (800) or the 500 volunteers who answer correspondence (ibid., 339).

Ever since Watergate there have been concerns over the size of the White House staff and, as mentioned, calls for its reduction. President Clinton, to demonstrate his serious intent to deal with the budget deficit and as a part of his overall pledge to reduce government by 12 percent, reduced the White House staff by 350 in the third week of his administration (Hart 1995, 48). His symbolic gesture caused more pain than gain, however, as well-experienced staff performing key correspondence and other functions were let go and there were often not enough people to handle the workload.

Meanwhile, the larger debate about the role of political appointees has continued along with the growth in appointments. The Volcker Commission joined the debate about the optimal number of political appointees and concluded that, in the words of two of its members, "fewer is better." They note the power PASs possess; they "sit at the top of the executive branch hierarchies and have the power to make policy, reorganize their agencies and hire and fire people, within the limits of the law. Their numbers may be relatively small, but their power is highly leveraged" (Richardson and Pfiffner 1991, 56).

The Reagan appointees' desire to change government quickly was coupled with a near-unanimous desire for more political appointees, because it was felt "you need to have people with you who you can trust immediately. . . . You need more political slots so you can have a team that can hit the ground running" (Ban and Ingraham 1990, 118).

The wish to maximize control led many of the appointees to push for placement of appointees deep down in the line agencies. In their haste they seemed unaware of or unconcerned about the danger that having more appointees would most likely insulate them further from their career staff, thus actually working against their ability to control them or even to establish good working relationships with them (ibid., 118–19). They seemed also not to have learned Nixon's lesson that more appointees equals less, not more, control.

On the other hand, there were those in the Ban and Ingraham study who expressed reservations about working with other appointees, precisely because they are so subject to external political pressures and may not really understand how the game is played: "They think they understand the political process, and most of them don't." Additionally, some questioned the competence of the appointees, particularly the noncareer SESs: "Over one-third of the *political* executives we interviewed offered unsolicited critical comments about their fellow appointees: 'A lot of political people don't know a hill of beans about their area. Those who are confirmed by the Senate are generally good, but at the lower levels, they don't have a lot of background, and have to rely on the career people'" (ibid., 121).

Tom McFee, longtime career executive, joins the debate: "Numbers, alone . . . are not the most critical issue. . . . but, rather, *the types of positions* that are filled by political appointments." Although PAS positions increased significantly (they more than quadrupled from 1965, when there were 152, to 1992, when there were 639), he feels that this increase was mostly justified as it kept pace with the growing size and complexity of government and was part of an overall management plan.

> The types of PAS positions which have experienced the most growth are those of the assistant secretary or agency head or their deputy level, or, in some cases, major program directors. . . . these positions require an act of Congress to be established [and] are normally scrutinized as part of the legislative committee process. [They] are only established after Congress and the administration agree that their mutual interest in the incumbents of these positions justifies their establishment. (McFee 1991)

However, beyond the increase in numbers, per se, is the related issue of loss of career positions through a process by which they are converted into noncareer positions. For example, the position of assistant secretary for administration or management (ASAM), was originally established as a career position in line with recommendations of the First and Second Hoover Commissions (1949 and 1955). Over time, however, these positions have been converted to PAS positions to meet demands for political responsiveness. Part of the problem was the manner in which the conversions were handled: there was no coherent congressional or executive plan to provide order and rationale for such a realignment.

Another problem is the premature "topping out" of civil service careers as the positions at the top of its career ladder disappear into the political ranks. In late 1992 only three of these ASAM positions remained filled by careerists, McFee being one. He agrees with the Volcker Commission recommendation that these positions should be returned to career status and suggests that they be established under the direction of a new political position of undersecretary for management (ibid.).

The SES General category allows positions to be filled by either career or noncareer persons and creates "a hodgepodge of reporting relationships wherein noncareer appointees can report to career managers and executives, etc. This wreaks havoc in our performance management processes and in the bonus system, as well, producing much confusion in the day-to-day chain of command" (ibid.).

To address these problems, McFee suggests the elimination of the SES General category and that the system return to the original supergrades that were career unless an exception was made. He also recommends that the 10 percent cap governmentwide be made to apply to each agency (currently individual agencies can have up to 25 percent noncareer SES positions, as long as the overall 10 percent cap is maintained). He speculates that this would result in career appointments being safeguarded from inappropriate political encroachment (ibid.).

There are few voices calling for more political appointees. One belongs to Republican Edward Lynch. In contrast to McFee, Richardson, Pfiffner, Light, and others, Lynch (having served as a Republican political appointee with seven federal agencies) argues that reducing the number of political appointees is not the answer; doubling them is. He appears to see the principal enemy as the Congress, rather than the careerists in the executive agencies. Apparently disdaining the Constitution's balance of power, his winner-take-all philosophy is seemingly offended that the Congress might think to thwart the president's intentions: "Responsive government requires a close link between the political ideas that win elections and the policies of government. . . . The executive branch cannot reflect the consent of the governed when the legislature constrains its ability to provide the leadership that is the rightful consequence of winning elections" (Lynch 1991, 55).

While Lynch would rather see exact parity between political and congressional staffs, "giving the executive one person to respond to each staffer who can ask questions of a political nature," he acknowledges the larger financial realities and would settle for twice as many appointees as currently exist, thus "assuring the President one appointee for each five staffers available to Congress" (ibid., 55).

Pfiffner offers three reasons to reverse the trend toward more political appointees to improve government's functioning "without sacrificing political accountability or responsiveness." First, in order for the bureaucracy to respond to the policy changes of a dynamic democracy, its permanent leadership must be up to speed, have a larger vision of government, and be comfortable working at its upper reaches. Bureaucracy cannot serve democracy if it is completely decapitated with each change of administration.

Second, excess appointments work against the policy interests of the president. The more layers of appointees there are between the bureau chief and the bureaucrats who actually implement her or his policy, the longer it takes to establish control. Presidents thus lose valuable honey-moon and "election mandate" time while appointees secure staff and try to establish control. And finally, the White House personnel office cannot keep pace with the current staffing needs (Pfiffner 1987c, 63), as vacancies of 15 to 20 percent testify.

Conclusion

It is clear that political appointments can be a mine field for unwary presidents. While they present an opportunity to put their stamp on the office, they also present a danger, as the assassination in 1881 of President James Garfield by a "disappointed office seeker" attests. Though not usually in such dramatic fashion, appointees can put their own stamp on a presidency (or president), as many a president has discovered to his dismay.

While presidents in the modern era have taken various approaches from indifference to active direction, no president can give personnel his or her full attention for long, and all have found it to be a headache. It is clear that the president must depend on her or his people to manage the government. But as the number of appointees has grown and the broker-ing power of the political parties has diminished, pressure has increased on the president from various quarters and special interest groups for their interests to be represented. Early planning and giving high priority to fill-ing vacancies and high visibility to the Presidential Personnel Office are crucial to personnel success. Mutual accommodation from the cabinet on down would ease working relations in the agencies while maintaining the White House tie. It is difficult to escape the conclusion that the number of political appointees should be reduced. While reducing the number of appointees would decrease the political capital of the spoils system, it would sharpen the process considerably, give the president more control over it, and reduce the workload on his already overburdened personnel office. It would have the added advantage of returning more power to the careerists, the people who "know how to put their hands on the right switches."

The gridlock with the Senate causes unnecessary delay and grief all around. Both sides should cooperate to ease the confirmation process, par-ticularly the paperwork part of it. Certainly, the personal investigation process should be tightened and confidentiality guaranteed to prospective appointees.

5

⊙♦♦♦⊙

PAS Quality and
Qualifications: Anything More than
a Roll of the Dice?

In innumerable ways, presidents live and die by their political appointments. Yet, how are they to determine before they actually make the appointment which appointee will enhance their political life and which will destroy their political capital? What qualifies a person to be a presidential appointee, per se? Qualifications for PASs are difficult to establish in advance because there is no single standard for competence, evaluation is necessarily (though not totally) subjective, and qualifications can be personal, professional, and political. Neither are the criteria consistent for finding "the best person" for any given position. Further, any one PAS, much like the president himself or herself, has to please a number of disparate elements in both the government and in society. What one group may consider a positive attribute or policy, such as willingness to implement budget cutbacks, another, such as a group affected by the cutbacks, may consider a negative.

The president may be seeking to please or at least not offend a particular group, may need age, gender, racial, or geographic representation, may owe favors to various individuals or groups, or may need to secure future political capital by creating obligation (Mackenzie 1981, 240).

Some positions require technical expertise that cannot be circumvented, some require other skills such as lobbying or networking with congressional leaders. An additional factor is that the definition process of coming to the "best person" is often a collegial one, with all the subjectivity and special interests that those in the process may bring.

Even when all those issues are addressed, there is still the problem of

finding persons who meet the "'softer' criteria for a job, people with political sensitivity, thick skins, good interpersonal skills, and loyalty to the
aims of an administration," criteria that cannot always be known in advance. Another problem is that the White House alone cannot know the
skills and characteristics of a large number of people. It must rely on third
parties to render judgment, which limits the search. "In relying on third
parties, [the] search for the 'best person' for the job becomes in reality a
search for the 'best person' known to [the] network of contacts" (Mackenzie 1981, 240).

The element of guesswork in the search process is complicated by the
fact that there are "few known test tracks [for] high-level government service. No job outside of government requires quite the same combination
of talents and attitudes that many government positions require." Presidential personnel officers are left with making what are hoped to be educated and informed choices in an atmosphere of uncertainty. Or, to put it
simply, as one former Bush PAS said of the chances of matching jobs and
qualifications, "It's a crapshoot."

Where, professionally, do PASs come from and what is their level of
preparedness for running the government? The 1985 NAPA survey of
PASs serving between 1964 and 1984 indicated that

> Many of them come from other positions with the federal government.
> Forty percent of political appointees are transferred or promoted from
> other positions with the federal government. We can assume that these
> people are reasonably prepared for the context, if not the scope of their
> new jobs. But 60 percent come from other occupations: 24 percent from
> business, 16 percent from the academic and research communities, 12
> percent from the legal profession, and 7 percent from state and local gov-
> ernments. Their level of education is relatively high, with 19 percent
> holding bachelor's degrees, 21 percent master's degrees, 17 percent PhDs,
> and 34 percent law degrees. (Pfiffner 1987b, 142)[1]

Complicating the picture is the fact that appointees who come from
outside the public sector are used to playing by a different set of rules. The
ethics and norms of government can seem very foreign to one coming
from the private sector. "There are unwritten rules of the political arena,
in which quid pro quo is the norm, and the negotiating of compromises is
basic to survival" (Bonafede 1987a, 123). Appointees who fail to learn or
heed these rules may find their worst nightmare come true—complete
agency breakdown and their transgression front-page news in the *Washington Post*.

Additionally, expectations are different in government.

Remarked Tom Korologos, a former Nixon White House congressional liaison aide and Reagan transition advisor, "Those who hadn't been here before and who come from the business community find things don't occur when they should, that they don't happen fast enough and often don't work. They become frustrated because they have so many bosses and discover that they don't have the impact they thought they would." (Ibid., 142)

Even *asking* about qualifications of PASs is a politically charged venture. Although many can cite examples of PASs who are in over their heads, there is no standard list of qualifications that one can use to determine if PASs measure up to the job requirements. While the issue of qualifications for specific positions may be addressed more thoroughly in the future,[2] for now perhaps the best one can do is to look to the personal characteristics and overall experience that tend to make for success in PAS positions.

The conservative think tank, the Heritage Foundation, is very clear about its requirements for PAS appointees. First is "character, toughness, reliability," followed closely by loyalty to the president and his agenda, and then by skills. But, clearly, "the greatest of these" is loyalty:

Loyalty is the cement which binds a team together. This can be tested by questioning whether an individual knows what the president has said he wants; whether the applicant for agency head has, in general, agreed with the president's positions in the past; and whether he has a reputation for sticking by his friends. . . . the president must ask whether the individual has the proper mix of leadership ability, management skills, and program knowledge. He must guard against falling into the trap of appointing someone who has gained program knowledge by spending many years in an industry or field with which the agency has a close relationship. Often such people are the worst appointees, because they cannot subordinate loyalty to a special interest group to the loyalty they owe the president. The selection should not be based primarily on technical qualifications, but rather on *who is the most qualified of those who meet the first two criteria, character and loyalty.* (Heatherly and Pines 1989, 806)

While this sentiment rightly warns against the danger of capture of agencies by the industries PASs regulate, it also suggests a nostalgic throwback to the days of Andrew Jackson's administration. In the reforms of public service in the early nineteenth century it was popularly assumed that running the country was a task that virtually any citizen could handle, regardless of education or training. Specialized knowledge and prior experience were assumed to be unnecessary, and perhaps a sign of elitism inappropriate to a democratic nation. The populism of the late-twentieth-century conservative movement with its distrust of professional bureaucrats harkens back to this older form of bias against expertise. It finds its modern-day voice in the odd bedfellows of Ronald Reagan and Ralph Nader. It overflowed into the legislative branch, finding its full expression in the 1994 midterm elections when expertise of any sort seemed to discredit candidates and *incumbent* became a dirty word.

"Trusting the Family Heirlooms to a Two-Year-Old": PAS Tenure and its Effect on the Bureaucracy[3]

Ban and Ingraham's study of the Reagan SES found a correlation between the agencies that had the most political-career tension and those with the shortest political tenures:

> As one might expect, higher levels of tension were clearly evident in those agencies, such as HUD and OPM, where this administration's policies were sharply divergent from those of past administrations. These are also the agencies in which political appointees have the shortest tenure in position. Thus, in the agencies where one might expect it would take the longest to forge relationships of trust, the time available is shortest. The result is often what one would predict. As one appointee described it: "There is no doubt that it will always be East is East and West is West and never the twain shall meet in regard to political and career relationships. You have good relationships with the people you work with every day, but not a sense of commonality of mission." (Ban and Ingraham 1990, 114)

The tenure figures for Senate-confirmed appointees are higher than the eighteen to twenty-four months usually cited for political appointees in general. For the period of July to December 1979, for example, tenure for PASs was slightly more than thirty-one months. Meanwhile,

> the figure for noncareer SES members was significantly lower; their average tenure was only 1.7 years, or roughly 20 months. This may not seem problematic, but the gross average hides some dramatic patterns. Addi-

tional analysis reveals that during this period fully 40% of political executives government-wide occupied positions for less than one year. By
comparison, Heclo (1977, 104) found that 16% of undersecretaries and
22% of assistant secretaries had a tenure of less than 12 months on the
job.

    This turnover did not reflect high inter-agency mobility. Rather, it
indicates total numbers leaving government, as well as extensive movement *within* agencies. . . . [During the Reagan administration] fully one-
third of political executives either changed jobs or left government each
year. *Inter-agency* moves remained infrequent. In the highest year (the
first nine months of 1985), there were only 34 such moves governmentwide. (Ban and Ingraham 1990, 112–14)

    This degree of change indicates "a surprising level of continuous tur-
bulence among political appointees, and of continual change" far beyond
what could normally be attributed to a new administration. As one careerist put it, "Five years [into the Reagan presidency] we are still circling
one another in this agency, and there is still a we-them mentality." Considering that it takes approximately a year to get "fully 'up to speed' . . .
the consequences of short tenure may be both decreasing competence and
increasing mistrust of the career bureaucracy" (ibid., 114). This has negative consequences for presidential policy direction in agencies generally
at odds with that direction. When PASs bring

    little substantive experience and high levels of mistrust of the career bu-
    reaucracy, the remarkably high percentage of appointees remaining in po-
    sition for less than a year poses a major problem for political manage-
    ment—managers who cannot learn one job before they move on to
    another, and whose potential for either competent management or for de-
    veloping working relationships with the career bureaucracy is necessarily
    lower than that of longer-term employees. The paradox is that those
    agencies where the greatest amount of change is desired may be popu-
    lated by political executives with the least capacity to direct it. (Ibid., 115)

    Short tenure also puts political appointees at a distinct disadvantage
vis-à-vis the career executives, who are typically in place much longer. It
is clear that "without a steep learning curve . . . political appointees are
likely to find that their capabilities for effective action have matured at
about the time they are leaving office" (Heclo 1977, 110).

    The transient nature of political appointees limits both their tenure and their commitment to the bureaucracy and its workings. This is not a recent phenomenon. In Eisenhower's administration it was observed that political appointees "tended to stay in Washington for 'a social season and a half and then leave.'" A 1967 Brookings study found that from Roosevelt's administration through Johnson's, only 52 percent of PASs stayed in one agency as long as two years, 29 percent stayed more than three years, and a mere 14 percent stayed four or more years (Ingraham 1987, 428).

There are several reasons for the frequency of this movement:

1. lower-level political executives are utilized as generalist managers (much in line with the original intent of SES) by higher-level political appointees; 2. the appointees themselves are anxious to gain as much experience as possible and often have a "preferred" appointment toward which they are progressing; 3. many of the younger political executives view their government service as a job market, one that must be utilized to the maximum extent possible in the short time available. (Ibid., 429)

Regardless of the reasons for the movement of political appointees, longer tenure in position is crucial to good management. Short tenure and the many demands on their time considerably limit PASs' scope and vision for public service.

Just as it does in the private sector, a high turnover rate in government leads to emphasis on short-term results and neglect of long-term planning. Political appointees tend to operate in a "firehouse environment of day-to-day crises and immediate concerns. Decisions have to be made on White House, congressional or industry requests, budget, legislative and regulatory proposals, and other assorted pressing issues related to department management." One can see how agency heads feel they are being, as one DOT official put it, "nickeled and dimed to death." (Thoryn 1983, 78–79)

Tenure in the first half of the modern era (1933–60) fared not much better than in its later years. According to a 1967 Brookings Institution study, assistant secretaries in that period typically averaged 2.7 years in their position. (Brauer 1987, 175)

However, the trend is toward even shorter tenures (see table 5.1). "Significant percentages served far less than the average. . . . thus a third served 1.5 years or less—and 14.3% served 1.5 to 2 years. 41.7% of cabi-

Table 5.1. PAS Tenure—Johnson to Reagan 1

President's Term	Average PAS Tenure (in years)
Johnson	2.8
Nixon	2.6
Ford	1.9
Carter	2.5
Reagan	2.0

Source: Carl Brauer, "Tenure, Turnover, and Postgovernment Employment Trends of Presidential Employees." In *The In-and-Outers: Presidential Appointees and Transient Government in Washington,* ed. G. Calvin Mackenzie (Baltimore: Johns Hopkins University Press, 1987), 174–75.

net secretaries served 1.5 years or less and a full 62% of deputy secretaries and 46.3% of undersecretaries had equally short tenures" (ibid., 175).

As noted previously, 85 percent of PASs in the NAPA study had prior government service, 80 percent of them in the federal government, often in the same agencies where they later served as a PAS. These statistics mitigate somewhat tenure and turnover figures, since, presumably, those appointees with government experience require less on-the-job training. Nevertheless, regardless of party change in the White House, total tenure in the agencies, as well as total service in the federal government, has been declining (ibid., 177).

The NAPA study found little correlation of tenure with previous employment, except among those who had worked for state or local governments immediately prior to their PAS service. The tenure of that group was 3.5 years, a full year longer than average. While it found negligible difference between female and male PASs, the study found that younger appointees tended toward shorter tenure (ibid., 175–77).

The study also found that longer tenure correlated positively with the time left in the president's term at the time of the PAS's appointment and the confidence PASs had in career executives, though it is unknown if longer tenure caused greater confidence or vice versa.

Shorter tenure correlated positively with: 1. the difference, not between pregovernment salary and PAS salary, but between the PAS's government salary and the next position she or he held; 2. the level of PASs' interpersonal skills (perhaps because those skills are highly in demand in both the public and private sectors); 3. Republican party affiliation (perhaps reflecting presidential disdain for government and the bureaucracy as evidenced by Nixon and Reagan); and 4. the number of hours worked weekly (Joyce 1990a, 140–41).

Joyce offers a useful context corrective to any whose angst over PAS turnover would be without qualification:

> The primary reason for high turnover and short tenure among these appointees is probably structural rather than motivational. Political executives stay on the job for a relatively short period of time *because they are political.* It is likely that the factor that influences the decision to exit more than any other is the realization that the appointive president's term will soon be over. Pragmatism dictates that the political executive will at this point seek another job. . . . This end-of-term turnover is built into the system. (Ibid., 142)

That perspective addresses end-of-term turnover, but what of earlier departures? They "leave more unexplained than explained. . . . we should not be convinced that we have anything close to a complete understanding of political executive motivations," according to Joyce. His analysis suggests at least four reasons for early departure: "1. salaries are not high enough to keep officials in the public sector; 2. executives are overworked; 3. political executives do not place enough faith in career executives; and 4. executives appointed by presidents lacking in commitment to traditional government service tend toward relatively rapid exit" (ibid., 143).

Why should the public be concerned about PAS turnover? As the NAPA study concludes: "If talented Americans decline the opportunity for public service, if they endure it for only short periods of time and if they are ill-prepared for the challenges they face in the public sector the system will not deliver fully on its promise" (NAPA 1985, 3).

"I Can't Afford It Anymore": Salary and Tenure

Salary constituted a major source of concern among PASs. Of those in the NAPA study, 55 percent reported some or a very significant financial sacrifice immediately upon accepting their appointment.[4] Indeed, as noted above, while low salary may keep many potential appointees out of government service, "the lure of higher salaries after doing without for a time" is what impels PASs to leave it. "This could mean that political appointees come to their jobs for reasons other than salary, but are not willing to do without indefinitely. It also supports the notion that political appointees really do see their government service as part of an overall "career path" and intend only to stay as long as it takes to make them marketable to someone who is willing to pay them a higher salary" (Joyce 1990a, 141).

Regarding earning power after government service, not even 17 percent of the NAPA respondents indicated that their service in government had significantly increased their subsequent earning power; 46 percent said that government service had no effect on it. One fifth of the appointees said that they left government to seek better-paying employment in the private sector, but very few appointees in any administration achieve "celebrity status;" far more often, appointees who leave for financial reasons do so in relative obscurity (Brauer 1987, 179–92).

Countering the cynicism of some, such as TRB and Thoryn (discussed below), Brauer observes, "although presidential appointments add value to people's careers and to their earning power, the cynical caricature of people who come to Washington to do good and end up doing well is neither fair nor accurate." He continues, "In fact, very few presidential appointees even stay on in Washington if they have not lived there prior to assuming their appointments. Of those surveyed, 49.5% reported living in Washington immediately prior to their appointments, while only slightly more, 52.7%, remained in Washington after them" (ibid., 186).

The 1984–85 Commission on Executive, Legislative, and Judicial Salaries, chaired by Nicholas F. Brady, noted the troubled history of linking congressional salaries with judicial and senior executive salaries. Congress had hoped by the linkage to achieve broad political acceptance of salary increases for itself; it did not work out that way. The Congress beat a hasty retreat in the face of the firestorm of protest over congressional salary increases; no group got a raise. The historical parallels are instructive. "In 1857 Supreme Court Justice Benjamin R. Curtis resigned because of financial pressures . . . 122 years later, undersecretary of health, education, and welfare, Hale Champion, quit office to return to academic life, declaring, 'I'm broke, I can't afford it anymore'" (Bonafede 1987b, 134). Similar complaints about salary were heard throughout the judiciary, such that Chief Justice Warren E. Burger in 1985 stated, "The consequences of continuing on the present course could undermine the federal judiciary for a generation" (ibid., 135).

The Brady Commission report showed that there was a near–40 percent decline in real wages for top-level federal officials in the sixteen years between 1969 and 1985. It is no coincidence that the average tenure of presidential appointees declined over the same period. Although declining real wages alone is not the only reason why average tenure has been getting shorter, it is an important one. It also explains in part why so few presidential appointees return to take another appointment after leaving one.

A salary study of the years 1977–1981 demonstrated that, in the words of Charles Bowsher, comptroller general of the GAO, "the executive pay ceiling has been increased by only 5.5%. During that same period, *retired* federal executives received annuity cost-of-living adjustments totaling 55%; federal white-collar pay rates have increased by 38% and private sector executive pay has gone up about 40%" (Grace Commission 1983, 112).

When combined with the high level of stress under which PASs operate, low salary is a potent disincentive to enter or continue public service. "A political executive would have to have an exceptionally strong commitment to public service or a particular president in order to choose remaining in a $50,000 job working 70 hours a week over a $100,000 private sector job working 40 (or even 50) hours per week" (Joyce 1990b, 19). What the Brady Commission called "the quiet crisis," the erosion in public service, is largely responsible for "the long, vexatious, and troublesome history of the attempt to set the salaries and compensation of top level federal officials, including members of Congress, judges, cabinet officers and agency executives" (Bonafede 1987b, 134).

Other factors that drive people out of public service—inadequate fringe benefits, lack of reimbursement for job-related expenses, disclosure and divestment requirements—also keep veteran appointees from returning to it and newcomers from entering it (Brauer 1987, 192–93). As the Brady Commission report observes, "We are drifting toward a government led by the wealthy and by those with no current family obligation. If candidates for high public office are to be drawn from such a narrow base, the quality of our government leadership will be seriously impaired" (Bonafede 1987b, 134).

It is clear, then, that salary has long been a bone of contention among PAS executives and a principal reason for many to turn down federal appointments. In many cases, states and local governments were paying higher salaries than the federal government, and people simply would not move to Washington, take on an unstable, high-stress political job, *and* take a pay cut. As noted, executive salaries were linked with those of the Congress and any attempt to increase them was met with outrage from the public-at-large, mostly directed at the Congress itself. That was the situation until 1991.

After years of fruitless discussion, Congress, in 1989, held a protracted debate about federal executive salaries and finally voted to increase them all significantly. The by-now familiar popular uproar and anger at Congress for increasing its own salaries forced a recision of that vote, however. That meant that again the promised pay raise for PAS and SES members was likewise rescinded. According to a Bush transition team member, this action prompted at least fifty-four individuals to turn down PAS positions with the new Bush administration and the second and third choices for many of the positions often followed suit.

In the 1990 congressional debate executive salaries were finally uncoupled from congressional salaries and a very large increase was ultimately passed for PAS and SES executives. While the General Schedule employees got their usual single-digit increase (4.1 percent in 1991), PAS and SES employees saw increases of 22.2 percent to 29.5 percent, worth $16,000 to $31,600 annually for that one catch-up year. In 1992 their raises returned to the more familiar 3.5 percent range; 1993 saw raises of 3.2 percent. The 1996 Executive Level salaries ranged from $108,200 to $148,400; SES salaries ranged from $94,800 to $115,700.

The one-time salary increase given government executives in 1991 was credited by many with single-handedly lengthening tenure among PAS employees, and it certainly served to increase the satisfaction level of SES members. As noted in the GAO study of the SES, the percent of those satisfied with their salary jumped from 11 percent to 77 percent in the first year of the increase (GAO 1992, 4). A sideline factor is that Social Security pensions are based on a combination of total years of service and the three highest annual salaries in the last five years of employment. The salary increase gave older employees an incentive to stay in office, thus lengthening average tenure for the Bush appointees. One Bush administration official in the Presidential Personnel Office indicated that PAS tenure was indeed increasing. As she said, "No one's leaving. They're all waiting for their high three."

Washington's Revolving Door

Some have questioned the motives of those seeking public service. Ambition and desire for power join money as incentives for some to seek a political appointment. Thoryn (1983), for example, categorizes the majority of political appointees as those nearing retirement, joined by those in their thirties and forties who see government service as a valuable experience or as a stepping-stone for work in industry.

TRB, the anonymous columnist for the *New Republic*, writing in

1985, picks up the stepping-stone metaphor to further the inquiry into political appointees' motives. He demonstrates little sympathy for complaints that people take a major financial loss to work for government:

> First, it may be that most of these people can make more money *now* in private life than they make in government, but many were making less before they got their high government posts. . . . Second, having held a high government job is often the only reason these people can expect to make huge incomes when they leave it. Their government connections, reputations, and experience is what makes them valuable. . . . Third, when these people talk of returning to "the private sector," they do not mean they are moving to Des Moines to manufacture widgets. They are remaining in Washington to leech, in some way, off the government, usually by peddling influence. (TRB 1985, 4)

"Cashing in is simply the last act in the standard four-act Washington epic tragedy," according to TRB. Act One is idealism, in which the person gets involved in politics on the basis of belief. Act Two is pragmatism, wherein one learns the value of compromise and working within the system. Act Three is ambition, wherein success for its own sake becomes the goal. Act Four is corruption, in which politics has become an instrument for personal enrichment rather than for ideological agenda (ibid.).

TRB feels political appointees are getting to Act Four faster than ever, for which he blames the Reagan administration: "Power is out; money is in: the exchange window is open." He further blames "the professionalization of political campaigns, which allows political skills to be marketed retail instead of wholesale," and the increased activism of corporate interests, which furthers the marketing of those skills. He also believes that the stigma attached to blatant influence peddling has disappeared, noting former Senate Majority Leader Howard Baker's $800,000 salary as an "influence broker" in the Washington office of a Texas law firm (ibid.). Baker's firm earned $1.6 million in 1990 representing Japanese industries. Jordan and Iraq are among his many other international clients, the latter having retained him at a rate of $500,000 a year, plus expenses.

More recently, the revolving door has sent PASs into numerous lobbying positions, often for foreign governments' trade or political interests. William E. Brock, the former senator from Tennessee and labor secretary in Reagan's first administration, left to work for Taiwan, Mexico, Panama, and the Bahamas. Karna Small was deputy assistant to Reagan for national security until she left in 1986 to lobby for Turkey. Steven Grossman, former deputy assistant secretary at Health and Human Services in the Bush administration, became a lobbyist for Hong Kong. Kristin Paulson, formerly deputy assistant secretary of commerce, left in 1989 to lobby for Japan. Steven Piper, on the U.S. trade representative's staff, left in 1987 and began working for Japan in 1988. Customs Commissioner William von Raab left that post in 1989. In 1991 he started working for a Swiss firm. Others stayed closer to home to lobby, such as Bush Transportation Secretary Andrew Card, who became head of the American Automobile Manufacturers Association.

Sometimes the revolving door ushers individuals into government service from a background in lobbying. Carla A. Hills, for example, the U.S. trade representative, was a registered lobbyist for Korea and Japan before assuming her position in the Bush administration in 1988.

The General Accounting Office conducted a study of 5,650 former senior-level officials who left government service between 1986 and 1991. It found that "82 of the officials had registered as foreign agents, including two senators, one member of the House, seven White House officials, 33 senior congressional staff members and 39 executive agency officials" (GAO 1992).

Critics of the revolving door argue that it serves the interests of foreign competitors at the expense of the United States. "The revolving door puts the United States at an economic disadvantage because those who flow in and out of government are analogous to insider traders who are privy to classified information, which then is used to benefit foreign interests."[5]

The revolving door, whether it ushers former officials into foreign or domestic enterprises, can have a corrupting influence on administration officials in place. They know they have limited tenure, even in the best of circumstances, and so may conduct the work of their office with one eye toward the future and their job prospects in it. This may or may not serve the interests of the administration, and it certainly could work against the best interests of the nation.

Because activities of the legislative branch are beyond the scope of this book, it only will be noted that the revolving door is as well-oiled for members of Congress and their staffs as it is for those in the executive branch. It has been estimated that nearly 40 percent of those who leave the Congress go into lobbying. While they cannot lobby Congress directly for a year after their departure, they can plan legislative strategy and lobby the executive agencies while they wait for the year to pass.

Indicators and Costs of PAS Success

What makes for a successful PAS? Certain personal and professional qualities recurred in the literature and in interviews with PASs and others. The Council on Excellence's *Prune Book* suggests that successful appointees possess at least a majority of the following qualities:

> 1. An informed and flexible intellect. Respect for the facts, including a readiness to discard inaccurate preconceptions and pet theories. 2. The ability to absorb large amounts of information quickly, discern its essentials, and identify workable solutions among conflicting views and currents. 3. Functioning political instincts and a robust skepticism. The courage of one's own convictions, but the wisdom to know when compromise is the better, or only, road. 4. Skill in getting acceptable and timely results from colleagues and staff. 5. Personal integrity. 6. Friendships or working contacts in upper echelons of the professions, business, government, or journalism. 7. Experience in public speaking and handling the press. 8. Influence in the selection of the deputy. 9. An ability to deliver testimony before Congress' committees and deal easily with its staff members. (Trattner 1988, 15–16)

Hess adds other personal qualities for PAS executives: persuasiveness, personal stability, broad intelligence, flexibility, a sense of duty, a thick skin, patience and impatience (and the knowledge of when each is required) (Hess 1988, 206–07).

Light suggests eight sets of skills that appointees need. They are:

> negotiating skills, analytical skills, public speaking and other communication skills, congressional relations skills, substantive knowledge of relevant policies, familiarity with Washington politics, management skills, and interpersonal skills.

> [He found that] in every case, appointees who consider themselves very adequately prepared find themselves better able to work with careerists and find careerists very helpful. Yet only slightly over half of the appointees considered themselves very adequately prepared in any of the eight areas. The highest perceived preparation was in the area of interpersonal skills, where 55% of the appointees rated themselves very adequately prepared; the lowest was familiarity with Washington politics, where 12% rated themselves very adequately prepared.

> Only half of the appointees studied by NAPA rated themselves very

adequately prepared in relevant policy skills. In addition, NAPA reports
that fully 79% of the appointees in their study received no orientation
prior to assumption of their duties. These data clearly indicated that "on
the job training" is an important part of the appointee's public management career. (Ingraham 1987, 430)

Ingraham discusses the experiential qualifications of PASs. Generally
well prepared for their positions, "slightly over one-third of the appointees in the Brookings study and nearly one-half in the NAPA study
have had considerable experience in the public sector. Despite this apparent level of preparation, however, there are deficiencies in the management and/or policy skills of many of the appointees" (ibid.). Light also
points to the need for expertise and its corollary, preparation: "Preparation for the job, whether defined in terms of management experience, negotiating skills, congressional relations, or personal style, makes a difference. Skills do matter" (Light 1987, 163).

These skills have particular relevance when it comes to an appointees' ability to work with the careerists to the administration's advantage. Regardless of party or ideological conviction, those appointees
"who know what they want and how to obtain it" are able to make the
best use of career expertise "in terms of substantive policy, congressional
relations, management of the bureaucracy, or technical analysis" (ibid.,
163). There are three reasons this is so:

1. Where appointees enter office with a short-term perspective, good
preparation will help them mobilize the resources of their bureaucrats. 2.
Preparation gives an appointee certain abilities to recognize the strengths
and weaknesses of the career service. . . . Well-prepared appointees know
enough to ask good questions. 3. . . . the most important preparation of
all is interpersonal. Appointees who have some appreciation for human
relations appear to have the greatest respect for the careerists. . . . The
public sector may be even more dependent on interpersonal skills than
the private. Lacking the financial resources to reward performance, public officials must rely to a much greater extent on their personal skills,
their ability to call upon the careerist's dedication. (Ibid., 165–66)

Political appointees themselves suggest that successful appointees
are those who "have had previous staff experience and who know the
town and how it works" (an oft-repeated refrain). As one PAS stated it,
they must "have a combination of skills that indicates they can operate

in Washington. Where most political appointees trip up is in three areas: inability to deal with Congress, with the media, and with interest groups." One former PAS suggested that successful appointees are

> open minded, willing to learn and trust, and they possess a sixth sense of when to delegate and when to make the decision themselves [because there is] a fine line between responsibility and authority. They stress competence over agenda. Those who are cause-oriented tend to let agency management go downhill while they push one or two pet causes. Those who are apolitical technocrats simply don't have a feel for how the town works. The most successful are the generalists and political animals who understand the political process and possess a sense of how the town and the country work. Their principal task is to manage the organization they inherit. Too many PASs come in with an agenda—they want to accomplish one or two things. This is a fatal flaw. You have to deal with everything that's on your plate. You can't let everything else go in the name of agenda. Those who see their role as steward and manager will have a more lasting impact than those pushing their agenda.

As noted earlier, concerns over the neophyte status of the PASs are somewhat assuaged by studies showing that many have experience working in the agency to which they are appointed or are from congressional staffs, think tanks, and interest groups based in Washington. Given this, the EPA's Linda Fisher wonders "whether 'in-and-outer' is still a valid characterization of presidential appointees in a time when so few of them come 'in' to the government from very far 'out'" (Mackenzie 1987, xvi). Certainly, *amateur* is an inadequate characterization of many; *short-timer* or *short-termer* is perhaps the more accurate designation.

Assessing what will make for the success of PASs is even more difficult than measuring qualifications because "success" has different definitions. The same former PAS who stressed management over agenda measured success by "the degree of change in an agency, the number of programs scuttled, and an absence of scathing IG (inspector general) or GAO reports. A successful appointee is one who doesn't embarrass the administration or produce any scandals, real or trumped-up." PAS success is not an unalloyed virtue, however; it can carry costs for both the bureaucracy and the president. Within the agency one of the "organizational costs of political executives' success" may be that the new PAS's agenda for change will likely disrupt or displace the previous PAS's agenda. Also, change in one part of the organization will affect other parts of the organization, perhaps lowering performance of the agency as a whole. Additionally, PAS-led change may create divisions among the career executives, causing a reduction in the agency's "capacity for effective cooperation and advice when the next appointee comes along with a different agenda . . . it may be precisely the demoralized segments that the next appointee needs most to draw upon. The result is an imbalanced organization that can walk with only its right or left feet" (Heclo 1985, 372–73).

As goes the old saying, "Be careful of what you wish for; you may get it." The success of one appointee may be the undoing of the next. Better one should take a holistic view of governance, looking at the entire government and its interworkings in evaluating PAS success, because, as Heclo notes, "government is a web of actions, reactions, and anticipations spread across the political landscape" (ibid., 374).

External liabilities that can come from PASs "'successes' in translating their agenda into bureaucratic behavior" are that the PAS may become a lightning rod for mobilizing outside groups to counter her or his policies or that the PAS may make necessary compromises that "tie the president to a set of understandings that reduce his future room for political and bureaucratic maneuver." Also, as with internal agency repercussions, change in one agency may adversely affect another. The result of uncoordinated successes may be an "increase in the muddle of the whole" in terms of the larger government (ibid., 373–74).

Benefits of the Short-Termer System

For all its flaws, the short-termer system has points to recommend it.

The appointment power is simple, readily available, and enormously flexible. It assumes no sophisticated institutional designs and little ability to predict the future, and it is incremental in the extreme: in principle, each appointment is a separate action. . . . By taking advantage of these attractive properties, the president is uniquely positioned to try to construct his own foundation for countering bureaucratic resistance, mobilizing bureaucratic competence, and integrating the disparate elements of his administration into a more coherent whole. Given his general lack of resources and options [and the time constraints of his term limitations], these are enticing prospects indeed. (Moe 1991, 142)

The system provides the flexibility to move people between agencies on short notice and to make modifications to agency commitments. It also provides safe "cover for shuffling out men who [can] not perform" (Rehfuss 1973, 131).

Even those who criticize the short-termer system acknowledge its utility to the country: "The injection of outsiders into high-level positions brings vitality to government, prevents the bureaucracy from becoming encrusted and too powerful, and makes government more responsive to the will of the people as expressed through the election of the president. A fringe benefit is that the private sector is enriched by the return to it of executives broadened by government experience" (Brauer 1987, 193).

Vitality is another of the benefits of the present system: "In a world where bureaucratic routine can easily suffocate innovation, this vitality is a considerable advantage to the work of the executive branch." There are other benefits of the short-termer system, such as its potential for political control that provides an opportunity for a highly focused administration such as Reagan's "to truly shake up the bureaucracy and implement its mandate" (Heclo 1987, 207).

Additionally, many PASs bring skills to deal with political pressures. They must "be able to navigate among competing demands of the White House, Congress, interest groups, and their own bureaucracy," not to mention the ever-present media. Short tenure carries the freedom to shortchange family and personal time and income needs, when one knows that it will not last forever. This has been characterized as "come in, burn out, move on." Furthermore, migration back and forth across the amorphous boundaries of government and nongovernment worlds infuses government with the outside perspectives of business and academia and lends deeper understandings of government to the nongovernment institutions of society (ibid.).

Good PAS appointments redound to the glory of the president who makes them, such as JFK's "best and brightest." "It was the coterie of talented aides he assembled rather than Kennedy alone that gave his administration the somewhat luminous quality for which it ultimately came to be remembered—by the public if not by historians" (Rourke 1991b, 124).

Regardless of Truman's assertion that the buck stopped at his desk, PASs provide political cover to a president, deflecting or absorbing abuse or blame that might otherwise be his.

Secretaries of agriculture have suffered this kind of martyrdom since at least the days of President Eisenhower's appointee, Ezra Taft Benson, as they struggled valiantly, if unsuccessfully, with the endless problems of

American farmers. White House aides can also absorb punishment for a president by performing unpleasant tasks like firing people. Sherman Adams played this role for President Eisenhower ["better you than me," said the latter to the former], as did H.R. Haldeman some years later for President Nixon. (Ibid., 124–25)

More recently, Bush Veterans Affairs' Secretary Edward Derwinski faced a concentrated attack by the veterans' lobby when he suggested closing or redefining the mission of underutilized VA hospitals to cut costs and provide care for underserved poor civilian communities. The resulting furor from the veterans' lobby during the 1992 presidential campaign so panicked Candidate Bush that he jettisoned Derwinski and his plan in hopes of an endorsement that never came.[6]

The deficits of the short-termer system are well known, documented in these and other examples. However, as Pfiffner points out, while the system is often inefficient and suffers rapid turnover and abrupt policy shifts, efficiency is not the only value in a democracy. And, in fact, inefficiency "is a small price to pay for a system that brings with it the ability to respond rapidly to the wishes of the electorate," as the political appointments system does at its best (Pfiffner 1987c, 62).

The short-termer system has other advantages:

In addition to providing this democratic link. . . . It brings into the bureaucracy fresh ideas and "new blood" to try them out. It brings in people who have not been worn down by the system and who can afford to work at full speed for the president's program for several years and return to their previous careers when they approach the burnout stage. It brings in people who are working on the cutting edge of new technologies or management practice, people who can transfer new ways of doing things to the government. (Ibid., 62)

Bureaucratic Costs of the Short-Termer System: Responsiveness and Effectiveness

There is, however, a downside to a personnel system that inherently features frequent turnover. It is possible to have too much of a good thing.

Turnover at the excessively high rate American government has today makes it much more difficult to achieve the political responsiveness that lies at the very heart of the in-and-outer system. In addition to making it harder for presidents to establish coherent and effective administrations, it makes government less efficient, leaving the career civil service alternately either without a clear sense of direction or too much affected by narrow bureaucratic interests. Finally, and with increasing significance as the world becomes more interdependent, excessively high turnover puts at a disadvantage presidential appointees who have to deal with foreign governments. (Brauer 1987, 193–94)

The "unplanned evolution" of the presidential appointments process away from the theoretically "rejuvenating, energizing potential of the in-and-outer system" has led to "a troubling paradox. As excellent leadership becomes an ever more important ingredient in effective government, excellent leaders are ever more difficult for government to recruit and retain. For those who wonder about the future capacity of American public administration to confront and solve the complex problems that now crowd the public policy agency, it is a chilling prospect" (Mackenzie 1987, xix).

Though previous government service gives seasoned PASs a leg up on the whole initiation process, Heclo feels that the duration of executive relationships is even more important than tenure and government experience. The instability caused by short tenure certainly also applies to those new to government who have the added burden of figuring out even the basics of how it all works. As noted above, if it takes six months for a new PAS to get acclimated to Washington's political climate and another six months to begin operating well in it, given the average turnover rates of eighteen to twenty-two months, PASs have barely a year or so of effective performance (Rehfuss 1973, 130).

Additionally, as discussed previously, the replacement of career executives with appointees in the government means that civil servants' careers now top out earlier than in previous generations. The deputy assistant secretary positions were the top career positions from the 1950s to the early 1970s. Deputy assistant secretaries managed thousands of employees, hundreds of millions of dollars, and major public policies. By the 1980s, however, most of these positions had been converted to political appointments (Richardson and Pfiffner 1991, 56). As of late 1993 there were only three careerists in deputy assistant secretary positions (Executive Level 4 equivalent) in all of government service.

As previously noted, the elimination of this top career position means that careerists are more likely to leave government service out of frustration, as the positions to which they formerly could have aspired are now occupied by short-time appointees "who may often have less experience, expertise, or competence. The resulting lack of high-quality career managers in the executive branch will hurt individual presidents. But more importantly, it will undermine the longer-term capacity of the government to function" (ibid., 56).

The topping out caused by downward PAS infiltration removes the incentive for career upward mobility; it also guts aspirations for excellence or innovation. According to John Gardner,

> There are far more political appointees, and the political tests of those appointees are narrower and sharper, certainly more deeply partisan over the past 15 years. Also, the degree to which they subordinate the career people under them, diminishing the integrity and dignity of the career people, is increasing. You can't have an effective government with people who are cowed and dumped on. (Qtd. in Pfiffner 1987c, 63)

The argument that the president needs to have his or her "own people" in place to strengthen the executive branch vis-à-vis the Congress is undercut by the fact, previously observed, that many PASs have other loyalties, i.e., to the Congress, interest groups, or the party, whose members may have sponsored their appointment. So having more appointees may even exacerbate, rather than solve, the problem (Richardson and Pfiffner 1991, 58).

Furthermore, the more political appointees there are, the thicker is the layer between the upper levels and the careerists, and the harder it is to build good working relationships. The more layers, the more time is needed to build relationships, but time is a very scarce commodity for appointees who are focused on short-term goals and quick turnaround. The many layers, then, impede contact between the two and slow down hoped-for change, à la Nixon. As Light notes, "It may be increasingly the case that the two worlds of political and careerists never collide at all, because the two groups move through separate space with little or no opportunity for contact (Light 1987, 157).

Limited contact leads to less effective control and more appointee frustration with bureaucracy. Interestingly, however, this frustration does not seem to devolve onto the career bureaucrats with whom appointees work. It is a truism that "political appointees love their bureaucrats, but hate bureaucracy" (Moe 1991, 157). PASs believe the careerists with whom they work

> are competent and responsive. Those views do not vary much across presidential administrations, party, ideology, number of hours worked per week, gender, year appointed (first, second, third, or fourth), or race. In-

deed, if there is any single lesson that PAS appointees would pass on to
the future, it is that the career servants should be accepted as competent
professionals, and should be used wisely. (Light 1987, 158)

In the NAPA study, 80 percent of the Reagan PASs found their careerists to be both responsive and competent. Why, then, did 50 percent
of them say that there should be more political appointees?

With limited political capital in Congress and the public, an administration must conserve its scarce internal resources—time, energy, expertise,
and information. Although careerists may have ample stocks of resources, which can certainly reduce the amounts a political appointee has
to spend, the initial investments may be too large for most appointees.
Again, there may be too little time, and too many layers, to make the connection between the two worlds. (Ibid., 160)

Another reason for the desire for more political appointees may be
found in PASs' frustration with the slow pace of government. Respect for
the civil service was lowest among the one-quarter of the Reagan PASs
who named that pace as their greatest source of frustration. It could be
that they blamed the individuals for the failures of the system. Or, "it
may be that Reagan appointees simply do not know whom else to blame."
While the Carter officials felt the same frustration, only half as many of
them favored increasing the number of political appointments as a solution (ibid., 162).

It is often observed that appointees have been progressively more negative toward the career service since the Eisenhower administration. This
is due to many factors, among them the rise of the short-term presidency,
limited PAS tenure, the ongoing trauma of dealing with a deficit in the
billions of dollars, the inability of the neophyte PASs to use the career resources of their department, and expansion of political appointments
down into the bureaucracy.

This latter factor often leads to lack of leadership, especially when political vacancies leave departments leaderless and unable to fight budget
cuts. "With unfilled slots at the assistant secretaryships and below, newly
appointed secretaries have little access to the kinds of information and expertise they need to win budget battles." Leaving the lower-level positions vacant can then easily sever the political-career connection and seriously weaken an agency. This can be both the outcome and design of a
deliberate administrative strategy, one Reagan was quick to exploit (ibid.,
163).

There are numerous problems with the PAS system: Short-termers tend to live for the moment because that may be all they have, given their tenure patterns and lack of job security. With great expectations imposed upon them by the White House and little time to meet them, PASs have an incentive to care more about the immediate and leave the problems that perspective creates to the careerists and their political successors.

Another problem is that agencies' programmatic lives face what Heclo calls "cycles within cycles of discontinuity." Because PASs' success is not based primarily on the health of the agency they administer, "their comings and goings in the executive branch are more likely to be based on calculations of personal benefit rather than the needs of government. . . . [One result is that they] have enough time to make mistakes but often not enough time to put the resulting lessons to use." (Heclo 1987, 208). Further, because there are so many appointees at the lower levels, political authority is diffused, making it harder for higher-level appointees to work in an agency rife with lower-level appointees (ibid., 209).

Another problem is "creeping appointeeism—the reproduction of pint-sized political executives throughout government." The more PASs there are and the farther down into the bureaucracy the administration plants them, the less desirable political positions become. More experienced persons will not take the lower-level jobs; they become filled by people of lesser ability and "young climbers . . . who are resume-building for the private sector or higher-level political appointments." As Elliot Richardson observed in 1985, "This administration is full of turkeys who have undercut the quality of public service in their areas" (Pfiffner 1987c, 63).

Another problem is the tendency toward bias in recruitment due to the costs imposed on the individual PASs. Beyond the obvious oversupply of middle-aged, white male PASs of means are other issues, such as the types of persons who are able to accept these positions. Those who are younger and have fewer financial obligations can accept political appointments without sacrificing much, particularly if they are single or have an easily employable spouse. Nonlocals with young children will be reluctant to move to the District of Columbia, given the realities of its public school system and expensive private schools. Those who are older and established in their careers (generally already in Washington, and whose spouse may be employed there as well) can afford to take a brief break for government service. Also, those whose professional lives will be enhanced by it, such as those in academia or think tanks, are more able to take the time for government service. Others, however, will find it a liability to have served in an agency that regulates an industry in which they hope to be employed in postgovernment service. Further, ethics regulations place restrictions of one year or more on the type of work they can perform, post-PAS service. Others cannot afford the break in their careers or the drop in salary such positions may carry (Heclo 1987, 210–11).

The increase and downward filtration of PASs lead to what one PAS termed a bureaucratic lobotomy, because with a change of administrations or even the departure of a lower-level appointee, "the people who could educate the assistant secretaries were gone too," thus seriously hampering an agency's effectiveness (ibid., 208). According to Fred Malek, Nixon's personnel chief, "In many cases, the effectiveness of an agency would be improved and political appointments would be reduced by roughly 25% if line positions beneath the assistant secretary level were reserved for career officials" (Pfiffner 1987c, 63).

Additionally, the overabundance of lower-level PASs and their claims to a political mandate lead to devaluation of "the coin of political executive leadership" in others' eyes. As one Reagan PAS put it, somewhat wistfully, "Washington is filled with people who used to be something, so that we're not really anybody anymore" (Heclo 1987, 209).

There are other factors that contribute to make political jobs less desirable:

> Washington positions, even when avidly sought, are generally seen as short-term appointments. They are accepted to cap a political avocation, to take a career break, or more often, as a duty which must be rendered to the party, candidate or nation. Although this may be changing, an executive rarely receives a tangible reward from his law firm or company for serving his country. He may even lose his place on the promotion ladder. (Rehfuss 1973, 131)

These factors make for a lessened commitment that imposes an additional bureaucratic burden on the system in terms of energy and shortened tenure.

There are other pressures on the PASs. As they work at the pleasure of the president, there is no job security, legal recourse if fired, or severance provisions. The workload is intense, with work weeks of sixty to seventy hours the norm. PASs' actions are subject to second-guessing in Washington's fishbowl atmosphere, with press and professional peers watching every move. Rehfuss's evaluation of the situation in 1973 is no less relevant today: "A reputation can be made and unmade in a few short days, and the necessity of protecting one's positions from attack is always present" (ibid., 135).

The crucial asymmetry between PASs and careerists discussed in chapter 4 means that the short-termer system and its practitioners can operate entirely independently of support from the careerists. While "political interests and outside policy constituencies" will fill in the political gaps allowing that system to function, "without good faith efforts at the highest political levels, the upper reaches of the [career] bureaucracy go to seed" (Heclo 1987, 202). A self-fulfilling prophecy operates in this kind of a system:

> When senior political appointees fail to include higher civil servants in substantive policy discussions, there is little reason for permanent career staff to acquire more than a narrowly technical, routine perspective. . . . they inevitably become divorced from the "big picture." When they are denied the sense of having a fair hearing for their views among the top political decision makers, permanent officialdom retreats into disgruntlement, backbiting, and, in extreme cases, sabotage. And so it is that by not being consulted, senior careerists over time become less worth consulting and less worth appointing to the more responsible departmental positions. (Ibid., 202)

PAS instability also imposes opportunity costs on the agencies and their career executives who must train their supervisors. One career executive described the care and feeding of new PASs:

> I don't know how many assistant secretaries I have helped break in. And you just divert an awful lot of time [doing it]. And there is always a propensity for a new guy to come in and discover the wheel all over again. And then you have the classic case of a political officer who is going to make a name for himself, and therefore he is going to identify one golden chalice he is going after, and he will take the whole goddamn energy of an organization to go after that golden chalice. He leaves after eighteen months, a new guy comes in, and his golden chalice is over here. "Hey guys, everybody this way." (Brauer 1987, 178–79)

The ongoing distraction of training and following an endless succession of new appointees is a clear drain on an agency's ability to pursue its mission.

PAS Interbureaucratic Relations:
A Government of Strangers or a Government of Colleagues?

Political executives, wrote Heclo in 1977, "exist in a 'government of strangers.' They are strangers to career bureaucrats, to other political executives, to Congress and congressional staff, and even to the president who appointed them" (Heclo 1977 qtd. in Joyce 1990a, 130). The daily reality of PASs' lives is that, while they all work for the same president, as the chief of a particular bureau or department, they may sometimes find themselves in a difficult position vis-à-vis their PAS colleagues:

> A major element of the life of political executives is the necessity both to compete and to cooperate publicly with other agencies. The necessity for executive branch teamwork conflicts with the value of departmental pluralism and the need for the executive to advance his agency's program. The effective executive carries water on both shoulders. Often a representative of one agency will be called to testify before a congressional committee on one side of an issue, and his counterpart in another department will present the opposite view. On occasion, divergent economic views will be presented to industry boards and committees. (Rehfuss 1973, 135)

The competition inherent in government bureaucracy is made all the more difficult if these same agency heads are strangers either to one another or to Washington. The reality of government by executives who are strangers to one another is closely related to the difficulties produced by tenures of eighteen months—PASs are unable to form good working relationships with one another and with their career subordinates, because there simply is not enough time.

However, Heclo made his assessment in an era in which the White House had changed parties several times with no president holding onto it for two terms since Eisenhower. In 1992, at the end of twelve years of uninterrupted Republican rule, the situation had changed. And, in fact, the Bush PAS Survey results indicate that many of the PASs knew one another, talked on the phone frequently, and labored together in relative familiarity in interagency working groups.

Clearly, the notion of "strangers" was fading from relevance by the early 1990s. As one PAS observed, there was not really any reason for the Bush-Quayle PAS Association to meet other than for the yearly Christmas party because everyone at that level knew everyone already. (The Bush SES Association did hold regular meetings, however.)

Nonetheless, in early 1993, with a team of Democrats long exiled from the White House freshly on the scene, new life may have been breathed into the "stranger" ethos. While there appeared to be numerous appointees from the Carter presidency in Bill Clinton's administration, groups long ignored or underrepresented were brought in to the centers of power by Clinton's commitment to gender, racial, and geographic diversity as he sought to create a government that, as he said, "looks like America." It is highly likely that most of these persons were strangers to one another. A fruitful area for future study would be the extent to which these appointees are able to meld into a cohesive force in his administration. Would they constitute a government of colleagues or a government of strangers? That awaits further inquiry.

Toward Improving the Nation's Governance

Early studies of the executive branch, such as those of the Brownlow Committee (1937) and the Hoover Commissions (1949 and 1955), dealt primarily with the structure of the executive itself, the inner workings and organization of the White House. Brownlow's call to action, "The president needs help," sums up the concerns of those studies. Additional examinations of the federal service grew out of these initial efforts, but it was not until the 1980s that serious attention began to focus on the process of staffing the many and growing federal agencies at the executive level in both its political and career manifestations.

A brief look at the most well-known and far-reaching of these studies of the executive staffing process, as well as some prominent theorists' contributions, proves instructive. While political appointees constitute the core of this chapter, appointees operate in unavoidable proximity to their career subordinates who must also be considered in order to understand the larger executive picture in government service. Therefore, career executives are included briefly in this appraisal.

The National Academy of Public Administration conducted four studies of political appointments and presidential transitions (1980, 1983, 1985, and 1988); they are considered together. The Twentieth Century Task Force (1987) examined the Senior Executive Service, and the Volcker Commission (1989) looked at the larger issues of public service. These six studies share a common concern about the quality of government given the country by its bureaucracy and about the factors threatening that quality. Each of the studies concludes that there are major problems in the bureaucracy, in the appointment process and its requirements, and in the relationship of career and political executives. Each makes recommendations for ameliorating, or at least addressing, the problems it perceives. In many cases their recommendations are the same.

The National Academy of Public Administration

The National Academy of Public Administration (NAPA) studied the presidential appointments process as it operated historically and as it operates today. The NAPA studies conclude that too many people lacking talents appropriate for the complexity of their jobs have found their way into high-level federal positions. Too little has been done to identify untapped sources of administrative talent or to recruit effectively from those sources outside the government that are already well known. The appointment process has not provided American presidents with the kind of support they need to construct their administrations in a wise and timely fashion. (Macy et al. 1983, 18)

NAPA's 1980 study of the presidency recommends improving the quality of the nation's government by improving the quality of its governors. It stresses managerial competence for PASs as fundamental. Noting that the complexities of modern government require more than party or personal loyalty to the president, it emphasizes "substantive knowledge and experience in administration and management" as fundamental attributes of PASs. They must desire and be capable of improving the internal operations and capabilities of their agencies (NAPA 1980, 32).

While the agency heads act as agents of the president, they "must be an integral part of any presidential decision affecting their agencies and must be at the center of the flow of information and advice from constituent units of their agency to the Executive Office." They must also share with the president responsibility for naming key political personnel in their agency (the double veto or mutual accommodation). Additionally, they must have a larger vision of government, "entering the process of joint decisionmaking as promoters of cross-cutting presidential perspectives . . . rather than as narrow advocates for their agency's position." This, not only because it is appropriate, but also as a way to stave off EOP intrusion in agency affairs (ibid., 32–33).

Feeling perhaps that the pendulum has swung too far in one direction, the NAPA report comments on the "pronounced shift" away from the Brownlow Committee's recommendation that the EOP be staffed primarily by career persons. Political staffing has deprived the EOP of continuity and consistency and staff who are experienced in staff roles and government management. It has also led to the EOP taking a controlling, rather than a coordinating role, making decisions that should be made in the agencies or by the president. NAPA encourages fortifying the president's capacity for leadership as a means "to strengthen the forces of cohesion and integration in the [entire] political system." The more effectively organized and managed the presidency is, the more Congress will be able "to fulfill its obligation of holding the executive accountable" (ibid., 3).

As Seidman and Gilmour explained it several years after the first

NAPA report, "Relatively youthful upstarts in the Executive Office of the President have stolen some of the glamour from the cabinet secretaries. Such Level II luminaries as the director of OMB wield more power and receive a greater press coverage than the heads of most executive departments" (1986, 265).

These luminaries, of course, are the political "amateurs" who run the United States government. As discussed above, the difficulty of recruiting those amateurs is caused by, among other factors, low salary, high stress, little actual power, high visibility, the long-term residual effect of the antigovernment rhetoric of the Carter and Reagan campaigns, the media's coverage of personnel recruiting efforts, private sector reluctance to lend employees to government service, and poor management of new appointees. To counter these trends, the NAPA study recommends:

1. Broadening the pool of willing, able, and competent people from which presidential appointees are selected; 2. Managing the recruiting and appointing process by reaching out to those in that pool; 3. Clarifying the rules, especially those concerning conflicts of interest and standards of conduct, that apply to federal officials; and 4. Easing the two-way transition between private and public sector employment, especially for younger and first-time presidential appointees. (Macy et al. 1983, xiii)

Ongoing concerns about the quality of political appointments led to NAPA's 1985 study of the presidential appointment system in which it surveyed more than five hundred present and former presidential appointees. Building on its earlier counsel to expand the pool of eligible applicants, NAPA made recommendations designed to improve the ability of the selection system to provide capable political appointees for government leadership. It focused on policy knowledge and administrative experience as the primary criteria for appointees; transition planning that begins shortly after the nominating conventions; streamlining of Senate examinations, FBI investigations, and OPM processes; simplification and liberalization of financial disclosure requirements; and a ban on discussions of private sector employment while in office.

To encourage longer tenure, NAPA recommends pay increases, severance pay to ease the transition out of government service, bonuses for those who stay more than three years, promotion within the ranks of appointees, reimbursement for job-related expenses, and support for networking and team-building efforts for appointees' spouses and families, as well as for the appointees themselves.

As did other studies, this NAPA report recommended a scaling back of appointed positions and reconversion of political positions to career posts as a way to tighten up the bureaucracy, as well as to address morale problems within the career executive force (NAPA 1985, 1–2).

NAPA's 1988 report had some forty-five recommendations for the presidential transition, twelve involving presidential appointees, many reaffirmed from the earlier study. New recommendations include:

> 1. The outgoing administration should prepare position lists, job descriptions, and a record of past personnel practices for the candidates; 2. Additional staffing should be provided temporarily to the offices responsible for the appointment and confirmation process; 3. The president should establish authority for personnel selection, balancing cabinet officers' needs with presidential prerogatives; 4. The president must set clear and high ethical standards for all public officials and respond swiftly and surely to any ethical lapses. (NAPA 1988, ix–x)

Additionally, the report urges the president to make a clear and public affirmation of the value of public service (particularly that of career employees) to the nation.

The Twentieth Century Task Force

While the career service was addressed in part by the NAPA studies, the Twentieth Century Task Force sought to address directly the problems plaguing the Senior Executive Service. The task force makes numerous recommendations to professionalize and reward senior career executives, with an eye toward excellence in government. It suggests that SES career executives be fully integrated into policy formation circles, dispensing with the notion of a politics-administration dichotomy once and for all.

> It's time to challenge the traditional justification that a president needs a loyal staff, sensitive to the administration's policy initiatives. . . . Overwhelming evidence supports the fact that career administrators, with few exceptions, follow political leadership faithfully—a fact that all modern presidents have ignored early, and embraced late, in their terms. . . . A strong case can be made that the number of political appointees in the federal government should be cut dramatically, with a corresponding extension of the career service to the assistant secretary or even undersecretary level. (Huddleston 1987, 63)

The task force also recommends that "selected positions in the management, budget, and personnel areas be designated 'career-reserved,'" to encourage retention of competent civil service employees by providing more career mobility (ibid., 8). It recommends upgrading the managerial skills of the political appointees to ease some of the stress of supervision. Friction is inevitable between career and political executives due to the interweaving of policy and administrative roles and the inability of the American system, with its inherent suspicion of strong bureaucracy, to address that friction adequately.

> As a nation we have sought to keep our bureaucracy weak and fragmented; we have populated our administrative system with technical specialists, discouraged breadth, emphasized carefully classified and circumscribed jobs, and forsworn any meaningful governmentwide personnel authority. And, as if these steps were somehow insufficient, we have also subjected the bureaucracy to extraordinarily close political control, insisting that as many positions as possible be in the hands of noncareer appointees and that the remainder be brought to heel through elaborate performance appraisal and compensation systems. (Ibid., 80)

While it was the impetus for reform that brought the SES to birth and a vigorous counter-reform movement that has denied it success, there is hope for the SES in further reform, difficult though it will be to institute: "there is no reasonable alternative to resuscitation. If the SES is allowed to slip quietly from the scene, neglected and unused, then the struggle will simply have to begin anew, for the need of the federal government for a competent and professional corps of senior executives is at least as great as the forces opposing it" (ibid., 32). In other words, if the SES did not exist, it would have to be invented.

The Volcker Commission

The nation's executive leadership, composed as it is of political and career employees, has served it well over the course of its existence. However, the Volcker Commission Report of 1989 cites problems in that leadership. The commission notes "evidence on all sides of an erosion of performance and morale across government in America. Too many of our most talented public servants—those with the skills and dedication that are the hallmark of an effective career service—are ready to leave" (Rosen 1989, 501).

The commission comments on the instability of the top level of government officials in relation to the career employees. In contrast to the long tenure of careerists, "the average tenure of Senate-confirmed presidential appointees (PAS) is about 2.0 years. The average tenure of noncareer SES members is 18 months, and *every year one third of them change positions or leave the government*" (emphasis added) (Volcker 1989, 215).

With the increase in political appointees and their filtration lower down into the executive ranks of the bureaucracy via Schedule C, there are now more of them at the GS 13–15 levels alone than there were total Schedule C appointees at all levels in 1976. As noted, this displacement means that fewer positions are now available for career employees, thus motivating an exodus out of public service. This has resulted in a brain drain and loss of morale: 52 percent of the career SES employees left government service between 1979 and 1982. Additionally, as observed, changes in presidential administrations mean that the entire top layer of an agency, as it is now often composed solely of political appointees, suddenly disappears, sometimes down to the Schedule C secretaries. In fact, any change of personnel often wipes out the next lower layers. The departing players leave behind no semblance of institutional memory; sometimes even basic knowledge of organizational functioning disappears with them. Continuity is thus lost and start-up time lengthened for the next troupe of political players (ibid., 215–16).

To reverse what the commission calls "the deterioration of the executive infrastructure of the government," it recommends, as have other studies, that the president give strong public as well as private support to the public service and improve the quality of political appointees. It also recommends a reduction of one-third, to two thousand in the combined political ranks of SES, PAS, and Schedule C, stating, as others have, that "excessive numbers of presidential appointees may actually undermine effective presidential control of the executive branch" by impeding communication between political and career executives (ibid., 17). While President Bush agreed with the overall direction of the commission's report, he rejected this counsel.

The commission calls for the movement of career executives into mid- and upper-level executive branch positions. To attract better noncareer executives it recommends improved orientation of newcomers, improved communications between the president and the appointees, a transition plan that begins with the party nominating conventions, and less rigorous financial disclosure requirements.

It is widely agreed that current financial disclosure requirements hinder the search for the best appointees. Waterman, for example, notes the effect of "the 1978 Ethics in Government Act, which kept many competent individuals from seeking government employment by requiring detailed financial reports and severely restricting post-government service employment options" (Waterman 1989, 31).

While recognizing the need for the president to set the policy agenda, the commission decries the centralization of the modern era and calls for greater decentralization of government management, including delegating to agency and department heads greater administrative discretion in managing their organizations and in hiring and firing decisions. This recommendation has two edges:

> Undoubtedly, greater administrative discretion would encourage more creativity and initiative in implementing public policy. At the same time, it would open the door wider for decisions that favor private and partisan interests. This underscores the importance of *matching more delegation with clear standards, effective oversight, and selection and orientation processes for political and career executives who need to be firmly grounded in serving the public interest* [emphasis added]. (Rosen 1989, 502)

Careerists should have greater administrative discretion and not be hamstrung by excessive adherence to predetermined rules. Focusing on results rather than rules as a means of judging bureaucracies would keep administrators and bureaucracies more responsive to public and official expectations (*PAR* 1991; Kelman 1982).

Heclo notes that "the present personnel system of political management is itself insufficiently managed." He observes that the short-termer "system, left to its own devices and put on automatic pilot, is a system likely to evolve in directions that confound the functioning of American national government" (Heclo 1987, 213–15).

His recommendations for "nudging the evolving design for political personnel in a more constructive direction" involve balancing the short-term perspective of PASs with "reliable, routinely accepted ways for pitting those fresh ideas against longer-term perspectives, without prejudice or recriminations on either side." He also believes that PAS positions must be taken seriously as "major centers of responsibility [and not be allowed] to proliferate haphazardly." He urges not permitting the enervating "personal dramas" of change-agentry "constantly [to] disrupt no less valuable elements of continuity in government that need to go on across a succession of political burnouts." Additionally, he stresses the need to protect "the virtue of democratic openness which creates 'citizen executives' from reflecting only the preferences held by those who happen to be mobilized to affect the government's work" (ibid., 212–13).

Conclusion

It is widely acknowledged that in significant ways the short-termer system, with its combination of technical competence/neutral responsiveness and political responsiveness, is well suited to the American political context and is here to stay. It allows flexibility and dynamism and provides political cover for presidential moves. However, it should not be allowed to grow untended. Its costs can easily outweigh its benefits when the growth of appointees creates inefficiencies in government, unnecessary layers of bureaucracy, and loss of institutional memory, and when it undercuts careerists' competence, ignores their political acumen, and curtails career mobility. Presidents must learn to resist the attractions of adding partisans to government and to govern with the people who know what they are doing.

The politically charged process of *choosing* the company the president keeps must be given high priority by the White House so that professional qualifications balance with competence the political qualifications of connections and loyalty. Further, as numerous studies recommend, the number of appointees at all levels should be reduced and as many positions as possible returned to the career service. The current system has not only gutted the morale of the careerists and distracted them with endless orientation and training of their new political bosses, it has also created excessive layers of government with too many top politicians too far away from the people who actually do the work.

Politicization of the budget function works against the administrations's credibility and should be cut back considerably, as was the case after failed attempts to politicize the personnel function in the first Reagan administration.

The negative image of government, "its aura of failure," has been fostered by events such as "Viet Nam, the overpromising in Great Society programs, and Watergate" (Heclo 1987, 212–13). Indictments and ethical charges against more than one hundred members of Reagan's administration and the Iran-Contra affair further tarnished Washington's image (Stengel 1987, 18–20). What will restore some of the political leadership's luster? While the new generation of political technocrats will have many negative examples and guidelines, [w]hat it is less likely to have is a usable lore for treating public service as a constructive enterprise. Something as loosely organized as the in-and-outer system is heavily dependent on people knowing what is expected of them, . . . sensing the institutional subtext that should shape personal calculations and appropriate behavior. We can be sure that a governing community in which "anything goes" among the participants will be one in which nothing goes particularly well. (Heclo 1987, 216)

George Bush took a significant step toward restoring respect for the public service. Unfortunately, he was followed by the "Republican Revolution" of 1994, a fundamental element of which was hostility toward Washington. The shutdowns of the federal government in late 1995 and early 1996 during the budget battles served to reinvigorate the Reagan-era animus toward federal workers. Only deeper cuts in the federal government, regardless of merit, will satisfy some critics; attempts to improve that government will carry little interest for those antagonistic to the majority of its manifestations, as many on the New Right (libertarians and the 1994 class of House "freshmen") are.

Nevertheless, presidents have a responsibility to lead. They can do so by appointing competent persons who place public service above self interest, who are well-rounded individuals loyal to their president's policy but not ideologues, and who have a commitment to managing their agencies well.

The administrative presidency in its various incarnations has had ample exposure on the public stage for a quarter of a century. What impact does the exercise of the administrative presidency have on the execution of government? To answer this question chapter 6 analyzes relations between political appointees and senior careerists in the modern era.

6

⟨✦✦✦⟩

Political-Career Relations
in the Modern Era:
"Articulating Society's Dreams and
Bringing Them Gingerly to Earth"

igh-level political appointees and their career subordinates engage in an elaborate, sometimes subtle bureaucratic dance as they draw boundaries, promote ideologies, and protect turf, ostensibly in the name of good, responsive, and effective government. Since neither side can run the government alone, a partnership built on mutual trust and respect is a crucial element in the dance. Each has a role in the choreography: "Presidential appointees provide the link between the decisions of the electorate in selecting a new president and the permanent bureaucracy. Senior career executives provide the professionalism and continuity required to manage effectively the complex programs of the federal government" (Rosen 1989, 505).

In Heclo's understanding, the traditional neutral competence of the career executives (as opposed to the responsive competence of the political executives)

> entails not just following orders but having the practical knowledge of government and the broker's skills of the government marketplace that makes one's advice worthy of attention. Thus, neutral competence is a strange amalgam of loyalty that argues back, partisanship that shifts with the changing partisans, independence that depends on others. (Heclo qtd. in Seidman and Gilmour 1986, 73)

The tension in political-career executive relations has existed since at least the 1930s. Yet, both sides contribute important positive elements to the bureaucratic mix: the political side with its short-term orientation brings change and new blood, the career, with its long-term orientation, brings continuity and institutional memory. The contributions of each are different but complementary, at least in classic politics-administration dichotomy theory.

> Political executives enunciate new directions and goals based on their interpretation of the public's will, while career executives help to translate new or modified policies into practical and effective programs. Bureaucracy needs the intermittent fillip of fresh questioning and outside redirection to counteract tendencies towards stultification and complacency, and political leadership needs the steadying anchor of institutional expertise and insiders' advice to avoid or reduce unnecessary errors and to obtain tactical sophistication. (Lorentzen 1985, 411)

This chapter discusses presidential relations with the bureaucracy, the Senior Executive Service (SES), and the results of bureaucrat bashing. It focuses on the key question of managing career executives and analyzes the different roles assigned politicals and careerists and the resultant tensions between them. It then turns to various models of political-career relations, including a typology of those of George Bush's administration.

The Administrative Presidency and Careerists: The President as Chief Bureaucrat

Presidents in the modern era have had decidedly mixed views of the federal bureaucracy. Relations between JFK and the permanent government, for example, were predominantly neutral in the early days of his administration but deteriorated over time.

> Kennedy and his advisors viewed the civil service with a low quotient of paranoia. They did not look upon the bureaucracy as a hotbed of covert political oppositionists. Yet before long they began to think of the rest of government not so much as a political resistance movement but as an *institutional* resistance movement [emphasis added], "a bulwark against change" and "a force against innovation with an inexhaustible capacity to dilute, delay and obstruct presidential purpose". . . . At times the White House staff may have confused the pace of the permanent government with its intent; the bureaucracy moved slowly, but it did not necessarily move in the opposite direction, nor was it totally immune to political leadership. The staff's suspicions of the civil service, however,

steadily increased in the Kennedy White House. They were to increase even more quickly under Johnson and to become pathological under Nixon. (Hess 1988, 82–83)

Johnson shunned the permanent government for guidance in policy development, believing it "too conservative and too incremental for rapid governmental change." Nevertheless, he did trust the bureaucracy to implement his programs and so devoted little attention to policing the bureaucracy, per se (Newland 1985, 139).

Perhaps the presidents most negative toward the bureaucracy have been Nixon, Reagan, and to a lesser extent, Carter. "President Nixon considered that President Eisenhower had committed a major error in failing to clean out the 'Democrat-infested federal bureaucracy. . . .' Distrust of the bureaucracy was a recurring theme in almost all of Nixon's public statements" (Seidman and Gilmour 1986, 99–100). However, "the evidence to support these White House suspicions is less than compelling." A study of the Nixon presidency based on data from 1976 "demonstrated that the 'clashing beliefs' between political officials and career administrators receded" over time, public rhetoric aside. Careerists need not have been considered the enemy. The indications are that

> senior bureaucrats, like Supreme Court justices, "follow the election returns." They will in fact defer to a president and support his programs even when they are not happy with either. This was certainly the case during the Nixon years with respect to programs enacted by Congress that had the full authority of law behind them. Where the White House got into trouble in its dealings with the bureaucracy was when it tried to pursue objectives that seemed illegitimate [such as the impoundment strategy]. . . . In any case, . . . the "pull" of the presidency is very strong as far as civil servants are concerned. (Rourke 1981, 137)

Whether the shift in Nixon's direction reflected careerist allegiance to neutral competence or simply an expedient listing to the prevailing political winds, "it bodes well for the ability of presidents to control bureaucracy" (ibid., 138).[1]

Jimmy Carter had feelings about permanent Washington similar to Nixon's, running as he did as an outsider against the government, determined to master it. He shared with Nixon "a profound distrust of the bureaucracy and faith that bureaucrats can be brought to heel through structural change" (Seidman and Gilmour 1986, 112). However, a more sanguine view of Carter's feelings about the bureaucracy might be more accurate:

> While Carter's preelection rhetoric was anti-bureaucratic, . . . unlike Nixon and Reagan, he did not identify the bureaucrats as the primary cause of the problem. His interest was less focused on dismantling particular bureaucracies and eliminating career jobs. This probably resulted in less conflict between the political appointees and career bureaucrats in the Carter administration, despite his apparent dislike for bureaucracy. (Joyce 1990a, 142)

It took Ronald Reagan in his campaign against Washington to turn the outsider's stance to full advantage. Rather than attempting a reorganization of the bureaucracy, he simply gutted and circumvented it. It was a strategy focused on command relationships and processes rather than on formal structure. It was, indeed, an administrative strategy of centralization that could bypass the recalcitrant Congress and bring the career bureaucracy to heel. The primary elements of this strategy were centralization of the budgetary, appointments, and decision-making processes and control and reduction of regulations (Seidman and Gilmour 1986, 127).

Reagan's assault on the bureaucracy was direct, unmistakable, and involved massive personnel changes.

> While moving ideologically screened appointees in, the administration also moved career federal employees out. From January 1981 to September 1983, the civilian (not including Post Office or Defense) employment of the government dropped by 92,000—7.4%—from 1,240,000 to 1,148,000. Twelve thousand employees lost their jobs as a result of reductions in force (RIFs) in FY 1981 and 1982. . . . Also, the administration made generous use of the provisions of the Civil Service Reform Act of 1978 to reassign executives from one job or geographic location to another, resulting in some controversial and well-publicized resignations. (Salamon and Abramson 1984, 46–47)

Reagan's policy of privatizing and providing (if pushed) but not producing services through contracting out had an additional unexpected impact on the career civil service, reducing its role and authority. The new style of "administration through third parties converted the role of many senior career executives to that of grant and contract administrators, paymasters, and regulation writers and enforcers." Less and less deliverers of services, they came more and more to be overseers of a process, regulation enforcers with little creativity or initiative of their own. It is little wonder, then, that a 1983 survey of federal executives found them so angry over a whole host of issues (including salary and political pressure) that more than 70 percent of them declared that they would advise bright young people *not* to seek employment in the federal government (Seidman and Gilmour 1986, 134–35).

Careerist morale and credibility were damaged not just by RIFs and transfers but by the administration's assault on the very legitimacy of the programs they managed, placing them

> in the awkward position of having to carry out instructions they felt were inconsistent with the statutes under which they [were] operating. Judicial rejection of many of the administration's regulatory interpretations testifies to the dilemma facing the career bureaucracy. Finally, the administration's tendency to appoint to subcabinet positions persons with strong ideological convictions and its efforts to plug information leaks from the bureaucracy have further undermined the opportunity for the bureaucracy to provide professional input that can influence policy decisions. (Salamon and Abramson 1984, 64)

Further, careerists who dared enter the fray between PASs and the Reagan White House risked dangerous shoals. While they could be key players in battles with the White House—supplying PASs with information, resources, and connections with the Congress and interest networks—their cooperation could backfire when the White House retaliated, as it inevitably would.

> The more careerists help appointees win skirmishes against the Office of Management and Budget and the White House staff, the more they may lose the longer-term war over the proper care of a competent civil service. The desire to be responsive to appointees in trouble at 1600 Pennsylvania Avenue may undermine future relationships with new appointees who have been carefully schooled in the disloyalties of the particular agency. (Light 1987, 161)

Presidents have several advantages over the career bureaucracy in the modern era. There has been a generalized decline in the willingness of the public to trust to expertise to solve the nation's problems. "When expertise loses its credibility, bureaucracy becomes less formidable as a competitor of the White House" (Rourke 1981, 139).

Also, the growth of government programs has created a concomitant tendency for agency jurisdictions to overlap. As the agencies compete for power in the decision-making process, none any longer enjoys sole power. While FDR excelled at the practice of divide and conquer within his bureaucracy, "modern presidents do not need to engage in such artificial contrivances. Today's agencies have a statutory mandate to compete for power" (ibid., 139). In the resulting stalemate, issues inevitably get pushed upward to the White House for resolution.

Additionally, interest groups have moved into the political mix and have created diverse constituencies that may work in concert with the White House against the agency, thus further eroding careerists' power base. The current era sees strengthened presidential control over the bureaucracy, given the factors acting to weaken the bureaucracies vis-à-vis the White House and the establishment of the SES and other management innovations (ibid., 140).

The Senior Executive Service: An Idea Whose Time Finally Came

The United States has been notably lax in developing theories of political administration. Rather than having "a coherent set of roles and relationships" between political and career executives, the United States has what Heclo terms "a widely varying free form exercise" as appointees and careerists seek to outmaneuver one another.

> For several generations now we have been accumulating a massive non-system of political management in the echelons between top agency heads and career officials in operating units. There are staffs to staff, offices atop offices, circles within circles. Almost no one can say yes to anything and almost everybody can say no—and even yes's are only provisional until the next no. In this situation the total amount of energy expended in defending boundaries and advancing personal projects can easily exceed the amount spent in accomplishing the purpose of government (Congress is no exception). (Heclo 1984b, 13)

Seeking to address this situation, the Carter administration initiated a reform of the civil service system. The 1978 Civil Service Reform Act was the result. A key component of the CSRA, the Senior Executive Service, was established in 1979 to provide the nation an elite specialized corps of civil servants. It was the product of long-sought reform and the Carter administration's desire for a civil service less independent and more responsive to presidential policy initiatives. The SES is a hybrid, not composed solely of career or political executives but rather a mix (albeit a lopsided one) of both. The establishment of the SES marked a reversal of the trend away from the politicization noted by Mosher (1968) a decade earlier.

Prior to the CSRA there was no coherent executive personnel system across the executive branch or even within agencies. In many cases Congress made the decisions about number, placement, and pay for federal executives. Congressional influence in the process led some careerists to see the Congress as their principal patron. Thus, their loyalties rested more in Congress or its subcommittees than in their agency head. In addition, the political appointees who headed the agencies had very limited power to reassign careerists internally, as rank-in-the-position made it difficult for them to move personnel to match changed agency priorities (Marzotto et al. 1985, 114).

The Senior Executive Service was designed to correct what were considered the worst flaws of the civil service system. When it was established there was a top limit of 10,777 positions allocated to the agencies and filled by them on request to the Office of Personnel Management. It is now composed of nearly 7,000 senior officials, approximately 90 percent of whom are career civil servants. The rest are noncareer political appointees.

In essence, "the SES encompasses the real managers of the American bureaucracy. Its members work at the strategic interstices of politics and administration—just below the president and his top political appointees." They are, for example: assistant and associate administrators, deputy assistant secretaries, directors of various government centers, research directors, and office and division chiefs of nearly every executive agency of the federal government (Huddleston 1987, 28–29).

The organizing principle of the SES was the forging of a

> unified, integrated higher civil service from the traditionally disparate shards of senior departmental administration. . . . the SES was to be America's answer to Europe's superbureaucrats—a general civilian officer corps, staffed by highly trained and broadly experienced men and women who could be shifted from assignment to assignment as the needs of government required. . . . the vigorous, competent, and spirited bureaucracy that democratic government requires. (Ibid., 29)

The SES has several key features. It makes performance a central principle; removes its members from traditional civil service protections; bases rank in the person rather than in the position; features enhanced pay, a merit-based bonus system, and broader opportunities with a wider range of placements over the course of the executive's career; and places SES personnel under the more direct control of political appointees. This last increases the likelihood of policy implementation, as well as the possibility of political harassment (ibid., 7).

Under the provisions of the CSRA, agencies have been empowered in new ways to control their internal personnel practices. The Office of Personnel Management (OPM) initially certifies persons to SES rank and allocates the number of them assigned to each agency, but the political agency head is free to decide where and how they will be used. Within limits, the PASs are also free to exercise more control over the SES members, punishing and rewarding them without the constraints of the merit system protections (Marzotto et al. 1985, 116).

The concept of a professional corps of federal bureaucrats has been around since at least the Hoover Commissions of 1949 and 1955. It had been rebuffed by successive presidents until Carter's reorganization. While Carter was successful in creating the SES, it continued to face opposition for various reasons. The SES

> clashed with the ingrained traditions of our federal civil service; one which has evolved as an unwieldy bureaucracy characterized by a large number of technicians and specialist managers; which is top-heavy with political appointees; which is based on a fragmentation of power between the executive and legislative branches of government; and which has an intricate, decentralized administrative structure that often fosters loyalties within bureaus and agencies rather than across the executive branch. The SES has also run counter to our historic suspicion of specialized knowledge, our traditional fear of strong, centralized government, and our antipathy to authority in hierarchical structures. (Huddleston 1987, 4)

Backlash was not far behind inauguration of the new system.

The Genesis of the SES Quiet Crisis in the 1980s

The backlash took the form of politics that quickly intervened to withhold what the new civil service reforms promised.

> First, Congress and the Carter administration came to believe that the SES bonuses were too generous and were given to too many people. Over the next several months, by law and regulation, the original provisions were amended by decreasing from 50 to 20 percent the employees eligible

for bonuses. This was the first of many actions that slowly disillusioned the SES members. Second, the personal development plans promised by the CSRA were scaled down (i.e., in the first six years of the SES, only 12 senior executives used the sabbatical provisions of the Act). Another disappointment to employees was the merit pay system for mid-level managers (GS 13–15), which was never adequately funded to provide attractive bonuses for high performers. Finally, reassignments and relocations, supposedly a positive feature of the new system, were sometimes used by the Reagan administration in its first years in a way many SES members regarded as punitive—as a means to get them out of the way or to force them to retire. (Levine 1986, 201–02)

Careerists' unhappiness with the system soon surfaced. A 1984 study found that "45% felt that the disadvantages of the SES outweighed the advantages. Only 45% of mid-level staff (GS 13–15) said they would join the SES if given the opportunity" (CRS 1987, 8).

According to many, "'Carter's gift to Reagan' . . . [the CSRA and SES] enabled the latter to gain easy control over a bureaucracy made more vulnerable by the CSRA" and contributed significantly to the politicization of the executive branch (Levine 1986, 202). As one careerist put it, "Scotty Campbell [the architect of the CSRA] did more to move careerists out of OPM than [Ronald Reagan's OPM chief,] Don Devine."

Over and above the politics of the SES, there is the bedrock systemic problem of continuity: only five years after its inception there was not a single person at OPM or the White House who was responsible for the original design of the SES. As is clear,

> There is no surer recipe for failure than to separate someone's personal stakes from the fate of the projects he or she is called upon to manage. Yet that is what we have done. . . . To ask temporary political appointees to superintend most of the major operations of the SES system is approximately comparable to entrusting the family heirlooms to a two-year-old, which is roughly how long most political appointees remain on the scene to account for their handiwork. (Heclo 1984b, 13–14)

The short-termer system as it currently operates builds into the larger structure disincentives for a competent career executive service. Because political appointees are temporary, they can escape the consequences of their actions. They do not have to worry about staff development or the long-term health of their agencies because they will likely be gone before any long-term problems they generate surface. In fact, "for political appointees it is personally rational to be institutionally foolish—not to worry about long-term resentments, not to worry about the executive development of officials who will be of use only to a successor administration, not to look past short-term responsiveness in judging performance" (Heclo 1984b, 14). Such a situation fairly cries out for trouble, which soon followed the creation of the SES.

Crashing Morale: The Wages of Bureaucrat Bashing

Despite grand hopes for it, the SES in its first decade was acknowledged by many (CRS 1992; GAO 1992, 1990, 1988, 1987a, 1985; Heclo 1986, 1984a; Huddleston, 1987; Levine, 1986; etc.) to be a system in trouble, a victim of low pay and pay compression, retrenchment on promised bonuses and career advancement, agency interference, general hostility to the concept of a managerial elite, less-than-competent coordination by the OPM, and the "widespread sense that the system has been politicized and that neutral competence is no longer valued" (Huddleston 1987, 30). As discussed above, declining morale in the SES was the inevitable outgrowth of these problems. Some career SES members even went so far as to sue the federal government, charging breach of faith over changes in bonuses and other aspects mentioned earlier. Between 8 percent and 16 percent left the service annually since 1980, further indicating dissatisfaction with the SES (CRS 1987).

A Merit Systems Protections Board survey of former members of the SES found in 1989 that while low pay and operation of the bonus system were the most frequently cited reasons given for their departure, large percentages left because of job dissatisfaction. It was revealed that "46% left the Federal service, in part, because they did not enjoy the work anymore and 42% . . . , in part, because their skills had not been used appropriately" (USMSPB 1989, 1).

The MSPB study also showed that SES careerists generally were not happy with their political bosses. They held

the nonpolitical skills and abilities of politically appointed senior executives in low regard. Fewer than a quarter of the former career executives believe[d] that non-career executives [brought] valuable experience, good managerial skills, or leadership qualities to their positions. Moreover, career executives who worked for noncareer senior executives and political appointees more frequently listed the following concerns as reasons for leaving the Service than did executives not supervised by noncareer and political executives: 1. the lack of competence of their immediate supervisor; 2. the politicization of their agencies, and 3. the ethics of higher management in their agencies. (Ibid., 2–3)

It is well-documented (USMSPB 1990) that career executives are faced with declining morale and career mobility as a result of bureaucrat bashing, the increase in political appointments, and the decrease in career appointments, among other factors. The increased numbers and placement of political appointees were discussed in detail in chapter 4. In this context, it is sufficient to note that the morale and mobility of the careerists are inextricably linked in inverse proportion to the increased numbers of their political counterparts. Between (fiscal years) 1980 and 1986, the numbers of noncareer (political) SES members and Schedule C employees increased 12.8 percent and 13.1 percent respectively, while the number of career SES members decreased 5.3 percent (GAO 1987b). Certainly, this growth affects their relationships, when political executives displace career executives in agencies, limiting the latter's sources of influence, power, and upward career movement and contributing to the politicization of the public service.

Other factors contribute to morale problems as well. Bureaucrat and government bashing have made public service less attractive to both career and political executives, as have salary caps, personnel cutbacks, and the sluggish state of the economy. Political replacement of career executives in OPM and in the Office of Management and Budget (OMB) politicized the personnel process itself. Also, pervasive doubts about the qualifications of the Reagan political appointees in particular contributed to the lowered morale of the career executives and the diminished esteem of the public service.

The "quiet crisis" literature assumes that the toll taken on the professional civil service has affected the quality of that work force. "There is evidence on all sides of an erosion of performance and morale across government in America. Too many of our most talented public servants—those with the skills and dedication that are the hallmarks of an effective career service—are ready to leave. Too few of our brightest young people—those with the imagination and energy that are essential for the future—are willing to join" (Volcker 1989, 1).

Both Jimmy Carter and Ronald Reagan fanned the flames of bureaucrat bashing. But while Jimmy Carter made much of being an outsider unencumbered by Washington politics, alliances, and obligations in his successful campaign for the presidency in 1976, Ronald Reagan turned bureaucrat bashing into a fine art as he rode a popular wave of discontent into the White House in 1980. The campaign appeal to "get the government off our backs" was no last-minute opportunistic gambit on his part. As early as 1976 he had said, "The best thing government can do is nothing" (Kelman 1982, 17). And while Reagan's interests were largely in the area of "regulatory relief," he made great electoral strides by attacking the bureaucracy in general, which enabled him to turn his sights to a social agenda.

Negative consequences of bureaucrat bashing soon followed Reagan's election and proved to be self-defeating for the health of the federal bureaucracy. According to some, many agencies lost their best people while the dead weight stayed; the sense of mission, so vital to public service, was damaged. Performance declined, and demoralization set in, thanks to RIFs, pay increases of less than half the rate of inflation, and static ceilings on the salaries of top careerists (ibid.). OPM chief Don Devine's personnel philosophy that "the public deserved a competent, but not necessarily stellar, federal workforce angered many employee organizations."[2]

Bureaucrat bashing only defeats the purpose of having a public service. Indeed, bureaucrat bashing brings its own punishment.

> The unavoidable conclusion, in sum, is that Reaganism's onslaught against the bureaucracy can only hinder any effort to eliminate the waste, fraud, and abuse that constitute the most wide-spread beef against "big government." The attack is likely to nurture indolence and incompetence by decreasing the proportion of able, eager people in career civil service positions, and by undercutting the ability of government agencies to instill the requisite sense of mission. (Ibid., 17)

Added to bureaucrat bashing is what might be termed government bashing and a generalized negative image of public service and its servants. Candidates Carter and Reagan both played to this image to advance their campaigns, though the latter significantly more than the former. "This phenomenon has several explanations, the most obvious being the general antipathy of Americans since colonial days toward 'big government' and 'bureaucrats.' To many citizens, 'big government,' 'fraud, waste, and abuse,' 'bureaucracy,' and 'bureaucrats' are terms synonymous with a system of government—and of government spending—gone out of control" (Levine 1986, 202).

Another factor contributing to poor morale among government workers in the domestic agencies was the all-out attack on most agencies' missions or on the agencies themselves by Reagan and his appointees.

Particularly since 1981, budgetary cutbacks, program terminations, and a general decline in program activism have combined to reduce the sense of achievement that prevailed during the sixties. Few people who have contributed to the creation, development, and growth of a program can be expected to approach its retrenchment with equal enthusiasm. Nor is it reasonable to suppose that adapting organizations and programs to cope with conditions of austerity will strike many potential federal employees as a rewarding challenge. (Ibid., 202)

Given all these negative factors, the wages of bureaucrat and government bashing should come as no surprise. Surveys continue to report federal executives' lack of enthusiasm for recruiting newcomers to their ranks. In the 1984 survey of the career members of the Senior Executive Service, "72% responded 'No' when asked if they would recommend a career in the federal government for their children" (ibid., 203). In 1988 only 13 percent of SES members reported that they *would* recommend a government career to young people (Ventriss 1991, 275).

All told, it remains to be seen which estimations are most accurate, the early hopes for the SES or the quiet crisis assessment.

The recent history of executive pay in the federal government is one of lost economic ground. As the purchasing power of federal executives fell, relative to the nongovernment sectors, it caused a brain drain as careerists topped out and then got out of government service. As discussed above, after several false starts the situation was finally remedied with the large salary increase that went into effect in 1991 as a result of the 1989 Ethics Reform Act.[3] This separated senior federal workers (PAS and SES) from congressional pay and established the increases at .05 percent below that of the civil service workers, GS-1 to GS-15, for increases after 1991. It is generally believed that tenure is increasing in the career SES ranks as a result of the salary jump.

Despite President Bush's exhortations about the value of public service and the absence of bureaucrat bashing in his administration, CSESs did not seem to feel any better about their situation than they had during the Reagan years. According to a GAO study, the percentage of career respondents dissatisfied with the public image of federal employees decreased only to 71 percent in 1991, though it was down from 85 percent in 1989 (GAO 1992, 4).

Interestingly, feelings of harassment by supervisors did not decrease significantly in Bush's administration. While 92 percent of both career and noncareer respondents indicated in 1991 that they had not themselves experienced abuse such as "shelving" (when an SES executive is reassigned to non-SES type duties), 51 percent of the careerists and 34 percent of the noncareerists believed that this has happened more than once in their department.

Only 53 percent felt that their supervisors viewed their job as an opportunity to make positive, long-term improvements to government. Even fewer (40 percent) agreed that their supervisors supported merit principles in hiring most or all of the time: 58 percent saw self-interest as a greater motivator for their supervisor's actions than public interest. While 90 percent saw political executives as working hard to carry out the Bush administration's policies, only 56 percent agreed that appointees make grants, contracts, loans, and loan insurance guarantees solely on the basis of merit, and 51 percent thought there were too many politicals for the job.

Career SES members gave political supervisors in the Bush administration mixed marks on leadership behavior and abilities: only 43 percent agreed or strongly agreed that their supervisor ensured that employees fully realize their potential, and only 55 percent said that their supervisor kept employees informed about events in their subunit. Others (43 percent) agreed that their supervisor often shared her or his experience and training, 41 percent said that their supervisor often provided them with sound job-related advice, and 30 percent felt that their supervisor provided needed technical knowledge. The barest majority (50.1 percent) agreed or strongly agreed that their supervisor was capable of getting the resources needed to get things done, and 59 percent agreed that she or he had the clout necessary or (63 percent) knew how to use contacts to get things done.

On the other hand, while 80 percent agreed or strongly agreed that their supervisor demanded compliance with her or his decisions, 69 percent said that their supervisor discussed the "big picture" of the subunit with them. Two-thirds (67 percent) felt that she or he gave appropriate praise and credit for employees' work; 75 percent that she or he showed trust and respect for the respondents; 73 percent that she or he consulted with subordinates and took their opinions and suggestions into account when making decisions; and 70 percent that supervisors delegated authority and responsibility to subordinates and allowed them to determine how to do their work.

Only 18 percent felt "subjugated" by their supervisor, while 24 percent felt that their supervisor made decisions in their area of work without consulting them. Close to three-fifths (58 percent) felt that their supervisor satisfied employees' needs and expectations for growth and development and that she or he met the subunit's goals.

Perhaps most telling as a sign of political-career trust, 78 percent felt that their supervisor allowed them to become involved in the formulation of agenda for policy. It is interesting to note, however, that this is *down* one point from 1989 when, presumably, the attitude of the Reagan appointees would have kept the career bureaucracy at arm's length from discussions of policy making.

Though the SES was designed to bring career and political executives into one service in a cooperative venture, suspicion and distrust still characterize feelings on each side, according to many careerists in the personal interviews. The problem is only partially one of miscommunication. The larger problem is that the two streams of executives compose two competing cultures that are defined to a certain extent by their opposition to one another. The irony is that the competing sides find themselves in a situation where "success, in the end, is dependent on their cooperation;" neither can live without the other (Huddleston 1987, 62).

This dismal picture was nearly universally painted prior to the 1991 pay raise, which may change the political landscape. In regard to the effect of the salary increase on job satisfaction, one measure of contentment is retention of employees. Retention has, indeed, gone up and, as noted, retirement has gone down significantly as careerists work through their "high three" years. Nevertheless, other measures will have to be analyzed in the next few years to determine if there has been real improvement in political-career relations or if the salary increase simply bought a short-term respite for a system in long-term trouble.

Sound Management as a Government Priority?

While there is consensus that the "presidential control apparatus" has grown, there is little analysis to indicate if that growth has improved public management. "The Reagan administration is especially troublesome in this regard. Good management was not an early priority," particularly in the first two years, according to Newland. "The focus was on confident and decisive change—implementing a fixed idea of governance—to the neglect of matters of importance to longer term success, including management" (Newland qtd. in Ingraham 1987, 425).

In the second half of his first administration Reagan did implement some management-oriented initiatives, notably "'Reform 88' which focused on managerial processes and systems: budgeting, resource management, and management information systems, as well as the broader area of 'general administration'" (Ingraham 1987, 425). Other initiatives, however, were directed at gaining political control over the career bureaucracy, for example, "the extensive use of carefully chosen political appointees, the aggressive pursuit of clearly defined partisan policy objectives in most federal agencies and programs, and, in some cases, the creation of new networks within the bureaucracy which permit[ted] political staff to bypass career executives" (ibid.).

As discussed previously, the political purpose of these activities was unambiguous in the Nixon and Reagan administrations. While giving lip service to the importance of solid policy formulation, quality implementation, and sound management practices in government, the operating principle of those eras was "you cannot achieve management, policy or program control unless you have established political control" (ibid., 425).

While "quality of management" is difficult to define with precision, the public administration community must continue to struggle with it. The political establishment of the day must also recognize that it is inappropriate and ultimately self-defeating to use managerial means to achieve political ends by filling what should be career positions with political appointees.

It is wrong to view the extension of political appointments to more management and line positions as benign. Further, "good management" initiatives do not fill the gap. They are somewhat akin to tinkering with the ship's engines while the vessel wanders aimlessly about the sea. At a minimum, "good" management requires clear direction, appropriate political and career management skills, full utilization of those talents, collaboration, and trust. On these rudimentary components, the present system is seriously deficient. (Ibid., 432)

Ingraham suggests that the search for solutions to management issues must be

both empirical and normative. . . . Not enough is known about political appointees, about what they want to achieve, about what they feel about their public service jobs, about why they change jobs so frequently. Of equal significance, a normative model is lacking for public service which is relevant to both political appointees and career managers. To achieve reasonable consensus . . . [it is necessary to achieve] a consistent and heightened awareness of the centrality of effective public management to the long-term public interest. (Ibid., 432–33)

Increased presidential control carries significant weight to largely negative effect. Based on recent developments in public service, Ingraham calls for "a new assessment of political direction and control." She notes four characteristics that mandate this new assessment: First, the greater number of political appointees and their increased infiltration of the bureaucracy through Schedule C and the SES results in political appointees in line as well as in management and staff positions. This reduces the role and influence of the careerists because it "allows top level political executives to bypass career executives and rely instead upon lower-level political appointees" (ibid., 426).

Second, "the extremely short tenure of the majority of political executives . . . creates a serious management void, . . . [with] a cadre of political executives almost constantly in flux." As noted previously, this means, in effect, that political executives spend the majority of their time learning their job and career executives spend much of their time teaching it to them (ibid., 426). The cultures of the two camps lead in opposite directions. As the name implies, careerists are making a career out of government service; they are in it for the long haul. Political appointees, on the other hand, tend to be policy experts with a particular agenda, not system managers. Indeed, Ingraham and Ban's 1985 interviews with careerists contradicted the widely accepted figure of the 18–24-month tenure of political appointees: "interviewees reported an average tenure by their superiors of 12 months. Some noted that appointees who stayed longer than eight months were considered 'old timers'" (Ingraham and Ban 1986, 155).

Third, political appointees often demonstrate a lack of preparation for their jobs. This may refer to "lack of management experience; lack of understanding of, and experience in, the public sector; and/or inadequate understanding of the programs and policies for which the political executive is responsible." The vaunted "fresh perspective" that political appointees are supposed to bring to government is virtually useless "unless it translates into constructive policy change, improved management, and enhanced public service." The lack of preparation and short tenure of political appointees decreases the chances of that translation occurring (Ingraham 1987, 426).

And fourth, the SES, though designed partially to enhance the morale and flexibility of senior executives and the personnel management system, was also designed, as discussed above, to increase political control over career executives through performance reviews, bonuses, and political decision making over career executives' assignments, transfers, and career paths. This increased political muscle in the personnel system was augmented by the ability to place political appointees in line positions (ibid.). This trend, too, must be assessed anew to consider its negative effects on the government's ability to do its work.

Within the context of presidential ambivalence (when not outright hostility) toward the senior career civil service, the siren song of bureaucrat bashing, the inherent conflict of political-career relations, and often minimal commitment to sound management principles, how do political and career executives actually relate to one another, and how might they better do so? Several models of political-career relations are next explored, beginning with the political models of conquest-bureauphobia, capture-bureauphilia, and comity-realpolitik. Then, the goal congruency and politics/administration models are discussed, followed by the technical models of neutral, responsive, and managerial competence, the moral-ethical models, the public service model, and finally, an assessment of relations within George Bush's administration.

Clearly, the models do not have clean lines of demarcation between them. They overlap nearly as often as they contradict one another. Nonetheless, an attempt to delineate them can clarify the complex issues of political-career relations.

Political Models: Conquest, Capture, and Comity

As noted, tension between the president and the bureaucracy was not the invention of Ronald Reagan. "In 1913, federal employees shuddered as the Democrats returned to the White House after a 16-year absence. William Jennings Bryan and other spoilsmen hoped to undo the merit system extensions of previous years, and despite the efforts of President Wilson, they had some successes. The Harding transition eight years later was essentially similar" (Maranto 1991, 248).

FDR's election brought a new approach to political appointments. Federal jobs became less a source of jobs outright, and more an instrument for policy implementation. Roosevelt simply bypassed the existing bureaucratic machinery and its Harding-Coolidge-Hoover conservatism to establish his New Deal outside the civil service system (though the New Deal agencies and their employees were soon blanketed into the merit system).

Eisenhower entered office with a distrust of the bureaucracy based on its twenty years of service to Democrats, combined with a basic distrust of big government that he bequeathed to his successors; presidential suspicions of the career civil service and anti–big-government campaign rhetoric continue to this day to one degree or another, regardless of party or house of Congress.

Conquest: Bureauphobia

The language used to describe this intrabranch tension borrows heavily from that of warfare, calling to mind macho images of conquest and surrender, victor and vanquished. Whipped up by the antibureaucracy rhetoric of recent presidential campaigns, most newly appointed appointees carry this warfare mentality into office with them: "many Washington denizens believe that either conquest or capture is almost inevitable. For example, one Heritage Foundation writer maintains that 'recurring, prolonged warfare doesn't go on—one side wins or the other gets captured'" (ibid., 248–49).

The conquest approach is, perhaps, best embodied in Richard Nixon, who

> warned his cabinet against becoming captives of the career bureaucracy: ". . . We can't depend on people who believe in another philosophy of government to give us their undivided loyalty or their best work. . . . If we don't get rid of these people, they will either sabotage us from within, or they'll just sit back on their well-paid asses and wait for the next election to bring back their old bosses." (Maranto, 1993, 1)

Theorists of this school seem to have an approach that is angry and personal as much as political. Butler, for example, comments that "The bureaucratic entrepreneur will not be content merely to block administration proposals; he wishes to impose his policy agenda on an unwary administration" (Butler et al. 1984, 492). Conquest is the goal when the White House chooses persons to head an agency who are fundamentally opposed to the mission of that agency. Their assignment is to serve as internal change agents, to bore from within. This was seen most clearly in the Reagan political appointees who: "'carried the campaign into office,' held career executives at arm's length, viewed any dissenting career advice as a sign of disloyalty, and in effect created a self-fulfilling prophecy in respect to their negative views on government and bureaucracy" (Lorentzen 1984, 8).

There is a broader politicizing trend inherent in the conquest mentality. It acts to the detriment of the larger public service and on both sides of the executive equation.

> Relations between political and career executives have become increasingly blurred as political levels have become bureaucratized and presidents have tried to gain control—especially in the higher career ranks and without the political orientation provided by old-style party ties. Yet this

situation damages the basic idea of a civil service far more than it threatens bureaucratic self-interests. Caught up in a politicizing trend, career officials have every incentive to neglect civil service norms of objective responsiveness and instead to survive by relying on their own buddy systems or by showing they can be as unquestioningly loyal as any personal aide who might be brought in (with the added asset of knowing how to work the system). In this sense, bureaucratized power can become more entrenched while the broader concept of a civil service declines. (Heclo 1977, 76)

In addition to the effects of White House reorganization of central agencies such as OMB and OPM, a generalized politicization removes decision-making power from career executives by various means. In the Reagan administration these means included:

the threatened use of sanctions on agency officials who did not follow administration policies . . . ; maximum use of . . . RIFs; greater use of political appointees at both higher and lower levels in agencies; ideological litmus tests for important bureaucratic positions; and the politicized OMB which emphasized political oversight and regulatory control. Presidential loyalty appeared, at times, to be more important than responsibility to the law. (Cigler 1990, 644)

The result of this general politicization was that career professional expertise was significantly excluded from the higher levels of policy and implementation. *"Public administration under President Reagan [was], to a significant extent, ideological political administration"* (Newland 1983, 2).

This conquest model, what Durant (1990) terms the bureauphobic perspective, is embodied in appointees who distrust careerists. They are likely to rely on threats and confrontations to accomplish administration ends. This approach is criticized for leaning toward authoritarianism and political rigidity.

A more subtle form of career exclusion and political control is what is referred to as "jigsaw puzzle management," another Sanera–Heritage Foundation concept:

Very little information will be put in writing. Career staff will supply information, but they should never become involved in the formulation of agenda-related policy objectives. Similarly, once controversial policy goals are formulated, they should not be released in total to the career staff. Thus, the political executive and his political staff become "jigsaw puzzle" managers. Other staff see and work on the individual pieces, but never have enough of the pieces to be able to learn the entire picture (Sanera 1984, 514–15).

This approach is also referred to bleakly as "mushroom management" because it keeps subordinates in the dark, covered with manure (Pfiffner 1985, 355).

The key role that agencies play in policy formation and the different perspectives of the career and political executives create fertile ground for conflict between the two camps of executives. The interpretive and implementational responsibilities of the executive agencies also mean that the potential for conflict of varying degrees of severity grows in inverse proportion to the specificity of the authorizing legislation. The clearer Congress is in its policy desires, the less room there is for interpretation and conflict between political and career executives. However, if Congress, for political or other reasons, chooses to leave its wishes ambiguous, policy making falls more directly to the agency and with it, greater potential for conflict between the political and career executives. Conflict is virtually guaranteed if the White House is opposed to the intent of the legislation itself.

The appointees themselves often work against complete political control of the bureaucratic process due to their inexperience or personal agendas. "'Political' appointees as a group have been distinguishable by nothing so much as by their common lack of experience in party politics, their unfamiliarity with agency programs and their general protectiveness of their organizational jurisdictions" (Heclo 1977, 79).

But political executives can be successful change agents for the president if they stay in place long enough, have sufficient skills (particularly people or political skills) to deal with both the internal and external politics, and avoid identifying with their organization or resorting to illegal practices.

Nonetheless, careerists are the determinant factor in agency change because the appointees "are often not a coherent management team. They are a dramatically disparate group of individuals who obtain policy direction and guidance from many different sources that may, but most frequently do not, include the president or White House staff. To expect coherent policy to emerge from such a setting is the stuff of exquisite fairy tales" (Ingraham 1991, 192–93).

PASs can compensate for their diffuse institutional character with adroit use of careerists. They can look to tools of the administrative presidency and attempt to "alter agency culture by promoting and recruiting careerists who share their goals and transferring or otherwise neutralizing others. . . . In effect, determined political appointees can make agency goals congruent to administration goals" (Maranto 1991, 248–49).

However effective this approach, it is an indirect one that further highlights the importance of careerists. The central place of careerists leads some to "question the underpinnings of theories such as those supporting the 'administrative presidency'" (Ingraham 1991, 192–93).

Capture: Bureauphilia

Capture is best expressed by the phrase *marrying the natives,* used derisively to describe the depoliticization that occurs when an appointee comes to identify, for whatever reason, more with her or his agency or its interest groups and less with the White House.

As discussed previously, depoliticization happens as appointees try to go deeply into the workings of their agencies and micromanage the work of the bureaucrats they supervise. They tend then to take on the perspective of their agency and become less responsive to political pressure from the White House. "Few political appointees are likely to be united by bonds of party loyalty," according to Heclo (1977, 106). While they may be in general agreement with the president's or the party's policies, they are unlikely to have been active in the campaign that brought them all to office and also unlikely to be moved by political rhetoric. Managing their agencies well becomes their priority. These are the PASs accused of "going native."

Capture is charged when an appointee supports a program the administration wants scrapped or argues against a budget reduction in her or his agency. According to Reagan EOP officials, there was no "good" reason to depart from such administration policy and the White House often retaliated for such defection by cutting funds, moving or reducing staff, or appointing more "trustworthy" subordinates to subvert the PAS's errant course. Surgeon General C. Everett Koop, for example, experienced this form of retaliation when he deviated from Reagan's social policy, particularly with regard to abortion, AIDs, and smoking. He suddenly found his key staff aide fired and himself isolated. Eventually, he resigned from office.

The capture or bureauphilic perspective gives primacy to the long-term careerists and their expertise in agency direction. It counsels short-term political appointees to cooperate with them and include them in policy making. This perspective is criticized as encouraging bureaucratic freewheeling unfettered by democratic (read: political) control.

Comity: Realpolitik and the Cycle of Accommodation

Once political appointees are in place they do not exist in a policy
vacuum, of course. They live and breathe the same bureaucratic air as do
the career executives, with whom they may have little in common, and
much to divide. Yet, the impression one gets when analyzing political bureaucrats versus career bureaucrats is that there is no "versus" involved.
Bureaucrats of either type "love their program, not the parties" (Heclo
1977, 148). That common focus tends to ameliorate the factors that divide
in favor of those that unify.

Pfiffner (1987b), Lorentzen (1985), Huddleston (1987), Maranto (1991),
and others observe what is called the cycle of accommodation in political-career relations. It seems to work broadly across all recent administrations. PASs may come into office breathing fiery distrust of the careerists, but if they stay long enough (two to three years), they learn to
work with their careerists. The comity that develops between them "results in a more sophisticated appreciation of the contribution of the career service and a mutual respect and trust" (Pfiffner 1987b, 60).

John Ehrlichman's change of heart is representative of many White
House officials. While he initially "saw relations with the bureaucracy as
"guerilla warfare," he later came to feel that the Nixon administration
lost ground by excluding "career executives from policy deliberations,
both because of their expertise and because of their ability to develop support for the administration's programs" (ibid., 60).

Indeed, the NAPA study demonstrated little variation among PASs of
whatever administration in their regard for their career colleagues, as the
following table indicates (ibid., 61).

While the Reagan administration officials, as might be expected, held
the careerists in lowest esteem, it is notable that they rated them only
marginally lower than the others and not below 77 percent in competence
or political responsiveness. Even Carter's appointees—whose boss, like
Reagan, ran against the Washington bureaucracy (but significantly, much
less against the bureaucrats, themselves, than did Reagan)—rated careerists similarly with other presidents' appointees. The Bush appointees
clearly reflected the more positive attitude toward the civil service that
their boss embodied, scoring the careerists the highest of all the PASs.
And, in fact, that attitude was reaffirmed in the PAS interviews.

It is widely acknowledged that most PASs come to see the value of a
"neutral" bureaucracy sooner rather than later.

Not only are [careerists] responsive, but they perform functions that are
essential to the proper operation of the government and to the success of

Table 6.1. PASs Evaluate Careerists' Competence and Responsiveness

	Percentage of PASs Surveyed	
Administration	PASs Rating "Competent"	PASs Rating "Responsive"
Johnson	92	89
Nixon	88	84
Ford	80	82
Carter	81	86
Reagan	77	78
Bush	94	92

Source: From the Bush PAS Survey of those who rated their career SESs as competent and responsive to a "moderate," "great," or "very great" extent.

the political appointees for whom they work. While we expect career executives to be responsive to political leadership, at the same time we expect them to resist illegal or unethical direction from above. . . . One example of appropriate bureaucratic resistance was the refusal of the Internal Revenue Service (IRS) to audit George McGovern's campaign aides' tax returns at the order of the Nixon White House. Thus we expect bureaucrats to be responsive, but not too responsive. (Pfiffner 1987b, 62)

Another example of comity is one brought on by external pressures. If conflict between careerists and appointees becomes public enough to

attract attention from powerful external actors, the White House may appoint more moderate (or at least politically competent) individuals, either piecemeal or en masse. The latter occurred with the departure of embattled Administrator Anne Burford and many others from the Reagan Environmental Protection Agency (EPA). Indeed, some suggest that since bureaucrats implement programs supported by Congress, interest groups, and public opinion, it is misleading to assume that presidents and their appointees alone can control the bureaucracy. Instead, "the best way is to work with the bureaucracy and not against it". . . . The short tenure of PASs suggests that there might not be a single transition but rather a continual series of transitions over the course of an administration, varying with leadership changes in particular organizations. (Maranto 1991, 249, and Waterman 1989, 170)

Heclo (1977) looks at the givens of Washington's political scene and opts for his version of comity, the realpolitik response. The givens are: the transient nature of the political appointees; their babes-in-the-woods status vis-à-vis the career bureaucrats and the Washington power game; their inability, real or perceived, to fire or even transfer recalcitrant civil service subordinates; the alienation in which they live and work, having little sense of community within their own agency and even less among their appointee peer colleagues; and pressures from the White House, that competes with pressures to identify with their agency.

Heclo's is a contingency-based approach that uses exchange theory and is grounded in the values of the public service model (discussed below). His vision of exchange theory is illustrated in what he calls "conditional cooperation," that is, cooperation that is conditioned on the mutual performance of both political and career executives, a sophisticated and sometimes subtle game of "you scratch my back, I'll scratch yours." Established as an informal but powerful quid pro quo, its reward and punishment structure can operate in very indirect ways: A political appointee can invite career executive presence and participation at key meetings or she or he can practice policies of exclusion and control. A career executive can warn political appointees of impending disaster or simply step aside and let them suffer the inevitable consequences of ignorance, can counsel neophyte appointees in the appearances-is-everything mentality of Washington or silently let them lavishly redecorate their offices and wait for them to be lambasted in the dreaded *Washington Post*.

The federal bureaucracy is not a monolith; career and political appointees should understand that each side has different perspectives and motivations. Appointees can use this knowledge to advance their political goals. Heclo identifies four genres of bureaucrats (program, staff, reformers, and institutionalists), with four types of reactions to appointee overtures (opponents, reluctants, critics, and forgottens). He counsels political appointees to employ strategic leadership in working with their career subordinates and to use the diversity of the bureaucracy to evoke conditional cooperation rather than depending on invocations of formal authority to move their political agenda.

Only major crises create opportunities for what Heclo calls "Big Change" procedures that involve major shake-ups in organizations and expectations, and perhaps the creation of a new agency. Given their rare occurrence and the reality that "there are no magical management systems or organizational changes for 'getting control of the bureaucracy,'" he recommends that political executives seek out a strategy of cooperation with their career counterparts, rather than trying to change the norms and standard operating procedures of an organization with which they will have limited tenure. As he notes, "For those both tough and sensitive enough, it is a job of managing a pluralistic, changing consensus with limited strategic resources" (Heclo 1977, 220–21, 233).

Heclo's exchange theory of conditional cooperation emphasizes the need for both sides to work at relationships that depend on the contingencies of one another's actions, not on preconceived ideas of strict supervision or harmonious goodwill. It assumes that career executives can recognize self-interest in the success of their political supervisors and can be motivated to work to ensure that success. Likewise, political executives can see the benefits to be gained by granting credibility and discretion to their career counterparts. Both are motivated to operationalize conditional cooperation. As Durant notes, "The real basis of conditional cooperation lies in making bureaucrats creditors rather than debtors to the political executives; that is, giving them a stake in (the appointee's) future performance" (Durant 1990, 321).

Heclo's concern for a middle ground between political rigidity and bureaucratic freewheeling is echoed by others. Durant, for example, asks, "How can a polity best reconcile its needs for bureaucratic responsiveness and accountability, presidential influence within the bureaucracy, and a neutrally competent civil service?" His answer builds on Heclo's system that is conditionally cooperative *and* grounded in a "public service model of appointee-careerist relations which embodies notions of mutual responsibility and respect, joint tempering and concern for the public interest" (ibid., 319).

After the Reagan years of bureaucrat bashing, this approach is absolutely necessary. To reach the middle ground of conditional cooperation means that:

1. Appointees must acquire more sophisticated, realistic, and less polarized expectations about the nature and legitimacy of careerist behavior and dissent than those typically informing the present debate; 2. They must be afforded the heuristic tools and strategies necessary for anticipating, understanding, and constructively engaging careerists, responding disparately to their initiatives; and 3. Careerists must appreciate what presidentialists already understand and what protean empirical evidence over the past four presidencies readily supports: If political direction and career expertise are to "season and temper" each other, appointees must increasingly wield the tools of the administrative presidency with political and strategic prowess. (Ibid., 319–20)

Durant's typology extends to bureaupolitical responses to policy initiatives that range from mutual accommodation to manipulated agreement, adversarial engagement, and disintegrative conflict. The response of the careerist to policy initiatives, which he calls the noncompliance delay effect (NDE), depends on the degree of threat she or he perceives to the mission and program of the agency as a result of resistance; the greater the threat to the agency, the lesser the resistance, and vice versa.

Using the NDE as a diagnostic tool, Durant advises appointees to assess careerists' readiness to adjust to new policy initiatives and encourages them to nurture rather than demand change in their subordinates' levels of readiness. He employs Hershey and Blanchard's (1988) concept of "follower readiness" to provide a model for when appointees should provide greater or lesser supervision of careerists. Durant's "strategic approach informed by the NDE allows appointees to identify leadership styles, tactics (telling, selling, participating, and delegating strategies), and targets most critical for crafting accomplishment in ways that also advance the values associated with a public service model of appointee-careerist relations" (ibid.,1990, 326).

What is the career side of this interaction? Zuck advises careerists to recognize that change in policy direction is part and parcel of democratic government and that career staff will be employed in service of that change. Therefore, careerists should behave in a professional manner, providing their "best advice, information, and insight which . . . experience has provided." He urges careerists not to withhold negative information in the name of "loyalty." Also, careerists need to think beyond their own bureaucratic horizon to creative ways of accomplishing goals, cutting through red tape, and providing to appointees options and their likely consequences to appointees. Perhaps his most salient (if not comforting) word is that careerists should expect to have their advice regularly ignored or rejected. "Not only is it likely that one's advice is not always sound, but also each administration and political appointee has the right to fail. It is the career official's responsibility to provide the most professional advice he or she possesses, but recognize the right and responsibility for the final decision to be made by the appropriate political executive" (Zuck 1984, 18).

In the "balancing-and-controlling" routine that characterizes the bureaucratic game, each side has powers to exercise. The careerists' include "the power of relative independence in status and tenure, the power of expertise and specialized information, the power of permanence and stability, i.e., to 'wait and delay,' and the power of providing or withholding their services." The political appointees' powers include "the power of legitimacy and formal credentials, the power of the purse and budgetary decisions, the power to select and set goals, and the power to establish new bureaucratic rules and internal support" (Lorentzen 1984, 10–11).

It is important to maintain realistic expectations of improving political-career relations. Tension, power plays, strategizing, and differing motivations are inherent in the body politic. Arguing against the hidebound politics/administration dichotomy that posits a role for careerists confined strictly to carrying out the orders of their political superiors, Lorentzen argues for the development of collaborative working relationships between the two groups of executives. A relationship built on trust and a mutual understanding of perspectives and orientations would allow careerists a role in policy formulation as well as implementation and make for greater success in government administration. "These features of executive branch life are not only inherent in the American democratic system of government, but ultimately are operational aspects of how we have decided to pursue our fundamental political values: dispersed and not unitary power, multiple and not single controls, and consensus/compromise rather than efficiency" (ibid., 11).

The point is not to abolish the game or take away one player's powers, but rather to give its participants "a more supportive environment and better skills for constructive interactions." Both sides carry responsibility for developing this more trusting environment for the creation of collegiality. Careerists must initiate the start of constructive relations; PASs must let them know that such overtures are welcome and that dissent will not incur retaliation (Lorentzen 1985, 413).

The Goal Congruency Model of Political-Career Relations

Aberbach and Rockman (1988), Brauer (1987), and Maranto (1991) note the limitations of a theory of political-career relations that assumes an inevitable clash between the two groups of executives, as do the three political approaches discussed above. They suggest a fourth approach to understanding those relations, goal congruency: "If there exists high goal congruence between a presidential administration and a federal organization, relations between careerists and political appointees are likely to start well and remain that way. If, on the other hand, organization and administration goals are at odds, one can expect relations to start badly and take some time to recover" (Maranto 1991, 249–50).

Some agencies are likely, thanks to goal congruency, to escape political pressure and to enjoy smooth political-career relations from the start. Those are the defense agencies. Maranto's research suggests that no cycle of accommodation is evident in defense organizations because none is needed—political-career relations start well and continue in that vein. The popular and presidential support of the military and the defense buildup during the Reagan years make it a less-contentious arena than many of the domestic agencies he studied. "It is," Maranto observes, "notable that no president since Eisenhower has been less than highly supportive of the military"[4] (ibid., 262).

The more appointees there are in an agency, the greater the opportunity for conflict, because the growth of appointees was likely due to the actions of a president seeking to exercise political control and probably came at the expense of career positions. On the other hand, agencies dealing with highly technical or scientific tasks or noncontroversial issues are likely to be more heavily, perhaps even entirely career and, thus, to be free of political tension (ibid., 251). They are also less likely to experience the turbulence of short tenure.

Maranto finds that while the cycle of accommodation does operate in some domestic organizations in the throes of policy change even before controversial appointees are replaced, his data suggest that the cycle would be short-circuited were the leadership not to change. In other domestic organizations where the cycle of accommodation is one-sided and only operates among appointees but not among careerists, there is no improvement in their relations. This suggests that

> the goal congruence of an administration and organization has a strong impact on relations between career and noncareer executives in the organization. . . . Even in conflict-prone organizations, the attitudes of incoming noncareer executives may shorten or prolong the era of bad feelings associated with the transition. If this is the case, better preparation of appointees could help. The relatively experienced Bush cabinet and the president's experience in, and respect for, the federal government should account for better relations in the current administration than in the two past terms, particularly since there has been no change of party. Early discussions of the Bush presidency in fact fail to note significant tensions between appointees and careerists. Indeed, had Michael Dukakis won, it is quite possible that *his* appointees would have distrusted the careerists who served a GOP president for so long. (Maranto 1991, 263)

The Politics/Administration Dichotomy Revisited: Power Without Competence? Competence Without Power?

A third set of models deals with the relationship between political and career executives and seeks to separate the policy roles and responsibilities of each in the traditional politics/administration dichotomy. While attempting to exclude careerists from key policy-making functions and positions, however, these models fail to develop in the appointees the skills, experience, and networks to fill the resulting void.

The we-they mentality that results from the exclusion of career managers in these models is advocated by theorists such as Nathan (1985), Rector and Sanera (1987), and others at conservative think tanks such as the Heritage Foundation. As discussed, it was put into practice by the officials of the Reagan administration. This administration saw a nostalgic return to the politics/administration dichotomy in a presidential control model in which political appointees sought to make all decisions, and careerists were to offer expertise only to implement political dictates but not themselves to advocate policy positions (Ingraham and Ban 1988, 12).

These models of exclusion have developed over time and do not take into account the fact that the roles of political and career officials are, in fact, converging.

> Both make policy, both represent interests, both have policy objectives. . . . The moral dilemma posed by bureaucratic policymaking is power without responsibility; the dilemma of policymaking by politicians is power without competence. Excessively bureaucratic policymaking may lead to a crisis of legitimacy, but excessively political policymaking threatens a crisis of effectiveness. (Ingraham and Ban 1986, 153)

There are two other problems that are not adequately addressed by any of the three models. For one thing, political appointees have no incentives to be expert managers. Any failings in the system eventually get laid at the feet of the career managers—politicals are long gone by the time they appear. The second, and perhaps more troubling, deficiency of these models is "the absence of direct consideration and pursuit of the public interest." While each model addresses the public interest, it is only an indirect and glancing consideration, according to Ingraham and Ban (ibid., 158–59).

Competence-Based Models

In contrast to the technical competence models of political-career relations—neutral, responsive, and managerial competence—are the moral-ethical models that seek to address the broader purpose of public administration. They ask, public administration to what end? Directed to career civil servants, they seek out the special responsibility of those servants to promote the public interest that is missing or downplayed in the other models.

Neutral competence is grounded in the politics/administration dichotomy that assumes separate realms for political and career responsibility. It can be defined as "the ability to do the work of government expertly, and to do it according to explicit, objective standards rather than to personal or party or other obligations and loyalties" (ibid., 152).

Political leaders determine policy and the civil service carries it out, in this view. "Neutral competence assumes that the public interest is best served by objective applications of career expertise." The central values are economy and efficiency. The development of a professional civil service best serves the needs of efficiency, providing "stability and the institutional memory to balance the rapid turnover of political executives" (ibid., 159, 152). However, this view is too limited.

> It is simply naive and wrong to believe that the role of the career service is to "do what they are instructed to do." At least since the Nuremberg trials, the defense of individual responsibility and accountability for one's actions cannot be based upon the proposition that one was ordered by a higher authority to execute a particular action. Society expects our public officials, whether political or career, to act in ways reflecting high ethical and moral character. (Zuck 1984, 16)

Watergate, and then the Iran-Contra scandal, add more recent frames of reference of this lesson that even presidents and their surrogates (whether political or career) acting in their name, are not above the law. "The oath of office taken by career staff is the same as that taken by political executives; . . . career executives have also sworn to uphold the laws of the land and defend the Constitution" (ibid.).

Simply put, there are no solid, easy-to-define boundaries between politics and administration. American society and government are too complex and interrelated to make such clean divisions of labor. It is clearly unwise to ignore the knowledge, experience, and skills of the careerists in the development and evaluation of policy options.

Responsive competence is seen by some as an attractive antidote to counter what is perceived as insularity and excessive professional or agency loyalty on the part of careerists. Defined as competence "at the disposal of and for the support of, political leadership," responsive competence leans in the direction of presidential control and centralization of power in the White House and the expansion of political appointees across and down the executive agencies. It correlates the public interest with partisan interest and is less concerned with efficiency, per se.

> This model asserts that the line between politics and administration is a fuzzy one, since many decisions made in administering a program have

policy consequences. Therefore, even line administrators need to "buy in" to the administration's programs, and political appointees need to play a direct role in line operations. Inefficiencies which result are an acceptable cost of democracy. (Ingraham and Ban 1986, 153)

Like the neutral competence–politics/administration dichotomy model, the political responsiveness model fails to comprehend the complexity of modern government. Appointees are inevitably at some disadvantage because they generally "do not know 'how to put their fingers on the switches'. . . . In contrast, careerists know not only the switches but also which ones are most likely to work." While the value of expertise is unclear in this model, "in the hierarchy of policy choice . . . political demands are clearly superior to program expertise as well as to other public values (ibid., 158). Bluntly stated, "a strict application of this theory is that the role of the career service is to 'do what you're told to do' by political officials. Any contrary conduct is perceived as being 'disloyal' to the political executive or as the bureaucracy's demonstrating traditional impediment to carrying out administration policy" (Zuck 1984, 15).

Managerial competence contains elements of both neutral and responsive competence and draws heavily upon private sector business management practices with an emphasis on eliminating structural barriers to management flexibility. It "assumes that 'good' management practices include consideration of the public good." Its failings are that managerial competence relies on private sector definitions of competence, which often are not appropriate for the public sector, and it neglects to ask the question, "managerial competence for what purpose?" (Ingraham and Ban 1986, 153, 158–59).

Moral-Ethical Models

Another set of models is addressed to the career service and seeks to deal with the gaps in the three technical competence models. They are the moral-ethical models of social equity, regime value, and public interest.

The social equity model "proposes an activist-administrator who, by virtue of the public responsibility inherent in her-his career choice, is driven by moral and ethical concerns for social justice." The regime values model relies on the Constitution and its inherent values to guide public administrators to discern the public interest and direct their actions in its name. "The oath of office legitimates a degree of professional autonomy for the administrator and . . . the object of the oath, the Constitution, it-self can keep this autonomy within acceptable bounds" (Ingraham and Ban 1988, 10).

> The public interest model. . . . identifies an emergent or perceived public interest as the overarching guideline for administrative action. . . . Though definition of the public interest is problematic, theorists in this group argue that definition is possible. . . . [This model argues for an] "agency perspective," a particular view of the public interest (and the public service) derived from the programs, policies, and organizational culture of the agency in which the careerist is employed. Thus, it reflects commitment to a particular government function or service and to a par-ticular segment of the citizenry. (Ibid., 10–11)

While the technical models see good administration as an end in it-self, the ethical models see it as "the means to a higher good." The ethi-cal models present "an exalted view of the public service, . . . a service which is . . . 'fameworthy,' [one in which] individual morality and the public good are jointly served." Public service in the ethical models offers "a 'calling,' an opportunity to serve, an opportunity to be a part of a greater good" (ibid., 11).

The Public Service Model

Ingraham and Ban see a need for an alternative model, that of the pub-lic service, to incorporate both the public service and political perspec-tives and to address issues of "'balance' in terms of public policy processes and outcomes" (ibid., 11).

A public service model of political-career relations counterbalances the we-they mentality and makes good use of what can be creative ten-sion between the two. This model "is based on the clearly normative as-sumption that both career administrators and political appointees have a legitimate role to play in the public policy process." It does not limit ei-ther group by or to specific functions and assumes both are guided by a larger vision of the public interest (ibid., 9, 12). Both also carry a dual re-sponsibility:

> The responsibility to develop and maintain excellent management and program skills is obvious. Less obvious, but of critical significance, is the constant responsibility to ask: Why are these skills important? For what purpose are they being utilized? [It is to be noted] . . . that this dual re-

sponsibility resides with *all* the members of the public service. The responsibility to serve the public interest must be as keenly a part of the political public service as of the career service. Failure to recognize this duality seriously distorts administration and trivializes the political role in public management, no matter how many appointees there may be. (Ibid., 13)

Certainly, it is difficult to define with precision so ephemeral a term as "the public interest." It serves as much as an opening for debate as an actuality.

"The public interest is a standard of goodness by which political acts can be judged; action in the public interest, therefore, deserves approval because it is good." Baily, while labelling the reality of the concept a myth, also notes the value of the ideal: "The phrase 'the public interest' is the decisionmaker's anchor rationalization for policy-caused pain. . . . It is balm for the official conscience. It is one of society's most effective analgesics . . . ; 'the public interest' is the central concept of a civilized polity. Its genius lies *not in its clarity*, but in its perverse and persistent moral intrusion upon the *internal* and *external* discourse of rulers and ruled alike." (Ibid., 13)

The aspect of moral intrusion keeps the politics-merit debate about the public interest lively. There need be no expectation of any final resolution between politics and merit, politicians and careerists, only that the debate continue. The wider public interest ultimately benefits from the ongoing discussion of means and ends.

The public service model differs from the others in the following respects: It explicitly includes both political and career public servants, valuing the roles and perspectives of each as important to a democratic society. It endorses "mutual, bilateral respect and collaboration between political executives and career managers." It sees the public service holistically, focusing on effectiveness and efficiency for "a higher, broader purpose, which crosses program, policy, and partisan lines." And it keeps foremost the concept of the public good as the purpose of a public service, "driven and constantly informed by broader societal concerns" (ibid., 14).

A public service model is characterized by:

1. A consistent awareness of the public service as a democratic institution for political appointees and for career managers. 2. A joint commitment to management competency which also recognizes the unique qualities and demands of public management. 3. A mutual respect for the

skills, perspectives, and values each set of managers brings to the organization, and 4. A consistent awareness of, and active concern for, the public interest, broadly defined. For political appointees, this will mean moving beyond election results. (Ibid., 14)

How is this ideal model to be achieved? The Senior Executive Service, at least in theory, was a step in the right direction because it attempted to create a unified executive service in which career managers were given a significant policy voice while simultaneously being subject to political control. However, as noted, the larger political dynamics and the problems inherent in the SES soon doomed this good intention to serious difficulty. The public distrusted any sign of perceived elitism, bonuses and other incentives were cut, the percent of those eligible to receive bonuses was reduced from 50 percent to 20 percent, and personal development plans were drastically scaled down. Ronald Reagan's appointees came into office determined to cut the careerists out of policy discussions and used reassignment and relocation provisions of the system punitively to enforce their will on careerists they considered subversive (Levine 1986, 201–02).

Despite this history, the climate of relations between political and career managers can be improved within the public service model with some determined effort. Presidents and political appointees need first to stop bureaucrat bashing: "Appointees cannot arrive at their appointed positions proclaiming that all bureaucrats are incompetent and expect to be viewed [by them] as legitimate managers." Also, political appointees must commit to longer tenure in office and be better schooled in management and the legal restraints on their actions. Education of future career managers must include a component of democratic and ethical concerns to match their technical expertise. Additionally, SES members must maintain a pride in their calling and a belief that they are performing a valuable service to the nation (Ingraham and Ban 1988, 17).

The politics-career tension is probably as old as the bureaucracy. Each side in turn has predominated.

In times of political excess and abuse we turn to the concept of a neutral career service for expertise and balance. In times of frustration with the slowness and isolation of the public bureaucracy, we turn to the dynamic political system for energy and balance. . . . the vitality of the system depends upon the value of both the career civil service and the political management system. (Ibid., 16–17)

While the *public interest* inherent in the public service model is an amorphous concept, the debate itself will continue to be a key ingredient to the model. The debate about its definition is and "always has been at the heart of the public policy process; it is also an essential part of the public management process." It remains to be seen whether a broad public interest can overcome narrow political ideology. It is, however, "a worthy goal to pursue that 'well ordered polity' [in which] . . . 'politicians and bureaucrats can each do what they are best able to do: politicians articulate society's dreams and bureaucrats help bring them gingerly to earth'" (Ingraham and Ban 1986, 159).

Contextual Images of Political-Career Relations

Aberbach, Putnam, and Rockman (1981) approach the question of political-career relations from a content-context basis, more than from a rules-and-regulations basis. Growing from their fundamental assumption that both camps are policy makers in one way or another, their "images" of these relationships are intended to illuminate patterns in the data that has been gathered about these players.

The first of their images is the standard politics/administration dichotomy, wherein partisans are to decide policy and bureaucrats are to implement it, cut and dried, no questions asked. Image II moves more into the area of context apart from authority and assumes that both politicians and bureaucrats make policy but with different focuses. The dichotomy here is between facts and interests. The politicians must balance and mediate among diverse and conflicting claims. They ask if a policy will pass political muster with relevant constituencies. Bureaucrats ask the more technical question, will it work? While the politicians pass value judgments, the bureaucrats pass technical judgments.

Image III posits a dichotomy of energy versus equilibrium. It moves even more into the context area, focusing on the world in which each camp lives within the same bureaucracy. The politicians live in a broader world in which they confront the conflicting interests of unorganized individuals. They have an interest in helping to surface the claims of unorganized persons and interests as a means to create greater political capital for themselves: as such, their goal is to bring more people into the process. Bureaucrats, on the other hand, deal with organized groups; their focus is more narrow and limited. While politicians operate on the macro level and seek to reconcile and bridge conflicting interests, bureaucrats operate on the micro level and, lacking the overall picture, are not disposed to integrate diverse claims and interests across boundaries. They have a tendency to fix on what is in their current scope, while politicians' tendency is to look beyond the present reality to the potential.

Temperament plays a significant role in these two camps' tendencies. "Prudence, practicality, moderation, and avoidance of risk are the preferred traits of a civil servant; only a politician could have termed extremism a virtue and moderation a vice," as did Barry Goldwater in his presidential race against Lyndon Johnson in 1964. The Republican presidential contenders in the 1996 election, each seeking to claim the mantle of the most conservative, were only following in Goldwater's footsteps. As the authors note, "The natural habitat of the politician is the public podium, whereas the bureaucrat is found seated at a committee table." Politicians' souls are stirred (and they are more apt to stir the souls of others) by passions and appeals to philosophical principles; bureaucrats are more likely to practice conflict management and to avoid controversy (Aberbach et al. 1981, 12).

Aberbach et al. note a convergence of roles from the second half of the nineteenth century in which Image I's politics/administration dichotomy reigned, to the first half of the twentieth century when Image II's acceptance of a limited policy-making role for bureaucrats was accepted, to the third quarter of that century, which saw an expanded policy-making role for bureaucrats.

This growing overlap of roles culminates in Image IV, the pure hybrid caused by the increasing need for expertise in both camps in the last quarter of this century. This need has significantly erased the dichotomy between politics and administration as the two tasks have become integrated.

This integration can be seen in several places, notably in the White House staff that brings in large numbers of careerists in key policy-making roles, particularly in OMB. The clearest sign of this integration in the larger bureaucracy is the Senior Executive Service. As discussed above, the SES was created in 1978 specifically to be political, to give partisans more control over the bureaucracy. While only 10 percent of its members are political appointees, the other 90 percent are top careerists who have traded civil service job security for increased power, salary, and mobility. The Bush PAS Survey, in which the PASs gave ample evidence of their dependence on their top careerists, demonstrates clearly the validity of this hybrid model in the current era.

One additional location of note for this hybrid is in the congressional staff, particularly those assigned to committees, which have become larger and more specialized to counter the growth of the executive branch's bureaucracy. Congress will continue to demand more staff with program and policy expertise, particularly in times of divided government.

Competent Comity in the Public Service:
George Bush's Model of Political-Career Relations

Given the above description and illuminations of political-career relations, into which does George Bush's style fit? His administration did not match neatly any one of these various models but might best be described as a combination of the comity-realpolitik, competence, public service, and Image IV models. Bush clearly valued the public service and the skills and dedication of its practitioners; he encouraged his appointees to work with, rather than against, their career subordinates. He did not place appointees in agencies to undermine their mission, as had Reagan, and he did not generally engage in subversion of the agencies' work (with the exception of the Competitiveness Council, which could unilaterally reverse agency regulations, thus overturning agency rule-making authority in the interests of free enterprise and unfettered capitalism).

As noted, there are realpolitik givens of the political-career relationship: the transient nature of political appointees, their relative inexperience and naivete vis-à-vis the careerists, the sluggish nature of a civil service system that frustrates efforts to move, demote, or fire employees, and the conflicting pressures on appointees that pull them simultaneously downward into their agency and outward to the White House. These givens lend support to the comity model that suggests a positive working relationship between the two partners in the bureaucratic choreography so they can get on with the dance. The Bush people appeared to recognize the utility of comity in political-career relations.

Bush also stressed competence in his appointees to a greater degree than had his immediate predecessor. He focused on managerial competence, placing great faith in lessons carried over from the private sector and its business practices (such as the Competitiveness Council and "regulatory relief"). The problem with this approach is that it enshrines practices that are not at all foolproof and, more seriously, fails to recognize the inherent differences between the public and private sectors. It also can work against the public interest as it seeks to promote or protect business interests, rendering moot any grand assertion that Bush's was a pure public service model.

The public service model is a positive, forward-looking standard that respects both partners and assumes that each has a legitimate role in the dance and that each is guided by a concern for the public interest. Given Bush's support for the public service, this paradigm was certainly a significant component of his model of competent comity in political-career relations.

It is also clear that the hybrid model was employed in the Bush administration with public service and its bureaucrats granted significant respect and support. Given the increasing demands on government and their complexity and government's shrinking resources to meet those demands, future administrations will continue to utilize the hybrid model, giving more policy-making discretion to bureaucrats and further integrating them into the policy-making process.

Conclusion

The often turbulent recent history of relations between the political and career directors of the federal government's bureaucracy must be seen in context to be fully understood. There has been tremendous growth in both camps in the modern era. Beyond the inevitable strain of growing pains is the underlying issue of confusion that arises from the constitutionally mandated separation of powers.

One factor that exacerbates the problem is the burgeoning number of political appointees of all types. The White House could take a significant step toward resolving two of the levels of confusion by reducing the number of appointees and eliminating as many levels of bureaucracy as possible. A flatter hierarchy led by politicals that are fewer in number but committed to the president's agenda and closer to the careerists would make better use of both White House leverage and careerist skills.

Conflicts between political and career executives are an inherent component of democratic life as practiced in the United States. They can be seen as a destructive but necessary evil or as a source of creative tension within the body politic. As numerous theorists have noted, bureaucracy and democracy need one another to ensure the proper functioning of both; there is an intimate relationship between them.

> One of the great paradoxes of representative government is that in order for democracy to flourish, bureaucracy must thrive as well. . . . Bureaucracy is the side of government that gets things done—the side that builds roads, safeguards our air and water, protects our rights, and defends our freedoms. Without bureaucracy, we have no government. Without government, we have no civilization. (Huddleston 1987, 27)

Understanding one another's culture, clarity of political purpose and open, "clean" fighting between the two competing camps will lay the groundwork for appropriate compromise and cooperation that will in the long run serve the interests of an open and democratic system. As Alexander Hamilton noted in *The Federalist* (Number 68), "The test of a good government is its aptitude and tendency to produce a good administration."

The quiet crisis in public service demands credible solutions if there is to be the good administration that is the prerequisite for a good government. Some solutions can be found in the style of mutuality that Heclo calls conditional cooperation and in Ingraham and Ban's public service model. If they are right, conditional cooperation and commonality of purpose can improve working relations and general morale in the agencies where they are practiced. Meanwhile, as the roles of the two camps continue to overlap, Aberbach's hybrid model will more firmly establish itself, creating more support for cooperation and mutual respect.

Greater respect between the two camps of political and career executives would yield important benefits for the political, career, and overall agency positions. The political side would see greater facility in recruitment, higher quality, and longer tenure for political appointees. On the career side, improved self-esteem and morale would follow from a renewed sense of the importance and value of public service and acknowledgement of the key role of the career civil service leadership in it. On the agency side, an increase in workforce quality and morale would lead to improved performance, agency esteem, and general credibility, particularly in those agencies that make appropriate use of career expertise in the policy-making arenas.

As discussed in the next two chapters, while George Bush took appropriate steps to restore respect for the career bureaucracy in general, his appointments were not met with rousing cheers. Further, he did not make any moves to reduce the number of political appointees or to reclassify key political positions as career reserved, as the great majority of theorists and studies urge. This task awaits future administrations.

The challenge for the next generation of presidents and political appointees is to create a viable system that is both responsive and competent to meet the nation's needs. How can this be accomplished? The following chapters suggest solutions by answering the identity, qualifications, and intra- and interbureaucratic relationship questions surrounding a particular cohort of presidential appointees, those of the Bush administration. Who they were, what their senses of accomplishment and their reputations were, among their peers and their subordinates as well as within the larger political context, can prove instructive for those who succeed them, both in appointing and in serving.

7

OWWO

The Bush Senate-Confirmed
Presidential Appointees:
Political Hacks or Savvy Politicians?

W ho were the presidential appointees of George Bush's administration? What were their basic demographics (gender, race, age,
party affiliation, etc.)? How did they achieve their PAS positions? What were the benefits and sacrifices of accepting their jobs? Further, what were the Bush PASs' backgrounds and experience in and
knowledge of government? How did their tenure and relations with the
White House and with other PASs affect the quality of the PAS workforce? In both categories, identity and qualifications, how did the Bush
PASs compare with those who had gone before them, particularly Ronald
Reagan's PASs? To what extent is the conventional wisdom about PASs
(that they are unqualified political hacks) an accurate characterization of
George Bush's appointees?

The data to answer these questions and those posed in subsequent
chapters came from three sources: an initial set of interviews with nineteen persons in government, a survey of PASs in the Bush administration
that was administered in the summer of 1992 through the auspices of the
General Accounting Office, and a series of confidential interviews that
was subsequently conducted with PASs (twenty-nine individuals) and
others in government (seven). The various interviews are the source of
any unattributed quotes used throughout (see the appendixes for the complete survey, survey and interview methodologies, interview questions,
and lists of interviewees).

Identity: Who Were the Bush Appointees?

There were few surprises in the Bush PAS Survey results. In fact, they so closely paralleled the popular image of a senior political official that one could hazard a characterization of the "typical" PAS and probably be right on point. To wit:

The typical Bush PAS in the Bush administration was a white, married, male Republican, aged fifty or older. He was comfortably upper or upper-middle class. He was well educated. His undergraduate degree was in the liberal arts, political science, science, engineering, business, or history. He held at least a master's degree, Ph.D., or law degree. He lived in the larger Washington, D.C., metropolitan area prior to accepting his Bush PAS appointment and had served previously in various levels of government and in at least one of the Reagan administrations. He worked in what might be termed middle management at Executive Level (EL) 3 or 4 in the Bush administration (see table 7.1).

The typical PAS had no or very limited previous experience supervising staff or bearing direct responsibility for budgets over $10 million. Immediately prior to his current PAS service he worked in government at the federal, state, or local level, or in the business sector. After his PAS service he expected to go into the business sector, research, or academia, or to be self-employed, rather than return to government.

He was basically satisfied with most aspects of his job and would continue in it or in another PAS position, should the occasion arise. He was unhappy with the job protections for civil service workers in that he felt unable to dismiss or reassign them easily. However, he was generally well-satisfied with his ability to direct and work with senior career employees.

He thought highly of the responsiveness and competence of his executive colleagues and subordinates, both political and career. He consulted them frequently on all phases of policy from feasibility to implementation, on staff and budget decisions, and on most of his work tasks. He felt he was held accountable for his work to a significant degree. He found working the federal budget process the most difficult of his tasks.

While he took a financial loss to accept his job, he expected a significant gain when he left it. If he were to leave his job prior to the end of the Bush administration, it would probably be to pursue a career opportunity with a higher salary elsewhere, although the stress of his job would factor into any decision to leave early.

He was well-connected to the Republican party and President Bush and knew many other PASs in the administration. He believed recruitment of capable persons to PAS service would be helped by raising salaries and by shortening and simplifying the appointment and confirmation process, particularly the White House, FBI, and Senate clearances. The following tables and discussion add detail to the picture of this "typical PAS."

Table 7.1. Who Were the Bush PASs? (in percent)

Age	
30–40	10
41–50	25
51–60	33
61–70	28
71 +	4
Gender	
Female	17
Male	83
Race/ethnic origin	
Caucasian	81
Hispanic	6
African-American	4
Other	5
Marital status	
Married	87
Unmarried	13
Undergraduate major	
Liberal arts	20
Government/Political Science	20
Science	17
Engineering	16
Finance/business	14
History	12
Highest college or graduate degree	
B.A./B.S.	22
M.A.	23
Ph.D., L.L.D., M.D.	53
Party affiliation	
Republican	70
Democrat	18
Independent	6
Executive level	
EL 1	4
EL 2	8
EL 3	22
EL 4	56
EL 5	8
Other	2
Prior location, local to D.C. area	59

Source: The Bush PAS Survey
Note: Between 165 and 180 PASs provided descriptive information in the above categories.

PASs came to their initial PAS position in the Bush administration through a variety of channels, some overlapping. Eighty-nine were recommended by a cabinet member, agency head, or colleague, thirty-six by President Bush, thirty-five by a member of Congress, twenty-two by their party, while eighteen were self-referred, thirty came through other means, and curiously, nine were uncertain how they came to the attention of the White House Presidential Personnel Office (PPO).

As discussed above, a constant source of complaint has been the amount of time it takes for an appointee to be confirmed after the president's nomination. While the time varied greatly, with some processes lasting many months, a comparison of nomination and confirmation dates reported in the Bush PAS Survey revealed that the median number of days for confirmation was only seventy, though the mean was eighty-three days, indicating that some confirmations took a very long time.

There was a fairly representative spread among respondents to the Bush PAS Survey throughout the five executive levels of PAS service. Additionally, a few were in other categories that are comparable to ELs 4 or 5 or, surprising in status-conscious Washington, did not know their executive level.

The majority of appointees lived in the metropolitan Washington, D.C., area prior to assuming their initial PAS position in the Bush administration. When they leave their job most of the locals will stay in town, as will some, but not most, who moved there to assume their PAS position. One Democratic PAS mover was "ready to go home unless a new and interesting position developed in the Clinton administration." He noted that "some people forget why they came here and will do a lot to stay here once they get Potomac fever." For many of the newcomers the move was seen as a temporary adventure, resume enhancer, or as service to their country or president, and they were quite ready to go back home. "This has been a nice run," said another, but he was ready to resume his former life, as he had always planned. Said another, "I'm going home after this. I don't have Potomac fever. I'm not 'a survivor.'"

Post-PAS salary expectations pointed to both the financial value and the cost of political service. As discussed in chapter 5, PAS salary, per se, is a potent disincentive for long tenure for many. Yet many PASs hope their experience will translate into a significant post-PAS salary boost, as attested by the 36 percent who believed their salary would increase anywhere from 51 percent to more than 200 percent post-PAS service (see table 7.2).

It is possible that those expecting large increases were substantially the same group that reported a moderate-to-great sacrifice in accepting

Table 7.2. Financial Expectations, Post–PAS Service (in percent)

Previous salary	
$50,000–$99,999	57
$100,000–$149,000	20
$150,000–$200,000	8
Over $200,000	9
Overall financial effect of	
accepting PAS job	
Great sacrifice	21
Moderate sacrifice	30
Moderate benefit	19
Great benefit	3
Salary expectations post–PAS job	
No change/decrease	35
Increase <50%	29
Increase 51–100%	15
Increase 101–200%	17
Increase >200%	4

Source: The Bush PAS Survey
Note: Between 165 and 180 PASs provided information.

their position (51 percent), now planning to resume their previous earning power. Interestingly, the percent of those who indicated they had taken a moderate-to-great financial loss in accepting their Bush PAS position was very close to that reporting the same loss in the 1985 NAPA study of PASs who served between 1964 and 1984 (55 percent). This is not surprising, since PASs of any administration are drawn largely from the same socioeconomic classes.

Some planned to leave the administration for financial reasons even if Bush had been reelected. Energy Secretary James D. Watkins, for example, felt he could not afford the loss of military retirement pay he sustained when he signed on with the administration. "I can't afford it any more. I have had to give up $300,000 in retirement pay," he said.[1]

On the other hand, in the NAPA study of previous PASs, only 16.5 percent indicated that their service in government actually had significantly increased their earning power. It is likely that the expectations of the 36 percent of the Bush PASs who anticipated a significant raise, post service, were out of line with reality. This sad supposition seems to have come true in the wake of the Bush defeat, when many Washington-based PASs found themselves a surplus commodity on the political employment market, according to several *Washington Post* articles chronicling their fate.

It was clear from the Bush PAS Survey that in terms of identity, the PASs were a relatively homogeneous group as far as gender, race, education, and class were concerned. Given that many had recycled from Ronald Reagan's administrations, it was unlikely that the Bush PASs differed demographically in great detail from their immediate predecessors. How they may differ from their successors remains to be seen.

Qualifications: Revisiting the Conventional Wisdom

The lack of qualifications of many of the Reagan appointees has been enshrined in conventional wisdom (see chapter 2 for this discussion). To what extent did the Bush appointees fit that picture?

One means of assessing qualifications for PAS service is to consider previous employment. Thanks to the two previous Republican administrations (Reagan 1 and Reagan 2, as they are called), nearly half of Bush's PASs came directly from government (another 38 percent came from the business sector, law firms, and academia).

While some PASs were veteran presidential appointees, holding as many as six PAS positions over the past ten administrations, the Bush PAS Survey results indicated that for the great majority (79 percent), this was their first PAS position. This number, probably accurate, casts doubt on the claim of 67 percent of the Bush PASs that they had held a PAS position in Reagan 2. Most likely they were unclear about terminology (strange, if true, given their current positions); for many it was a political, noncareer SES or Schedule C position, rather than a PAS position that they had held previously. Indeed, many in the Bush PAS group (sixty-seven) had served in noncareer SES positions (median number of positions, one), Schedule C positions (fifty-eight: median, one position), or other federal employment (ninety-four: median, two positions). Because these groups overlap, it is difficult to determine the exact number of the PASs who had had previous federal government experience, but clearly, a very high percentage of the Bush appointees were *not* newcomers. This was in clear contrast to the PASs of Reagan 1, the great majority of whom had not served previously in the federal government.

A fair number of PASs had also had had personal experience in electoral politics beyond the presidency, some thirty having been elected previously to at least one office. City government claimed thirteen elected officials serving a range of two to eighteen years with a median of six years. Six persons had been elected to county government with a range of one to twenty-three years of service, also with a median of six years. Eleven had been elected to state government with a range of four to nineteen years (median six years) and two had been elected to serve in the federal government with a range of fourteen to twenty years (median seventeen years). These are in addition to others who had run unsuccessfully.

While many leave Washington after their PAS service, many also stay and recycle, if not into government, at least into the lobbying business. Washington's Revolving Door was still fully operational for the Bush PASs, despite the Republican loss of the White House in 1992; there were clearly those who gained a great deal, thanks to the contacts they made during their PAS time. Given where they came from, where did the Bush PASs expect to go after they left the administration? (see table 7.3).

Generally, the PASs sorted themselves out over the options offered for postgovernment service more evenly than they had for their pre-PAS employment (respondents were asked to check as many options as applied for the future). Clearly, many who had previously worked for the government (possibly in political positions) planned to go elsewhere after the election, even if Bush were to be reelected.

Table 7.3. Where Did The Bush PASs Work Before and Where Did They Expect to Work After Their Current Jobs?

Employment Setting	Pre-PAS Occupation (%) N=180	Post-PAS Expectation[a] (%) N=146
Federal, state, or local government	48	23
Business/corporate	18	46
Self-employed	6	38
College/research	11	37
Think tank	1	17
Interest group	1	8
Law firm	9	22
Nonprofit organization	3	20
Retirement	0	14
Undecided	–	16

Source: The Bush PAS Survey.

[a]Respondents were given the opportunity to check multiple responses for this category.

Many expected to go into the corporate sector, research firms, or think tanks, Washington's local cottage industry. Constance Horner, head of Bush's PPO, for example, landed at the Brookings Institution as a guest scholar. Others, such as Jack Kemp, secretary of Housing and Urban Development (HUD), and Richard Cheney, secretary of defense (DOD), went to the Heritage Foundation and the American Enterprise Institute, respectively, Washington bastions of conservative thought. Both men briefly nurtured presidential ambitions in the 1996 campaign. Some, such as White House Counsel C. Boyden Gray, founded their own think tanks to keep the Republican flame alive and strategize for the 1994 and 1996 elections. Others took to the airwaves for the same purpose, such as Lynn Martin, secretary of labor, who went to work as a radio commentator, and White House Chief of Staff John Sununu, who went into television.

Those choosing self-employment might be planning to go through the revolving door to market their access to Congress and the agencies they formerly supervised (within Office of Government ethics restrictions, presumably) as consultants or lobbyists to various business or even foreign interests. Edward Derwinski, secretary of veterans affairs, and Carla A. Hills, U.S. trade representative, among others, formed their own consulting firms.

Some went directly into lobbying. Manuel Lujan, Jr., secretary of the interior, for instance, became a lobbyist for a development company whose efforts to build a resort on Park Service land in New Mexico he had supported while in the administration. HUD's deputy secretary, Alfred DelliBovi, with no previous banking experience, became president of a specialized government-backed bank that lends mortgage money to savings and loans associations. His 1992 PAS salary was $129,500. His new salary: more than $250,000.

Others wrote books, formed political action committees (PACs), and went on the lecture circuit, some to assess presidential possibilities, such as William J. Bennett, Bush drug czar and former head of the National Endowment for the Humanities; Jack Kemp; Lamar Alexander, secretary of education; James A. Baker, III, secretary of state and Bush campaign chief; Lynn Martin; and Richard Cheney. Oliver North went stumping for a Senate seat from Virginia and became a millionaire in the process, thanks to book royalties and $25,000 speaking fees. Others did it just for the money, such as generals Norman Schwartzkopf and Colin Powell (the latter's standard speech fee is $60,000, and his book deal paid $6 million).

Some went into other government jobs, such as four-time PAS Constance Berry Newman, director of Bush's Office of Personnel Management who became deputy at the Smithsonian Institution. One Reagan PAS even recycled into the Clinton White House, to the astonishment of Washington wags. David R. Gergen, senior policy advisor to Reagan, previously having been recycled from Nixon, claimed no savings when he left Reagan's employ in 1984 for the television, think tank, news media, and lecture circuit. His White House experience paid off handsomely. A popular speaker and writer, his income shot up dramatically, such that he earned more than $1 million in the seventeen months of January 1992 through May 1993, when he joined the Clinton White House and dropped back down to the more mundane $125,000 salary for his EL 3 position.

A term or two as president proved a good revenue enhancer. Japanese tours seem to be particularly profitable—Ronald Reagan earned an infamous $2 million fee from Japan for two twenty-minute speeches and several appearances during a weeklong visit in 1989. George Bush gave his family values speeches for the controversial Unification Church of the Rev. Sun Myung Moon for a fee unspecified but widely assumed to be well into seven figures. Bush's post–White House standard stump fee was $80,000, but he made $100,000 for a single speech to the 1993 Amway Convention. Being a former first lady or vice president had its rewards, as well. Barbara Bush's usual fee for a single speech was between $40,000 and $60,000, while Dan Quayle's was around $12,500.

Quayle went back to his family business of newspaper publishing and joined the Hudson Institute as chair of its Competitiveness Center, while nurturing hopes of an eventual return to public office. Marilyn Quayle, outspoken defender of traditional womanhood and keeper of the home fires, added back her original family name (Tucker) and resumed her law career, joining a law firm in Indiana and leaving her husband in Washington to care for their four children for the remainder of the school year.

In the past two decades, law firms around the nation have seen the value of having a Washington office, creating a massive jobs program for recycled politicians. Many PASs, such as Lamar Alexander, James Baker, Secretary of State Lawrence S. Eagleburger, Attorney General William P. Barr, and Solicitor General Kenneth Starr, went that route.

Some PASs went into academia, such as Louis Sullivan, secretary of Health and Human Services, who became president at Morehouse College School of Medicine, and others went into public interest advocacy, such as William Reilly, Environmental Protection Agency chief, who became senior fellow at the World Wildlife Fund.

Some moves, while legal, prompted public outrage: Abraham D. Sofaer, a former federal judge and the State Department's top lawyer from 1985 to 1990, agreed for an undisclosed sum (widely believed to be at least

$500,000) to represent Libya in the attack on Pan Am Flight 103, in which 259 passengers and crew members were killed.[2]

Tenure and Quality

Because questions of quality are related to length of experience in office, we sought to assess the length of the tenure of Bush PASs. This proved to be impossible without White House assistance, which was not forthcoming. The alternative was to gather that information from the Bush PAS Survey respondents who, since they were still in office, obviously had not completed their tenure. Instead, we focused on tenure-related issues.

However, we encountered considerable difficulty in phrasing a question that would get at those issues for the various classes of executives in the agencies. We settled on two questions that elicited subjective responses, asking PASs, not if tenure were short or long, which proved too difficult to interpret, but rather their assessment of how tenure (of both political and career executives) in their agency impacted the effectiveness of operations there. Contrary to theory and to careerists' widespread conviction, PASs consistently expressed satisfaction with the level of turnover in their agency, with 79 percent saying PAS tenure resulted in "very" or "generally" effective operations; 73 percent said the same for noncareer Senior Executive Service (NSES) members, 79 percent for career SESs (CSES).

When we asked about factors contributing to executive employee turnover we found that many responded "no basis/not applicable," and few reasons were chosen by more than 50 percent of the respondents as having even "some" or a "moderate" impact on tenure. Two factors in particular, interpersonal conflict (52 percent for conflict with other PASs and 53 percent for conflict with NSESs) and stress on personal or family life (PASs' assessment of 57 percent for NSESs), did seem to take their toll on political appointees. PASs cited burnout (50 percent), stress on personal or family life (52 percent), and policy disagreement (62 percent) as major factors in CSES turnover. PAS stress level and the reasons for it are discussed in more depth in chapter 8.

Despite PASs' assertions that they were happy with the degree of turnover in their agency, there was no disagreement among them about the harmful effects of high turnover in the political leadership. As one PAS said, "the viscosity is higher in government due to turnover," it takes longer for agencies to move, to get things done. Additionally, rapid turnover hurts the agencies because the "time slippage" involved in getting a new secretary and her or his staff on board is repeated when the secretary leaves. As one survey respondent wrote, "By the time political appointees realize that career personnel can be trusted and can in fact be very supportive and loyal, the term of the appointee is over and the cycle begins anew with a new appointee. This way of thinking usually cuts government overall efficiency by 40–60 percent. The government cannot afford this kind of gridlock while the new appointee learns she or he can work with career people."

Another PAS observed, "If the secretary leaves, that is a revolution within the agency. Cabinet government is dictatorship. The departure of the secretary ends the agenda within the agency—it's life and death for the other PASs in the agency. . . . It's less of a problem when lower-level PASs leave; it has less impact on the agency. But when the top leadership goes, everything else grinds to a halt."

Another noted the companion effects of a vacancy at the top. The agency is left without an advocate in the larger political system and with a diminished ability to accomplish its mission: "It leaves a gap, leaves an agency leaderless. The staff can't take on any new initiatives and they lose their access to the external network to get what they need from the White House and the other agencies. An agency needs a political leader—nothing can happen in the agency without one."

What causes PASs to leave before the end of an administration? Lack of a promise to stay is a key factor. While Ronald Reagan made no effort to keep his appointees in office, both Jimmy Carter and George Bush asked their appointees to stay for the duration of their terms. Consequently, their appointees stayed longer than did Reagan's. As Frank Hodsoll, deputy for management at OMB, suggested, "Though we don't have involuntary servitude in this country, the White House should make a greater effort at the front end to secure a commitment that the person will stay a reasonable length of time. The greater the responsibility the job carries, the longer should be the time commitment."

The Senate became concerned with the effects of rapid PAS turnover during the Reagan administrations. Senator John Glenn, chair of the Governmental Affairs Committee, was most vocal about this problem. He made a habit of discussing with nominees their tenure expectations during their confirmation hearing and asking them to remain on the job throughout Bush's term.

As discussed above, finances play a part in some PASs' decision to leave early. The reality is that many PASs could (and did) make a great deal more money outside of government (viz., the 51 percent who made a moderate-to-great financial sacrifice to accept their PAS position). After a while, the stress and workload of political service start to make other offers sound tempting, particularly for middle-aged PASs who have children to educate. As one such PAS said, "Being a political appointee is like being a riverboat gambler, but it's not as easy being a riverboat gambler when you're forty-six and have kids in college." And, as another remarked, "The intensity is wearying. If you try to do the right thing, eventually people will come back to get you."

Gerald Shaw, general counsel for the Senior Executive Association, voiced sympathy with those feelings: "The job requires quite a bit of sacrifice. They [PASs] get ripped to shreds in the policy process. Everything you do is questioned, the media and others assign bad motives, your family is fair game, you face a lowered salary and public scrutiny. . . . This is a democracy where the prevailing view of the way you win is by destroying the other." Or, in the immortal words of President Harry S Truman, "If you want a friend in Washington, get a dog."

One PAS contrasted those new to government service with the in-and-outers who had done it before. The newcomers, particularly those coming from business, get frustrated with not getting their agenda through or with the slow pace of dealing with the bureaucracy. Also, through their work they make contacts that offer them good employment opportunities and it simply makes sense to go when they get a choice offer. They are not especially interested in government service, per se. The true in-and-outers, on the other hand, have less interest over time in "the big bucks" and more interest in the work of government. They stay in longer and are more likely to come back to it than are the "here-and-gone types."

The essentially transient nature of the assignment does not call forth much long-term loyalty. It is simply not a long-term job; as noted previously, the prevailing culture is that PASs *not* let any grass grow under their feet. Further, some people do not really know what they are getting into in PAS positions, or for personal reasons, cannot stay too long, or feel they have accomplished their own goals and it is time to move on. "The good ones moved less in Bush. Of those who left, most did so because their agenda was accomplished, there was no reason to stay," commented one careerist. Ambition drives others to leave who want to capitalize on their experience while it is still worth something on the open market.

This transient quality of political jobs can lead to a variety of problems. One PAS addressed the damage caused by

PASs with no experience in government who want to use it to pursue their own agenda and in a fairly ruthless way. They use people and don't understand how bureaucracy functions. It takes so long to learn that they are gone before they do learn. These are the senior officials who show up at the wrong meeting because they want to control everything—they gut their whole hierarchy by showing up inappropriately at lower-level meetings and taking over. They don't understand the system.

The most troubled government programs were those with the highest turnover. For example, the General Services Agency had three chiefs from 1987 to 1992. Health and Human Services had twelve assistant secretaries of housing in twelve years (ten in the eight Reagan years) before Secretary Sullivan came on board. His long tenure throughout the Bush administration provided the stability the agency needed to get its work done, partly because it kept the same political leadership in place throughout the agency. Doc Cooke, director for administration and management at the Defense Department and one of the most respected senior careerists, noted various incentives for PASs to leave early: "Some don't really like it that much; those who like it and are good at it get promoted as other vacancies arise; a certain number of them screw up in one way or another and get eased out; people coming from business think they're running a hierarchical line structure and they aren't. A certain number of businessmen never get it—they quit in frustration and blame the bureaucracy."

One PAS believed that turnover in itself was not necessarily bad: "Three and a half years are long enough because of the burnout factor." Echoing another, he continued, "But the gaps are more problematic. While the 'Acting X' is running things everyone's waiting for the real appointee to come. Everything's on hold."

However, as one careerist noted, two problems would arise for PASs if all appointees did stay the entire four years: They would all be out on the job market at the same time. Second, outwaiting the ethics code and conflict of interest strictures means that appointees have a one-year delay before being able to lobby their previous agency. They have to be out early enough in an administration to last that time and be available while their contacts are still worth something, that is, while their president still holds office. Timing, in this case, is everything if Washington's door is to revolve for them. Thus, the law of unintended consequences strikes—the ethics code becomes an inadvertent cause of shortened tenure among appointees.

Near the end of an administration a mix of tenure-related issues is at play. One PAS summed up the sense of things among the PASs late in what turned out to be the only Bush administration:

> At the end of the term in an election year the tension among PASs esca-
> lates—for most of them Bush's reelection is life and death. They have to
> figure out how to protect themselves in a presidential transition. Even if
> Bush is reelected the secretary may go or may not be reappointed, so
> lower-level appointees are all anxious. They're trying to find other em-
> ployment while not undercutting their effectiveness, programs, or boss.
> The secretary is also playing his cards [close to the vest]: "We're here to
> do our job, we came to serve this administration, we serve at the pleasure
> of the president," he says. Everyone pretends everything's calm but in re-
> ality everything's crazy beneath the surface. . . . PASs feel the need to get
> out while they still have some currency to get another job.

What Would Make for Better Recruitment?

Of the various suggestions offered in the PAS survey for recruitment
of highly qualified people to PAS positions, only two were rated as being
of "great" or "very great" help by a majority of the survey respondents: 55
percent thought salaries should be raised ("but the public won't buy it,"
as one said) and 72 percent thought the entire nominations and confirmation process should be simplified. This last was particularly telling,
given the frequency of complaints voiced by respondents both in the survey and in the interviews about the length and complexity of the appointment and confirmation process. As noted above, eighty-three days
was the mean number of days for confirmation from the time the nomination was received. The Senate study of confirmation delay indicated
that the White House was largely responsible for the protracted confirmation process. This was corroborated by the responses of 87 percent that
shortening the time it took for the White House clearance would be
"somewhat" to "very greatly" helpful in facilitating recruitment of
highly qualified people to PAS positions.[3]

Interviewees indicated that some parts of the process were in themselves enough to drive people away. The universally disliked FBI clearance, for example, was characterized by one as "horrible," going as it does
into all of one's activities since birth, including every address and one's
neighbors there, every job, every organization one ever belonged to or
gave money to, "from the Chamber of Commerce to Scouts to hospital
boards," and every drug (prescribed or illegal) ever taken. Investigators
also want to know about every trip out of the country and the traveling

companions who went along, the nominee's lifestyle, sexual orientation, finances, and tax returns. The investigation extends to her or his family, as well.[4]

There was also the fear among potential nominees that some behavior considered appropriate, or at least legal, in business would be unearthed and reported on the front page of the *Washington Post* in a way that would damage the reputation of the nominee. The Senate's investigation is more public and more open to leaks, making this a not unrealistic fear. (The stress of and dangers posed by the Senate confirmation process itself are discussed in greater detail in chapter 9.)

While no one wanted to ease the ethical considerations that had helped rescue political service from the depths to which it had sunk during the Reagan years, there was widespread conviction that the financial disclosure, divestiture, and revolving door restrictions made it difficult to recruit PASs and SESs into government service. This was particularly true in the Defense Department, which is more involved in procurement than are the domestic agencies. There are "fewer rising young tigers and more older retirees or lawyers [in PAS service] who can more easily move in and out of jobs than can younger persons and those in production industries," said one longtime careerist at Defense. One PAS wished that the divestiture and other requirements were not so restrictive because they made it difficult for "people like me [i.e., people of means] to serve."

How Difficult Are Political Positions? PASs' Perceptions

One approach to evaluating qualifications is to analyze PASs' sense of the ease or difficulty of various aspects of their job in relation to their past professional experience in order to determine if particular kinds of experiences led PASs to feel a greater sense of self-confidence in their work. In doing so we focused on PASs' occupation immediately prior to their initial PAS position in the Bush administration and their previous experience in management and in budgeting. We asked individuals to make an assessment of their own ease or difficulty of accomplishing their current job. While obviously a subjective judgment, it did allow a glimpse into the self-perceptions of the PASs.

A few, telling relationships were found between current ease or difficulty of job and a PAS's prior occupation or primary function. As might be expected, those coming from the federal government more often found directing senior civil servants easy (75 percent, as compared to 62 percent easy overall). Those whose primary function in their previous position was government relations were most likely to find such supervision easy (75 percent). However, those coming from academia or a research firm were much less likely to find directing senior civil servants easy (39 percent).

Those who had come from the business sector reported the most ease in dealing with the news media (55 percent of that group considered it easy, compared with 39 percent overall). However, this business-oriented group encountered the most difficulty dealing with the informal party networks that affected the work of their agency or department (35 percent, compared with 19 percent overall who experienced difficulty).

Those who were self-employed prior to their PAS service were more likely to find the lengthy, convoluted and consensus style of the decision-making procedures of their agency difficult (63 percent, compared with 43 percent overall who found it difficult). Those who had come directly from academia or research organizations reported the most difficulty in dealing with the White House (39 percent, compared with 16 percent overall).

As a group, PASs were notably inexperienced in personnel supervision. While PASs' prior direct supervisory experience with paid staff varied greatly (from those who supervised none to those who carried direct responsibility for sixty thousand employees), the median number they supervised was only seven employees. Supervision of volunteers was likewise varied. Some PASs had managed as many as fifty volunteers; 75 percent had supervised none directly.

Equally diverse were the numbers of employees in the organizational units for which PASs had previously been responsible. While they ranged from zero to as many as 150,000, the median was thirty-three paid staff employees. Volunteer employees ranged from zero to one thousand but again, most PASs (66 percent) had not supervised volunteers in their larger organizational units.

While a few PASs had had experience supervising large staffs, only 12 percent had directly supervised more than fifty, and fewer than one-fifth had had even indirect responsibility for more than five hundred employees. This relative inexperience in personnel supervision could have serious repercussions in government agencies where PASs are often directly responsible for many employees and indirectly responsible for hundreds, thousands, tens of thousands, or even hundreds of thousands more.[5] Given this, the PPO should take personnel management experience into consideration when it recruits, assesses, or trains candidates.

Although two-thirds of the PASs had had some direct budget responsibility, one-third had not. When added to the 37 percent who had had responsibility for budgets of only up to $10 million, that meant that 70 percent of the PASs had not had responsibility for budgets of more than $10 million (see table 7.4).

While the federal government is certainly replete with accountants

Table 7.4. How Much Prior Budget Responsibility Had PASs Had?

Amount of Budget (in dollars)	Percentage of PASs Responsible
Less than 1,000,000	22
1,000,000–4,999,999	19
5,000,000–$9,999,999	8
10,000,000–24,999,999	11
25,000,000–100,000,000+	11

Source: The Bush PAS Survey.

and each major agency now has a chief financial officer, PASs are ultimately responsible for vast sums of money as they manage the ever-growing federal budget.[5] Given the "typical" PAS's difficulty with the federal budget process (61 percent found it "generally" or "very" difficult), the PPO should consider budget acumen along with personnel management experience when it recruits, assesses, or trains candidates, particularly those in the big-ticket agencies.

How Competent Are Political Appointees and Careerists?
PASs Evaluate Their Colleagues

PASs generally rated one another highly, in terms of their competence and responsiveness to political policy direction. Of 167 PASs surveyed, 79 percent judged their colleagues to be competent, while 84 percent termed their colleagues responsive. The numbers were similar for the 154 NSESs questioned: 70 percent said their colleagues were competent, and 82 percent judged them responsive.

There were, of course, exceptions. One respondent in an independent regulatory commission (IRC) despaired of his colleagues who were then adjudicating law in an area in which they had not previously specialized "outside the Beltway" (that land of non-federal-government reality of which Washington's denizens and pundits speak fondly but to which few are prepared to move). "I don't know what the White House saw in their credentials or lack thereof," he wrote. As one interviewee observed, "Some of my (PAS) colleagues have to work pretty hard to do their job."

Other PASs felt that their own PAS colleagues were good, but mentioned problems at other agencies that get more than their share of incompetent appointees, particularly the well-known "turkey farms" or "dumping grounds," as they are unkindly called, agencies such as the Housing and Urban Development Department (HUD), the General Services Administration (GSA), and the Federal Emergency Management Agency (FEMA). One careerist observed that "agencies like HUD and GSA that have lots of political slots have to place the sons and daughters of big contributors, so there is less quality there."

One PAS noted that the status of the agency follows the status of its secretary. "The quality of secretaries varies by agency. Those with the best reputations are at State, Justice, Education, and Labor. Those with the worst are at Interior, Energy, and Health and Human Services."

As noted in chapter 4, Bush got particularly bad marks for his choice of ambassadors. With eleven of his nominees members of Bush Team 100 (those who gave at least $100,000 to his campaign), Bush gave the naked impression of jobs for sale that most presidents seek to avoid. Marvin F. Moss, chief of staff for Democratic Senator Paul Sarbanes, made this assessment:

> Ronald Reagan appointed a lot of truly incompetent people to ambassadorial positions around the world, such as his personal secretary, whom he sent to Denmark. . . . They created scandals in the countries they were sent to. . . . [But] the Senate had no solid basis to oppose them.
>
> Much more than had Carter, Ford, Nixon, and Reagan, though, Bush appointed to countries that had previously had professional foreign service officers [careerists] as ambassadors a series of Republican high rollers who had given $100,000 to the Bush campaign *and* were unqualified. Only three were not confirmed. One well-known case was [of someone] who had worked in advertising in the 1988 campaign. He was sent to Iceland where he spent his time there faxing, working on the campaign. He was an ambassador for 112 days before he rejoined the 1992 campaign.

Moss noted that it costs fifty to sixty thousand dollars to train each ambassador.

One careerist expressed dismay at some political ambassadorial appointments:

> Rampant patronage is a pretty shabby way for the United States to conduct its business in 1991. A big contribution to the party ought not constitute qualifications for political appointments. Higher standards are needed. Sometimes the standard is met, but often it is not. No other major country appoints its ambassadors with the frivolity that the United States uses. . . . No country's going to raise Cain because it's been given

a dunderhead for an ambassador, but lack of competence represents opportunities foregone to advance U.S. interests around the world.

Bush's nonambassadorial appointments were somewhat more kindly received. One Republican PAS, somewhat estranged from the administration, judged his colleagues as "not too bad," noting that he had nothing to compare them with, but, in any case, "It's not their competency I question, but their perspective." Others expressed appreciation for the skills of those PASs who had gotten their jobs because of their competence, not as political payoff.

Many PASs remarked on the very high level of cooperative relations among their colleagues, but noted also the competitiveness for resources, time, and turf that is everywhere apparent in politics. "I'm not possessive, but I protect my mandate," as one said. An outsider to Washington prior to his appointment, he was "bothered that government feeds on itself, with battles between and even within agencies." The lack of cooperation between agencies was particularly troubling for him because his agency was required by law to consult with other agencies but they had no limit on their response time. "Sometimes, it seems they don't understand we all work for the same government," he sighed.

One Democrat discussed the great lack of collegiality within her IRC. There were no policy discussions, no give-and-take, no mutual respect for the members, no teamwork. In her estimation, "Republicans don't value government, so they don't work hard to put the right people in the right jobs, so you end up with mediocre people in government."

Elliot L. Richardson, perhaps the quintessential in-and-outer, has served in numerous political positions since Eisenhower's administration. He observed that

> the ethos of the Bush administration tended to be competitive. It bore earmarks of his experiences as captain of the Yale baseball team [viz., Bush Team 100]. It was a team orientation with an element of loyalty to the team captain. PASs reinforced the notion that they were Bush loyalists. How long they had been with Bush, if not determinative, was more relevant than in any previous administration.

One Republican discussed turf issues at his agency. He thought the other assistant secretaries (ASs) felt threatened by him, that he was trying to enlarge his area at their expense. "They operate out of the six-glass theory," he said. "All six ASs are represented by six glasses with the exact same water level—when any glass's level gets too high it has to be lowered until it's the same as the others."

Others confirmed what has been reported in the public administration literature, that the worst PASs were those coming directly from the business sector and, to a lesser extent, those from academia. "The business types don't understand how government works. They think government works like business and they can sit in their offices and issue orders and expect them to be obeyed."

Many PASs and careerists stated that the best PASs are those who have had previous government, particularly staff, experience. "Dick Cheney, for example, came originally as a horse holder and learned how the town functions," said one former appointee.

Charles Grizzle, former EPA assistant administrator for administration and resources management, saw commonalities among successful PASs: they are open-minded, willing to learn and trust, and they possess a sixth sense of when to delegate and when to make a decision oneself, noting the fine line between responsibility and authority. The unsuccessful PASs share commonalities as well. They

> come in with an agenda; they want to accomplish one or two things. This is a fatal flaw. You have to deal with everything that's on your plate. You can't let everything else go in the name of agenda. PASs' principal task is to manage the organization they inherit. Stewards/managers will have a more lasting impact than cause-oriented PASs. Generalists/political animals (those who understand the political process) will have more success than the apolitical/technical people who don't have a feel for the political process or how the town or the country works.
>
> Success can be measured by the degree of change in an agency, the number of programs scuttled, if there are no scathing IG or GAO reports, and if the PAS hasn't done anything to embarrass the administration. In other words, avoid real or trumped-up scandal, or even the appearance of scandal.

Connie Newman noted that the competence and self-confidence of the appointees influenced their willingness to ask questions and seek the counsel of careerists. Overall, Bush appointee competence was good, she felt, noting that there were few scandals in his administration and that those making the news (e.g., the savings and loans and HUD scandals) were "old scandals, hangovers from Ronald Reagan." This level of competence was related to the fact that "Bush and his people have been around before (as opposed to Carter and his neophytes in Washington), and they have the combination of skills that indicates they can operate in Washington." But there are three areas where appointees are most likely to get in trouble—Congress, the media, and interest groups, she said.

Steven D. Potts, as director of the Office of Government Ethics (OGE), personally signed off on all PASs before they went to the Senate. He was very impressed with the agency heads in his contacts with them regarding government standards. He felt that the emphasis the Bush administration placed on ethics in government at the beginning of the administration had borne fruit: "There has been no scandal of real significance, compared to other administrations."[7]

One PAS, a former SES, spoke highly of the benefit to the country of requiring a Senate confirmation of appointees, feeling that it insured better quality. Along with many others, she observed that those PASs who came from government service tended generally to have the most success. However, she noted that they also tended to have the tougher confirmation trials because they had a reputation to defend. "If they have done *anything*, they have made enemies, particularly if they tried to change things. In confirmation your career is on the line—it's very public and partisan and *very* stressful."

She felt that political chiefs of staff and special assistants (NSESs and Schedule Cs) were more troublesome than PASs because, while they had not had the public exposure of a confirmation, they did have the power of a high-level position. "They are the right-hand person, the closest aide to the secretary who tries to push around and dominate the PAS structure and operate ruthlessly with the careerists. They aren't in charge of any line operations, serve their principal only and have personal loyalty only and no institutional loyalty."

Some had horror stories to tell about appointees in the Reagan administrations. Deborah Gore Dean, for example, a Georgetown socialite and bartender trying to grow her own business, became Samuel Pierce's assistant in HUD. Their scandals still reverberate in the halls of HUD and in the newspapers. Although Pierce escaped indictment, if not suspicion, Dean was convicted in late October 1993 on charges of using her job to funnel federal money to Republican insiders, friends, and Nixon's former attorney general, John N. Mitchell, her mother's companion.

The Civil Rights Commission was taken over by politicals during the Reagan era, completely changing its character. Its general counsel, a twenty-seven-year-old lawyer with a tax law background and no experience in supervision or civil rights law, headed an office of thirty-five lawyers, "a set-up not all that rare during the Reagan years," said one careerist.

One Bush secretary had a habit of surrounding himself with Schedule Cs, creating layers of bureaucracy between himself and the other appointees and between himself and the careerists, the classic problem of having too many appointees. As one careerist observed, "Maybe it's because he wanted to get things done in a hurry, but it's like putting a moat around the secretary."

One PAS, noting the claim that appointees bring fresh points of view and fresh blood to government, said, "Well, make of it what you will—not all of them are insightful and dynamic and not all [career] bureaucrats are tired. Judgment is the key ingredient for an able person."

Was There a Discernable Difference Between Reagan's and Bush's Appointees?

PASs' opinions about the differences between Ronald Reagan's and George Bush's appointees went in all directions. Few were for attribution; most of the comments that follow were made off the record.

Often, interviewees noted that many of the PASs in all three administrations (Reagan 1 and 2 and Bush) were the same people. The differences on which interviewees remarked usually started with the appointer. Ronald Reagan had a vision of what government should be—minimal: everything he did and every appointment he made was with an eye to that vision, to paring back government, which he defined as "the problem."

Table 7.5. Differences Between Ronald Reagan and George Bush

	Ronald Reagan	George Bush
Mission	clear goals	no mission, except to stay in office
Power	no power struggles among administration	lots of independent power groups
Structure	as long as you are accomplishing your goals who cares about structure?	lots of arguments over structure—little goal change from Reagan because no clear mission

Source: Gerald Shaw, Senior Executive Association counsel.

Gerald Shaw, counsel for the Senior Executive Association, characterized the differences between Reagan and Bush with a quick sketch (see table 7.5).

George Bush had trouble defining what he called "the vision thing," so he could not get to "the problem." As numerous pundits observed during the campaign of 1992, the reason he wanted to win was so that he could stay in office, where he felt he had a right to be: he wanted to win because he wanted to win. Unlike Reagan, who made his vision simple to the point of simplistic, Bush could not articulate a vision of where he wanted to take the country—he had no single, clear message around which voters could rally.

His appointments and personnel actions reflect that lack of focus. When the Far Right gave him grief he would give them an appointment— a surgeon general who did not believe in the right to abortion or a director of the office of family planning who did not believe in birth control, for example. Sometimes he offered up a head on a platter, such as John Frohnmayer's (chief of the National Endowment for the Arts), when the Religious Right became art critics, or Edwin Derwinski's (secretary of Veterans Affairs), when the veterans' lobby got angry over the closing or reassignment of underutilized veterans' hospitals. But no matter how much Bush gave them, he could never give his detractors enough to allay their deep suspicion that he was not one of them.[8]

According to some PASs, Bush often used IRC positions (except the chair) as political plums. This is a fairly safe thing to do, because the chair is the chief administrative officer and carries a great deal of weight in most IRCs. The other commissioners tend to follow her or his lead. However, when close votes are counted or lobbying is needed in Congress, the president does need strong, capable commissioners and so cannot afford to slough off on these appointments.

Most PASs were reluctant to distinguish between the two presidents' PASs. And, as many said Reagan's appointees were better as said Bush's were. Many did observe, though, that the Reagan White House was "more acutely attuned to political considerations" than the Bush White House. Said one, "It was a similar crowd, there wasn't a huge difference between them." But then he observed, "the Bush people were less ideological, more Washington-based, higher quality. Reagan dumped lower quality people, whom the PAS described as "low-quality hacks," at HHS and HUD, noting that one HHS chief of staff was convicted of fraud and served five months in prison.

Conversely, Bush was more likely, especially early on, to appoint people who believed in and cared about government.

Bush put in place a cabinet and a White House staff that [foretold] a style of governance—a conscientious, relentlessly mainstream Republican administration filled with pragmatists who prize public niceness. Bush promised fresh faces but hired old friends. . . . Packed with skilled, centrist Washingtonians, Bush's cabinet "could have been put together by the National Academy of Public Administration," Brookings Institution senior fellow Stephen Hess said. "These are people who won't make silly mistakes, people who are interested in governance." (Aberbach 1991, 239)

While no clear consensus about the differences in quality or competence between the Bush and Reagan people emerged in the interviews with the Bush PASs and careerists, some rather stark differences in characteristics did frequently appear (see table 7.6).

One PAS seemed somewhat wistful as she recalled the previous administration, noting differences not in skill or qualifications, but in philosophy and approach:

Ronald Reagan's PASs were more colorful, controversial, aggressive overall, and much more willing to fight. They had major knock-down fights over policy changes, blood all over the floor regarding export policies, for example. The Bush people seem to squelch fights down in the bureaucracy. This doesn't give the president the range of options he needs. Reagan allowed the turmoil to go on underneath—a lot more contentious issues went straight to him for resolution. In Bush, things get resolved lower down—any policy now going to the president has to have three policy options. . . . Colorful people don't show up as much in Bush's administration.

Ivan Selin, chair of the Nuclear Regulatory Commission, said,

The Bush people are much more professional than the Reagan people (that's not to say they're better). There is less personal aggrandizement, a higher ethical fiber. They're less likely to be looking out for themselves, thinking, "Where will this job take me?" than the Reagan people. However, there's less unity, less clear idea of where the administration is going. While Reagan had a simple, insufficiently nuanced policy, Bush is more pragmatic, less ideological. In general, his people are very competent—there's been no one like Energy Secretary Edwards [first head of the new department—a dentist with no energy policy experience].

When an administration brings in people who create scandals, isolate

Table 7.6. PAS-Reported Differences Between Bush's and Reagan's Appointees

George Bush's PASs	Ronald Reagan's PASs
Cabinet model of appointments at first, then White House model	Central clearance—White House control of appointments from the start
Less control in the 3rd and 4th levels of the bureaucracy	Careful placement deep in the bureaucracy down to the 4th level and Schedule Cs
Team players/Bush loyalists	Ideologues; as many as 80% came from Nixon's administrations
Trouble with "the vision thing"; No clear goals except to stay in office	Simplistic, clear message and mission—Reagan and PASs
"Government of colleagues" experienced in government	"Government of strangers." Newcomers, especially in Reagan's first term
Committed to government service	"What's in it for me?" Government service as a resume-enhancer
More professional/ administrative goals—managed agency well, did not push the administrative state	Agenda-driven; built on and extended Nixon's administrative state
Emphasis on tenure/lower turnover	No emphasis on tenure/high turnover
High ethical standards, few scandals	Many lapses, many scandals
Disdainful of Reagan's "party hacks"	They were considered "the party hacks"
More women and minorities	"Good old boys," some younger
Bush supported public servants; respected government, public service	Reagan attacked public servants; "Government is the problem"

Source: Bush PAS interviews.

themselves, or are incompetent, it not only makes the agency and ad-ministration look bad with the public, it also sours relations with the ca-reerists. That was the theme of the Reagan years. Overall, however, the Bush years did not carry that same motif. There was far less criticism of the competence of his appointees, according to one careerist.

Jerry Shaw recalled Reagan's agenda-driven focus. His people were

> extremely ideological. They wanted very quickly to stamp their presence on the federal workforce. They attempted to weed out Democrats, both political and career. . . . Political operative Lyn Nofziger's motto was their own early on: "Don't you ever forget, the best government is no govern-ment."
>
> According to [one estimate], 80% of Reagan's appointees had been in the Nixon White House and had done nothing in the four years they were out but decide what they were going to do when they got back in and what they wanted to do was "nothing" in the regulatory agencies. Their goal was to take control of the agencies and make those they didn't like ineffective. Many good career people left in the early years because of the ideological shift—they moved to the private sector.

Long-term occupation of the White House may be the dream of the political parties but it carries negative consequences for filling govern-ment's political leadership. According to Shaw,

> By Reagan 2 many of the ideologues had left because they had accom-plished what they wanted to. George Bush probably brought in less-qual-ified people in lower-level political jobs than was true in Reagan. It was probably a logical extension of twelve years of one-party rule. Bush's pay-back was less, not that different a crowd from Reagan. But in Bush, peo-ple in their twenties and early thirties who had never held a job were placed in very responsible NSES positions, especially in Education, Com-merce, and the Small Business Administration. Also, lots of young Hill staffers were placed in executive positions; some had falsified their SF 171 to make them appear more qualified—one had been in prison, one had run his business into bankruptcy.

Shaw noted further that a party's third term has fewer qualified peo-ple from which to draw. "The high flyers have come and gone; the ones who try to stay are those who don't have a good background, or qualifica-tions, or any place to go, or they would have gone already." As he and others observed, once agenda-driven appointees accomplish their goals they are ready to move on because "government gets old after a while."

Shaw spoke of what he considered Bush's obviously wise choices, "Sullivan at HHS, Newman at OPM, Shirley Peters at IRS, Gwendolyn King at SSA. But lower down at the deputy assistant secretary level, there was a lack of qualifications." He continued, "In Bush there were lots of young, arrogant appointees without executive or leadership skills who screamed and yelled at careerists. They didn't know any better, they were too young. But it was ulcer city among careerists. There were heart attacks, high blood pressure, alcoholism. It was a rough time."

Another careerist noted that

Reagan's PASs were more philosophical, ideological, agenda-driven, mission-driven than any previous president [in his experience]. It was much broader than just political objectives. Once in office they felt they had a mandate to implement their approach to government. It was very, very frightening. They were riding their individual, personal agendas more than Reagan's. Some had a way-out, political philosophy (libertarian) and they were trying to implement *Mandate for Leadership I*, which was never a Ronald Reagan paper. They were much more distrustful of government: Government was bad; bureaucrats were bad. George Bush's appointees did much less of this. His PASs were more into good government; they were institutional people into improving government.

Hill staffer Moss had this assessment:

Bush continued the same general trend regarding appointees. They were dismantlers, not improvers; it was less overtly political, but just as solid a trend. Many Reagan PASs were put in charge of programs or agencies they had strenuously criticized—AID, Legal Services Corp, Watts at Interior, the Park Service—it was the "fox in the chicken house" effect. Congress refused to confirm some of them. The 1982 tax bill, the reconciliation bill, made it clear that the Reagan administration was placing people who had a vested interest in seeing that programs did not work in agencies and programs to which they were opposed. This was a completely new departure in government that many found irresponsible and shocking.

The appointees to the SEC, ICC, FCC, and other regulatory agencies were all deregulatory people. They initiated legislation to further deregulate the agencies they managed. This resulted in some major disasters— the savings and loans scandal, airlines, and freight rail fees, in particular.

One reason for the poor relations between the Bush appointees and careerists was suggested by one high-level careerist: "The relationship with political appointees under Bush was much worse than under Reagan. The Bush people were smarter, and so they knew how to stop things when the president wanted them stopped. They knew the system better . . . and so they were able to get [Bush's] dirty work done" (Riccucci 1995, 225).

Nixon's and Carter's appointments drew praise from some careerists who noted a subsequent decline. Said one, in remarking that Bush's people were better than Reagan's,

> They are similar to Nixon's people in terms of qualifications, degrees, and experience. DOD is back to being run by military people, there are fewer politicals there now. The line between agencies that have traditionally been political (HUD, HHS, GSA) and those that haven't (EPA, DOD) was blurred by Reagan 1. DOD and EPA have been of high quality in Bush. The technical needs predominate, there is a limited number of PASs, NSESs and Schedule Cs.

Many PASs talked of and were disdainful of the party hacks who had discredited the Reagan administrations. This was also reflected in conversations with careerists, whose long-term orientation affords them an understanding of the larger issues of workforce morale. As Carol Bonosaro, executive director of the Senior Executive Association, observed,

> The difference between George Bush and Ronald Reagan is probably, as the president [Bush] would say, "the ethics thing." Early on, George Bush set high standards and communicated it very well to his appointees. Ronald Reagan's scandals (HUD, EPA) were very demoralizing to people in the SES "career core." The sense that the government was being run by a bunch of crooks made it difficult, aside from having to deal with them. The public image of the public service was damaged and with it the career service was [painted] with the same brush in the public eye.

Moss outlined the difference between the Democratic and Republican parties in their approach to government, as embodied in their leaders: Carter believed government had a role to play in almost every dimension of American life. Reagan believed government's role should be minimized. George Bush was only slightly behind Reagan's lead. Their appointees reflected their philosophy. Moss drew the contrast with Jimmy Carter's appointments, which were of good people who were interested in improving innovative programs, as opposed to the Reagan people who were opposed to the mission of their agency or who wanted to deregulate the IRCs. Reagan chose "Reagan Democrats," neoconservatives, for non-Republican IRC slots. This basis for selection carried over to lesser-known but important agencies, such as NLRB, which makes key labor decisions. . . . The Reagan appointees shifted the whole basis of labor law through the appeal process.

Moss felt that the quality of Bush appointees was not up to that of the Carter administration and had deteriorated in the past twelve years of Republican leadership. "Aside from ambassadors, Bush's choices *may* be marginally better than Reagan's. There have been no Jim Wattses in Bush's term (those so far out of the mainstream of American thought as to be egregious). George Bush is less ideological, less overtly interested in making government appear to be working less efficiently."

He did not see any differences between Reagan and Bush regarding political-career relations, however. "The professionals are generally superior to their political overseers," he said.

Elliot Richardson commented on the differences between Reagan and Bush:

> Generally, the Reaganites had a higher ratio of true believers. The right wingers never really believed Bush was one of them, despite his best efforts. . . . He nominated a lot of moderate Republicans, these were the early Bush people, pre-1990, so the loyalty litmus test brought in a different breed than the Reaganites.
>
> George Bush had fewer ideologues. He didn't treat seriously enough the third- and fourth-level jobs [the deputy assistant secretaries]. Reagan looked at those jobs and chose the fourth-level person in the campaign (the advance person) for the job. It was often a mismatch of skills—too many people in those jobs who were there due to patronage.

Moss noted that Bush talked more than Reagan did about appointing women and minorities, and he did, in fact, appoint women chiefs to many posts—OPM, Social Security Administration, Internal Revenue Service, Federal Labor Relations Agency, National Institutes of Health, Federal Trade Commission, Labor, Commerce, Peace Corps, PPO, Small Business Administration, and Surgeon General. Also, "minorities have done better than in previous administrations. Hispanics and Indians less so than Blacks. They feel slighted somewhat—only now are Hispanics getting organized."[9]

A careerist added that "Nixon was the first to advance women, Carter moved it on, but Reagan set it back—he claimed Schedule C secretaries in his count of women appointees. George Bush is pushing it up again, but it's still behind where it was, we're still in the dip from the Reagan years."

Conclusion

It seems obvious that, aside from the differences discussed above, the Bush PASs were a fairly homogeneous lot, both in their demographics and in their qualifications, so much so that a "typical PAS" could be described: the standard-issue PAS was a middle-aged, married, well-educated white male from Washington, D.C.

Questions of on-the-job competence continue to provide a political thicket for political theorists and others. While the *Prune Book* systematically analyzes qualifications for some jobs, there is no such handbook for the majority of positions. This is a responsibility the Presidential Personnel Office (PPO) should undertake at its earliest opportunity. The PPO is also the unit that should address federal budget and personnel management training for its PASs.

In general, it is clear that more pressure should be placed on the PPO to make qualifications at least as important a criterion as connections in political hiring.[10] As most PASs have relatively little power in hiring their subordinates, this pressure has to come from the top of the administration, as well as from the Senate.

PAS turnover continues to be a serious issue for any administration. While Ronald Reagan seemed oblivious to its importance, Jimmy Carter, George Bush, and some senators during the latter's term made it clear to nominees that they expected them to sign on for the full term. This trend is healthy and should be continued by future presidents and in the Senate confirmation process.

What many judged the excessive and intrusive nature of the FBI investigation should be reevaluated. It is not crucial to the health of the Republic that the FBI know every single address, membership, contribution, prescription drug, etc., going back over the entire life of a potential nominee. In most cases there should be a limitation of no more than fifteen years on the number of years back into a nominee's personal life that the FBI and the Senate dig. It is also not necessary for the Senate to make public all of its knowledge about a candidate and, certainly, to that end leaks should be firmly plugged.

There should be some significant streamlining of paperwork in the nomination process so that the same information is not demanded in different formats on different forms from the White House and the Senate, as it is now. It seems reasonable that staff cooperation could produce a basic questionnaire to which both sides could append their own questions.

Delay in nominations seems to rest with the White House more than with the Senate. While the growth in political jobs and increasingly tight ethics requirements since the Watergate era have been, to a large degree, responsible for this, the White House has been increasingly slow in choosing candidates and inordinately sluggish in the simple act of transmitting nomination papers to the Senate. This should be addressed and remedied in the PPO, supported by increased presidential attention.

While past excesses discourage any suggestion that ethics laws be loosened at this time, it appears that the financial disclosure laws and conflict of interest requirements are in need of revision to the extent that they keep otherwise qualified candidates from public political service. Likewise, postservice job restrictions should be analyzed to ensure that, in a frenzied public display of political morality, they do not excessively hinder recruitment or shorten tenure by encouraging early departure.

Bush maintained Reagan's antiregulatory stance, appointing like-minded people to the IRCs and agencies and strengthening the vice president's Council on Competitiveness, which, on its own authority, could overrule agency regulations of any sort if it deemed them harmful to capitalism or the market. He also extended Reagan's litmus test on abortion, most publicly in his appointments to the federal bench and the Supreme Court, but later in his term to many of his other PAS appointments, as well. This political criterion clearly limited the president's options.

George Bush appears to have at least cracked the conventional wisdom that posits political appointees as hacks, unqualified, agenda-driven ideologues who are more concerned with their own advancement than with the efficient and effective administration of their agency. However, because he stood so long in the shadow of Ronald Reagan and because so many of the key players were the same over both administrations, it is difficult to assess the width or depth of that crack. Nevertheless, the twelve years the Republicans held the White House meant that very often, even if appointees moved, they moved within government, not out of it, or if they did move out, they did not go very far and returned relatively quickly. Indeed, the fact that as many as 50 percent of the Bush people originally served Reagan's administration indicated that they received on-the-job training and so, often being their own predecessors, were more prepared and qualified by the time they served in Bush's. Although their experience in managing budgets and personnel was very limited, perhaps, at least, George Bush did not leave the "wisdom" about PASs as conventional as he found it.

While interviewees were of divided opinion as to which president's (Bush's or Reagan's) PASs were more competent, it was clear that George Bush's sense of team spirit mobilized his appointees in loyalty, if not in unity of vision. However, opinion was undeniably united regarding the unhappy combination of youth and inexperience in a PAS in any administration.

A word may be spoken regarding the potential end of "the age of macho" in Washington. With the advent of a nondefensive president who is not afraid to have equal partners in his spouse, the first lady, Hillary Rodham Clinton, and his vice president, Al Gore, there is, perhaps, hope that the new consciousness slowly dawning in the White House will filter down through the administration. Bill Clinton made a promise to create an administration that "looks like America," in terms of gender, ethnic, and geographic representation. He made a good start in that direction. It is therefore unlikely that the next cohort of PASs will be as easily typified as was George Bush's.

The following chapter analyzes the Bush PASs in light of various intrabureaucratic issues, with particular attention to relations among the various levels of federal employees, job satisfaction, and stress.

8

⚬〰⚬

Intrabureaucratic Issues: "Here, Ruining People Is Considered Sport"

B ecause PASs relate to numerous types of federal employees in many agencies in their federal service, they have to be flexible enough and experienced enough to tolerate a system that does not respond to a command-control style. They have to know whom to consult and when, and whose judgment to trust. They also have to walk a fine line of politics, knowing who their boss is and who their customer is at any given time, because they relate not only to the White House that appointed them but also to the Congress, the press, and the public that all hold them accountable. Additionally, they have to know their own values and what gives them satisfaction in their work and how to maximize it, as well as what causes them stress and how to minimize it.

PASs carry primary responsibility for the functioning of their agency. As the political overlords in the system they have to manage organizations of varying sizes and complexities, providing policy direction while administering political and career staff of equally varying sizes and complexities. Because some PASs may be the only political appointee in their agency or they may not have any Senior Executive Service (SES) subordinates, it is difficult to generalize about PASs as a group in discussing intrabureaucratic issues. However, some conclusions can be drawn from the results of the Bush PAS Survey; they are explored in the following sections dealing with intrabureaucratic issues—political-career relations, political-political relations, job satisfaction, and stress.

228

PASs Evaluate the SES: The System and Its Careerists

PASs were asked to rate SES members, both career and political, on their political responsiveness and competence. While PASs rated career SESs (CSESs) somewhat lower on responsiveness (reflecting perhaps real or imagined resistance to the Reagan-Bush agenda), they rated their competence higher than that of the political, noncareer SESs (NSESs).

Some respondents expressed frustration with the protections of the civil service system. A few wrote critical, even hostile, marginal comments in the survey about those protections and the roadblocks to change they believed these protections presented in their agency. This belief was echoed by many of the PASs who were interviewed. Though they strongly supported it in theory, they felt that the protections of the civil service system too often obstructed attempts at good management. Said one PAS: "The worst stuff is the personnel system—it protects individuals at the expense of the efficiency of the operation. One's abilities to deal with the anomalies are much more limited than in even the most unionized company. There should be audits but there should be more emphasis on efficient management, especially regarding personnel, not to put impediments in the way of it."

Another unwittingly expressed the paradox of the situation: "On balance the careerists are pretty good. They have a remarkable level of competence considering the level of protection they have. But they should have protection. I don't believe politicians should 'clean house.' On the other hand, they should be able to get rid of the bad ones."

Others had disparaging words for the SES system and its safety for careerists, calling it a "homestead provision" that insulated workers or a "closed society" too difficult for outsiders to enter. Said one, "Certain people [CSESs] are knighted and unless they stub their toe they're going to be there forever—and it takes an *awful lot* to stub your toe. They're golden for the rest of their career."

The Senior Executive Association's executive director, Carol Bonosaro, rebutted the politicians' complaint that it was nearly impossible to dispatch a CSES:

I'm stunned that people don't use the tools they have to get the performance they want—it's a mystery to me. In fact, it's very easy to get rid of careerists. Set performance standards of things to be accomplished. Either they do it or they go—rate them once as unsatisfactory, that's all it takes. I'm astonished that PASs do not exercise this option because CSESs basically have no rights, (except prohibited personnel practices).

On the other hand, her colleague, Jerry Shaw, SEA's lobbyist and counsel who represents careerists against administrative charges, said, "Any kind of adverse action against an employee results in a call to the IG of allegations against the supervisor, 100 percent of the time." The prospect of a long, drawn-out IG investigation is probably enough to deter all but the most serious of intentions on the part of most PASs.

Even the unhappy PASs, however, rated their career people highly. While, as one would expect, the PASs who were interviewed reflected the survey consensus, they placed greater emphasis on support for careerists in the SES. In fact, their praise of the CSESs was nearly unanimous, due, in some cases, perhaps, to low expectations. One PAS commented that he was "startled at the dedication of most of the federal workforce. They are unbelievably smart people." Another compared their intelligence to university faculty and said, "The CSESs won, no contest."

The praise for the CSESs was not unalloyed, of course. One not-so-happy reviewer said the careerists' attitude was,

> "I've seen five of you come and go and I'll still be here after you've gone." At the beginning of the term they have an incentive to work with you and you can accomplish some things. Toward the end you're more a lame duck and they engage more in foot dragging while they wait you out. They're also getting a little braver the stronger Clinton looks. . . . The system stinks—it has created its own good old boy network that makes faculty tenure look poor.

Another PAS had a mixed message. He called himself a big fan of the careerists and felt that George Bush, "the quintessential bureaucrat," had been a good president for the career civil service. But he noted that there were always tensions of some sort between the politicians and the careerists "because the institutional culture is to outwait. It's frustrating because institutional inertia makes it difficult to turn the ship." He felt that the government did not pay high enough salaries to attract good support staff, nor was he overly taken with long-term government lawyers who, he said, "tend to opt for lifestyle—9 to 5, no weekend work. Private law firm culture is more aggressive. For newcomers to government from private practice it's a step down in regards to workload, but they're still operating a step up from the ones who are already there."

The mission of an agency has a lot to do with the type of professional workforce an agency attracts. Some agencies' professionals spend their whole career doing the same small task or type of investigation over and over again. If there is a limited market for that specialty in the private sector they have few options and so stay in government, even though they are burned out by the work. An agency like the Environmental Protection Agency (EPA), however, can draw people who have skills that are needed in both private and public sectors, so "there is an active flow of people in and out of the agency and to and from the private sector," according to Linda Fisher, assistant administrator for pesticides and toxic substances.

Also, some agencies, such as EPA, have a mission that calls forth personal as well as professional commitment, and so attracts "an outstanding, impressive, very well-educated, highly motivated workforce," according to Fisher. She observed that when she had meetings with other agencies she came away far more impressed with the EPA people than with those at the other agencies. Likewise, banking regulatory agencies tend to attract better people than do the other regulatory agencies because securities lawyers have good job opportunities elsewhere, so turnover there is related to a better job elsewhere rather than to burnout, according to Susan Phillips, a governor at the Federal Reserve Board.

The ambient politics also affect the health and well-being of the career workforce. Donald Laidlaw, the assistant secretary for Human Resources at the Department of Education, saw "the yin/yang of politics" in the existence of his agency: "Ronald Reagan swore to kill this creation of Jimmy Carter but could not. George Bush, calling himself the 'education president,' resuscitated it. That kind of uncertainty takes its toll on career morale."

Interviewees were asked if they had any sense that the careerists harbored political opinions contrary to their own, and if so, if they sensed any difficulty there. Most said that they did not have a clue about their subordinates' politics and had no sense that it affected their work in any way. HUD's Keating, for example, was pleasantly surprised at the high quality of the workforce he found at his agency, given HUD's reputation (another example of low expectations being overtaken by experience). He noted that

> Kemp and company are not in sync with the majority of careerists but they've all gotten along well and the careerists respect Kemp's leadership. The agency has a Democratic culture of liberal Democrats but there is great agency solidarity among the political and career people due to Kemp's leadership. The careerists are more globalist than the administration but there's a good symbiosis there.

Frank Hodsoll, deputy director for management at the Office for Management and Budget, said he had no sense that politics affected the work of his careerists in that most political of places. He trusted their neutral competence and saw no difference between the career and the political people. "You need to develop a team that can produce the result. [The careerists'] job is to present options doable at the moment. They generally genuinely support whoever is in office—most senior careerists date back to Carter, some beyond. OMB is a very heady, elite place to be for careerists—it generally has the highest quality career staff in government."

That heady atmosphere carries its own problem, however, in that its workforce is removed from what Hodsoll called "the retail level."

> OMB advises the president, brokers budgets, and works the legislative process, but doesn't really do anything [i.e., produce a program or product]. You're the advisor to the public but you never get your hands dirty; you don't understand what it's like to run a program. Some [OMB careerists] have been there too long. The staff would be better off to go out to an agency or the private sector for a while to regain perspective. The game of brokering a budget (and it is a game) can become alienated from the real work of running an agency. This encourages agencies to look to their Hill committees for support (the iron triangle setup) and undercuts the White House.

Another mixed message came from a PAS who spoke of her support for careerists and "empowering them to do policy making." But she was clearly resentful of the power they wielded to block her moves:

> At my agency the careerists in the legal office and administrative office seek to curtail PASs. A lot of power is vested in entrenched career people. Treasury, State, OMB, and Commerce are heavily controlled by careerists, the entrenched bureaucracy. This acts positively as a brake, negatively to keep the status quo perpetuated. They can block needed change. Careerists will be careful of what kinds of issues they bring to PAS's attention for fear they'll muck it up, especially when the PAS is new.

Another PAS noted how the transient nature of political appointees in the federal government carried with it its own cost.

> Careerists [ostensibly] respect PASs' ability to talk to other appointees to make decisions, but deep down it's not really true, the appointees are more tolerated. . . . Careerists might be waiting. They expect change—a new appointee will come along and march them off in a different direc-

tion. The deference shown in the federal government is different from the deference shown to supervisors in state government and industry. There's much more movement of supervisors in the federal government.

Noted another PAS, "Career staff will accept leadership, but if you don't furnish it they will have an agenda of their own—nature abhors a vacuum."

Many PASs spoke of their trust in careerists, how much they depended on them for policy guidance, as well as to keep them informed about the culture of their own agency. One noted that he involved careerists and tried to keep them on board. "Careerists have it as a part of their culture to support the boss. I don't see careerists as Democrats or Republicans, per se. Their program identification is very high and they will tend to resist change there. My own success comes not from my political skills but from my bureaucratic skills."

Laidlaw placed responsibility for political-career relations squarely at the politicians' feet. "It's up to the political staff to set the right tone to give direction to the agency. After all, when the boat misses the harbor, it's seldom the harbor's fault."

Careerists had conflicting opinions on the quality of political-career relations in the Bush administration. Several expressed appreciation for Bush's first public appearance as president where, in a speech to the SES, he affirmed both public servants and the public service. This was in marked contrast to Ronald Reagan's bureaucrat-bashing, antigovernment campaigns that always seemed to spill over onto the civil service and its employees. As Bonosaro noted, "George Bush's support for the civil service probably permeated down to his appointees and depoliticized OPM [Office of Personnel Management]—both of his OPM heads were supportive of civil service and development, as opposed to Don Devine, who served as the lightning rod to grow the professional organizations and unions—he was the perfect enemy."

Most careerists, however, while welcoming the absence of a frontal attack from the Bush administration, did not think political-career relations had improved much over Reagan. "On a scale of hostility zero to ten (ten being low), under Ronald Reagan hostility between careerists and political appointees was maybe a five, now it's maybe a six," said one highly respected careerist. As noted earlier, Bush's late 1992 campaign proposal to cut salaries for senior executives damaged his relations with careerists and will doubtless color perceptions of his administration's political-career relations in future reflections on the subject.

PASs: Their Colleagues and Subordinates at Work

PASs exhibited a decided tendency to confer with their agency colleagues of all three executive categories regarding policy, budget, and staff decisions (see table 8.1).

It was clear that PASs relied heavily on their careerists. One PAS put it succinctly: "You can't develop policy without working with careerists." Indeed, most PASs did not exclude their career SES subordinates from any facet of policy making. In fact, they seemed to rely on them much more than they did on their noncareer SESs and often more than they relied on their PAS peers.[1]

PASs' feelings about CSES employees prior to their first-ever PAS appointment were assessed in order to discern if actually working with careerists changed their assessment of them. They were asked to recall their opinion of careerists prior to having worked with them. Then they were asked their opinion of careerists after having worked with them.

Though their reflections were doubtless colored by time and subsequent experience, the greatest change came with those PASs who were predisposed to be positive toward the career SES—those who previously believed that SES careerists would "greatly help" them in executing their duties (31 percent). After working with careerists, that percent increased to 48 percent. This spoke well of political-career relations in the real world of everyday work, as did the rest of the survey results and the interviews with PASs, confirming their reliance on careerists for policy making.

Table 8.1. Whom Did PASs Consult Most on Policy, Budget, and Personnel Issues? (in percent)

Issue	PAS N=170	NSES N=154	CSES N=169
Policy feasibility	75	62	72
Policy formulations and development	76	59	74
Policy implementation	72	63	77
Budget decisions	66	52	73
Staff selection and promotions decisions	53	45	66

Source: The Bush PAS Survey.

The SES performance plan won little praise from the PASs. It is composed of two cycles of evaluation, an annual pass/fail grading based on the individual's job description that is the basis for bonuses, and a triennial evaluation of job performance that is the basis for recertification within the SES. Beyond the minimum "C" grade acceptable for the annual review, the triennial review is expected to show above-average performance if an SES member is to retain SES ranking. An SES who does not make the grade can be returned to grade 15 or take early retirement with no loss of annuity. Good as it sounds, it was rated by only 59 percent of PASs as "generally" or "very" effective in holding CSESs accountable and by a mere 52 percent in holding NSESs accountable for their work; "a joke," said one SES.

PASs were asked to evaluate assistance rendered by the three levels of executives in their organizational unit. Although there were some minor signs of disaffection and many checked "no basis to judge/not applicable," well over two-thirds of PASs who responded rated their executive colleagues highly helpful in terms of accomplishing work tasks (see table 8.2).

While it might be expected that PASs would rely more on their political peers for relations with the Congress and more on their careerists for technical issues, it was clear that the politicals relied heavily on their careerists in every aspect of their work. There was no politics/administration dichotomy in their real-world lives.

Table 8.2. How Helpful Were PASs and SESs in Accomplishing Work Tasks? (in percent)

Task	PAS N=166	NSES N=150	CSES N=168
Mastering substantive policy details	83	86	87
Liaison with the federal bureaucracy	76	82	85
Liaison with Congress	80	74	72
Anticipating policy implementation problems	77	80	81
Handling day-to-day management tasks	69	80	86
Technical analysis of difficult issues	77	84	91

Source: The Bush PAS Survey.

The Inspectors General—the Internal GAO

The inspectors general (IGs) are a special breed of appointee, established by the 1978 Inspectors General Act. The only PASs in this study appointed to unlimited years in office, IGs are located in nearly every federal agency and perform the internal auditing function in the agencies. Their job is to identify and root out "waste, fraud, and abuse." There are sixty IGs located throughout the government; twenty-seven are political appointees at EL 3; the other thirty-three are "designated" careerists at GS levels 13 to 15, chosen by the agency head.

Agencies unused to political IGs did not always welcome them when the five newest political IGs were added in 1988. The OPM chief, for example, tried to locate her IG in a satellite building out of town, even though the law specified that they were to be housed in the agency headquarters. (Stern correspondence from OMB and the Senate Governmental Affairs Committee brought the IG into the headquarters in that instance.) IGs have, however, gradually earned respect for their function, which is to seek out waste, fraud, and abuse within the agency.

Much like the PASs of the independent regulatory commissions, the political IGs are very protective of their independence. "Politics are outside the IG office," is their credo. Their function and independent reporting to Congress make the IGs the parallel in some ways to Congress's investigative arm, the General Accounting Office (GAO). IGs send a semiannual report to Congress through the agency head who may add comments but may not change their report. Because the IGs try to stay politically neutral and because the issues with which they deal are rarely entirely clear-cut, the neutrality of the IG position is crucial, and learning the careful art of compromise is essential. IGs can make enemies on either side. "Being an IG is like trying to straddle a barbed wire fence—measuring the height is what's important," said one.

Barriers to effective administration (one aspect of the nefarious Washington gridlock) show up in the experience of the IGs, thanks to the hostility between the legislative branch and the executive branch agencies inherent in divided government (and not unknown in unified government). The IGs themselves would prefer that their function be a management tool rather than a management critique, but that is difficult to achieve with a public report that goes to a Congress controlled by the other party "always looking for ways to make the executive branch agencies look bad." A negative IG report will likely bring congressional calls for a GAO audit of the IG's agency, an unhappy agency chief, and an irate

White House. Said one, "IGs produce an annual plan of issues they expect
to cover for the year, then Congress picks it up and asks the GAO to investigate those specific issues. . . . GAO comes in and picks my cherries.
Fortunately, the GAO people are very professional and that helps to save
things; we work together."

Rarely is Congress the friend of the IG. One IG noted a lack of clear
direction from his congressional oversight committees. "Oversight hearings are muddled and I don't know what to expect from them, but usually
someone's going to get bloodied for political splash." Another described
his job thus: "I get my butt chewed out by Congress every day." He never
got any feedback or questions on his annual report and had no sense that
there was any real interest from his oversight committees, except to use
his reports to make his agency look bad. There was, he felt, an uncom-
fortable ambiguity to his service: "Who is the customer?" he asked, "the
president, the agency, OMB, Congress, or the taxpayer?"

The Bush White House was not the IGs' friend, either. In the Reagan
era, OMB respected the IGs and there were good relations between them.
The president always addressed the annual meeting of the professional organization of IGs, the President's Council on Integrity and Efficiency
(PCIE), and gave the association's annual award to an IG. When George
Bush was elected he sent the political IGs the standard letter all the PASs
got reminding them to resign, but most IGs refused to comply, citing the
independence of their office. This was supported by letters from the Senate Governmental Affairs Committee and the House Governmental Operations Committee and eventually the president had to back off.[2] (While
the president can fire a political IG, it is a riskier proposition than removing any other non-IRC PAS. The president, upon dismissing an IG,
must send a letter to Congress stating his reasons for doing so. No consent from Congress is required, but the public nature of the event might
give a president pause.)

This history is thought to be the reason for cool relations between the
Bush White House and the IGs (Richard Darman, OMB director, or Boyden Gray, White House counsel, were thought by one IG to dislike them).
After the first year of his administration, Bush never again addressed the
PCIE. As a consequence, "several IGs have run to Congress for their
strokes," according to one IG. The result is that Congress is referring or
directing more work to the IGs and using them as an internal agency-
based GAO; IGs who seek to promote their own careers try to satisfy their
oversight committees. As one IG observed, "IGs all have super egos that
need to be stroked."

Job Satisfaction

Clearly, PASs took their jobs seriously and felt personally responsible for the execution of their duties. They responded in clear majorities of two-thirds to 90 percent that they felt they were held accountable to a "great" or "very great" extent for meeting objectives for their organizational unit.

Satisfaction with PAS service in general can be seen in the numbers of those willing to continue in it, should the opportunity arise. Only fifteen of the survey respondents said they would decline additional PAS service and forty-one said they did not know what choice they would make. That 101 indicated they would continue in their current PAS positions and fifty-eight would accept a different PAS position gave clear evidence of a reasonably well-satisfied workforce, apart from the usual problems that go with the federal bureaucratic territory.

At the same time, only 21 percent who answered felt they would "definitely" or "probably" pursue career civil service status, with 8 percent undecided and 70 percent saying they probably or definitely would not. This latter is not surprising because, as one PAS former careerist noted, "It's awfully hard to go back, both ego- and status-wise, and also in terms of being accepted by your peers, once you've been a political appointee."

The Bush PASs registered strong opinions, both positive and negative, about specific aspects of their jobs. Substantial majorities of at least two-thirds reported being "generally" or "very greatly" satisfied with numerous aspects of their jobs. Between 172 and 179 PASs questioned indicated which factors gave them the most job satisfaction:

Dealing with challenging and interesting problems	99%
Having an impact; making a difference	96%
Meeting and working with stimulating people	94%
Working with CSESs	90%
Improving internal agency operations	86%
Reaction of CSESs to policy direction	83%
Managing a large government organization	83%
Working with other political appointees	81%
Promoting their own policy objectives	81%
Implementing the president's policies	81%
Public perceptions of PASs' role as federal manager	77%
Agency quality of life	70%
Dealing with the White House	67%

Many things brought job satisfaction to the PASs. Making a difference seemed to be high on the list for most—the sense of producing a needed product or "the ability to change things in the public interest from time to time." Said another, whose job is listed in *The Prune Book*'s "100 Toughest Jobs" and who admitted to great levels of stress, "It's the most exciting job I've ever had in my life—there's never been a boring moment. I get great satisfaction in seeing success, improved education, or a program succeed."

Others spoke of the satisfaction of being an agent for change, being able to work in public service, and feeling that theirs was a "higher calling." Some found satisfaction in being able to craft a compromise to reach a solution to government's problems. Some even admitted to enjoying working with Congress. Others spoke of the quality of the people they worked with, calling them "incredibly smart and dedicated." Many liked the independence and decision-making powers that came with their office. Others spoke of their fulfillment in "getting things done." Many discussed how much they enjoyed the challenge that their work and resolving complex issues brought them. As one said, "It's a lot less money but a lot more fun than if I'd stayed in the law firm."

Some spoke of their enjoyment of management, "making this a better place to work, having people be accountable." Anthony McCann, assistant secretary for administration at Veterans Affairs, spoke of "relations with the staff and redemption of lost souls" as his greatest sources of fulfillment. He found great satisfaction in being able to relocate careerists who had been sidelined or shunted aside, giving them something meaningful to do where their skills were best used. Once placed in different positions where their skills matched the job, they had flourished, to his obvious pleasure.

Others were attracted to public service by "the ability to be involved in public issues. You're far more involved in critical issues than if you work in the private sector," said one. Many spoke of the issues they dealt with, how extremely interesting and challenging they were. For example, the Fed's Susan Phillips said, "The Fed is Mecca for an economist. It is unmatched for the depth and scope of economic research, with tools, resources, visiting scholars, and conferences."

Many spoke of their pleasure at being able to make a contribution, of being able to give something back to their country. One PAS spoke of his desire to "achieve something, leave a legacy behind. There's a new landscape every day." He found "the intelligence business totally fascinating, entrancing."

Some spoke of the satisfaction of producing a product "that improves the quality of life and delivering it more effectively and cheaply with better management and more awareness of the taxpayer." Others spoke of their love of the policy-making process and their ability to get things done, to make the private and public sectors work together. For many, the chief joy seemed to be the ability to put their work where their ideals were, to test out their political beliefs and see if they were workable. It was clear that the PASs believed in what they were doing and that they were very committed to their work.

Job satisfaction was viewed through various lenses in the survey to isolate particular factors or conditions that might contribute to or detract from it. Those lenses or factors are executive level of the PAS, term or nonterm status (PASs appointed to an independent regulatory commission [IRC] and PASs appointed to an executive agency), and appointee numbers. The results follow.

Distinctions Among Executive Levels

Executive level (EL) offers an obvious approach to analyzing potential differences among PASs because it is clearly an objective condition—one's EL is not a matter of opinion. And, indeed, some distinctions in sense of job satisfaction were found among the PASs based on their executive level.[3]

Executive Level Ones (EL 1) occupy the apex of the federal panoply. They are the cabinet-level agency chiefs (e.g., the secretaries of the Departments of Labor, State, Treasury, Agriculture, Health and Human Services [HHS], Education, etc.), and a few others in the Executive Office of the President (EOP), such as the director of the Office of Management and Budget (OMB), the director of the National Drug Control Policy, and the U.S. trade representative.[4]

Clearly, the EL 1s were the most satisfied with their PAS job. They registered the greatest levels of satisfaction in the quality of life in their agency and in managing and improving their organization, implementing President Bush's policy objectives, promoting their own policy goals, and dealing with OMB and with OPM.

These results indicated a pleasant and politically useful synchronicity of agenda between President Bush and his top appointees, as well as between the appointees and OMB, often fertile ground for conflict.

While 62 percent overall were satisfied with their dealings with Congress (with 23 percent dissatisfied), 43 percent of the EL 1s were *dissatisfied* with those relationships. These particular results were not surprising, given the very public role assigned the cabinet officers. If a congressional committee is in a restive mood or angry at an executive branch agency, the cabinet officer is usually its first and very public target.

EL 1s were also the least satisfied with working with other political appointees. Out of the overall majority that was dissatisfied with the pace of government decision making, they were the most dissatisfied.

EL 1s (the highest paid and closest to the president) were the happiest of all the PASs with their salary, the amount of time their job required of them, and the impact of their job on their personal or family life. It seemed clear that the many demands placed on them and the sacrifices required of them were more than offset by the perks and the personal, professional, and political benefits they derived from their offices.

EL 2s are the deputy directors of the cabinet-level agencies, the heads of major noncabinet agencies, such as the National Aeronautics and Space Administration, OPM, the FBI, the Federal Emergency Management Agency, the military service branch chiefs, and the chair of the Federal Reserve System. They also include heads of EOP offices such as the director of the Office of Science and Technology Policy and the chair of the Council of Economic Advisors. The primarily public role and responsibility of the EL 1s of necessity takes them outside the internal workings of the agency they defend publicly. That responsibility falls to the EL 2s, who get the least public glory and the most internal agency criticism. In addition to doing all the "scut work" of running someone else's shop, they also have less direct contact with the president and the power that "access" or "face time" imparts.

Overall, it made sense, then, that the EL 2s appeared the least content with their lot, scoring themselves lowest in seven of the nineteen categories and highest in none. While the EL 1s rated most satisfied with aspects of internal agency life, the EL 2s sent a different message. They were least satisfied or most dissatisfied with managing their organization, the quality of life in their agency, dealing with the White House, public perceptions of their role as a federal manager, and dealing with organized groups that opposed their agency's policy. They were equally unhappy with the amount of time their job required and the impact of their job on their personal or family life.

EL 3s are agency undersecretaries, members of commissions whose head is an EL 2, such as the Fed and the Nuclear Regulatory Commission, or heads of other agencies and commissions, such as the General Services Administration, the Peace Corps, the Federal Maritime Commission, the Interstate Commerce Commission, and the Federal Trade Commission.

The EL 3s did not appear to have many sentiments particularly out of sync with the other PASs, though they did report the least satisfaction with their salary and the most dissatisfaction with their ability to dismiss or reassign civil servants.

EL 4s are assistant secretaries or administrators of major units in the major agencies, such as the Administration for Children, Youth, and Families or the National Institutes of Health of the Department of Health and Human Services (HHS); they are inspectors general and general counsels at the major agencies. They are also deputy directors whose boss is an EL 3, members of commissions chaired by an EL 3, and heads of smaller or specialized agencies such as the Federal Labor Relations Board, the U.S. Commission on Civil Rights, the Panama Canal Commission, and the Selective Service Administration. EL 4s appeared to be generally similar to their colleagues and did not stand out in any way as being particularly satisfied or dissatisfied.

EL 5s are deputies to EL 4s and directors of smaller agencies or large departments, such as the Asian Development Bank and the Smithsonian Astrophysical Observatory, the Administration on Aging (HHS), and the Farmers Home Administration (Agriculture). They are also assistant secretaries and general counsels in the smaller agencies.

EL 5s, the lowest in the PAS hierarchy (they and the EL 4s are parallel to the SES's highest levels [SES 4, 5, and 6] in salary), clearly have the least power and the greatest frustration with seeking to wield it. The key means of exercising power in government—staff, budget, access, and policy-making authority—are farthest from their grasp.

The EL 5s were least satisfied with the reaction of civil servants to political direction and their own ability to dismiss or reassign them, PASs' dealings with OMB and their frustrations in trying to control their own budget, dealing with organized groups that opposed agency policy, and success at promoting their own policy goals.

Interestingly, however, EL 5s were not without their point of light: despite their frustrations, they rated themselves 100 percent satisfied with their dealings with other political appointees, mirror images of the EL 1s at the top of the hierarchy who were, as noted, the least satisfied on that score.

IRC and Non-IRC PASs

As observed in the previous chapter, the PASs in the independent regulatory commissions (IRCs) as a group generally were not markedly different from the other PASs. Some clear differences along the indicators of job satisfaction did appear between the two groups of PASs, however (see table 8.3).

Table 8.3. Job Satisfaction Among IRC and Non-IRC PASs (in percent)

Job Satisfaction Factor	IRC	Non-IRC
Managing a large government organization	73 (N=52)	88 (N=100)
Dealing with OMB (N=177)	47 (N=47)	61 (N=95)
Implementing the president's policies	72 (N=54)	86 (N=98)
Dealing with Congress (N=177)	69 (N=64)	57 (N=100)
Time available to think creatively about issues	74 (N=70)	49 (N=103)
Time requirements of job	74 (N=72)	57 (N=102)
Dealing with groups opposed to agency policy	66 (N=64)	39 (N=82)
Impact of job on personal or family life	64 (N=72)	45 (N=102)

Source: The Bush PAS Survey.

Though the IRCs wield tremendous power and are sometimes responsible for vast amounts of money (viz., the Federal Reserve Board, which controls the interest rates and supply of money in the U.S. economy), their administrative structure is nearly flat, their administrative staff relatively small. Generally, the chair of the IRC is the chief administrative officer; thus, the great majority of the IRC PASs do not carry the stress of dealing with the personnel and management issues that plague the PASs in the executive agencies. As discussed earlier, IRC PASs carefully guard their independence from White House interference. Although they noted less satisfaction in dealing with OMB than did the non-IRCs, IRCs have direct formal access to Congress to dull OMB's budget-cutting knife. This, along with the fact that IRCs are usually bipartisan bodies, may account for IRC PASs' greater satisfaction in dealing with (and greater need for) Congress.

IRC PASs were also more likely to work a "normal" work week (relative, in Washington terms) and not to be on the edge of mental and physical exhaustion, as many of the other PASs seemed to be in the interviews.

Freed from many internal pressures and direct political oversight, more of the IRCs enjoyed the luxury rare in political government circles of actually having time to think and reflect. According to Susan Phillips, "The Fed is like being on a university campus without the students. We have access to some of the best minds in the country and we can bring them together for symposia or as consultants any time we need them."

Job Satisfaction and Appointee Numbers

Despite the Reagan-Bush growth in the number of appointees overall, PASs (by a plurality and often a majority) said the number of PAS, noncareer SES (NSES), career SES (CSES), and Schedule C employees should remain the same. This was most clearly seen in their own agency, where 81 percent of PASs said the number of PASs should remain as is. The same held for NSES (51 percent), CSES (45 percent), and Schedule C (57 percent) employees in the respondents' agency. This trend held governmentwide, where 57 percent of PASs said the number should remain the same, as should that for NSES (40 percent), CSES (43 percent), and Schedule C (46 percent) employees.

Given this debate over the appointee numbers, it is interesting that there was no relationship between job satisfaction and the optimal number of political appointees and career SESs. Pluralities, and often majorities, felt the number in all categories (PAS, NSES, CSES, and Schedule C) should remain the same, both in their agency and governmentwide, regardless of individual measures of satisfaction within the various indicators of job satisfaction.

It was particularly noteworthy that this sense that the numbers should remain the same held also for the two indicators that uniformly had the least number satisfied (ability to reassign or dismiss civil servants) and the most dissatisfied (the pace of government decision making). Apparently, unlike the Reagan appointees, most Bush PASs did not seek solutions to their problems in more appointees.

PASs clearly respected career expertise and the value of its neutral competence. Those who consulted most with CSESs on matters of policy feasibility, formulation, development, and implementation and on budget and staffing decisions uniformly believed there should be more rather than fewer CSESs, both in their agency and governmentwide.

Stress: Gnashing of Teeth as a Lifestyle

Great as were many of the satisfactions of PAS service, stress was barely below the surface for most PASs interviewed. These frustrations, all agreed, were the inescapable facts of government life: little or no control, little sense of completion, and the open-ended nature of government processes in which "nothing was ever over" and decision making was never brought to closure. Bureaucracy, administrative red tape, and the length of time it took to get things done were major causes of irritation for many of these action-oriented PASs. Again, most of the following comments, some painfully candid, were not for attribution.

One PAS named the problem as "not having a clear shot at making a decision—no authority to make a final decision—hundreds of people have the power to block any decision. Life in government is absolutely nutso, with all the relations between agencies that have to be built and bases that have to be touched. The system itself blocks authority and power. No one person has the authority to change the system."

Another PAS phrased his predicament as "never being in a position where I can command change in the way I want, both administratively and politically. I'm not able to make the changes I see need to be made in the agency or fix the things that need to be fixed." There was the sense, as one PAS expressed it, of "If I could just run that agency myself, god-damn it, I could fix it" (a not uncommon sentiment in Washington).

Financial limitations weighed heavily on some PASs, creating, as one put it, the pressure of "not being able to do everything that needs to be done, never having enough resources and people to do the job." Nixonian fears of PASs "going native" appeared not ungrounded—commitment to doing a good job seemed to override orthodox Republican devotion to shrinking both government and taxes. (Additionally, it makes no sense to assume that growth-oriented business people whose previous work life revolved around expansion of their domain were suddenly going to rein in their ambition simply because they worked for the government—Reaganite Republicans and Libertarians who succeed in getting their private-sector people into office should expect a certain measure of disappointment on this score.)

One PAS spoke of the turf battles he felt compelled to fight:

I'm bothered that government feeds on itself—there are lots of turf battles. Interior, for example has lots of problems—its divisions fight one another. My greatest disappointment in government service is the battle for turf—it's agency versus agency, department versus department, etc. But I do recognize that such is the way of Washington—rather than living by the code that we all work for the same country.

His agency was one of those noted previously that was required to consult with other agencies before issuing regulations. With no limit on their response time other agencies could, in effect, block his agency by delaying their answer.

Allan Bromley, director of the Office of Science and Technology Policy in the Executive Office of the President, spoke of how hard it was to keep the flow of people moving between the public and private sectors.

"Expertise is harder to borrow from the private sector. Conflict of interest strictures mean we can only bring in those who are retired or just out of school and not yet established."

Fred Hitz, inspector general at the CIA, felt the ethics regulations and other restraints were too intrusive into peoples' lives. The financial disclosure and blind trust requirements were onerous and had a detrimental effect on getting people of means to come into government.

Bromley noted another problem in an increasingly litigious society. "The rules are interpreted more narrowly by each generation of lawyers in the agencies. They are nervous and interpret the regulations in the most restrictive way so no one can blame them if things go wrong."

Others discussed the lack of annual leave (vacation) or sick leave. Because no one monitors their time, PASs are expected to build off-time and vacations into their schedules, but that can be nearly impossible in these high-stress jobs. As one PAS noted, "You can't be out of touch—and if you are, you're in trouble." They have the freedom to come and go as they please but lack the protection of having a supervisor or structure tell them when it is time to take a vacation.

There was also the pressure of being watched, both within the agency and without (the ever-present *Washington Post* loomed large in many interviews). As one said, "It's the frustration inherent in managing any large bureaucracy and the constant criticism the agency comes under, no matter what we do." Said another, "The IG watches you like a hound and has to investigate even anonymous allegations, no matter how far-fetched."

Phillips mentioned that, in addition to the requirements that they "give up everything, resign from everything, and make financial sacrifices," there is also some loss of intellectual freedom. PASs cannot serve on boards, cannot speak and write as much as they might like to, and cannot freelance theory. They have to be very careful because anything they might say or write carries disproportionate weight.

Time pressures were a constant feature of PASs' life. Some noted the lack of "quality time" to do strategic or long-range planning, with constant demands on their time, many beyond their control ("In an IG world the priorities are changing almost hourly"). There was also congressional pressure on their products (reports). Other factors and players beyond their control also contributed to stress. The eighteen-month federal budget cycle, for example, is beyond their control. Yet, they have to produce their agency's next year budget request while they still do not know exactly what their previous year's budget will be. Further, as discussed earlier, the federal budget process was baffling for many PASs. They were unsure of the players and the rules. One expressed frustration with the external constraints on what he could request and the fact that "no rationalization was given for budget decisions made on high."

Personal finances were a source of complaint for some. Retired federal employees called to PAS duty (reemployed annuitants) only receive the difference between their retirement pay and their PAS salary. Though they knew this going in, it still galled some. One noted that he was ill-prepared for the personal financial costs of the job. The costs of doing business come out of their own pockets in many cases and PASs are expected to operate on a high executive level, often on a lower salary than they enjoyed in the private sector. This is a major adjustment for those coming from the corporate world.

There is no free lunch for PASs—they cannot accept meals or various other "freebies" to which many had become accustomed as part of corporate life. Adding insult to injury, their career people were often the ones who had to explain the ethics rules to them, which put the careerists in the awkward position of being negative, of "saying no to the boss." The IGs in particular operate under more stringent ethics rules due to their policing function, while the other PASs do have more freedom because they are expected to act for a political agenda.

Congress came in for its share of criticism for its attempt to micromanage the executive branch agencies. This was seen as a natural executive-legislative tension, more related to turf than party. "The fault-finding and micromanagement wear you down. Taking a chance and the risk of producing a mistake are not tolerated. You take constant berating and battering and there's not much you can do about it—you don't have the leverage to make reform in the federal government. There's a lot of second guessing."

Vincent Foster, one of President Clinton and First Lady Hillary Rodham Clinton's top advisors and personal friends, committed suicide in July 1993. Although Foster was the victim of clinical depression, the particular reasons for his death remain largely a mystery. However, they seemed not unrelated to the strain of life in the national pressure cooker. A note Foster wrote to himself read, "Here, ruining people is considered sport." This seems an apt description of much of political and journalistic Washington. It was echoed by one male PAS: "There is little or no pleasure or joy in my job—just lots of misery. My agency is a macho environment—one proves oneself by besting one's opponents. People get caught up in a 'political appointee' syndrome, but that's not why we're here. People aren't being served by the system as it operates this way."

It was the atmosphere of "zero defects/zero tolerance for error" that made their jobs so difficult, according to many PASs. There was simply no margin for error. If it was not Congress, GAO, and the press looking over their shoulder, they had to worry about their own IG micromanaging their work, said some. As the Fed's Phillips observed, "In government there's much more of a premium on being right. You have to bring people along, build a consensus for decision making. In the private sector you can afford to be wrong. In the public sector you don't have that luxury."

Given the action-oriented nature of the PASs and the satisfaction they took in being able to "get things done," it is hardly surprising that the major areas of dissatisfaction were the ever-unpopular inability to reassign or dismiss civil service workers (73 percent) and the pace of government decision making (52 percent). Those coming from the business sector were most likely to feel irked by these factors. As one PAS said, "In the private sector you give an order and it tends to get carried out. In the public sector you give an order and it's the beginning of a negotiation." This sense of frustration was also borne out in the interviews, as discussed above.

OPM got only lukewarm support, with 40 percent of the Bush PAS Survey respondents being "generally" or "very" satisfied in their dealings with it, 19 percent being "generally" or "very" dissatisfied, and 40 percent being neither satisfied nor dissatisfied.

Some reasons for the overall low satisfactory rating of OPM were revealed in the PAS interviews. OPM has general administrative responsibility for the civil service employees, Schedule C, and Senior Executive Service members assigned to the agencies. Although the White House or the agency hires a particular political appointee, OPM designates the number of SES positions that each agency is allocated and its Qualifications Review Board certifies potential appointees as eligible for appointment. As one researcher remarked, "OPM is viewed as a bottleneck. They can always come up with ten reasons to tell you why you can't do what you want to do when what you want to do is legitimate."

OPM's problem might be similar to that of OMB—too-limited "retail level" experience. As explained by one frustrated PAS:

> OPM has limited vision for the needs and financing for field staff—what they can be paid, the overall intent and direction of our program. OPM just doesn't understand the needs of this agency; it insists on compartmentalizing departments according to some standardized format. There is a rigidity in the OPM structure that is loosening a little, but only

slowly. I can't raise salaries enough to bring in good people who carry major responsibility. For example, I can only pay $38,000 to a man who's responsible for making loans of $700,000 on his own authority.

As discussed above, frustrations with civil service protections featured strongly in many PASs' working lives. "The protection of the individual is beyond the level of adequacy. The federal government is slow to hire, slow to fire. This is good for stability and good for loyalty but it makes it tough to manage and change—it has its consequences." For example, after a year of trying to get rid of one CSES, Frank Keating at HUD found he could only do so by promoting the person laterally or "upstairs" (having first to find an available slot):

> GS people are even harder to get rid of. It's virtually impossible to do, it's maddening. The only thing you can do is treat them like grains of sand in an oyster—try to build a wall around them. I couldn't even get rid of the man responsible for hiring and protecting "Robbing Hood" [an employee in a prominent HUD scandal]—I had to reinstate him due to service protections.

Another area of dissatisfaction surfaced in the issue of hiring political subordinates. While an occasional secretary will come on board with carte blanche hiring authority from the president (James Baker at the State Department, for example), most cabinet secretaries do not have total control in staffing their agencies. The PPO will often operate with surgical precision, telling an agency which political appointee to place in which position.

Similarly, PASs on down the line do not exercise a great deal of leverage in choosing their own assistants, either within or across party lines. This has meant running battles between agencies and the PPO, sometimes throughout the entire first year of an administration.

This pattern also holds between secretaries and the assistant secretaries in the agencies. Assistant secretaries are rarely given a free hand in hiring their subordinates. Hiring is usually a process of negotiation between the secretary or deputy and the assistant secretary, with the former holding the decisive vote. In one agency the assistant secretary was brought on board with the promise that he could hire his own staff but found the secretary vetoing his choices after he had rejected one of the secretary's candidates because he felt the man was incompetent. Finally, one of the other assistant secretaries clued him in: the secretary wanted to have one of "his people" in each department and he was jeopardizing his own position by his refusal to take the secretary's choice. The assistant secretary gave in and took him, found him to be "a complete disaster, and spent the next nine months trying to get rid of him."

This same process also occurs in the IRCs. In most IRCs the chair is the administrative chief and the other commissioners may have little say in choosing their own aides. This led to the curious situation of Democratic IRC commissioners being assigned Republicans as their secretaries and confidential assistants by the OPM of the Reagan and Bush administrations.

Some PASs missed the satisfaction they found at other programs or in other lines of work: "At the higher policy positions you miss the direct benefits of seeing or producing a program, seeing you've *done* something."

Though the length of time it took to accomplish things was universally decried, several PASs also observed that there were occasional advantages to a system that requires many check-offs: "The flip side is that it sometimes makes for a better product," said one.

The NRC's Ivan Selin offered a less-than-sympathetic rejoinder to the multitudinous complaints about the restrictions on PASs' personal and professional lives. Noting the depth and breadth of PAS positions, he commented:

> The problems with disclosure requirements and press intrusion are true, but so what? It's all true but it goes with the territory. People in public service have no reason to be embarrassed about things they have no control over (like an errant brother in drug rehabilitation). The frustrations of public service are high but the stakes are enormous—you have a huge impact, you should expect the issues you deal with to be highly contentious. I started a company that now has four thousand employees, but what I do [now] on Monday morning affects a huge number of people, so of course there's going to be conflict.
>
> There's lots of chickenshit stuff in government (petty rules and regulations regarding gifts, the use of government cars), but why allow it to be a big deal? It goes with the territory.

PASs dealt differently with stress, depending, perhaps, on their age, personality, experience in government, and the particulars of their job. Several of the older male PASs mentioned the unexpected lesson their heart attacks and bypass operations taught them about slowing down and managing their stress appropriately. Others jogged every day to let off steam. As one said, "Health maintenance is a big item in this town."

Others, by virtue of personality or experience, delegated duties to subordinates. A few compared their current job stress favorably to previous occupations—university administration was far more stressful, according to two. On the other hand, one declared that his previous work as a law enforcement hostage negotiator was less stressful than his PAS IG work:

> At least in that job the issues were black and white with clear-cut goals and objectives. Now the stresses are more fatiguing, there are many more influences and ramifications and other government agencies to consult with. I cannot make a decision without doing it in a committee, it's not just based on objective factors and the best available information. Now decision making is a mental and diplomatic exercise more than anything else.

Some spoke of "the difficulty and enormity of the job, the long hours, the amount of material to be read and absorbed." Said another, "There are more successes and more frustrations in this job. There's a higher level of work, responsibility, exposure, and visibility."

The EPA's Fisher echoed Selin: "It's a high-stress job due to the weightiness of the decisions made, the number of controversial issues, the amount of interaction with the media and Congress, the complexity of the issues, and the personalities to deal with at EPA."

Said one whose job was listed in the *Prune Book*'s "100 Toughest Jobs," "My stress level has been *very* high from Day One. The goal of most PASs by the end of the job is to leave one's job and get out of town with as few scars as possible." Others spoke of how they "always" felt under high-level stress. Another, noting these very high levels of stress among PASs, attributed it to interest group pressure, Congress, self-imposed stress, and stress resulting from attempts to change things in a context in which "the status quo is the overriding influence in this town," a city of, as President Kennedy quipped, "Southern efficiency and Northern charm."

"Working for the government is akin to intellectual strip mining," one PAS's friend told him, but, he thought, "the intellect was the last thing it strips. Your energy is the first thing government strips. It doesn't actually use your intellect—there's too much to do, too much to read, too much preparation required" to make good use of one's intellect. Often he read material on the way to a meeting at which he had to make major financial decisions. He was very frustrated that "too much is decided on too little information."

His only advice to his successors regarding how to deal with stress was simply to expect it. He had not anticipated his current level of stress. He had experienced stress before, he observed, but "this is *Olympic* stress. You have to live this, there's no way to know it otherwise."

The end of an administration brings a curious mixture of slowdown and mania. Said one PAS, "The last nine months of the administration things lighten up, you don't initiate anything new. The main thing is to make sure there are *no surprises.*" Another called his own stress level "pretty low" but added that "everything's crazy under the surface with the election panic."

Washington is a very expensive town where professional and social obligations mean a certain amount of entertaining and black-tie dress, which placed a significant financial burden on some. One remarked that his work and social obligations meant his wife was expected to be an unpaid worker for the government.

Family stress was mentioned by many of the PASs. Many traveled a great deal; fifty- to seventy- or seventy-five-hour work weeks are the norm in Washington's highest echelon. One mentioned that he and his wife were separated, a fact "not unrelated" to his travel schedule and stress. Many times the spouse of a PAS is a highly educated professional who is unemployed or working at a level below her or his capacity. This, too, contributes to stress at home.

Many mentioned the lack of time to spend with their spouse and children, or a family living out of the area, as part of their stress load. Those whose family did not relocate to Washington usually traveled home on the weekends, which got them out of the nation's pressure cooker, but made for solitary week nights alone in Washington. When they were home, accumulated details and a spouse weary from being a weekday single parent added more stress.

Conclusion

Intrabureaucratic conflicts continued, for all intents and purposes, nearly unabated during the Bush administration. While the Bush PASs expressed obvious support for the careerists with whom they worked, there was a clear schizophrenia in their feelings about them. They respected their expertise but at the same time resented it because of the power it gave them. It was not apparent that there was a significant improvement in political-career relations from the Reagan administrations that had so vociferously attacked the public service and its servants. Whether or not this lack of improvement can be attributed to the nature of government, the basic Republican stance toward government, or any other factors (or combination thereof), it is clear that the objective of improving political-career relations toward the goal of improving government is still elusive.

Presidential appointees indisputably derived great satisfaction from their work. As might be expected, those at the top of the hierarchy were the most satisfied, those in middle management the least. Those serving a specified term in flat structures (the IRC PASs) tended to be more satisfied and less stressed than those serving at the pleasure of the president in tall structures in large, complex agencies. For most appointees, the intellectual stimulation, policy involvement, ability to "make a difference," and their location at the center of the policy-power nexus compensated in large measure for the stress of the job. They relished breathing the rarefied air of power, even if they were not always able to exercise it directly themselves.

However, stress undeniably figured in the life and work of the Bush PASs, dominating all too often. To a certain extent, of course, it goes with the territory, given the enormous responsibility they carry, the many players on the scene, the Constitution-based separation of powers, the high stakes involved, and the nation's zero tolerance for error. Nonetheless, not all stress is unavoidable; certainly, less would be preferable. The PPO should lead in educating PASs about the dangers of excess stress and ways to deal with it, both personally and institutionally.

The president could also lead by example and directive, though there was little hope of that with the frenetic workaholic Bush in the White House. It would be interesting to know if Reagan's PASs took their cue from their frequent-napper boss and slowed down or if they had to work even harder to pick up the slack. In any case, following the tragic suicide of Vincent Foster, Clinton's close friend and aide, the president did publicly state the importance of maintaining a balanced life. On the other hand, Clinton EPA chief Carol Browner thought it a major advance to organize her staff schedule so each person got home before 9 o'clock at least one night a week.

It is difficult to assess the extent to which George Bush's and Ronald Reagan's PASs, and thereby their administrations, differed. Certainly Bush, "the quintessential bureaucrat," did not mount the full frontal attack on government to the extent that Reagan had. He supported the public service both in concept and in reality, at least until he lost his bearings late in the 1992 election.

As had every group of PASs before them, the Bush PASs stressed the crucial importance of the career staff and their belief that they could be trusted. Early PAS orientation by the Bush PPO included, apparently for

the first time, a brief segment on working with careerists. Only a concerted effort by the White House will move new PASs quickly beyond
whatever anticareerist prejudice they bring into office with them. They
should not have to spend the first year on the job learning that lesson.

This lesson is particularly important for an incoming administration,
many of whose members would likely mistrust the careerists who labored
long and faithfully for the previous administration or party. Newcomers
should recall the solid recommendation given careerists by Republicans
in similar situations, as well as studies that indicate that as much as 44
percent of senior careerists are not affiliated with either majority party.
Independents, along with party-related careerists, are inclined to follow
political leadership, mostly out of allegiance to professional standards of
neutral competence and partly out of simple expediency. New presidents
and their people should play to the strength of professionalism and not
fear residual pull from the previous administration.

There is also a certain cynicism about government by those who
know it from the inside, accompanied by a desire for change in the agencies, that works to the next administration's advantage. As one careerist
observed,

> The agencies are eager for change. Twelve years of one party is too long.
> The system is dependent on the dynamic of change. My agency loves cri-
> sis and heroes—it focuses attention on issues—it likes opportunity, new
> directions. Careerists see themselves in the white hats, very committed
> to the agency and its mission, rather than to the public service, per se.
> They don't really care who wins, they just want change.

These factors should assure incoming PASs that they need not fear
sabotage or disdain policy input from their careerists. In fact, as many
Bush PASs acknowledged, the politics/administration dichotomy lives, as
it always has, more in theory than in fact. They used and valued careerists
for policy as well as administrative advice. Incoming PASs of either party
would do well to do likewise.

9

⊙〰⊙

Interbureaucratic Issues:
The End of Village Isolation

Heclo's 1977 claim that federal executives were operating independently in isolated villages (executive branch agencies) was rendered obsolete by three terms of one-party control of the White House. Because President Bush chose as much as one-half of his initial political executive force from the Reagan cohort, very many of the Bush PASs already knew one another at the start of the administration. The initial getting-to-know-the-players time was thus significantly shortened for Bush's team: after twelve years, most PASs knew one another and did not have as much need to get together. They had already "arrived" so they had less need to network (read: jockey) for personal power.

This chapter addresses three larger issues of bureaucratic life—PASs' interaction and sense of collegiality and solidarity across the government, and their relations and experiences with the White House and with the Congress, including the sometimes-hellish confirmation process. The primary basis for this analysis is data from the Bush PAS Survey and personal interviews with PASs and others.

The Villages Form a Colony: PASs Governmentwide

What nurtured the Bush PASs' sense of collegiality? One factor beyond the aforementioned familiarity is that most PASs met with or talked with their colleagues in and beyond their own agency often during the week. Nearly 95 percent of the PASs reported working contact by telephone or in meetings with PASs in other agencies; 68 percent had at least one contact per week, 35 percent had four or more per week. Fewer than 6 percent reported no contact at all outside their own agency.

Personal communication in the modern era of government has been facilitated by interagency task groups, which have become a very common form of governing, or at least of problem solving. In fact, 77 percent of the Bush PAS Survey respondents reported at least some involvement in an interagency working group. Government's functioning is mandated by interagency task forces because so many of the issues are interrelated that the agencies have to work together to get anything accomplished. As one PAS said of her work, "EPA issues absolutely *fall* over everybody else's issues because EPA regulates federal facilities and energy plants, and relates to agriculture and trade issues."[1] The staff of the various agencies often informally work out issues among themselves. (If a settlement cannot be reached among the agencies, the PASs may have to elevate issues to OMB or the White House for resolution.)

However, some also commented on a sense of isolation and tunnel vision within the agencies, quoting Henry Kissinger's dictum that "the immediate drives out the important." PASs are usually so absorbed in their daily activities of their villages that they do not often step back and assess the larger picture.

Some, by virtue of their position, are not really able to connect with other PASs. Inspectors general, for example, always have to remain a little outside the politics of the agency. Similarly, with those in the agencies that regulate other agencies (such as OMB, OPM, and the Federal Labor Relations Authority [FLRA]), there is a need for neutrality. The FLRA's Pamela Talkin observed how her role makes personal or social relations awkward. They are "the cop in the federal sector" so they cannot get too close to other PASs who might at some point be litigants in a case.

Certainly, Independent Regulatory Commission (IRC) Democrats serving the Republican administrations were odd politicians out, as noted above. Conservative enough to be appointed by Reagan or Bush, they were "Reagan Democrats, out of step with Republicans and out of step with other Democrats." They had few or no relations with Congress or with other Democratic PASs because their interests were localized in their agency, though some reported social connections around town.

Because there are so few women PASs (only 20 percent), Democratic women PASs were even more isolated. While there was a women's PAS group, one Democrat reported that she attended once and found the group's focus was on how to get Democrats out of the Senate. She "sneaked out with a 'respectable' member who had to leave early and never went back."

Spouses were often the forgotten people in the federal pressure cooker, called upon for social functions with little to support their own personal fulfillment. There was a group for wives of PASs, and another for husbands of PASs (the latter called the Denis Thatcher Society after the husband of former British prime minister Margaret Thatcher), both geared for spouses' support and social needs.

Orientation to PAS duties was stressed more in George Bush's administration than it had been in Ronald Reagan's, perhaps due to the former's emphasis on team spirit. While the Bush one-day orientation could do little in the way of training, it did set the tone of the administration and introduced PASs to the White House staff. This strategy was one way to make the PASs feel connected with one another across agencies: it was also a way to remind them of their obligations to the White House. An official of the PPO indicated that the White House was making a concerted effort to get every new PAS to an orientation session. If the PAS did not attend on the first invitation, it was reissued two more times.

While those who had previously served as a PAS might not feel the need for an orientation on how the federal bureaucracy operated, it is interesting to note that 54 percent of the total respondents indicated that they had attended a Bush White House orientation session, perhaps to get on board with the Bush administration per se, its people, agenda, and way of doing things (read: team spirit. Also, 19 percent attended orientation sessions in their own agency.) This stood in marked contrast to the 79 percent of the PASs in the 1985 NAPA study who indicated they had received no orientation.

PASs clearly (by 94 percent) chose ethical guidelines as the most important aspect of orientation to federal management. This is particularly key, given the ethical lapses of some appointees in the Reagan administrations.[2] PASs considered the following areas to be of very or very great importance for discussion during an orientation is listed below (173 to 178 PASs responded):

Ethical guidelines	94%
Public policies relevant to PAS's agency	80%
The president's policy objectives	79%
Interactions with Congress	77%
The federal budget process	73%
The federal personnel system	60%
Relations with the news media	60%
OMB's decision-making process	59%

It was also clear that appointees felt the need to learn the basics of how Washington works—public policy, the budget, the White House apparatus, personnel, the media, the Congress. Obviously, a one-day orientation is not the venue to satisfy this extensive agenda, but the PPO is the unit that should respond with appropriate training and resources.

Because the goals that appointees have going into an office will likely influence how they will approach their tasks, those in the Bush PAS Survey were asked to rate the importance of particular agency goals. The Bush PASs' primary goals for their agencies are listed below (178 PASs responded). Only four goals were rated definitively (by 70 percent or more) as being of "great" or "very great" importance:

Improving their agency's effectiveness	93%
Improving operational efficiency	89%
Developing new policies/regulations	81%
Changing public perceptions of agency	70%
Improving public perceptions of civil servants	52%
Reducing regulations	51%
Enhancing size or scope of agency	20%

It was particularly interesting that in a strenuously antiregulation Republican administration, only the barest majority of its PASs felt that reducing regulations was a significant goal, while more than 80 percent wanted to create *new* policies and regulations. Meanwhile, only 20 percent claimed enhancing the size or scope of their agency was of "great" or "very great" importance, 31 percent saw it as of "somewhat" or "moderate" importance, while more than 49 percent claimed it was of "little or no" importance. One wonders what tricks of administrative legerdemain nearly half would employ to create more federal regulations without the administrative apparatus to back them up.

Congress: Political Games and Gauntlets

Dealing with Congress was an integral part of bureaucratic life for most PASs. As discussed in earlier chapters, the Democratic Congress was more often seen by Republican PASs as the enemy than as the colleague branch in government.[3] Interviews tended to confirm this perspective.

While several PASs spoke of the importance of maintaining good relationships with key members of Congress and their staffs, and there seemed to be many staff-to-staff contacts that greased the wheels of legislative-executive work, there was, nonetheless, some discontent with the size and demands of congressional staff. "Senators have big staffs that make a lot of requests," said one PAS, who felt his agency expended too many resources on congressional requests. "We waste money, time, and effort responding endlessly to congressional oversight rather than pursuing our mission."[4]

One survey respondent wrote about "intrusive staff who apparently desire to micromanage executive agency policies and, at times, even personnel. I believe there are far too many congressional committee staff members who do little except create extra paperwork and stress on senior agency personnel in most instances. They wield far too much authority and have little or no accountability for the extensive mischief they can create."

A PAS at Health and Human Services agreed with the assessment that Congress had "way overdone document requests" by demanding too much documentation. He also felt that his agency in particular got more budget grief from Congress even than from OMB: "HHS has taken a cut in terms of real dollars and yet the work has grown every year." Long-simmering congressional anger at HHS often erupted inappropriately in micromanagement, he said. For example, "shortsighted and petty vindictiveness from Congress resulted in a near freeze of the travel budget for this year," because some members were angry at the number of political appointees from the Public Health Service who went to the international AIDS conference. In retaliation, they imposed a freeze on the agency travel budget. However, this tactic backfired: "It kept [career] health fraud investigators nailed to their desks but didn't affect the political appointees who had a separate budget for travel."

Anger at Congress came not just from its attempts to micromanage the work of the agencies but also because its GAO did not address what was all too often the root problem in government—insufficient funds. This frequently expressed sentiment is particularly noteworthy in light of the conventional Republican bias for less government and the "read my lips, no new taxes" motto of their boss, George Bush. Said Veterans Affairs' Anthony McCann, "GAO goes to the authorizing committees with reports of problems it finds in the agencies but the agencies already know about the problems but often don't have the funds to fix them. DVA gets beaten up pretty badly by Congress. But GAO doesn't go to the appropriations committees (which is where the programs live and die) to get better funding so the problems could be addressed."

Then GAO would compound the problem of cumbersome and slow bureaucracy by demanding additional internal red tape. "GAO reports always say more review is needed by the secretary. GAO has no concept of the Office of the Secretary. It demands that the secretary review even little things that should be decided further down the line (like the location of telephones at the VA hospitals)."

The EPA's Linda Fisher echoed this perspective on Congress and the budget. "The great untold story is that the Hill has been cutting EPA's budget, coming in at $50–$100,000,000 less than the president's request. The Hill is more of a problem than OMB. The environmentalists are not as aware of EPA's budget as they have been of legislation. They need to be more aware of the budget." However, others observed that Congress was sometimes their friend in a budget or ideological fight with the White House, as in the case of the ICC staff cuts discussed previously.

Nevertheless, budget was often the area where PASs had the most difficulty with Congress, particularly in regard to hearings. Said one, "they often display a willful ignorance of economics—hearings are grandstanding without knowing or bothering to learn the details." Said another, "Congress likes to hold hearings to yell about things. Congressmen are petty tyrants running a circus—hearings are shows to get headlines, publicity."

Agreed another:

> Congress, without a question, is the hardest to deal with. They lack clear direction. They scream like stuck pigs when you want to do something, like close an office. The Hill is trouble for budget requests. The whole budgetary process is desperately in need of a revamping. Why? "Special interests"—that says it all. I lay the problem squarely at the feet of the chairs of appropriations committees in both Houses.

On the other hand, Science and Technology Policy's Allan Bromley saw advantages to having day-to-day contact between his "apolitical science and technology staff" at the White House and the congressional staff. Good working relations helped smooth the way for upcoming legislation, in his experience. He had invested a lot of time in developing and rebuilding the bridges with Congress: "It's extremely important to have cooperation with Congress if you're going to get anything done." This view was echoed by others, as well.

Another PAS made this assessment of the Congress: "The Congress puts too much pressure on the system for the benefit of their constituents. This is a fact of life in a presidential (rather than parliamentary) system. Each person in Congress has to be elected as an individual. If they do a bad job of protecting their constituents, they lose their job. Congress is very reasonable to deal with on issues, but less so on legislation."

Or, as another PAS put it, "Inefficient government is the nature of Congress—it's endemic to Congress, it's the nature of the beast."

Confirmation: "Nineteen Other Reasons for Holdups"

The confirmation process is an issue about which few PASs have no opinion. For the several who described their confirmation hearing as "cordial, positive, matter-of-fact, very fast" (three weeks in that particular case) or "nondescript and noncontroversial," there were many more who had "horror stories" to tell of being "badly bruised" by senators, of rude behavior by them, such as those who smoked "fat, smelly cigars," chatted with one another or with their staff who popped in and out, did other work during the hearing, or simply did not show up at all. Other indignities included long delays, invasive and time-consuming FBI investigations, and confirmations being held hostage to a variety of political games and issues unrelated to the nominee. The process itself could be daunting enough to discourage any but the most tenacious.

A few cases, perhaps, are illustrative. Democrat William Albrecht was approached and interviewed by the Presidential Personnel Office (PPO) for a seat on the Commodity Futures Trading Commission (CFTC) late in Ronald Reagan's second term in a recess appointment. Then he heard nothing for many months. He found out about his appointment when a newspaper called him in Iowa to check out the story. When he called the PPO he was told they were "in the leak phase." Due to ambivalence in the White House regarding recess appointments,[5] it took a while for the president to make the formal appointment, which required an FBI investigation. When Albrecht finally came on board, he did not plan at that point to stay more than a year.

For the regular appointment by Bush that followed, another FBI check was required. It was late summer 1989 before Bush nominated him; by then, Albrecht knew the people on the Agriculture Committee and found no problems there, but still the chair and others did not move on his confirmation. His hearing was held up because of hostility toward the Republican CFTC nominee who was up for confirmation at the same time. The committee felt they could not hold a hearing on Albrecht without holding one on the Republican as well. The Senate refused to move on it, saying "the White House wouldn't like it."

Finally, Albright himself started home-state pressure on Senator Tom Harkin. Former Senator Richard Clarke (for whom Albrecht had worked at one time) pushed the committee chair to schedule the hearing; then the process moved smoothly. He was nominated in August 1989 and confirmed in November of that year. (The Senate committee never did hold the hearing for the Republican nominee.)

Albrecht observed that, had he known better, he would not have moved to Washington and rented out his home in Iowa until he had the confirmation in hand. Sometimes the delay is the fault of the White House, sometimes the Senate, but as he suggested to any potential candidates, "Be prepared for an extended, uncertain process. And don't burn any bridges until it's done."

The NLRB's Dennis Devaney, another Democrat, also discussed the essentially political nature of the confirmation process, which focuses more on larger partisan issues than on the qualifications of the nominee herself or himself, particularly in the more controversial agencies, such as his. Three Bush nominees to the NLRB had been blocked in the Senate, "some by the left (labor), some by the right (business)," he noted. This, his third confirmation, was "tough, the other two were easy." As had other interviewees, he declared that the White House had imposed no litmus test on him, but as he was already well known as a conservative, a Reagan Democrat, that hardly seemed surprising. He agreed with many others about the FBI investigation. "The FBI stuff was a pain—we've gotten off track with how much we muck around in people's lives."

Much like Albrecht's, other PASs' confirmations were held hostage to a larger dispute between their agency and the Congress, some for many months. Linda Fisher's confirmation for EPA, which she described as "uneventful," was held up over the Alar apple pesticide controversy that was unrelated to her candidacy. She echoed the comment of a PAS quoted earlier that if one had formerly worked on the Hill, one was likely to have made some enemies; previous as well as current staff conflict could also contribute to the delay. As she noted, "There are always nineteen other reasons for holdups on confirmation besides the nominee."

OMB's Frank Hodsoll had a similar tale of an unrelated issue delaying his confirmation—it was inadvertently linked with a rule-making dispute.[6] His solution was to hold up his own confirmation until the rule-making dispute quieted down. Eventually Senator Glenn put his confirmation forward as a separate issue.

One PAS observed that he was "not treated well" in the confirmation process. He was nominated in the first week of May but not confirmed until the last week of November. The chair of his agency's oversight committee was from his home state and had bottled his nomination in reaction to criticism that the candidate had been named to please him. Finally, the secretary pushed it, demanding a vote up or down. He was confirmed unanimously.

Added to the uncertainty of the process, the intrusive nature of the FBI investigation rankled many. One PAS called it "burdensome; it serves neither the Congress nor the administration." As noted previously, in addition to the four to five hours of FBI interviews (and thirty-five interviews of one's friends, family, employers, employees, acquaintances, and neighbors), the paperwork load is intensive. The nominee may have to pay considerable costs for an accountant to provide the required financial information. One interviewee reported that he needed his financial advisor and secretary to help him handle all the forms; he estimated the paperwork alone consumed a total of one hundred hours.

William Studeman, deputy director of the CIA, described his confirmation process as "like running the gauntlet—a hell of a paperwork drill," requiring several different forms for the same information. "There were forms, then pages and pages of specific questions. . . . [And then,] confidential answers provide fodder for the later public hearing." He remarked on the "huge studying required in preparation." He felt he was treated well by the Senate, where he was known from his previous stint as director of the National Security Administration; but even on a fast track, his confirmation took three to four months.

Veterans Affairs' Ed Timperlake remarked on the "chilling effect" of the FBI investigation and the financial disclosure requirements. "They're the scary part of the process. Things get written down on a sheet of paper and can stand alone. Allegations, even if unsubstantiated and disproved on the next sheet of paper, can be used against you. The country has turned to government bashing, it's more puritanical. The burden of proof is now on the person, not the process. You're guilty until proven innocent."

OPM's Connie Newman felt the confirmation process was longer and tougher now as a direct result of Watergate. Her appointment to head OPM was her fourth presidential appointment and "each time the confirmation process was longer and deeper than the one before." However, as she observed, "the limitations are such that even the most thorough investigation may not correlate to later corruption. For example, Sam Pierce [HUD secretary] had nothing in his background that would give even the slightest hint of his later corruption, so there was nothing there for even the toughest investigation to ferret out."

The PPO handles all the appointment details up to the submission of the nomination to the Senate oversight committee responsible for a particular position. In most cases it provides a summary of the FBI investigation but not the raw data to the Senate, so each committee requires its own forms to elicit information it thinks important. One question on the Senate form asks if there is anything in one's background that would be an embarrassment to the nominee. "The forms are public information so whatever you tell them is indeed going to embarrass you," one PAS observed dryly, having found out too late that copies of his completed forms were out on a table at his nomination hearing for anyone, including the press, to take. He speculated that the hassles involved in the process caused 5 to 15 percent of potential nominees to withdraw from the process enroute.

On the other hand, the FLRA's Talkin described her confirmation as slow but "a breeze. Senator Glenn [chair of Governmental Affairs], sets rules and follows them." She observed, however, that the confirmation process itself was the real lesson in how to get through it. "You need to have someone to guide you through it, tell you to contact senators' staff, schedule meetings, etc." Nominees may meet with or pay courtesy calls on as many as fifty senators or their top staff.

The SEA's Jerry Shaw termed the Senate confirmation process a mystery. He could not see "any real reason why one person got confirmed and another got worked over," whether for political or qualifications reasons. "Most of the confirmations are very quiet processes," he stated.

Tedious, drawn-out confirmations do more than slow down the political process and hamper agency operations. They can also wreak havoc in an individual's personal life, as mentioned above. One PAS's confirmation took eleven months due to "political games." The uncertainty meant he could not move his family to Washington. By the time he was at last confirmed, his children were well into a new school year and his wife had finally accepted a promotion in her job. He ended up commuting home every weekend. His was not a unique case.

The White House and its agencies use subtle and not-so-subtle means of persuasion to get recalcitrant candidates to sign on for the long, difficult, and sometimes offensive confirmation process. Often desperate themselves for warm bodies, they implore candidates to take the job, telling them how much they need them and that they cannot find anyone else to take a particular position, while they "hum the national anthem in the background," as one said. For those who did not really want the job and had to be courted (and there are quite a few and many turn-downs), the subsequent intrusive investigations, protracted confirmation process, public exposure, and skirmishes between the legislative and executive branches constituted an insult that continued to sting years later.

Another PAS felt that the chilling effect of the process had a negative impact on the quality of people willing to enter short-term government service.

It's hard to get top people into public service, with the investigations and deep digging into one's private affairs, expectations that political appointees be perfect, never have any problems and be shot at all the time. Who wants that? The result of the unrealistic situation in which [PASs] are expected to serve is that the government doesn't get the most creative, fit, or qualified people in public service.

Newman agreed: PASs serve only at the pleasure of the president and can be fired instantly with no severance pay. They also face ethics restrictions of one or two years during which they cannot lobby their former agency, with some activities barred for life. Given all this, "the job kind of loses its charm," she observed.

PASs within the federal workforce are invariably pulled in two directions at once, inward and outward, causing the personal and political conflict of divided loyalties. Not unlike the careerists, they are judged on two criteria that may be contradictory—competence and political responsiveness. Drawn inward into their agency and its needs, they must provide leadership to and oversight of their career staff. The respect accorded them internally is based in large measure on their competence at managing their agency.

At the same time, PASs are pulled outward into the White House and its demands. In that arena they are judged primarily according to their responsiveness, their ability and willingness to adhere to the president's policy objectives, even if that spells a shrinking mission or budget for their own agency.

In addition, part of PASs' job is to represent both their agency and the White House to the Congress. Not only do they have to deal with this prime player (Congress), but they may also have contradictory impulses related to their bifurcated responsibilities (to their agency and to the White House and its very powerful OMB).

While, on balance, the many strains of their job are outweighed by the satisfaction they derive from it, stress, not unrelated to their dual loyalties, is an ever-present and largely unhealthy feature of PAS life.

Relations with the White House and OMB

The Bush White House was felt by some appointees to be populated by lesser lights than in Reagan's day, though some felt Bush had recently begun to "pump up the White House with heavy people." Its Presidential

Personnel Office came in for some criticism. Said one PAS, "The PPO has gotten progressively worse from Carter onward—Bush's is the worst."

Although there were some informal White House briefings, they were not felt to be of much help. This PAS expressed a desire for a more formalized training system, especially training in politics and "how the town works" for those new to Washington.

Even though conservative Reagan Democrats were the Democrats most likely to be in the IRCs, for them, relations with the Republican White House were "still like being a fish out of water to be in the off-party community," though one PAS observed that "being a Democrat in a Republican administration is a lot easier if you are in agreement with the administration's policy." As a conservative Democrat who liked Reagan's economics, however, he felt "it's harder to know what Bush stands for; he's a backslider."

Gail McDonald, Democratic vice-chair of the Interstate Commerce Commission (ICC), observed the pressure the 1992 election imposed on new appointments: "The PPO is turning even more hard right as the election nears; there's more [anti-]abortion pressure." An ongoing dynamic between her agency and the White House was that the Republicans since Reagan had been trying to close down the ICC, the nation's oldest IRC, and were particularly determined to abolish its office of public assistance.

One Republican PAS felt that the Bush people were more political than the Reagan people, to the point of removing "Reagan-appointed chairs from IRCs because Bush didn't want any Reagan people heading any of the agencies. The Reagan people were better mannered, more communicative; the Bush people are rude and crude," she said.

The Bush White House was at least consistent in its ethical stance, according to the OGE's Steven Potts, who, with somewhat faint praise, called it "more a help than a hindrance." He judged OMB as also being helpful.

PASs' opinions of OMB were often directly related to whether or not OMB had taken aim at their budget. Relations seemed to be workable as long as the PAS's agency or program was not on OMB's hit list and the agency did not ask for any budget increase. As one PAS explained, he has "fine relations with the White House and OMB. I'm reasonable; I don't seek to expand my programs. The OMB is amenable to reasonable arguments."

As Frank Keating, HUD's general counsel, noted, White House intervention in agency affairs "depends on the degree of the president's interest in the agency's issues. What shows up on the president's radar screen" is what attracts OMB's budget axe, the most direct way an administration forces agency or policy compliance. He called HUD's relationship with OMB "difficult but professional. OMB sees itself as the self-proclaimed conscience and soul of the administration, though not necessarily the last word. If there are disputes between HUD and OMB, the White House counsel or others in the White House break the tie."

Talkin judged relations with the White House to be good. "It never interferes and OMB is easier on FLRA than it had been on the Equal Employment Opportunity Commission [where she had been chief of staff]. We get the money we need."

When IRCs do not get the money they feel they need there is one place of refuge from OMB's budget-cutting knife: Congress is the court of last resort when the administration's budget short-changes an agency. For example, the White House forced the ICC chair to accept a substantial staff cut over the unanimous objections of the commissioners and sought to micromanage the commission by directing a department-by-department budget breakdown. Over White House objections, McDonald and the other Democratic commissioners were able to persuade the Congress to restore the budget to its current level.

Said one PAS, whose IRC has good relations with both the White House and Congress (and which also employed only a little more than half of its allotted number of employees), "We have good relations with OMB—and Congress is there to help raise limits if OMB balks."

A consistent theme among the PASs was the frustrations that arose with OMB when its budget watchdog role slipped into a policy role. These comments came from conscientious PASs trying to do too large a job on too little money. One PAS felt that "OMB has been too constraining of funding for my agency. It has suppressed our ambitions; it controls everything. There are twenty-four steps in the appropriations process and OMB controls every gate in terms of what the administration brings to the Congress in that interaction."

One assistant secretary said, "In relation to OMB, mostly what I do is deal with conflict. I need nearly twice as much money to do the job I've been given, but I can't get it. OMB is very rigid and difficult to deal with, but that's their role and function and they do a good job at it."

Because OMB speaks for the administration and makes budget decisions, "it is very powerful and has gotten stronger over time. It is literally the gatekeeper on any major policy or legislation." OMB's power extends beyond the budget, as well. Said one PAS, "The department and OMB prescreen my testimony before Congress and change it if they don't like it.

Dancing to the tune of the political arena is all part of the bureaucracy."

OMB's method of control came in for severe criticism from another PAS, who observed the power of long-term careerists there.

> At all levels, political and career, OMB consistently serves to thwart, limit, and derail new, exploratory initiatives and fundamental policy creation and idea formulation. OMB should be held accountable down to the GS-12 level careerists who badger and "instruct" senior PAS officials through testimony and other policy. OMB's culture is not to help or assist, but to intimidate and even ridicule. Political appointees have to yell and escalate the conflict to get it kicked up to the White House. Once you have their attention they will support the political people, but otherwise the careerists at OMB run things.

The Independent Regulatory Commissioners

The one group among the survey respondents that was overrepresented was the 42 percent of the PASs (seventy-five individuals) who indicated they held a statutory term appointment in an independent regulatory commission, or IRC (the 141 PAS allocated positions in this category comprise 22 percent of the 639 PAS allocated positions). Apparently, nearly twice as many term-appointed PASs as their overall percentage in the Bush PAS Survey universe responded to the survey. Although at any given time there is a certain number of vacant positions, it is likely that the term nature of the appointment makes for a lower vacancy rate for IRC appointees than for the other PASs, which may explain in part its overrepresentation.

This group is composed largely of those serving on the thirty-one regulatory agencies, collegial bodies, and commissions in the executive branch (herein referred to collectively as IRCs). The Democratic and Independent appointees and survey respondents are most likely to be in these positions as most of these bodies are required by statute to have no more than a majority from one party. Members of such bodies usually number three to five and serve fixed terms, generally from four to six years, though some may serve longer (as in the Fed, whose seven commissioners serve fourteen-year terms).

Another group within this designation does not sit on such commissions but does serve in term appointments. It is composed of such persons as the surgeon general, the director of the National Institutes of Health, the commissioner of the Food and Drug Administration, the postmaster general, and the director of the FBI. They were included in the Bush PAS Survey because they are located in the executive branch.

Conversely, others are appointed by the president to term offices but serve the legislative branch and so were not included in the study. They include the comptroller general and deputy comptroller of the United States (General Accounting Office), the librarian of Congress, the architect of the Capitol, the public printer and deputy public printer (Government Printing Office), the nineteen judges of the U.S. Tax Court, and the three members of the Copyright Royalty Tribunal.

Those serving in the regulatory bodies constitute a specialized genre of presidential appointee. Though appointed by the president and confirmed by the Senate to serve in the executive branch, they, unlike the other PASs, are not subject to presidential discipline. Their term appointment protects them from removal, either by the president who appointed them or by his successor. While the president can replace the chair, that person continues to serve out her or his term on the IRC. Only resignation, death, or malfeasance in office can separate commissioners from their positions before their term expires.

Therefore, IRC PASs are spared many of the overtly partisan pressures that their other PAS colleagues face. And, indeed, in the interviews the IRC PASs, much like the inspectors general, asserted their independence from the White House. Often, the cases that come before their commission have a White House component or interest, so executive contact with the IRC PASs (ex parte communication) is strictly forbidden. Said one PAS, "The 'I' is very important. It makes the IRCs almost a fourth branch of government." "The IRC has tremendous independence to 'call them as you see them,'" said another, noting that this is particularly healthy for the development of regulatory law.

Pamela Talkin, a Democratic member of the FLRA, for example, said that she "never felt any pressure from the White House to be or say anything other than what I believed. I feared there would be a time when I might have to take a stand—it's never come. We were told to take a low profile regarding Bush's reelection campaign. I found myself actually shocked at the lack of partisan pressure and how committed people are to doing their jobs beyond the politics."

Of course, this did not prevent the White House from exerting pressure on the commissioners. Nevertheless, the IRC PASs interviewed all stressed the independence of their agency. As one put it, "The White House leaves us alone. . . . We can submit our budget directly to Congress, bypassing OMB if we want to."

Of all the PASs interviewed, the IRCs seemed the most relaxed as a group, the ones most likely to have the time to think about the larger picture, about the philosophy of law and its application in government, and perhaps, the ones most likely to have time to respond to a GAO survey.

Another study might look only at the PASs in this category or might exclude them altogether in order to get a clearer picture of the more purely political appointees who serve solely at the pleasure of the president who appoints them.

Nonetheless, little difference emerged between the responses of term-appointed PASs and the others. For example, their responses were within three percentage points of one another in judging CSESs' responsiveness to political direction and competence. However, a few of the Bush PAS Survey's twenty-six indicators for job satisfaction did elicit a significant difference between the IRCs and the other PASs, as noted in table 14 in chapter 8.

Hiring and Firing PASs

Of issue in every administration is the degree of independence each cabinet secretary is given in choosing her or his subordinates. While Reagan closely controlled this process, Bush, as discussed previously, started his term with a cabinet government, in which the secretary has primary appointing authority within her or his agency. He soon shifted away from that model, however, and in the second round of hirings changed to a more White House-dominated style.

As expected, feelings among the PASs about cabinet government fell along two demarcations. HUD's Keating felt it resulted in "a more viable and functioning team because the secretary can create her or his own team. Outstanding secretaries bring in outstanding people. Less competent secretaries attract less competent people."

Ted Barreaux, who worked in the Bush transition, said that Bush let his cabinet members choose their own team more than any other president. In contrast to Keating, he felt it was a mistaken strategy.

> The secretary builds a team loyal to her or him. When she or he leaves, if the team stays it is loyal to neither the new secretary nor to Bush. Reagan chose people more on personal loyalty to himself than on philosophy. Consequently, there was little ideological theme to the Reagan pudding, with disastrous consequences (i.e., scandals in the SEC and FCC). . . . Reagan was not interventionist in the regulatory mode. He trusted the business community to "do the right thing." Instead they took the opportunity to make money.

Barreaux judged the Kennedy White House the best in terms of getting a team in place that was generally competent and loyal to the president. "Clark Clifford ran the JFK transition. He got rid of all the Eisenhower appointees by January 20th. He knew the cabinet member would rely on his or her own team."

The flip side of hiring is, of course, firing. How do PASs actually get fired? There is no clean and easy way to do it and some, such as the inspectors general, have argued that they cannot be fired, short of malfeasance in office. Also, as discussed above, firing a political appointee can be politically hazardous, alienating the PAS's friends and constituency or implying poor judgment in hiring on the president's part.

According to Barreaux, when the decision is made that a PAS has to go, the agency head is invariably the one who goes to the White House to initiate the proceedings. First, she or he and the agency's chief of staff go to the head of the PPO and then to the chief of staff at the White House. Personality and policies are the usual causes for dismissal, though occasionally sexual harassment rears its ugly head and does seem to be taken seriously.

At the assistant secretary level the head of the PPO contacts the PAS and usually offers her or him an alternative position, sometimes a lateral transfer to an equal position, but usually there is at least a subtle downgrading of position. Sometimes the PAS is transferred to a lesser job, perhaps an SES position, which is usually refused for ego reasons. Sometimes a person is just pushed out one small step at a time, "dying the death of a thousand cuts."[7] If the PAS has another job to go to she or he leaves immediately or sets a date of resignation effective upon the confirmation of a successor and then leaves. Because there is no accumulated leave time for PAS positions, departing PASs usually set a date far enough in advance to include vacation time they have not been able to take. Then there is what Barreaux called "the traditional exchange of polite letters: 'Dear Mr. President, thank you for the opportunity to serve; sorry I can't stay, etc. . . . ' 'Dear (PAS), Thank you for your dedicated service. I'm sorry you have to go; best wishes, etc.'"

Once the decision has been made to get rid of a PAS, the search for a successor is usually expedited. In these cases the White House generally has a candidate in the pipeline and can go through the confirmation process in as few as six weeks. A quick FBI investigation can be cursory and completed in a couple of days, if necessary. The thirty-five interviews required for a PAS (or twenty for a noncareer SES) can be handled by sending thirty-five (or twenty) agents out into the field and doing the interviews in one day.

That, according to Barreaux, was how firings and replacements were handled in the Bush administration. Sound and intelligent advice on ways to avoid this fate and be a successful PAS were offered by the interviewees to their successors of either party and are discussed in chapter 10.

Conclusion: Strangers No More

Despite the many satisfactions of PAS work, the conflicting pulls on the PASs (inward and outward) created significant tensions both within their agency and within the PASs. The strains of political life, including dealing with the White House and the Congress, will continue to visit the appointees of any future administration. As several PASs noted, it was important for them to understand the realities of politics and the many players in the status-conscious, high stakes, pressure-cooker, fishbowl atmosphere of Washington. They saw the need to realize that any real change would be incremental at best, to take pleasure in small victories, and to take care of their own physical, emotional, and mental health.

The Bush PASs may have felt a certain sense of isolation that came with their territory and agency responsibility, but they did not evidence any interagency lack of connection among themselves. In fact, their early orientation, frequent contacts, and interagency working groups maintained a sense of cohesiveness, if not always unquestioning cooperation, among them. That so many had worked in Reagan's administration gave them something of a long-term sense of collegiality, as well. If the Reagan PASs had a unified sense of vision, the PASs of the Bush administration had a distinct sense of the interconnectedness of their mission, even if they were not always certain of its exact nature. Further, while competition for budget marks any bureaucrat's life, and a certain defense of "mandate" was noted by some of the PASs, it was obvious from the interviews that not only did they understand their boss's preference for team players, they knew personally most of their teammates. This smoothed communication among them, even if it did not always resolve their differences.

Clearly, George Bush's administration was no "government of strangers" in Heclo's sense. As much as possible, given the nature of modern government, it could be termed a "government of colleagues."

Notwithstanding this, friction over PASs' natural desires to expand budget and mission over and against the standard Republican commitment to cutting budgets led to the internal conflict common to any administration. However, political dissension may have been more muted for public consumption in the Bush administration than would be the case in a Democratic administration.[8]

Nonetheless, Republicans were wise to fear that their appointees would be "captured" by the bureaucracy. Despite the stridently antiregulation tone of three Republican administrations, only a bare majority of their PASs felt reducing regulations was a key goal, while four-fifths wanted to create *new* policies and regulations. Frequently voiced complaints by Republican PASs about the lack of budgetary resources to do their job should also give antigovernment politicians and tax-cutters pause. A political appointee, like any other conscientious and ambitious employee, wants to do the best job she or he can, and doing so requires resources. Because the demands of the populace are seemingly limitless, there is always more that could be done. Reality tends to overtake ideology for most PASs.

The reality is that running the government takes money. While directives to streamline operations and eliminate waste, fraud, and abuse are all to the good and can be counted on to claim headlines, there is no escaping the conclusion that government will not get what it is unwilling to finance. There is only so much that can be cut in a democratic system replete with growing needs and demands, checks and balances, special interests, and divided powers. Antigovernment Reaganite Republicans, Libertarians, and others are doomed to perpetual angst in such a situation.

10

⟨✦⟩

Conclusion and
Future Directions

The PASs of any administration are in a unique position to offer wisdom to their successors. Many of George Bush's did this, and graciously. It was also clear to the author that certain trends have appeared in the institution of the presidential appointment system and its appointees, and that they have implications for research on these high-level political appointments. These are the subjects of this final chapter.

The Christmas Help and the Permanent Staff:
PASs Offer Advice to Their Successors

In the course of the personal interviews with PASs, they were asked what advice—professional, political, and personal—they would pass along to their successors.[1] While, as one PAS put it, "Some things you can only learn by being here—you have to live it; no child's guide to government will do," most were willing to offer some suggestions for survival, and beyond that, success. The most astute advice fell into three not totally distinct categories: administrative, political, and personal.

The advice they gave was sound, useful in any administration regardless of party label, and is offered for PASs of future administrations. However, if experience is any guide, it will be ignored soundly by them, having, apparently, to be learned firsthand by each generation of appointees.

Counsel for Successful Agency Administration

Good personnel choices are crucial for PASs once they successfully navigate the confirmation process themselves. Ted Barreaux, Bush Transition Team member, advised that new PASs first choose the "top four, the most important members of the team." They are the congressional relations staff, the counsel ("to keep you out of trouble"), the deputy (the chief operating officer of the agency), and the public affairs staff.

> Congressional relations is the most important of the four. That person keeps Congress from screaming at you. If you get off to a bad start with Congress you can spend the rest of your time in office testifying, dealing with congressional staff. It makes for a miserable experience. Best to co-opt Congress, get it on your side. [One chief at] USIA is the classic example of someone who didn't do this. He felt dealing with Congress was beneath him, felt his mission in life was to travel. He got run out of his job, slipped off to Belgium as ambassador.

PAS interviewees often said that too many PASs came into office with an agenda—they wanted to accomplish one or two things and that was all that was on their horizon. But few interviewees said, as did one, "Survival is not the point—having a goal is important. Be prepared for conflict in order to accomplish it." This single-minded approach constitutes a fatal flaw, according to many.

Frank Hodsoll at the Office of Management and Budget (OMB) agreed with this analysis and said PASs should plan on spending 80 percent of their time in basic management of their agency. However, early on, preferably prior to their confirmation, they should establish some political priorities for their tenure.

> Think through early the two or three things you'd like to do in the two to three years you have and plan to devote maybe 20 percent of your time to them. Think through why those particular things are important and how you would accomplish them. Consult with the career staff to inform yourself about the choices of the two or three things. Assess in the first six months on the job who can help get the job done and establish a team approach to do it. Establish a safety net to make sure nothing terrible happens to the rest of the program while you're working on your specific goals. Keep it all in reasonable perspective.

Hodsoll suggested that PASs focus on "specific areas with fixable problems to work on, especially high-risk areas and scandals or those in the making, such as the Housing and Urban Development scandals and Department of Defense inventory reporting."

Political appointees can inflict damage on their successors more readily than they can repair damage inherited from their predecessors. Steven Potts, head of the Office of Government Ethics, offered a cautionary word to counter the standard feeling of appointee newcomers that they should be "super careful and protect themselves" from the careerists. His advice was to consider that feeling carefully to see if it was really necessary or helpful. "There's a danger of building a wall between yourself and the career staff. You can do damage to the agency if you shut them out. *Rely on the careerists.*" He noted how helpful this advice had been in his own experience in cementing his relationship with his career staff. He was able to restore the relationship with them and heal scars left by a previous agency director who had seriously alienated them.

To a person, the PASs spoke highly of the careerists with whom they worked. Many PASs addressed the importance of establishing good relations with career people, not only because of their high level of competence, on which most remarked, but because, as one said, "Government is consensual. Who does the work? Not the political appointees. You have to get the line people behind you."

PASs were keenly aware of their limited tenure; that, after all, is the nature of political jobs. They were equally aware of the key role the stability of the permanent bureaucracy plays in getting anything done in Washington. Simply put, they knew all too well how dependent the country is on the careerists and how relatively dispensable politicians are in the day-to-day management of agency business. As one said, "They look at us as the Christmas help. They know we'll be gone pretty soon. You need their support to get anything done."

Many interviewees discussed the larger nature of politics in Washington. Fred Hitz, inspector general (IG) at the CIA, suggested PASs "take the long view, don't think you're going to get everything done in a short time—the system will beat you bloody. It wages a war of attrition." Despite the warfare imagery, Hitz, along with others, considered government "fun—it's more fun than selling tires."

The Politics of Success

PASs as a breed are action- and results-oriented. Many in the Bush PAS Survey, especially those who came from the private sector, expressed amazement and frustration at "how long it takes to make anything happen. You have to remember to touch all the necessary bases." In general, PASs sometimes have trouble understanding that there are limitations on their ability to accomplish things because they have to operate vertically throughout their own agency and up to the White House, as well as horizontally within their agency and with other agencies in the federal bureaucratic maze. One compared the process to the drawn-out nature of labor negotiations.

As one former PAS observed, "This government requires an element of trust and a high degree of comity to work. Washington is a city of cocker spaniels more ready to be loved and petted than to wield power." Whether this is a cause or effect of the consensual nature of government is a matter of speculation.

The EPA's Linda Fisher advised,

> People underestimate how hard these jobs are and how much intellectual heavy lifting you have to do to solve the public policy issues. It is substantive hard work. Be prepared to work hard. Be prepared to question the experts. You need to fully understand all sides of an issue; not everything is there at once. You have to consider what comes to you versus what hasn't come to you. What hasn't bubbled up may be more important than what has.

Others expressed surprise at the variety involved in their work, the heavy workload, the number of hours they had to devote to their work (fifty-five to seventy or more hours a week is standard), and the amount of reading they had to do, simply to keep up. Many issues are not clearcut and require a certain level of sophistication in negotiating them. The fact that they often dealt in shades of gray intrigued some PASs, as did the complex nature of the nation's problems. As one PAS said, only half-facetiously, "In Washington you can only keep things from getting worse— you can't change things for the better."

Inspectors general (IGs), in particular, have to be aware of the pitfalls of their position. As one advised, "Always honor your integrity and independence or you're dead as an IG. Don't bend one way or the other. Your job is to collect and report the facts and stick to that."

Many were not prepared for the rough game that is politics in Washington. "Be very sensitive to your environment, be prepared for ruthless intensity," said one. The CIA's William Studeman suggested that PASs practice what he called "the conservation of enemies" because the various players "may be allies one time and enemies the next."

One PAS expressed surprise at "how mean it is—politics is a rougher game than I thought it was. You're the personal target, particularly in a political [election] year." Another urged nominees to prepare themselves for "the nasty things people say about you during the confirmation process." And once in office, "get a thick skin. The easiest thing is to say no, you can always say no. The hardest thing is to say yes because that means you're going to create change. . . . Doers often are not liked in their own building but may have a good reputation outside."

Another PAS noted wryly his naivete in coming to Washington. He was not alone in thinking that he could just concentrate on his job to be a success. He had "done little in the way of networking or socializing or 'schmoozing' and figured the best way to help the president was to do a good job." He soon learned that networking and schmoozing are part of the job. He also committed the near-fatal error of not accepting White House personnel suggestions. Consequently, he was seen as not being a team player, and not being a team player could be the kiss of death in George Bush's administration.

This PAS soon came to understand that political appointees have to be more attuned than he had been to politics, to the party line expected of appointees, and to the prevailing ethos of you-scratch-my-back,-I'll-scratch-yours. He urged that appointees learn ahead of time what it means to be a political appointee. "The 'political' part carries a lot of weight. Ask yourself what the payoff is you're looking for, if it's realistic to expect to find it in a political job, and if it's worth the price."

Two groups in general came in for special scorn from the PASs—the media and special interest groups. "I have no or low respect for the media. I don't trust them. They are headline-grabbers always looking for scandal, whether or not it exists," said one.

On the other hand, the Nuclear Regulatory Commission's Ivan Selin noted that he had "more sympathy for the media and Congress than do most PASs. The media are the avenues to the people—every public servant should consider it part of the job to deal with the media. It's the prime way to deal with their employers (the public)."

PASs saw themselves as public servants serving the public interest. It was a bit of a stretch to think of themselves as "the enemy," as they sometimes appeared to be to advocacy or special interest groups. HUD's Frank Keating counseled, "Watch your backside from the special interest groups . . . that are utterly agenda-driven. If you don't agree completely with them, you're the enemy. You can't think out loud with them or treat them like a peer. They will stab you in the back if they have a chance. They're always playing 'gotcha.' They see the world in a frantic, revolutionary sense."

Succinct advice for basic political survival was offered by Veterans Affairs' Anthony McCann: "Trust the judgment of careerists regarding substantive issues. Delegate—do not get swamped in the minutia; let it go.

Don't deal with too much yourself. Figure out where the secretary is coming from. Keep your relations close with the IG. This last helps when things go wrong—and there's always something going wrong in an agency."

Those from the private sector clearly valued the opportunity to work in the public sector but, warned one, "It's a very protected environment. People [civil servants] can get comfortable with no driving force in government to keep them competitive, to bring out the best."

Selin recommended that persons not be appointed to high-level posts until they have had experience in the private sector. They "should plan on making their money in the private sector first and then going into public service a little later in life." He also felt they should work in government at the GS-15 level or lower before taking a political appointment to get a sense of how government operates. He noted a difference between the public and private sectors: "Government service is hard in the sense of having a wide impact. The private sector is more narrow. There, one can concentrate on maximizing a few things, focusing on a few things and doing them well. But in government, you have to satisfice, to balance many interests and needs."

Many PASs talked about the consensual nature of federal politics. One always needs to "keep one's eyes open" and be aware of the politics of the situation and the reaction of Congress. As Elliot Richardson noted,

> Decisionmaking is the easiest thing you do, say one-seventh of the job. Then you have to get the support of the staff, OPM, OMB, the Hill, interest groups, the president, and the general public. All the players have to be at least considered and in some cases brought on board. The complexity of the governing process increases and grows faster than any of the trends that contribute to it.

The nature of democracy itself is largely responsible for the complexity within which political actors operate. Perhaps the final word of political advice belongs to Richardson.

> The function of the political process is to make choices among competing claims. There are no simple answers or easy decision making and there is no objective way to decide among them. Any politician who doesn't waffle doesn't understand the problem. Politicians should have the imagination and intelligence and empathy to understand the jostling of competing claims.

Personal Survival at the Policy Nexus

Many expressed the view that PAS service was a privilege and an honor: "It's a great experience to come in and serve the country." However, PASs have to learn to protect themselves and to build in successes along the way, if they are not to burn out in the process of serving their president and country. As one PAS noted, "The opportunity to feel you've done something is less than it is in academia where you can build up a program or develop a school. You have to create those opportunities" to do something.

As discussed in previous chapters, the nomination and confirmation process can be one of extended length, great complexity, and stressful uncertainty. Sometimes confirmation delay is the fault of the White House, sometimes the Senate, but rarely is it pleasant or easy.

Self-protection in the face of personal criticism loomed large in many PASs' comments. "Be prepared—it's not a glory job, prepare yourself for criticism. Regardless of what you do, Congress will just criticize, not praise," said one.

Others spoke of the intensity of the work, particularly in hot-button agencies like Health and Human Services where PASs are likely to work eighty-hour weeks and receive calls at home at all hours of the day and night. The toll this takes on one's family was a point of consideration for more than a few. Stress, as discussed in chapter 8, is an ever-present problem for PASs. As the CIA's Studeman said, "Managing your health is a big issue around town. You have to develop stress management techniques or this town will run you over and kill you deader than a doornail. You have to avoid getting emotionally tied to it." Said another, "You have to keep stress under control or you don't do the job well, you can't be effective, and you end up cheating your family."

The social pressures of Washington also got to some. "Washington is a very demanding, expensive town—the in-crowd social expectations could easily dominate your entire life," said one PAS.

Trends in the Institution of the Presidential Appointment System and Its Appointees

While political prognostication is always a risky proposition, it seems to be the favorite pastime in the nation's capital. Some trends, issues, and questions relevant to the future of the institution of the presidential appointment system and its yield, the PASs, can be culled from the Bush PAS Survey and interviews: they are worth noting.

Here to Stay But "Maxed Out" on Numbers

It appears that the trend of having more appointees placed deeper in the agencies finally came to its end in the Bush administration. Although Clinton promised to trim the federal government by some 272,000 career positions (12 percent), it was for financial, not management or political theory reasons. But even if he had had the financial resources, it was unlikely that the Clinton administration would have adopted this Eisenhower-Nixon-Reagan administrative presidency strategy of superimposing political appointees over a dispirited bureaucracy.

A Rebirth of a Government of Strangers?

With Democrats taking back the White House after an absence of twelve years, there were some Carter people in the Clinton administration, but the aura of a "failed presidency" (however fair or unfair an assessment) still haunted them. Young newcomers (particularly those coming from Arkansas who had not had Washington experience) did not know the old hands or how the town worked. Strangers, they likely irritated the old hands and one another. A future study will have to address this question.

On the other hand, the phenomenon of government by interagency task force will continue to grow with the complexity of the nation's problems and the overlapping missions of the various federal agencies. The demands of this type of governing will likely mean that its political leaders from whatever source will not long remain strangers to one another.

A Setback in Political-Career Relations?

As noted, Democrats probably mistrusted careerists who loyally served three Republican administrations. The clear message from the Bush PASs (echoing the Reagan PASs) was that careerists could be trusted and politicians should not waste valuable time trying to circumvent or disempower them. Also, if what careerists report is true, the agencies themselves are eager to move on; they depend on party changes to rejuvenate them—the new political bosses have little to fear from their careerists. However, if history provides any model, that lesson will likely have to be learned anew by the incoming tenants of the White House.

Qualifications and Training Will Continue to Be Important

The need remains to push qualifications as a key criterion for appointees. Training—even on-the-job training and particularly in understanding and working the federal budget, agency management, and the basic politics of the administration and town—will often be critical to PASs' success.

Slowness in Nomination of PASs Will Persist

The troublesome trend of nomination delay has grown unabated for the past several decades. While the White House is not the sole cause of this problem, there are things it can do to ameliorate it. For example, a new president should make early nomination a priority for his or her administration, enhance the stature of the PPO by giving it high-level visibility and access to his time and attention, place reasonable limitations on the FBI investigation, and reduce the paperwork required of nominees. The White House should also work more closely with the Senate committees to streamline the paperwork and process.

Turnover Will Continue to Be Highly Dependent on the Chief Executive

The president (along with the Senate) must make clear to nominees his expectations regarding tenure in office if he hopes to alleviate the many administrative and political problems caused by frequent turnover.

PAS Service As a Lose-Lose Proposition?

The nation's hostility toward Washington will continue to increase in direct proportion to the growth of the nation's problems and its expectation that Washington solve them. Balanced-budget activism,, Republican anti–big-government rhetoric, Perot-style populism, and Libertarian hostility to the very existence of most of the government will make public service even more unattractive to many potential nominees. Unless the financial disclosure and post-PAS employment restrictions are loosened, PAS service will be less and less appealing to highly skilled individuals. Only those just starting in their careers or nearing retirement will be able easily to afford (in financial and career terms) to accept a PAS position.

The Politics-Administration Dichotomy: A New Paradigm?

One logical extension of the centralized presidency could be a revised, revitalized version of the politics-administration dichotomy. In this version, the PASs could find themselves assigned the neutral competence (administration) position formerly allotted careerists. As decision-making power (politics) continues to accrue to the president's aides in the Executive Office, particularly to the chief of staff and the OMB, the political appointees in the agencies could find themselves more often assigned the role of policy implementer, rather than policy maker. This would make PAS service even less attractive to policy activists.

Stress as a Fact of Life

Contradictory pulls inward (to the agency) and outward (to the White House) will continue to plague PASs. It is important for them to understand the realities of politics and the many players in the high-stakes, status-conscious, pressure-cooker, fishbowl atmosphere of Washington. As had their predecessors, they have to deal with the tension of trying to do a good job in an era of expanding demands, contracting budgets, and generalized belligerence. Because PASs are by nature action- and results-oriented, they need to realize that any real change will be incremental at best and to learn to take pleasure in small victories. In the midst of their fifty-five-to-seventy-hour work weeks, they also need not to lose sight of their responsibility to take care of their family, personal relations, and their own physical, emotional, mental, and spiritual health while they are serving their president and country.

Questions for Future Research

What implications from this study pertain to the ongoing institution of presidential appointments in the federal government? What would make for a stronger PAS workforce and a more smoothly functioning government? As discussed throughout the preceding chapters, questions arose whose answers might prove useful barometers of PASs' attitudes and aptitudes.

One recurring point of conflict between the administration and the PASs and among the PASs themselves at different executive levels was the decision-making power for hiring PASs in the agencies. Would mutual accommodation smooth political relations? The possibility of a more shared decision process with a double veto or, put more positively, mutual accommodation on both sides (PPO/PAS; PAS/PAS) should be explored. In a succeeding survey of Clinton appointees, exploration should be undertaken of how PASs' feelings about the PPO relate to their job satisfaction.

Given PASs' general unease with the federal budget, it would also be valuable to explore in some depth the extent to which previous budget experience and responsibility relate to competence in a particular PAS position. Does previous experience in budget or personnel supervision matter? In that context, it would also be useful to know the budget PASs handle in their current position, as well as the size of their previous budget, as the Bush PAS Survey asked. Further, it would be useful to know the extent to which the PPO looks for this kind of expertise in potential nominees.

Similarly, it would be valuable to know how important previous personnel experience is to the success of PASs and also the extent to which the PPO evaluates this kind of experience in its potential nominees.

Is there any real difference between IRC and non-IRC PASs? While there were few differences observed in the survey results between those PASs who served term appointments on independent regulatory commissions (IRCs) and those who served at the pleasure of the president in the executive agencies, they do constitute two distinct groups. Investigation into differences between IRC and non-IRC PASs might prove fruitful, particularly in terms of exporting to the non-IRCs the greater job satisfaction the IRC PASs enjoyed in some arenas. These arenas were: dealing with Congress and groups opposed to agency policy, the time requirements of their job, the time available to think creatively about issues, and the impact of their job on their personal or family life.

An IRC-only study would also prove instructive as IRC PASs often outlast their president. Because IRCs cannot be composed of more than a simple majority of one party, Reagan and Bush appointed "Reagan Democrats;" Clinton most likely appointed "Clinton Republicans" (though that term was not bandied about) to these collegial boards. Because the sitting president designates the chair, who often determines the overall character of the board, after twelve years of Reagan-Bush appointments, how did the next eight years of Democratic appointments affect the internal workings and policies of the IRCs?

Perhaps most germane to a study of PASs is an examination of what happens in the succeeding PAS community when long dominance of the White House by one party is ended. Did the Clinton appointees construct their own village government? With Bill Clinton's administration, was there a reemergence of the village of strangers in which appointees lived in their own isolated agencies, taking on their perspective against the White House's? Or, with the growth of government and political appointees during the Republican reign and the advent of interagency task forces and working groups dealing with cross-cutting issues, has there been a paradigm shift in the way government is conceived and operated? Is it even still possible to *be* isolated in modern government?

Further, did Clinton's people feel the need to reinvent the political-career relations wheel? As had every administration before them, did they come into office with a bias against the careerists or were they more open to careerists' participation in policy making? What effect did the massive reinventing government initiative and subsequent downsizing have on political career relations?

The claim that the short-termer system revitalizes the government is generally accepted by both the political and the career partners in the dance of bureaucracy: relevance "Outside the Beltway" continues to be the ultimate reality check. A future study could explore the extent to which "outsiders" bring the advantage of a different perspective to Washington. Does "new blood" really make a difference? These outsiders would have to be genuine newcomers, though, not the local short-termers who never move out of the nation's capital but simply recycle in succeeding administrations, perhaps skipping an administration or two (or three). Crucial though they certainly are to the nation's governance, local short-termers tend to adopt the prevailing Washington mentality and so lose whatever advantage exists in true outsiders' perspectives.

While the outsiders have some advantages, they also carry the disadvantage of naivete. Whether they come in as new presidents, representatives, senators, or appointees, political newcomers to Washington, especially those coming from the business sector, do not really know how the federal government works, how slow and convoluted is its movement. Their cocksure approach and self-confidence are quickly eroded and can turn into disillusionment and cynicism when faced repeatedly with political reality. One can only wonder what would have happened to Ross Perot's breezy manner once he had really gotten "under the hood," as he was fond of saying, had he succeeded in his on-again, off-again presidential campaign.

However, it is always pertinent to ask what use Washington makes of any alternative perceptions of those imported from beyond the Beltway. To what extent are they listened to and to what extent are they simply overrun and co-opted by the prevailing perceptions, attitudes, and "business as usual" approach of the status quo?

The questions and issues raised throughout this book will and should be raised by practitioners of government as well as by its students. Government is an art as much as a science. In practicing this art, government's leaders should strive for the most creative solutions to the country's problems, the most qualified political personnel, the most graceful performance of the bureaucratic dance by its political and career partners, and the most complete shared understanding of the value of the public service to their nation. If the goal of government is to produce the best government of, by, and for its people, then perhaps the questions are nearly as important as the answers.

Appendix 1

The Methodology of the Bush PAS Study

This study employed two approaches to the analysis of presidential appointees. The first was a written survey[1] of the full-time political appointees in the executive branch who were appointed by President George Bush to positions subject to Senate confirmation (PASs). Most were located in the agency headquarters in Washington, D.C., Maryland, or northern Virginia.

Ambassadors, federal judges, U.S. attorneys, U.S. marshals, and part-time commission members were excluded from the universe because they constitute very different and distinct groups among the presidential appointees. They are spread geographically throughout the nation and the world. The judges are in the judicial branch; the marshals and attorneys are all in one agency, the Department of Justice. Inclusion of the latter two would have given Justice disproportionate representation among the agencies.

The second approach was a series of personal interviews conducted with PASs who volunteered via the Bush PAS Survey. Interviewees were selected to provide a diverse and representative mix of the executive levels among the federal agencies.

The Bush PAS Survey constituted a collaborative effort with the General Accounting Office (GAO). It was based on a combination of factors: the author's dissertation proposal for the GAO doctoral fellowship, GAO interests, and a request by the former House Subcommittee on Civil Service, Committee on Post Office and Civil Service, that the GAO examine political-career relations with an eye toward their improvement.

The purpose in conducting the survey and interviews was twofold: First, to present a picture of the PAS population, circa mid-1992. Aside from a NAPA study of presidential appointees from 1964 to 1984, little recent attention has been devoted to them as a whole. This is especially true of the Bush appointees. The survey afforded a unique opportunity to gauge the background, experience, and perspectives of this group.

The second purpose of the survey and interviews was to assess the general qualifications of the Bush presidential executives. The conventional wisdom regarding presidential appointees (particularly after two Reagan administrations) was that they were often unqualified political hacks[2] with few legitimate credentials, who got repaid for their service in getting their candidate elected by being placed in government where they could do varying degrees of damage to the federal bureaucracy. Ambassadorships in particular seem often to be awarded on the basis of campaign contributions, particularly in the Bush administration, which otherwise enjoyed a somewhat cleaner reputation for appointing qualified people than did the Reagan administration.[3]

While qualifications for particular positions are notoriously difficult to ascertain on a broad scale due to the widely differing demands of federal jobs, the survey sought to determine where these individuals had come from, their degree of prior experience in managing people and budgets, and their attitudes toward public service and the federal workforce, as an avenue of general assessment.

Another bit of conventional wisdom is that Republicans, traditionally hostile to big government, brought with them an agenda of limiting or severely weakening its power. This was certainly the reputation of the majority of the Reagan appointees. One goal of the survey and follow-up interviews was to ascertain the degree to which that was an accurate characterization of the Bush appointees, as compared to the Reagan appointees.

SURVEY DESIGN

Individual preliminary consultations were held with sixteen persons in Washington, D.C., to suggest areas for exploration in the survey instrument itself and in follow-up interviews with PAS executives. These persons included Senate staffers, current PAS executives, former PAS executives, Senior Executive Service (SES) members, think tank members, White House officials, and academics.

SAS 5.18 was used to analyze the survey. Medians and modes were most often used to describe PASs' years and types of experience and supervisory background. As is usual with survey research, not every respondent answered every question. In some cases respondents answered only parts of a question, depending on their experience. If enough of a survey was useable, it was included in the data set. Responses sometimes total more than 100 percent due to computer rounding or multiple responses. Generally, percentages were used throughout this book, though numbers were occasionally included for clarity. In questions that encourage multiple responses but do not have component parts (e.g., Questions 5, 16, 43, 45, and 53) it is difficult or irrelevant to report solely a percentage for analysis. In those instances both percentages and numbers are given, and percentages are generally rounded to the nearest whole number, as they are throughout this book.

Additionally, in order to avoid skewing the responses, we decided to eliminate "no basis to judge/not applicable" responses in computing answers to questions that provoked large numbers of such responses. This was particularly important in questions dealing with job orientation programs, recruitment of PASs, relations with other PASs and with Senior Executive Service members (both noncareer [political] and career), turnover of executive staff, accountability of both themselves and other executives, and job satisfaction and difficulty.

Though many PASs would have other PASs, noncareer SESs (NSESs), and Schedule Cs close at hand, many individuals were often the only political appointee in their immediate unit. This was particularly true of those in the regulatory commissions. Unfortunately for purposes of this study, PASs did not always seem to know the distinctions among the PAS, NSES, and career SES (CSES) categories. PASs' estimates for numbers of each in their own units and agencies were often wildly inaccurate (sometimes more than twice the number governmentwide) and so must be disregarded.[4] However, their comments about their relations with other political and senior career employees do provide valuable insight into the interpersonal workings of the government and so should not be discounted.

As was clear from some interviews and marginal comments written on the surveys, some PASs who did not have any SESs in their agency counted senior professional civil service staff as if they were SES. In these cases, responses to SES-based questions were discarded, as GAO was interested in gauging reactions to the SES members themselves. A few, not from ignorance but from principle, refused to separate the SES into noncareer and career categories, feeling, as one put it, that this "set up artificial divisions in government and there were more than enough of those already."

Job satisfaction and how various conditions affected it was of particular interest. Job satisfaction was crosstabulated with numerous factors such as executive level, type of agency (regulatory commission or executive agency), satisfaction with salary, and relationship with career SES members. Those results, along with others, are reported in chapter 8.

The Bush PAS Survey questions were distilled in large measure from the 1984 NAPA survey of PASs. However, the questions were often altered to meet GAO's interests, needs, and methodological requirements.[5] This rendered difficult the original plan of providing a comparison between the past and present PASs. Nonetheless, the survey did serve to present a broad picture of the current PAS population and to establish a baseline for comparison with future administrations' PASs.[6]

The survey instrument was pretested with five PAS executives—one each at Veterans Affairs, Health and Human Services, the Peace Corps, the Export-Import Bank, and the Federal Trade Commission. As with earlier interviews, these individuals' cooperation was obtained by referrals and by cold calls. The survey pretest was administered in personal interviews by the author and one or two staff members of the GAO's Design Methodology Technical Assistance Group (DMTAG), who worked on its design. We employed the standard GAO method of intensive individual pretesting, evaluation, revision, and additional pretesting. The survey was also sent to the White House and the Office of Personnel Management (OPM) for comment.

The survey covers areas such as PASs' background, qualifications, education and experience, orientation to their job, relationship with careerists and other political appointees, the White House, and the Congress, feelings about public service, job satisfaction, and stress.

SURVEY ADMINISTRATION

Because only 639 allocated PAS positions constitute the entire universe for this survey, it was decided to survey all the PAS executives in the executive branch agencies and independent regulatory commissions, with the exceptions noted above. The handful of PASs in non–executive branch agencies, such as GAO and the Copyright Royalty Tribunal, was excluded from the survey.

Securing a mailing list of PAS executives proved to be a daunting task. There were no readily available lists outside of government and attempts to secure one or address labels within the government were complicated by orders from the White House to at least two individuals (the deputy secretary at the Housing and Urban Affairs Department and the head of OPM) not to participate in the enterprise in any way. Evidently, the project aroused considerable anxiety at the White House.

The author was informed on numerous occasions that, as the survey was a project of the GAO (an agency of the Congress), the White House feared the survey was a setup, a congressional attempt to "get" the White House, and that it had created quite a controversy. She was also told that, had she been merely a lone researcher working on her own, she would most likely have encountered little resistance and more assistance along the way.

Nonetheless, when a draft of the survey was sent to the White House for comment, its officials inexplicably reversed course and offered to mail it to the PASs. Apparently (as the author was told by one PAS interviewee), they decided that the survey was innocuous and that the White House might find the information useful, so it was best to obtain the information directly from the PASs themselves, via the survey. Further, at least one Democratic PAS was called by the White House, told to expect it, and told that participation in it was voluntary. Clearly, the White House switched from a hostile to a neutral stance over the course of the project.

Unfortunately, the damage had already been done: The hostility sown by early White House suspicion had quickly filtered through the PAS grapevine. One result was that the numbering system on the surveys made the whole project suspect in some PASs' eyes. They felt the GAO was not being honest about confidentiality, even though the need for a numbering system and the promise of confidentiality were explained in both the cover letter and the survey introduction.

Some who might otherwise have completed the survey did not participate because they feared they would be identified, according to one PAS who attended a political luncheon where the survey was mentioned. Some who did participate voiced suspicion of GAO and its motives, either in the interviews or in personal notes on the survey itself. Yet they participated, they said, because there were no loaded questions and they felt it was a good survey.

A few who completed the survey obliterated the number; one even went so far as to cut the number off his survey cover but then signed his name to the survey. The logic of these responses was initially difficult to decipher. However, a quick reflection on the often paranoid, small-town, gossip-driven, pressure-cooker, high-stakes nature of the nation's capital lends a degree of understanding to the puzzle: PASs' desire to be heard overcame their fear, but they still were not taking any chances.

The process of actually distributing the survey took several months, given all the negotiations with the White House. There was one insurmountable problem with the mailing list, however: We never got to see it. Citing the Privacy Act, the White House steadfastly refused to allow anyone from GAO (including the author) to have access to or even see the mailing list.

There were other problems: In addition to reluctant and belated White House aid, the mailing list was not without its limitations. Numerous persons who received the survey called or sent notes to say that they had resigned their position, some as long ago as one-and-a-half years. OPM, which keeps a separate listing of federal personnel, had similar problems of different, outdated, or missing information. In fact, OPM statistics (data personally given to the author) as of June 30, 1992, listed only 565 PAS allocated positions, in contrast to the White House's count of 639. OPM also registered 480 positions as actually filled, a vacancy of 15 percent, in contrast to the White House tally of a 20 percent vacancy.

Yet another snag (one of many) developed to thwart our efforts to maximize the survey response rate. One military service branch chief called to ask if the other Senate-confirmed chiefs had been sent the survey. He had intended to complete it until he found out that the White House had not sent surveys to his peers. Even though they are all PASs, he was the only one on this particular White House mailing list: He refused to participate. Clearly, in-house politics of some sort were at work here.

The survey was finally administered via mail to the PASs' homes, packaged by GAO with a cover letter and a stamped return envelope preaddressed to the author at GAO. The survey packets in franked mailing envelopes were numbered and sealed at GAO and taken to the White House, where its staff matched numbers to names, affixed address labels on the survey packets, and mailed them.

Although there are in this universe 639 PAS positions authorized by the Senate, as noted, some 20 percent of the positions are vacant at any given time and filled by "acting" staff, sometimes political, sometimes career. Consequently, only 505 surveys were sent to Senate-confirmed appointees in the first mailing, according to the White House tally. The first mailing was sent June 8, 1992, with a cover letter over the signature of GAO's assistant comptroller general for general government programs. The second mailing was sent a month later using the same procedure. A third mailing had been planned but the White House inexplicably refused to participate further and, without access to the mailing list, we had to be satisfied with two mailings.

Numerous surveys were completed but discarded for various reasons. For example, some were from PASs in legislative branch agencies, some were returned by the Post Office as undeliverable, others were completed by individuals who were not PASs or who had long since resigned their office. Some surveys did not have enough completed answers to be of use. Of the 474 surveys believed to have reached the appropriate population, 182 were completed, for a response rate of 38.4 percent.

While the intransigence of the White House regarding the mailing list prevented verification of the identity of the individuals to whom it was sent, from the responses received it was clear that, overall, the surveys had gone to the appropriate individuals. Further, calls from numerous PASs requesting additional information, and signed surveys (indicating a willingness to be interviewed in connection with the project) came from PASs in a wide variety of federal agencies. Some 35 percent of the respondents (sixty-four) signed their survey, which provides an interesting answer to suspicions of the White House and others (some among the signers) who had expressed distrust of the GAO and its motives.

Another indication that the survey reached its intended constituency was that the executive levels of the respondents were roughly representative of their frequency in government, as was the gender and ethnic mix among the respondents. While the White House refused to give detailed demographic information about the PASs, it eventually allowed OPM to release some statistical data. Again, the problem of the difference in OPM and White House personnel counts presents itself. Nonetheless, percentages may present a useable point of comparison (see table A.1).

Table A.1. Demographics of PAS Survey Response Rate and OPM PAS Statistics (in percent)

	OPM^a (N=480)	PAS Survey (N=182)
Female	20	17
Caucasian	86	83
EL 1	3	4
EL 2	7	8
EL 3	18	22
EL 4	64	56
EL 5	9	8

Source: The Bush PAS Survey.
^{a}As of June 30, 1992.

PAS INTERVIEWS

The second methodological approach used the postsurvey interviews. These interviews, from an hour to an hour and a half in length, were conducted in the late summer and early fall of 1992 with twenty-eight PAS executives who completed and signed their surveys, volunteering for an interview.

Scheduling conflicts created insurmountable difficulties with some PASs. Nevertheless, those interviewed represented Executive Levels (ELs) 2 through 5 in a wide variety of executive agencies and independent regulatory commissions (IRCs), as well as in the Executive Office of the President (EOP). For example, the agencies included Agriculture, Labor, Health and Human Services, Interior, Commerce, Education, NASA, the CIA, and OPM. The IRCs included the Federal Labor Relations Board, the Interstate Commerce Commission, the Commodity Futures Trading Commission, and the Nuclear Regulatory Commission, among others. EOP offices included the Office of Science and Technology and the Office of Management and Budget (OMB). One cabinet secretary (EL 1) had volunteered to be interviewed but canceled due to campaign demands on his time as the presidential election approached.

The twenty-eight interviewees included six women, two minorities, eight independent regulatory commission members, and four inspectors general. The majority, as might be expected, were Republicans, five were Democrats (in the

IRCs); one (not IRC) did not care to specify party identification. They were grouped in ELs 2 (three individuals), 3 (seven), 4 (sixteen), and 5 (two).

Additionally, eight long-term SES careerists and former PASs were interviewed, postsurvey, to gain further perspective, particularly on the differences between the Reagan and Bush appointees.

The author interviewed the PASs and others alone in their offices confidentially, informing them that the interviews were primarily for the purpose of the study and not for GAO. She took handwritten notes with interviewees' permission and did not use a tape recorder. In some cases individuals did not want it known that they had even spoken with her, fearing identification by association; their names are omitted from the listings of interviewees in the appendices. In other cases, only some parts of the conversation were off the record, while the rest was not. All persons quoted by name gave permission to be quoted. Those who did not want to be identified are quoted anonymously.

The author asked questions similar to some of the survey questions, probing in more depth in areas such as the experience of the nomination and confirmation process, PAS's professional background and work prior to and in government, and their views of public service. She also asked about their working relationships with the White House, other political appointees, career employees, and with the Congress, and their sense of job satisfaction and stress.

Designed to gather supplemental data through anecdotal material, the interviews added color and flesh to the composite picture of the PAS executives and presented a broader picture of PASs' attitudes and relations with their career colleagues. The interviews also served to confirm many of the NAPA observations about PASs, as well as those noted in the literature and discussed throughout this book.

In conclusion, the two dissertation methodologies met with overall success in terms of eliciting information from a reluctant executive branch. While we would have preferred the three mailings of the original plan, the response rate of more than 38 percent from the first and second mailings was representative of the PAS population and thus enabled us to draw useable, if limited, conclusions about the PAS population as a whole. The interview approach was very successful: appointees were open and willing to talk about their experiences in and perceptions of government.

While having the imprimatur of the GAO was an initial deterrent to gaining White House cooperation, it was generally more useful in securing entree to the PASs themselves, many of whom voiced respect for the GAO's work. The interviews gave the author an unparalleled opportunity for an "outsider" to acquire an understanding of Washington's politics, with its complex customs, convoluted dynamics, and many players who live and move and have their being within the nation's pressure cooker.

Appendix 2

The Survey of Senate-Confirmed Presidential Appointees with Composite Response Set

Senate-Confirmed Political Appointees in the Federal Government

Introduction

The U.S. General Accounting Office (GAO), an agency that assists Congress in evaluating federal programs and operations, is conducting a study of Senate-confirmed presidential appointees (PAS) at the request of the Subcommittee on Civil Service of the House Committee on Post Office and Civil Service.

The purpose of this questionnaire is to gather information from PAS executives to provide a better understanding of areas relevant to their federal service. These areas include (1) PASs' professional background and experience, (2) improving PAS recruitment and orientation process, (3) PASs' relationship with career SES members, (4) factors influencing PAS executives to remain in or leave government service, and (5) the sacrifices and benefits of accepting a PAS appointment.

This survey is being sent to all Executive Level I through V full-time, nonjudicial presidential appointees in the executive branch. Your responses will provide valuable baseline information that may assist future PAS executives in moving quickly and effectively into their agencies.

Your participation in this survey is voluntary. Your responses will be treated confidentially, combined with other responses, and reported only in summary form to Congress. The questionnaire is numbered only to aid us in our follow-up efforts and will not be used to identify you with your responses. After the questionnaires have been processed, the link between you and your responses will be destroyed, and no one will be able to identify how you or any other individual responded.

The survey should take no more than 30 minutes to complete. Please check the boxes and fill in the blanks as indicated. There is space at the end of the questionnaire for any additional comments you might have.

Please return your completed survey in the enclosed preaddressed, postage-paid envelope within 10 days of receipt. If you have any questions, please call Judith Michaels at GAO's headquarters, (202) 275-5734. Please return the survey to:

> U.S. General Accounting Office
> Dr. Judith E. Michaels
> 441 G Street, NW, Room 3150
> Washington, D.C. 20548

Thank you for your cooperation.

* * * * *

Definitions

Presidential Appointments with Senate Confirmation (PAS) - For purposes of this survey, these positions are full-time nonjudicial presidential appointments that require Senate confirmation.

Initial PAS Position or Appointment - This is the first position to which you were appointed in the current administration.

Current PAS position - This is the position that you now hold. It may or may not be the same as the initial appointment.

---

1. Are you currently a full-time PAS appointee? *(Check one.)*

   N=182

   1. ☐   Yes *(Continue to Question 2.)*   100%

   2. ☐   No *(STOP. This survey is   0% intended for full-time, Senate-confirmed presidential appointees only. Please do not complete this survey, but return it in the enclosed envelope. Thank you.)*

I. Professional Background

A. Position Immediately Prior to Your
   Initial PAS Appointment in the
   Current Administration

*Please note that Questions 2 through 11 ask about
the position you held immediately prior to your initial
PAS appointment in the current administration.
Please exclude from your answers any paid or
volunteer Bush campaign or transition team work.*

2. Which of the following best describes the type of
   organization for which you worked immediately prior
   to your initial PAS appointment? *(Check only one.)*

   N=180

   1. ☐ Federal government   77 / 42.8%
   2. ☐ State or local government   10 / 5.6%
   3. ☐ Business or corporate sector 32 / 17.8%
   4. ☐ Self-employed   10 / 5.6%
   5. ☐ College, university, or   19 / 10.6%
        research organization
   6. ☐ Political party   0 / 0.0%
   7. ☐ Think tank   2 / 1.1%
   8. ☐ Interest group (e.g., Business 2 / 1.1%
        Round Table, VFW, etc.)
        (Please specify.) _____
   9. ☐ Law firm   17 / 9.4%
   10. ☐ Labor union   0 / 0.0%
   11. ☐ Nonprofit organization   5 / 2.8%
   12. ☐ Other *(Please specify.)*   6 / 3.3%
         _____

3. For the position you held immediately prior to your
   initial PAS appointment, how long were you in that
   position? *(Enter years/months.)*

   N=175   N=142
   Range = 0 to 39   Range = 0 to 11
   Median = 6   / Median = 3.5
   (Years)   (Months)

4. What was the geographical location of the position you
   held immediately prior to your initial PAS
   appointment? *(Check one.)*

   N=172

   1. ☐ Washington, D.C.   101 / 58.7%
        metropolitan area
   2. ☐ Other *(Please specify.)* 71 / 41.3%
        _____

5. Which of the following were your primary functions in
   the position you held immediately prior to your initial
   PAS appointment? *(Check all that apply.)*

   N=180   (Note: Percentages total to more than
           100% due to mulitple responses.)

   1. ☐ Administration   57 / 31.7%
   2. ☐ Management   97 / 53.9%
   3. ☐ Legal affairs   39 / 21.7%
   4. ☐ Political affairs   16 / 8.9%
   5. ☐ Government relations   20 / 11.1%
   6. ☐ Sales   5 / 2.8%
   7. ☐ Education   17 / 9.4%
   8. ☐ Training   4 / 2.2%
   9. ☐ Other *(Please specify.)* 35 / 19.4%
        _____

6. In that position, how many paid and volunteer
   employees reported directly to you? *(Enter numbers.)*

   Number of employees

   1. Paid employees
      N=171
      Range = 0 to 60,000
      Median = 7

   2. Volunteer employees
      N=72
      Range = 0 to 50
      Mode = 0

7. In that position, overall, how many paid and volunteer
   employees were in the work unit for which you were
   responsible? *(Enter numbers. Include the numbers
   entered in Question 6.)*

   Number of employees

   1. Paid employees
      N=170
      Range = 0 to 150,000
      Median = 32.5

   2. Volunteer employees
      N=67
      Range = 0 to 1,000
      Mode = 0

8. Did you have direct responsibility for a budget in the position you held immediately prior to your initial appointment? *(Check one.)*

   N=180

   1. ☐ Yes *(Continue to   121 / 67.2%
          Question 9.)*

   2. ☐ No *(Skip to Question 10.)*   59 / 32.8%

9. What was the budget amount for which you had direct responsibility? *(Check one.)*

   N=120

   1. ☐ Up to $500,000   19 / 15.8%

   2. ☐ $500,001 to $1 million   15 / 12.5%

   3. ☐ $1,000,001 to $5 million   23 / 19.2%

   4. ☐ $5,000,001 to $10 million   10 / 8.3%

   5. ☐ $10,000,001 to $25 million   13 / 10.8%

   6. ☐ $25,000,0001 to $100 million   14 / 11.7%

   7. ☐ More than $100 million   26 / 21.7%

10. Which of the following categories best describes your annual salary in that position? *(Check one. Include only your personal salary and other cash benefits such as bonuses and commissions, before taxes.)*

    N=179

    1. ☐ Less than $50,000   12 / 6.7%

    2. ☐ $50,000 - $99,999   102 / 57.0%

    3. ☐ $100,000 - $149,999   35 / 19.6%

    4. ☐ $150,000 - $200,000   14 / 7.8%

    5. ☐ Greater than $200,000   16 / 8.9%

11. How much of a financial sacrifice or benefit, if any, resulted from the acceptance of your initial PAS appointment? *(Check one. Please consider your total family financial situation immediately prior to your initial PAS appointment.)*

    N=180

    1. ☐ Great sacrifice   37 / 20.6%

    2. ☐ Moderate sacrifice   55 / 30.6%

    3. ☐ Neither a sacrifice   48 / 26.7%
           nor a benefit

    4. ☐ Moderate benefit   35 / 19.4%

    5. ☐ Great benefit   5 / 2.8%

B. Federal Government Employment

Questions 12 and 13 ask only about federal civilian employment work history. Do not include military service.

12. How many federal government positions have you held and how many years have you served in each of the following job
     categories? *(Include your current PAS position and enter numbers.)*

	Job Category			
	PAS position(s)	SES position(s)	Schedule C position(s)	All other federal employment
1. Number of positions held	N = 168 Median = 1	N = 67 Median = 1	N = 58 Median = 1	N = 94 Median = 2
2. Number of years served in each	N = 165 Mean = 4.8	N = 60 Mean = 4.0	N = 51 Mean = 2.6	N = 90 Mean = 10.1

13. In which administration(s) and for how many years in each administration have you served in any PAS position? *(Check all
     that apply and enter number of years, as appropriate.)*

ADMINISTRATION	Served? Yes (1)	No (2)	If yes, number of years?
1. Bush 1/89 - 1/93 N=175	175 100.0%	0 0.0%	Median = 3
2. Reagan 1/85 - 1/89 N=106	71 67.0%	35 33.0%	Median = 4
3. Reagan 1/81 - 1/85 N=76	34 44.7%	42 55.3%	Median = 3
4. Carter 1/77 - 1/81 N=56	5 8.9%	51 91.1%	Median = 2
5. Ford 8/74 - 1/77 N=56	8 14.3%	48 85.7%	Median = 2
6. Nixon 1/69 - 8/74 N=58	8 13.8%	50 86.2%	Median = 2
7. Johnson 11/63 - 1/69 N=52	0 0.0%	52 100.0%	N/A
8. Kennedy 1/61 - 11/63 N=52	0 0.0%	52 100.0%	N/A
9. Other *(Please specify.)* ____ N=6	1 16.7%	5 83.3%	N/A

C. Elective Office

14. Have you ever run for <u>and</u> been elected to public office? *(Check one.)*

N=182

1. ☐   Yes *(Continue to*   30 / 16.5%
          Question 15.)

2. ☐   No *(Skip to PART II,*   152 / 83.5%
          next column.)

15. At what level of government have you served in elective office and for how long? *(Check all that apply and enter number of years served.)*

Level	Number of years
	N=13
	Range = 2 to 18
1. ☐ City	Median = 6
	N=6
	Range = 1 to 23
2. ☐ County	Median = 6
	N=11
	Range = 4 to 19
3. ☐ State	Median = 6
	N=2
	Range = 14 to 20
4. ☐ National	Median = 17

II. PAS Selection and Orientation

The questions in this section deal with the process through which you were recruited, selected, and oriented to PAS service.

16. There may be several ways through which you became a PAS appointee. Which of the following sources led to your initial PAS position? *(Check all that apply.)*

N=180   **(Note: Percentages total to more than 100% due to multiple responses.)**

1. ☐   My party (e.g., worked   22 / 12.2%
          on campaign)

2. ☐   President Bush   36 / 20.0%

3. ☐   A Cabinet member,   89 / 49.4%
          agency head, or
          professional colleague

4. ☐   A member of Congress   35 / 19.4%

5. ☐   Self-referred   18 / 10.0%

6. ☐   Other *(Please specify.)*   30 / 16.7%

          _____

          _____

7. ☐   Uncertain/Unknown   9 / 5.0%

17. Have you attended any orientation program(s) given only to PAS appointees since your initial PAS appointment? *(Check one.)*

N=179

1. ☐   Yes *(Continue to*   136 / 76.0%
          Question 18.)

2. ☐   No *(Skip to Question 20.)* 43 / 24.0%

18. Which of the following organizations <u>sponsored</u> any PAS orientation program(s) (<u>do not include issue briefings</u>) that you attended and what was the year(s) of attendance? *(Check one box under Column A in each row. If "Yes," enter year of attendance in Column B.)*

ORGANIZATIONS		A. Sponsored orientation program?		B. If yes, year(s) of attendance.
		Yes (1)	No (2)	
1. The White House	N=132	130 98.5%	2 1.5%	
2. The department or agency to which I was appointed	N=57	25 43.9%	32 56.1%	
3. Office of Personnel Management	N=51	9 17.6%	42 82.4%	
4. The Kennedy School of Government at Harvard University	N=48	5 10.4%	43 89.6%	
5. The Brookings Institution	N=46	2 4.3%	44 95.7%	
6. The American Enterprise Institute	N=45	1 2.2%	44 97.8%	
7. The Heritage Foundation	N=45	1 2.2%	44 97.8%	
8. Other *(Please specify.)* _____	N=13	2 15.4%	11 84.6%	

19. Overall, of the orientation(s) you attended, was each of the following areas of government policy management addressed? If yes, how adequately or inadequately was each area covered? *(Check one box under Column A in each row. If "Yes," check one box for each row, as appropriate, in Column B.)*

AREA OF GOVERNMENT POLICY MANAGEMENT	A. Addressed?		B. If yes, adequately covered?					
	Yes (1)	No (2)	Very adequate (1)	Generally adequate (2)	Neither adequate nor inadequate (3)	Generally inadequate (4)	Very inadequate (5)	No basis to judge/ Cannot recall (6)
1. The federal budget process N=112	85 75.9%	27 24.1%	22 26.5%	35 42.2%	13 15.7%	13 15.7%	0 0.0%	0
2. The federal personnel system N=109	85 78.0%	24 22.0%	20 24.4%	39 47.6%	14 17.1%	6 7.3%	3 3.7%	1
3. Public policies relevant to my agency N=107	47 43.9%	60 56.1%	16 35.6%	18 40.0%	7 15.6%	3 6.7%	1 2.2%	0
4. The President's policy objectives N=123	111 90.2%	12 9.8%	46 42.6%	48 44.4%	10 9.3%	4 3.7%	0 0.0%	0
5. White House decisionmaking procedures N=109	72 66.1%	37 33.9%	28 40.6%	28 40.6%	6 8.7%	6 8.7%	1 1.4%	0
6. White House staff structure N=114	94 82.5%	20 17.5%	41 46.1%	37 41.6%	3 3.4%	6 6.7%	2 2.2%	0
7. The OMB decisionmaking process N=106	52 49.1%	54 50.9%	13 26.5%	20 40.8%	9 18.4%	6 12.2%	1 2.0%	0
8. The OPM decisionmaking process N=100	26 26.0%	74 74.0%	8 32.0%	7 28.0%	6 24.0%	3 12.0%	1 4.0%	0
9. Interactions with senior career employees N=107	69 64.5%	38 35.5%	23 34.3%	30 44.8%	9 13.4%	4 6.0%	1 1.5%	0
10. Interactions with Congress N=103	70 68.0%	33 32.0%	18 26.1%	33 47.8%	12 17.4%	4 5.8%	2 2.9%	0
11. The federal rulemaking process N=100	25 25.0%	75 75.0%	11 44.0%	6 24.0%	5 20.0%	3 12.0%	0 0.0%	0
12. Congressionally mandated regulatory systems N=97	22 22.7%	75 77.3%	6 27.3%	6 27.3%	6 27.3%	3 13.6%	1 4.5%	0
13. Ethical guidelines for presidential appointees N=129	126 97.7%	3 2.3%	81 67.5%	33 27.5%	5 4.2%	1 0.8%	0 0.0%	0
14. Relations with the news media N=108	78 72.2%	30 27.8%	23 30.7%	41 54.7%	7 9.3%	2 2.7%	2 2.7%	1
15. Other *(Please specify.)* _____ _____ N=11	7 63.6%	4 36.4%	5 71.4%	2 28.6%	0 0.0%	0 0.0%	0 0.0%	0

20. Based on your PAS service, how important is it that the following areas of government policy management be included in an orientation program for PAS executives who are new to the federal government? *(Check one box in each row.)*

AREA OF GOVERNMENT POLICY MANAGEMENT	Little or no importance (1)	Somewhat important (2)	Moderately important (3)	Very important (4)	Very great importance (5)	No basis to judge/ Not applicable (6)
1. The federal budget process N=177	12 6.9%	10 5.8%	25 14.5%	66 38.2%	60 34.7%	4
2. The federal personnel system N=176	13 7.5%	13 7.5%	44 25.4%	59 34.1%	44 25.4%	3
3. Public policies relevant to my agency N=177	12 6.9%	6 3.5%	17 9.8%	58 33.5%	80 46.2%	4
4. The President's policy objectives N=176	7 4.1%	8 4.7%	22 12.8%	65 37.8%	70 40.7%	4
5. White House decisionmaking procedures N=176	13 7.6%	24 14.1%	52 30.6%	53 31.2%	28 16.5%	6
6. White House staff structure N=177	20 11.7%	39 22.8%	50 29.2%	47 27.5%	15 8.8%	6
7. The OMB decisionmaking process N=176	15 8.8%	20 11.7%	36 21.1%	69 40.4%	31 18.1%	5
8. The OPM decisionmaking process N=177	21 12.3%	47 27.5%	51 29.8%	38 22.2%	14 8.2%	6
9. Interactions with senior career employees N=176	14 8.1%	22 12.8%	44 25.6%	50 29.1%	42 24.4%	4
10. Interactions with Congress N=175	5 2.9%	8 4.7%	26 15.2%	75 43.9%	57 33.3%	4
11. The executive branch rulemaking process N=172	14 8.4%	23 13.8%	49 29.3%	53 31.7%	28 16.8%	5
12. Congressionally mandated regulatory systems N=173	13 7.9%	26 15.9%	54 32.9%	47 28.7%	24 14.6%	9
13. Ethical guidelines for presidential appointees N=178	1 0.6%	3 1.7%	7 4.0%	55 31.3%	110 62.5%	2
14. Relations with the news media N=173	10 5.9%	15 8.9%	43 25.4%	56 33.1%	45 26.6%	4
15. Other *(Please specify.)* _____ _____ N=6	1 16.7%	1 16.7%	0 0.0%	3 50.0%	1 16.7%	0

21. How helpful, if at all, would the following suggested changes be in facilitating the recruitment of highly qualified people to presidentially appointed positions? *(Check one box in each row.)*

SUGGESTED CHANGES	Little or no help (1)	Somewhat helpful (2)	Moderately helpful (3)	Greatly helpful (4)	Very greatly helpful (5)	No basis to judge (6)
1. Ease conflict-of-interest strictures N=176	39 23.9%	17 10.4%	42 25.8%	28 17.2%	37 22.7%	13
2. Ease financial disclosure requirements N=175	29 17.4%	30 18.0%	51 30.5%	36 21.6%	21 12.6%	8
3. Simplify and limit FBI investigation N=173	48 28.2%	34 20.0%	41 24.1%	30 17.6%	17 10.0%	3
4. Shorten time for White House Counsel clearance N=175	22 13.1%	32 19.0%	48 28.6%	41 24.4%	25 14.9%	7
5. Make the Senate confirmation process less intrusive N=176	30 17.0%	25 14.2%	49 27.8%	43 24.4%	29 16.5%	0
6. Raise salaries N=176	25 14.5%	20 11.6%	32 18.6%	55 32.0%	40 23.3%	4
7. Waive double dipping restrictions N=173	45 31.5%	27 18.9%	27 18.9%	24 16.8%	20 14.0%	30
8. Simplify the entire process N=172	10 5.9%	11 6.5%	27 15.9%	53 31.2%	69 40.6%	2
9. Other *(Please specify.)* _____ _____ N=11	0 0.0%	0 0.0%	0 0.0%	3 27.3%	8 72.7%	0

II. Current Position

The questions in this section deal primarily with the
following aspects of your current PAS position:
characteristics of position, relations with other executives,
accountability, job satisfaction, and employment intentions.

A. Characteristics of Position

22. For your current PAS position, please enter the dates
you were nominated and confirmed. *(If confirmation
is pending, check the box.)*

N=165
Range = 2/4/74 to 6/18/92

1. Date nominated: |____|____|____|
                       mm   dd   yy

N=173
Range = 4/28/74 to 5/9/92

2. Date confirmed: |____|____|____|
                      mm   dd   yy

   OR

   ☐ Confirmation pending   **N=3**

23. Is your current PAS position a statutory term
appointment? *(Check one.)*

N=179

1. ☐   Yes *(Continue to*   **75 / 41.9%**
           Question 24.)

2. ☐   No *(Skip to*   **104 / 58.1%**
           Question 25.)

24. If yes, when does your term expire? *(Enter date.)*

N=71
Range = 6/15/91 to 1/31/04

|____|____|____|
  mm   dd   yy

25. Where is your current PAS position located? *(Check one.)*

N=181

1. ☐ Department or agency headquarters — 175 / 96.7%

2. ☐ Regional office — 1 / 0.6%

3. ☐ Area field office, field office or installation, or the equivalent — 5 / 2.8%

26. What is your Executive Level (EL)? *(Check one.)*

N=171

1. ☐ EL I — 7 / 4.1%

2. ☐ EL II — 14 / 8.2%

3. ☐ EL III — 37 / 21.6%

4. ☐ EL IV — 96 / 56.1%

5. ☐ EL V — 13 / 7.6%

6. ☐ Other *(Please specify.)* — 4 / 2.3%

B. Relations with Other Executives

27. Prior to your <u>first</u> PAS appointment by <u>any</u> president, how much, if at all, did you believe career SES executives would help you (encourage, share information, etc.) in or hinder you (discourage, withhold information, etc.) in executing your PAS responsibilities? *(Check one.)*

N=180

1. ☐ Greatly help — 55 / 30.6%

2. ☐ Generally help — 63 / 35.0%

3. ☐ Help more than hinder — 22 / 12.2%

4. ☐ Help as much as hinder — 7 / 3.9%

5. ☐ Hinder more than help — 6 / 3.3%

6. ☐ Generally hinder — 0 / 0.0%

7. ☐ Greatly hinder — 1 / 0.6%

8. ☐ No opinion — 26 / 14.4%

28. About how many PAS, noncareer SES, and career SES executives are there in your organizational unit and in your agency? *(Enter numbers.)*

		Your organizational unit (1)	Your agency (2)
1.	PAS	N=148 Range = 0 to 22 Median = 1	N=147 Range = 0 to 200 Median = 5
2.	Noncareer SES	N=115 Range = 0 to 100 Median = 0	110 Range = 0 to 1,248 Median = 3
3.	Career SES	N=129 Range = 0 to 900 Median = 4	N=124 Range = 0 to 1,500 Median = 25

29. Currently, in working with PAS, noncareer SES, and career SES executives <u>in your agency</u>, to what extent, if at all, do you generally consider them to be responsive to policy direction and competent?   *(For each colleague group, check one box in each row.)*

	Very great extent (1)	Great extent (2)	Moderate extent (3)	Some extent (4)	Little or no extent (5)	No basis to judge/ Not applicable (6)
PAS						
1. Responsive to policy direction N=167	63 44.4%	56 39.4%	15 10.6%	6 4.2%	2 1.4%	25
2. Competent N=167	63 40.9%	59 38.3%	22 14.3%	6 3.9%	4 2.6%	13
NONCAREER SES						
1. Responsive to policy direction N=154	39 33.9%	55 47.8%	16 13.9%	5 4.3%	0 0.0%	39
2. Competent N=154	33 28.0%	50 42.4%	28 23.7%	7 5.9%	0 0.0%	36
CAREER SES						
1. Responsive to policy direction N=170	43 27.6%	63 40.4%	36 23.1%	13 8.3%	1 0.6%	14
2. Competent N=171	56 35.0%	67 41.9%	27 16.9%	9 5.6%	1 0.6%	11

30. In general, how often, if at all, do you involve any other PAS, noncareer SES, or career SES executives <u>in your agency</u> regarding the following processes? *(For each colleague group, check one box in each row.)*

	Seldom, if ever (1)	Some of of the time (2)	Often (3)	Very often (4)	Always or almost always (5)	Not applicable (6)
PAS						
1. Policy feasibility N=170	5 3.3%	12 8.0%	20 13.3%	30 20.0%	83 55.3%	20
2. Policy formulation and development N=171	5 3.3%	10 6.6%	22 14.6%	21 13.9%	93 61.6%	20
3. Policy implementation N=169	7 4.8%	9 6.1%	25 17.0%	23 15.6%	83 56.5%	22
4. Budget decisions N=171	14 9.8%	14 9.8%	21 14.7%	22 15.4%	72 50.3%	28
5. Staff selection/promotion decisions N=168	23 15.8%	26 17.8%	19 13.0%	24 16.4%	54 37.0%	22
NONCAREER SES						
1. Policy feasibility N=154	7 6.9%	12 11.9%	19 18.8%	25 24.8%	38 37.6%	53
2. Policy formulation and development N=154	6 5.9%	14 13.9%	21 20.8%	20 19.8%	40 39.6%	53
3. Policy implementation N=154	8 8.1%	11 11.1%	18 18.2%	23 23.2%	39 39.4%	55
4. Budget decisions N=154	15 15.6%	14 14.6%	17 17.7%	16 16.7%	34 35.4%	58
5. Staff selection/promotion decisions N=154	20 20.4%	19 19.4%	15 15.3%	16 16.3%	28 28.6%	56
CAREER SES						
1. Policy feasibility N=169	7 4.5%	8 5.1%	28 17.9%	43 27.6%	70 44.9%	13
2. Policy formulation and development N=169	5 3.2%	9 5.7%	27 17.2%	43 27.4%	73 46.5%	12
3. Policy implementation N=169	3 1.9%	9 5.8%	23 14.9%	35 22.7%	84 54.5%	15
4. Budget decisions N=169	6 4.0%	11 7.3%	24 15.9%	30 19.9%	80 53.0%	18
5. Staff selection/promotion decisions N=169	14 9.3%	13 8.6%	24 15.9%	29 19.2%	71 47.0%	18

31. Currently, in working with PAS, noncareer SES, and career SES executives in your organizational unit, overall, do they help or hinder you in accomplishing the following tasks? *(For each colleague group, check one box in each row.)*

	Greatly help (1)	Generally help (2)	Help as much as hinder (3)	Generally hinder (4)	Greatly hinder (5)	No basis to judge/ Not applicable (6)
PAS						
1. Mastering substantive policy details N=166	45 39.5%	49 43.0%	16 14.0%	2 1.8%	2 1.8%	52
2. Liaison with the federal bureaucracy N=166	34 30.9%	50 45.5%	19 17.3%	5 4.5%	2 1.8%	56
3. Liaison with Congress N=166	33 29.7%	56 50.5%	13 11.7%	4 3.6%	5 4.5%	55
4. Anticipating potential policy implementation problems N=166	37 32.7%	50 44.2%	15 13.3%	9 8.0%	2 1.8%	53
5. Handling day-to-day management tasks N=165	34 31.5%	41 38.0%	24 22.2%	5 4.6%	4 3.7%	57
6. Technical analysis of difficult issues N=165	37 33.0%	49 43.8%	17 15.2%	6 5.4%	3 2.7%	53
NONCAREER SES						
1. Mastering substantive policy details N=150	30 34.1%	46 52.3%	9 10.2%	2 2.3%	1 1.1%	62
2. Liaison with the federal bureaucracy N=149	28 32.2%	43 49.4%	12 13.8%	3 3.4%	1 1.1%	62
3. Liaison with Congress N=150	25 30.5%	36 43.9%	15 18.3%	4 4.9%	2 2.4%	68
4. Anticipating potential policy implementation problems N=150	23 26.7%	46 53.5%	11 12.8%	4 4.7%	2 2.3%	64
5. Handling day-to-day management tasks N=150	30 34.9%	39 45.3%	13 15.1%	3 3.5%	1 1.2%	64
6. Technical analysis of difficult issues N=150	34 39.5%	38 44.2%	10 11.6%	3 3.5%	1 1.2%	64
CAREER SES						
1. Mastering substantive policy details N=169	71 48.3%	57 38.8%	15 10.2%	0 0.0%	4 2.7%	22
2. Liaison with the federal bureaucracy N=169	63 43.8%	60 41.7%	14 9.7%	5 3.5%	2 1.4%	25
3. Liaison with Congress N=167	37 27.8%	59 44.4%	29 21.8%	4 3.0%	4 3.0%	34
4. Anticipating potential policy implementation problems N=167	56 38.6%	61 42.1%	21 14.5%	4 2.8%	3 2.1%	22
5. Handling day-to-day management tasks N=168	71 48.0%	56 37.8%	18 12.2%	0 0.0%	3 2.0%	20
6. Technical analysis of difficult issues N=166	87 59.2%	47 32.0%	9 6.1%	2 1.4%	2 1.4%	19

32. Now that you have worked with career SES executives, how much, if at all, do you believe they help you (encourage, share information, etc.) in or hinder you (discourage, withhold information, etc.) in executing your PAS responsibilities? *(Check one.)*

    N=174

    1. ☐ Greatly help   83 / 47.7%

    2. ☐ Generally help   60 / 34.5%

    3. ☐ Help more than hinder   13 / 7.5%

    4. ☐ Help as much as hinder   8 / 4.6%

    5. ☐ Hinder more than help   2 / 1.1%

    6. ☐ Generally hinder   1 / 0.6%

    7. ☐ Greatly hinder   1 / 0.6%

    8. ☐ No opinion   6 / 3.4%

33. In your opinion, does the length of service (tenure) of PAS, noncareer SES, and career SES executives result in effective or ineffective operation(s) <u>in your agency</u>? *(Check one box in each row.)*

	Very effective (1)	Generally effective (2)	Neither effective nor ineffective (3)	Generally ineffective (4)	Very ineffective (5)	No basis to judge/ Not applicable (6)
1. PAS N=165	50 33.8%	67 45.3%	21 14.2%	5 3.4%	5 3.4%	17
2. Noncareer SES N=149	26 25.2%	49 47.6%	23 22.3%	3 2.9%	2 1.9%	46
3. Career SES N=165	47 32.4%	68 46.9%	19 13.1%	9 6.2%	2 1.4%	20

34. To what extent, if at all, do you attribute PAS, noncareer SES, and career SES turnover in your agency to the following factors? *(Check one box in each row.)*

FACTORS	Little or no extent (1)	Some extent (2)	Moderate extent (3)	Great extent (4)	Very great extent (5)	No basis to judge/ Not applicable (6)
PAS						
1. Burnout N=166	54 45.8%	25 21.2%	23 19.5%	9 7.6%	7 5.9	48
2. Stress on personal/family life N=165	38 31.4%	28 23.1%	26 21.5%	17 14.0%	12 9.9	44
3. Better job offer N=166	25 19.8%	22 17.5%	27 21.4%	34 27.0%	18 14.3%	40
4. Pursue career opportunity N=166	26 20.8%	15 12.0%	35 28.0%	32 25.6%	17 13.6%	41
5. Higher salary elsewhere N=164	25 19.8%	21 16.7%	27 21.4%	29 23.0%	24 19.0%	38
6. Policy disagreement N=166	66 54.5%	34 28.1%	14 11.6%	5 4.1%	2 1.7%	45
7. Interpersonal conflict N=166	48 40.7%	44 37.3%	17 14.4%	6 5.1%	3 2.5%	48
8. Time-limited appointment or change of administration N=165	23 18.5%	8 6.5%	22 17.7%	23 18.5%	48 38.7%	41
9. Other *(please specify.)* N=16	0 0.0%	0 0.0%	0 0.0%	0 0.0%	2 100.0%	14
NONCAREER SES						
1. Burnout N=153	39 47.6%	21 25.6%	14 17.1%	7 8.5%	1 1.2%	71
2. Stress on personal/family life N=152	23 27.4%	30 35.7%	18 21.4%	9 10.7%	4 4.8%	68
3. Better job offer N=154	11 12.4%	16 18.0%	20 22.5%	23 25.8%	19 21.3%	65
4. Pursue career opportunity N=153	13 14.8%	11 12.5%	24 27.3%	23 26.1%	17 19.3%	65
5. Higher salary elsewhere N=153	16 18.2%	15 17.0%	16 18.2%	20 22.7%	21 23.9%	65
6. Policy disagreement N=153	52 62.7%	19 22.9%	9 10.8%	2 2.4%	1 1.2%	70
7. Interpersonal conflict N=153	33 39.3%	26 31.0%	18 21.4%	4 4.8%	3 3.6%	69
8. Time-limited appointment or change of administration N=152	24 29.3%	10 12.2%	12 14.6%	14 17.1%	22 26.8%	70
9. Other *(please specify.)* N=26	0 0.0%	0 0.0%	0 0.0%	0 0.0%	1 100.0%	25

(QUESTION 34 CONTINUES ON NEXT PAGE.)

(QUESTION 34 CONTINUED.)

To what extent, if at all, do you attribute PAS, noncareer SES, and career SES turnover in your agency to the following factors? *(Check one box in each row.)*

FACTORS	Little or no extent (1)	Some extent (2)	Moderate extent (3)	Great extent (4)	Very great extent (5)	No basis to judge/ Not applicable (6)
CAREER SES						
1. Burnout N=163	61 50.0%	36 29.5%	20 16.4%	4 3.3%	1 0.8%	41
2. Stress on personal/family life N=163	51 41.8%	40 32.8%	23 18.9%	7 5.7%	1 0.8%	41
3. Better job offer N=163	22 18.0%	30 24.6%	20 16.4%	30 24.6%	20 16.4%	41
4. Pursue career opportunity N=163	20 16.3%	33 26.8%	27 22.0%	28 22.8%	15 12.2%	40
5. Higher salary elsewhere N=163	28 23.0%	26 21.3%	19 15.6%	26 21.3%	23 18.9%	41
6. Policy disagreement N=163	75 61.5%	30 24.6%	11 9.0%	5 4.1%	1 0.8%	41
7. Interpersonal conflict N=160	54 46.2%	44 37.6%	13 11.1%	3 2.6%	3 2.6%	43
8. Other *(please specify.)* _____ N=15	0 0.0%	0 0.0%	2 66.7%	1 33.3%	0 0.0%	12

35. How often, if at all, do you have working contact (i.e., by phone or in meetings) with PAS executives in other agencies of the federal government? *(Check one.)*

    N=178

    1. ☐ No phone calls or meetings   10 / 5.6%

    2. ☐ Fewer than 3 contacts   48 / 27.0%
           per month

    3. ☐ 1 to 3 contacts per week   58 / 32.6%

    4. ☐ 4 to 6 contacts per week   24 / 13.5%

    5. ☐ 7 to 9 contacts per week   6 / 3.4%

    6. ☐ 10 or more contracts   32 / 18.0%
           per week

36. Are you currently or have you been involved in a formal or informal interagency working group? *(Check one.)*

    N=179

    1. ☐ Yes   138 / 77.1%

    2. ☐ No   41 / 22.9%

C. Accountability

37. To what extent, if at all, do you, as a PAS, feel you are held accountable for meeting the following objectives <u>for your organizational unit</u>? *(Check one box in each row.)*

OBJECTIVES	Very great extent (1)	Great extent (2)	Moderate extent (3)	Some extent (4)	Little or no extent (5)	No basis to judge/ Not applicable (6)
1. Formulating policy N=178	126 74.1%	26 15.3%	8 4.7%	6 3.5%	4 2.4%	8
2. Improving operations N=176	111 64.5%	26 15.1%	19 11.0%	11 6.4%	5 2.9%	4
3. Improving the unit's capacity to perform its mission (e.g., staff development, systems, processes) N=178	99 56.6%	36 20.6%	27 15.4%	8 4.6%	5 2.9%	3
4. Meeting measurable program outcome indicators (e.g., quality, cost, timeliness, customer satisfaction) N=178	95 55.2%	31 18.0%	23 13.4%	12 7.0%	11 6.4%	6
5. Meeting affirmative action goals in hiring, promoting, and retention in the higher grades (GS 13-15, SES) N=177	84 50.6%	33 19.9%	21 12.7%	10 6.0%	18 10.8%	11
6. Long range planning N=177	92 53.5%	33 19.2%	27 15.7%	11 6.4%	9 5.2%	5
7. Representing my agency to the public N=178	123 70.3%	24 13.7%	21 12.0%	6 3.4%	1 0.6%	3
8. Establishing working relationships with other federal agencies N=178	86 50.0%	29 16.9%	33 19.2%	14 8.1%	10 5.8%	6
9. Other *(please specify.)* _____ N=7	4 100.0%	0 0.0%	0 0.0%	0 0.0%	0 0.0%	3

38. How effective or ineffective is the SES performance plan in holding noncareer and career SES executives accountable <u>in your organizational unit</u>? *(Check one box in each row.)*

	Very effective (1)	Generally effective (2)	Neither effective nor ineffective (3)	Generally ineffective (4)	Very ineffective (5)	No basis to judge (6)
1. Noncareer SES N=156	8 9.2%	37 42.5%	16 18.4%	16 18.4%	10 11.5%	69
2. Career SES N=171	20 14.6%	61 44.5%	21 15.3%	22 16.1%	13 9.5%	34

D. Job Satisfaction

39. Please rate the general level of satisfaction or dissatisfaction _you_ derive from the following aspects of your PAS service.
    (Check one box in each row.)

	Very greatly satisfied (1)	Generally satisfied (2)	Neither satisfied nor dissatisfied (3)	Generally dissatisfied (4)	Very dissatisfied (5)	No basis to judge/ Not applicable (6)
Internal Agency Relationships						
1. Working with other political appointees N=176	51 29.5%	89 51.4%	25 14.5%	8 4.6%	0 0.0%	3
2. Working with career SES appointees N=172	48 29.4%	98 60.1%	13 8.0%	3 1.8%	1 0.6%	9
3. The reaction of career SES executives to policy direction N=174	35 21.9%	98 61.3%	18 11.3%	8 5.0%	1 0.6%	14
4. Ability to reassign or dismiss civil service employees N=176	0 0.0%	7 4.7%	33 22.3%	56 37.8%	52 35.1%	28
Internal Agency Operations						
5. Improving my organizational unit's operations N=178	62 35.8%	86 49.7%	11 6.4%	11 6.4%	3 1.7%	5
6. Managing a large government organization or program N=178	68 44.2%	60 39.0%	19 12.3%	5 3.2%	2 1.3%	24
7. Ability to control my agency's or unit's budget N=178	37 22.8%	48 29.6%	32 19.8%	37 22.8%	8 4.9%	16
8. Agency quality of life N=178	48 27.7%	73 42.2%	29 16.8%	18 10.4%	5 2.9%	5
9. Time available to think creatively about the issues with which I have to deal N=178	22 12.5%	80 45.5%	22 12.5%	45 25.6%	7 4.0%	2
External Government and Public Relationships						
10. Dealing with the White House N=178	31 20.7%	69 46.0%	31 20.7%	15 10.0%	4 2.7%	28
11. Dealing with the OMB N=177	13 9.0%	69 47.9%	34 23.6%	24 16.7%	4 2.8%	33
12. Dealing with the OPM N=177	8 6.4%	42 33.6%	51 40.8%	18 14.4%	6 4.8%	52
13. Dealing with the Congress N=177	16 9.6%	87 52.1%	26 15.6%	29 17.4%	9 5.4%	10
14. Dealing with organized groups that oppose agency policy N=178	5 3.4%	70 47.0%	50 33.6%	19 12.8%	5 3.4%	29
15. Dealing with the news media N=178	15 9.1%	80 48.5%	45 27.3%	20 12.1%	5 3.0%	13

(QUESTION 39 CONTINUES ON NEXT PAGE.)

(QUESTION 39 CONTINUED.)

Please rate the general level of satisfaction or dissatisfaction you derive from the following aspects of your PAS service. *(Check one box in each row.)*

	Very greatly satisfied (1)	Generally satisfied (2)	Neither satisfied nor dissatisfied (3)	Generally dissatisfied (4)	Very dissatisfied (5)	No basis to judge/ Not applicable (6)
General Governing Issues						
16. Implementing the President's policy objectives N=178	53 34.2%	72 46.5%	25 16.1%	3 1.9%	2 1.3%	23
17. Dealing with challenging and interesting problems N=179	116 65.2%	60 33.7%	1 0.6%	1 0.6%	0 0.0%	1
18. The pace of government decisionmaking N=177	10 5.7%	49 28.2%	24 13.8%	75 43.1%	16 9.2%	3
Career/Personal Issues						
19. Meeting and working with stimulating people N=179	102 57.3%	66 37.1%	7 3.9%	3 1.7%	0 0.0%	1
20. Promoting my own policy objectives N=179	52 31.1%	83 49.7%	29 17.4%	3 1.8%	0 0.0%	12
21. Having an impact/making a difference N=179	97 54.2%	75 41.9%	4 2.2%	2 1.1%	1 0.6%	0
22. Enhancing my long-term career opportunities N=179	27 18.0%	49 32.7%	69 46.0%	5 3.3%	0 0.0%	29
23. The amount of time my job requires N=178	23 13.0%	89 50.3%	34 19.2%	26 14.7%	5 2.8%	1
24. My current salary N=177	12 6.8%	85 48.3%	43 24.4%	26 14.8%	10 5.7%	1
25. The impact of my job on my personal/family life N=178	13 7.3%	80 45.2%	33 18.6%	41 23.2%	10 5.6%	1
26. Public perception of my role as a federal manager N=179	31 18.2%	100 58.8%	24 14.1%	10 5.9%	5 2.9%	9
OTHER						
27. Other *(please specify.)* N=3	1 50.0%	0 0.0%	0 0.0%	0 0.0%	1 50.0%	1

40. To you, how important, or not, is each of the following goals for your <u>agency</u>?   *(Check one box in each row.)*

GOALS	Very greatly important (1)	Greatly important (2)	Moderately important (3)	Somewhat important (4)	Little or no importance (5)	No basis to judge/ Not applicable (6)
1. Improving efficiency of my agency's operations N=179	110 61.8%	48 27.0%	15 8.4%	3 1.7%	2 1.1%	1
2. Improving effectiveness of my agency N=178	124 69.7%	41 23.0%	9 5.1%	2 1.1%	2 1.1%	0
3. Developing new policies and/or regulations N=178	81 46.6%	59 33.9%	25 14.4%	7 4.0%	2 1.1%	4
4. Reducing regulations N=179	41 25.3%	42 25.9%	46 28.4%	20 12.3%	13 8.0%	17
5. Changing public perceptions of my agency N=178	72 41.9%	49 28.5%	32 18.6%	10 5.8%	9 5.2%	6
6. Enhancing size or scope of my agency N=178	16 9.5%	17 10.1%	32 19.0%	20 11.9%	83 49.4%	10
7. Improving public perceptions of civil servants N=178	47 28.0%	40 23.8%	45 26.8%	17 10.1%	19 11.3%	10
8. Other *(please specify.)* _____ _____ N=2	1 100.0%	0 0.0%	0 0.0%	0 0.0%	0 0.0%	1

41. Recognizing the complexity of government management, how easy or difficult are the following aspects of your job?
(Check one box in each row.)

ASPECTS OF JOB	Very easy (1)	Generally easy (2)	Neither easy nor difficult (3)	Generally difficult (4)	Very difficult (5)	No basis to judge/ Not applicable (6)
1. Managing a government organization or program N=177	16 9.6%	39 23.4%	35 21.0%	62 37.1%	15 9.0%	10
2. The substantive details of the policies with which I deal N=177	12 6.9%	51 29.5%	42 24.3%	53 30.6%	15 8.7%	4
3. The decision-making procedures of my department or agency N=177	16 9.0%	44 24.9%	42 23.7%	63 35.6%	12 6.8%	0
4. Directing senior career employees N=177	23 13.9%	79 47.6%	41 24.7%	21 12.7%	2 1.2%	11
5. The informal network within my political party that affects the work of my agency or department N=174	10 11.0%	21 23.1%	43 47.3%	13 14.3%	4 4.4%	83
6. The bipartisan networks that affect the work of my agency or department N=174	10 8.3%	32 26.4%	47 38.8%	26 21.5%	6 5.0%	53
7. The federal budget process N=176	5 3.3%	19 12.6%	35 23.2%	69 45.7%	23 15.2%	25
8. Defending my budget N=175	12 7.9%	46 30.3%	37 24.3%	46 30.3%	11 7.2%	23
9. Defending my programs N=174	12 7.6%	63 39.9%	41 25.9%	36 22.8%	6 3.8%	16
10. Dealing with the White House N=176	17 12.2%	53 38.1%	47 33.8%	18 12.9%	4 2.9%	37
11. Dealing with the OMB N=175	6 4.1%	50 34.2%	48 32.9%	35 24.0%	7 4.8%	29
12. Dealing with the OPM N=175	7 6.3%	27 24.1%	54 48.2%	18 16.1%	6 5.4%	63
13. Dealing with the Congress N=175	8 4.9%	52 31.7%	46 28.0%	38 23.2%	20 12.2%	11
14. Dealing with interest groups N=176	7 4.5%	47 30.3%	51 32.9%	40 25.8%	10 6.5%	21
15. Dealing with the news media N=177	12 7.4%	53 32.7%	61 37.7%	30 18.5%	6 3.7%	15
16. Dealing with changing expectations of public officials N=173	4 2.9%	23 16.8%	64 46.7%	40 29.2%	6 4.4%	36
17. Other *(Please specify.)* _____ _____ N=3	0 0.0%	2 100.0%	0 0.0%	0 0.0%	0 0.0%	1

42. Based on your own experience and observations, should more or fewer positions in your agency, and governmentwide, be filled by PAS, noncareer SES, career SES, and/or Schedule C employees, or should the numbers remain about the same? *(Check one box in each row.)*

	Many more positions (1)	More positions (2)	Remain the same (3)	Fewer positions (4)	Many fewer positions (5)	Don't know/ No opinion (6)
YOUR AGENCY						
1. PAS N=178	3 1.8%	16 9.5%	136 81.0%	11 6.5%	2 1.2%	10
2. Noncareer SES N=170	1 0.7%	45 32.6%	71 51.4%	15 10.9%	6 4.3%	32
3. Career SES N=174	3 1.9%	53 33.3%	72 45.3%	25 15.7%	6 3.8%	15
4. Schedule C N=172	1 0.7%	32 22.1%	83 57.2%	23 15.9%	6 4.1%	27
GOVERNMENTWIDE						
1. PAS N=173	4 3.1%	19 14.8%	73 57.0%	29 22.7%	3 2.3%	45
2. Noncareer SES N=169	2 1.9%	31 29.2%	42 39.6%	26 24.5%	5 4.7%	63
3. Career SES N=171	2 1.7%	33 28.2%	50 42.7%	25 21.4%	7 6.0%	54
4. Schedule C N=169	1 0.9%	21 18.9%	51 45.9%	28 25.2%	10 9.0%	58

E. Future Employment Options and Intentions

43. Following the end of the current administration, if you were asked to continue your federal government PAS service, which of the following might you choose? *(Check all that apply.)*

   N=176   (Note: Percentages total to more than 100% due to multiple responses.)

   1. ☐ Decline — 15 / 8.5%
   2. ☐ Accept same position — 101 / 57.4%
   3. ☐ Accept different position — 58 / 33.0%
   4. ☐ Don't know — 41 / 23.3%

44. If you were to continue your federal service, would you be interested in pursuing career status? *(Check one.)*

   N=170

   1. ☐ Definitely yes — 14 / 8.6%
   2. ☐ Probably yes — 22 / 13.5%
   3. ☐ Undecided — 13 / 8.0%
   4. ☐ Probably no — 37 / 22.7%
   5. ☐ Definitely no — 77 / 47.2%
   6. ☐ No basis to judge — 7

45. Which of the following categories best describe where you are likely to work after your PAS service? *(Check all that apply.)*

N=146 (Note: Percentages total to more than 100% due to multiple responses.)

1. ☐ Federal government — 25 / 17.1%
2. ☐ State or local government — 8 / 5.5%
3. ☐ Business or corporate sector — 67 / 45.9%
4. ☐ Self-employed — 55 / 37.7%
5. ☐ College, university or research organization — 54 / 37.0%
6. ☐ Political party — 2 / 1.4%
7. ☐ Think tank — 25 / 17.1%
8. ☐ Interest group (e.g., Business Round Table, VFW, etc.) *(Please specify.)* — 12 / 8.2%
9. ☐ Law firm — 32 / 21.9%
10. ☐ Labor union — 0 / 0.0%
11. ☐ Nonprofit organization — 29 / 19.9%
12. ☐ Retirement/Do not plan to work *(Skip to Question 47.)* — 21 / 14.4%
13. ☐ Other *(Please specify.)* — 4 / 2.7%
14. ☐ Don't know/undecided — 24 / 16.4%

46. How much of an increase or decrease in salary, if either, do you expect in the position immediately following your current PAS position? *(Check one.)*

N=165

1. ☐ Some decrease — 20 / 14.5%
2. ☐ No change — 28 / 20.3%
3. ☐ 1% to 50% increase — 40 / 29.0%
4. ☐ 51% to 100% increase — 21 / 15.2%
5. ☐ 101% to 200% increase — 23 / 16.7%
6. ☐ 201% to 300% increase — 3 / 2.2%
7. ☐ More than 300% increase — 3 / 2.2%
8. ☐ No basis to judge/Not applicable — 27

III. Personal Background

47. Which of the following categories best describes your age group? *(Check one.)*

N=178

1. ☐ Under 30 — 0 / 0.0%
2. ☐ 30 - 35 — 3 / 1.7%
3. ☐ 36 - 40 — 15 / 8.4%
4. ☐ 41 - 45 — 17 / 9.6%
5. ☐ 46 - 50 — 28 / 15.7%
6. ☐ 51 - 55 — 32 / 18.0%
7. ☐ 56 - 60 — 26 / 14.6%
8. ☐ 61 - 65 — 30 / 16.9%
9. ☐ 66 - 70 — 20 / 11.2%
10. ☐ Over 70 — 7 / 3.9%

48. What is your sex?   *(Check one.)*

    N=180

    1. ☐   Female   31 / 17.2%

    2. ☐   Male   149 / 82.8%

49. What is your marital status?   *(Check one.)*

    N=180

    1. ☐   Married   ⎫   154 / 85.6%
                            ⎬ *(Continue to*
    2. ☐   Separated   ⎭ *Question 50.)*   3 / 1.7%

    3. ☐   Widowed   ⎫   2 / 1.1%

    4. ☐   Divorced   ⎬ *(Skip to*   11 / 6.1%
                            ⎪ *Question 53.)*
    5. ☐   Single   ⎭   10 / 5.6%

50. Which of the following best describes your spouse's
    employment status, if any?   *(Check one.)*

    N=156

    1. ☐   Employed in the federal   15 / 9.6%
           government *(Continue to*
           Question 51.)

    2. ☐   Employed but <u>not</u> ⎫   69 / 44.2%
           by the federal   ⎬ *(Skip to*
           government   ⎭ *Question 53.)*

    3. ☐   Not employed   72 / 46.2%

51. In which of the following branches of the federal
    government is your spouse employed?   *(Check one.)*

    N=16

    1. ☐   The executive branch   10 / 62.5%

    2. ☐   The judicial branch   1 / 6.3%

    3. ☐   The Congress   1 / 6.3%

    4. ☐   The legislative branch   1 / 6.3%
           other than Congress

    5. ☐   Other *(Please specify.)*   3 / 18.8%
           _____

52. At which of the following levels is your spouse
    employed in the federal government?   *(Check one.)*

    N=16

    1. ☐   PAS   2 / 12.5%

    2. ☐   Noncareer SES   0 / 0.0%

    3. ☐   Career SES   1 / 6.3%

    4. ☐   Schedule C   2 / 12.5%

    5. ☐   Other *(Please specify.)*   11 / 68.8%
           _____

53. Which of the following best describes your racial/ethnic
    heritage?   *(Check all that apply.)*

    N=179   **(Note: Percentages total to more than
                 100% due to multiple responses.)**

    1. ☐   Do not care to respond   11 / 6.1%

    2. ☐   African American   8 / 4.4%

    3. ☐   American Indian/Inuit   3 / 1.7%

    4. ☐   Asian American   1 / 0.6%

    5. ☐   Caucasian   145 / 81.0%

    6. ☐   Hispanic, Caucasian   11 / 6.1%

    7. ☐   Hispanic, African American   0 / 0.0%

    8. ☐   Other *(Please specify.)*   4 / 2.2%
           _____

54. With which political party, if any, are you currently registered or affiliated? *(Check one.)*

N=178

1. ☐ Republican   125 / 70.2%

2. ☐ Democratic   32 / 18.0%

3. ☐ Independent   11 / 6.2%

4. ☐ Other *(Please specify.)*   0 / 0%

     _____

5. ☐ Not registered/Unaffiliated   10 / 5.6%

55. What is the highest level of education or degree that you have attained? *(Check only one and note area of concentration or major, where applicable.)*

N=179

1. ☐ High school graduate or equivalent   1 / 0.6%

2. ☐ Graduated from a 4-year college   38 / 21.2%

3. ☐ Master's degree   41 / 22.9%

     _____
              (Area)

4. ☐ Doctorate/Law/Medical degree   95 / 53.1%

     _____
       (Area of specialization)

5. ☐ Other *(Please specify.)*   4 / 2.2%

     _____

56. What was your undergraduate major or area? *(Enter major or area. If not applicable, enter "N/A".)*

N=164

Liberal Arts	33 / 20.1%
Government/Political Science	32 / 19.5%
Science	28 / 17.1%
Engineering	26 / 15.9%
Accounting/Finance/Business/ Economics	23 / 14.0%
History	19 / 11.6%
Other	3 / 1.8%

     _____
        (Major/area)

IV. Other Comments

57. If you have any comments on this survey, or on questions we should have asked but did not, please enter them in the space provided below. Also, if there are any other areas of your PAS service on which you would like to comment, or if you have any suggestions for changes in working relationships with senior career executives, please use the space below.

58. If you would be willing to be interviewed in connection with this survey, please enter your name and phone number below.

Name: _____

Telephone number: (_____) _____
                 (Area code)   *(Number)*

Thank you for your time and care in filling out this questionnaire.

GGD/966512/5-92

Appendix 3
Pre-Survey Interviewees

Theodore C. Barreaux—Counselor to the Comptroller General, General Accounting Office (extensive career as both career federal executive and political appointee; transition team member in Bush administration)

Mark Goldstein—Staff, Senate Governmental Affairs Committee

Charles Grizzle—Senior Vice President, The Jefferson Group (former PAS, Assistant Administrator for Administration and Resources Management, EPA)

Kirke Harper—Director of Human Resources Development Group, Office of Personnel Management (Career SES)

Rosslyn C. Kleeman—Director, Federal Workforce Future Issues, General Accounting Office (Career SES)

Ron Klein—Staff, Senate Judiciary Affairs Committee

Sally Kraus Marshall—Director, Public Service Consortium (Career SES)

Tom McFee—Assistant Secretary for Personnel Administration, Department of Health and Human Services (Career SES)

Constance Berry Newman—Director, Office of Personnel Management (PAS, EL 2)

Roger Sperry—Director of Development and Operations, National Academy of Public Administration

Elsa Thompson—Acting Special Assistant to the President and Associate Director of Presidential Personnel, the White House (Political appointee)

Edward A. Timperlake—Assistant Secretary for Public Affairs, Department of Veterans Affairs (PAS, EL 4)

John Trattner—Vice President, Council for Excellence in Government

Judy Van Rest—Chief of Staff, Office of Personnel Management (Noncareer SES)

Alan Wendt—Ambassador, Senior Representative, Strategic Technology Policy, State Department (Career SES)

Appendix 4

PAS Survey Pre-Test Interviewees

Constance B. Harriman—Director, Export-Import Bank of the United States (EL 4)

Wade F. Horn—Commissioner, Administration for Children, Youth and Families, Department of Health and Human Services (EL 4)

Roscoe B. Starek—Commissioner, Federal Trade Commission (EL 4)

Edward T. Timperlake—Assistant Secretary for Public Affairs, Department of Veterans Affairs (EL 4)

Barbara Zartman—Deputy Director, the Peace Corps (EL 4)

Appendix 5
Post-Survey PAS Interviewees

Anonymous (1)

William P. Albrecht, Ph.D.—Commissioner, Commodity Futures Trading Commission (EL 4)

Martin L. Allday—Chair, Federal Energy Regulatory Commission (EL 3)

Michael J. Astrue, Esq.—General Counsel, Department of Health and Human Services (EL 4)

John W. Bartlett, Ph.D.—Director, Office of Civilian Radioactive Waste Management, Department of Energy (EL 4)

D. Allan Bromley, Ph.D.—Director, Science and Technology Policy, Executive Office of the President (EL 2)

Eddie F. Brown, Ph.D.—Assistant Secretary for Indian Affairs, Department of the Interior (EL 4)

Bill D. Colvin—Inspector General, NASA (EL 4)

Julian de la Rosa—Inspector General, Department of Labor (EL 4)

Dennis Devaney, Esq.—Member, National Labor Relations Board (EL 4)

Linda Fisher, Esq.—Assistant Administrator, Pesticides and Toxic Substances, Environmental Protection Agency (EL 4)

Carol Pavilack Getty—Commissioner, U.S. Parole Commission (EL 4)

Frederick P. Hitz—Inspector General, CIA (EL 4)

Frank Hodsoll—Deputy, Management, Office of Management and Budget, Executive Office of the President (EL 2)

Frank Keating—General Counsel, Department of Housing and Urban Development (EL 4)

Herbert Kouts—Board Member, Defense Nuclear Facilities Safety Board (EL 3)

Donald A. Laidlaw—Assistant Secretary, Human Resources and Administration Office, Department of Education (EL 5)

Edward J. Mazur—Controller, Office of Management and Budget, Executive Office of the President (EL 3)

S. Anthony McCann—Assistant Secretary, Finances and Information Resources Management, Department of Veterans Affairs (EL 4)

Gail C. McDonald—Vice Chair, Interstate Commerce Commission (EL 4)

Patrick McFarland—Inspector General, Office of Personnel Management (EL 4)

Susan Phillips, Ph.D.—Governor, Federal Reserve System (EL 3)

Stephen D. Potts—Director, Office of Government Ethics (EL 3)

Ivan Selin—Chair, Nuclear Regulatory Commission (EL 2)

William O. Studeman—Deputy Director, CIA (EL 3)

Pamela Talkin—Member, Federal Labor Relations Authority (EL 5)

Roland R. Vautour—Under Secretary for Small Community and Rural Development, Department of Agriculture (EL 3)

Deborah Wince-Smith—Assistant Secretary, Technology Policy Office, Technology Administration, Department of Commerce (EL 4)

Appendix 6
Supplemental Post-Survey Interviewees

Anonymous (2)

Carol A. Bonosaro—Executive Director, Senior Executive Association (Career SES)

Doc Cooke—Director, Administration and Management, Department of Defense (Career SES)

Thomas F. McFee—Assistant Secretary for Personnel Administration, Health and Human Services (Career SES)

Marvin F. Moss—Chief of Staff, Senator Paul Sarbanes

Elliot L. Richardson—Attorney in private practice (former PAS—Secretary of Health, Education, and Welfare, Attorney General, Ambassador to Great Britain, Director of Presidential Appointments, Legislative Assistant for Majority Whip)

Gerald Shaw—Counsel, lobbyist, and founding director, Senior Executive Association (Career SES)

Appendix 7
Post-Survey Interview Questions

1. Relations with careerists—have they changed over time—when you first arrived to now? How do you feel about careerists?

2. To what extent do you include careerists in policy discussions?

3. Do you have the sense that your careerists' partisan, political, or ideological views differ from your own? If so, does that make any difference in their work?

4. Do you have the sense that careerists have ever tried to sabotage your policy directives?

5. Do your careerists have close ties to Congress? Does this help or hurt your agency?

6. Do you perceive a "quiet crisis" in the career workforce? If so, to what do you attribute it?

7. What is your assessment of the quality of the workforce?

8. Describe the various sources of pressure for/against agency policy.

9. How would you characterize your relations with the Congress?

10. How would you characterize your relations with the White House?

11. To what extent does the White House intervene in agency affairs?

12. How would you characterize your relations with other PASs—in your agency, in other agencies? How much of a sense of collegiality/competition/alienation do you feel?

13. What factors do you think contribute to the relatively high rate of turnover among PAS members?

14. From your perspective, what effect does the turnover of PAS executives have on federal programs?

15. What differences, if any, do you see between the Bush and Reagan PASs?

16. In general, how do you assess the qualifications and skills of the current PASs?

17. What has been the biggest source of satisfaction in your work?

18. What has been the biggest source of frustration in your work?

19. What do you wish you had known prior to accepting nomination to a PAS position?

20. What advice would you give incoming appointees?

21. How do you assess your stress level, and that of the agency overall?

22. What originally pulled you into public service?

Notes

1. Introduction

1. The institution of political appointments has evolved into a system of some complexity and large numbers in the modern era. Located primarily in the executive branch, there are some 1,163 full-time and 1,565 part-time PAS positions, 561 high-level political positions that do not require Senate confirmation (PAs), 459 excepted political positions, 95 "other" positions, 723 positions in the Senior Executive Service, and 1,794 Schedule C positions. Additionally, there are 903 federal judgeships in the judicial branch (*The Plum Book*).

2. Appendix 1 details the trials and tribulations of efforts to gain cooperation from the Bush White House to execute the Bush PAS Survey, as well as the methodologies of the survey and interviews.

3. This particular bit of conventional wisdom happens to have solid basis in fact: Some 71 percent of Reagan's early appointees had *no* previous government experience (Newland 1983, 3).

2. Presidential Appointees in the Modern Era

1. The conservative partisan sauce deemed good for the goose is likewise good for the gander in Nathan's schema: "when the wheel of government rotates again to the liberal side on domestic issues, this is precisely what social policy liberals must do in their turn" (Nathan 1985, 376).

2. President Bill Clinton's two years of Democratic control of the Congress did not mean the end of the administrative presidency. He discovered to his chagrin, as had Jimmy Carter before him, that unified government does not equal united government. Even before the Democratic party lost both houses in 1994 the Democratic Congress could not have been expected to follow unhesitantly its president's lead in all, or even most things, given that so many of its new members came to office riding the anti-Washington wave. The House, with its gung-ho, increasingly conservative, reform-minded new class (not unlike the 1974 post-Watergate class), and the Senate, lacking a filibuster-proof majority of sixty, constituted a significant challenge to President Bill Clinton's leadership. In 1995, with both houses in Republican hands for the first time since 1955, the president might have found the administrative presidency a particularly attractive strategy.

3. Conveniently for Oliver North, the White House refused to make public the secret documents he claimed he needed for his defense. Consequently, two

major charges against him had to be dropped. This carried the added benefit to the White House of protecting Reagan and Bush from further exposure to charges of complicity that might have been found in the documents.

4. See chapter 3.

5. Administrative discretion is also within the purview of careerists; subsequently, court involvement has curtailed their power, as discussed below.

6. Discussion of this concept follows in chapter 3.

7. This group of inexperienced PASs (71 percent, 101 of 142) stands in marked contrast to the Bush PASs, of whom, according to the Bush PAS Survey, 71 of 182 had been in a PAS position in Reagan's second administration, 34 in his first, 8 each in Ford's and Nixon's, and 5 in Carter's administrations. Sixty-seven of Bush's PASs had served in at least one SES position, 58 in at least one Schedule C position, and 94 in some other type of federal (nonmilitary) employment. Additionally, 77 had moved directly from federal government service to their initial PAS job and 10 came directly from state or local government service. Pfiffner reports that of the initial Bush White House staff, 24 of 29 had previous White House experience (Pfiffner 1990, 66). Clearly, the Bush people were a group well-versed in the ways of government service.

8. R. H. Melton and Bill McAllister, "From Watergate to Whitewater, Ethics an Issue," *Washington Post,* October 21, 1996, A1.

9. Howard Kurtz. "The Big Sleazy," *Washington Post,* March 26, 1995.

10. Ibid.

11. Melton and McAllister, "From Watergate to Whitewater," A1.

12. "Nixon Suggests Vandalizing RNC Offices," *Washington Post,* February 15, 1997.

3. Politicization and Depoliticization in the Nation's Pressure Cooker

1. Over time, the presidential superstructure came to embrace the Council of Economic Advisers, the National Security Council, the President's Special Trade Representative, the Council on Environmental Quality, the Office of Science and Technology Policy, and other offices, all with sizeable staff. By 1987, the Executive Office of the President ran a budget of more than $114 million and a staff of more than sixteen hundred: 620 in the budget bureau alone and 325 in the White House proper (Smith 1988, 301).

2. See Appendix 1 for further details of negotiations with the White House over the Bush PAS Survey.

3. GAO audit in progress at the time of this writing.

4. Testimony of Hugh Heclo, U.S. Congress, House Committee on Post Office and Civil Service, Hearings on Civil Service Reform, 95th Congress, 2d Session, 1978, 339.

4. Appointments and Appointees in a Politicized Atmosphere

1. Since LBJ, though, the two positions have not been combined under one person and are now separated by law.

2. Delay and vacancies early in the administration continued throughout Bush's term. At the time of the PAS survey late in Bush's administration, June

1992, 20 percent of the PAS positions were vacant, most filled by "acting" personnel, some, PASs-in-waiting anticipating their own confirmation, others, career deputies awaiting a new boss and acting as her or his surrogate in the meantime.

3. *Washington Post*, March 2, 1993.

4. *Baltimore Sun*, April 7, 1992.

5. Ibid.

6. "Cabinet government is dictatorship," as cabinet watchers are fond of saying. When a secretary leaves, the top political level is likely to go with her or him or be replaced by the next secretary who wants to bring in her or his own people. With the low tenure of secretaries an unfortunate given, secretary choice only increases political instability and mismanagement in the agencies.

7. See chapter 9 for additional discussion of hiring and firing PASs.

8. *Washington Post*, November 27, 1996.

9. See the reports of the Volcker Commission 1989; Twentieth Century Fund Task Force 1987; National Academy of Public Administration 1980, 1983, 1985, and 1988.

10. The history of the EOP has been one of continuous growth accompanied by calls to prune that growth, particularly since its misuse during Nixon's Watergate era. Even though the White House staff shrank by more than half between the Nixon administration and the end of the Carter administration and continued to decrease in the early 1980s, the recent upward trend has lingered. The White House staff numbered about 1866 in September 1992; political and career staff in the EOP have increased 20 percent since 1986, according to OPM. This, however, does not include the staff of OMB, CEA, or NSC. Taken altogether, they number close to five thousand, not counting detailees.

There is also what is termed the "hidden White House budget" of nearly $720 million, in addition to the $280 million generally acknowledged. This comes from allocations in the budgets of the Defense Department, State Department, Coast Guard, FBI, Secret Service, National Archives, General Services Administration, and National Park Service. These agencies protect the president and vice president and their families, as well as international dignitaries; they manage diplomatic events, store presidential documents, and generally maintain the institution of the presidency. *Baltimore Sun*, December 19, 1992.

5. PAS Quality and Qualifications

1. See chapter 7 for comparable data on the Bush PASs.

2. The Council for Excellence in Government's *Prune Book* and *The 100 Toughest Technical and Scientific Jobs in Washington* do just that for a relatively small number of appointive positions.

3. See chapter 7 for Bush's PAS tenure-related factors.

4. See chapter 7 for comparable Bush PAS data.

5. *Washington Post*, April 9, 1993.

6. Additional evidence of the power of this particular special interest group came early in President Clinton's administration. On the ninety-ninth day of the media-hyped "First 100 Days," the veterans lobby forced him to reduce the dollar amount of his public-service-for-education plan (AmeriCorps) from $20,000 to

$13,000 per student, because the lobby was determined that these benefits would not surpass the GI Bill's education benefits for veterans.

6. Political-Career Relations in the Modern Era

1. On the PAS side, however, there is a pull to the bureaucracy, particularly by those experiencing frustration with the White House, lending "credence to Nixon's fear that his appointees would be captured by their departments." And despite the best efforts of the Executive Office of the President (EOP) to separate the politicians from the careerists, the Nixon appointees generally gave high marks to the civil service. So, "if confidence in the career service is one indicator of capture, Nixon's inner circle was right to worry about losing control" (Light 1987, 159–60).

2. "Quality of Work Force Seen as Not in Decline." *Washington Post*, August 12, 1992.

3. In 1991, the catch-up year, SES salaries rose between 22.2 percent (at the first level, ES-1, from $71,200 to $87,000) and 29.6 percent (at the top level, ES-6, from $83,600 to $108,300). Thereafter, the salary increase was more in line with the usual raise (e.g., 3.2 percent for 1992).

4. Clinton's youthful indiscretion, that is, committing to writing his honest feelings about the military and the draft, was a constant source of irritation to the military, both establishment and enlisted. His ongoing problems with the military weighed heavily on his presidential campaign in a time that also saw the end of the Cold War and the beginning of more serious intentions to cut the military budget. He was helped somewhat by the few top brass who came to his aid and throughout his first term he was notably deferential to military sensibilities and budget requests, with one early exception, his commitment to ending discrimination against lesbians and gay men in the military. Following the ensuing hysteria in the military and the general public, he staged a strategic retreat, leaving the matter to the courts. Regardless, distrust of him by veterans' groups and some active-duty military people continued long into his term.

7. The Bush Senate-Confirmed Presidential Appointees

1. *Washington Post*, October 3, 1992.

2. Sofaer had crafted the government's justification for the U.S. military strike on Tripoli and the economic sanctions against Libya that many think were the impetus for the Libyan attack on the airliner. Washington's anger over the questionable ethics of accepting this job caused Sofaer to drop it within several days of its becoming public in July 1993.

3. Simple transmission of completed nomination papers from the White House to the Senate can be inexplicably slow; some PASs reported a delay of as long as two months. On the Senate side, there is an automatic three-week hold on a new nomination while the nominee runs the gauntlet of courtesy meetings with senators; even then, the committee chair can hold up consideration indefinitely. Additionally, any senator can anonymously request a one-week delay in the confirmation process.

4. The author can speak from personal experience about the rigorous-to-the-point-of-imbecility security check. A one-year doctoral research fellowship with the GAO with no security clearance required fingerprinting, completion of a ten-

page form, and an hour-and-a-half personal grilling by two OPM investigators, both form and interrogators asking most of the PAS-related questions (going back fifteen years) in an atmosphere of dispassionate suspicion. It was a weird and intrusive experience, one difficult to imagine being willing to undergo to the depth required of PASs.

5. One example tells the story: The assistant secretary for health (EL 4) at HHS is responsible for a total staff of fifty thousand in a wide range of offices and departments, including the Surgeon General's Office, the Food and Drug Administration, the Centers for Disease Control and Prevention, the Indian Health Service, and the National AIDS Program.

6. The same HHS assistant secretary mentioned above oversees a budget of $20 billion.

7. There are always exceptions, of course. In August 1993 Robert Bostik, a Bush associate deputy undersecretary of labor for international labor affairs, pleaded guilty to violating federal conflict-of-interest laws. While working on the North American Free Trade Agreement he accepted an interest in a Mexican housing development. He was to receive 10 percent of the profits of a housing development. His take: between $250,000 and $1 million.

8. It is worth noting that President Bush's first public speech (to the Senior Executive Service) is often cited as a show of presidential support for the public service and its servants. He said,

> You are one of the most important groups I will ever speak to. . . . Our principles are clear. That government service is a noble calling and a public trust. I learned that from my parents at an early age, and that, I suspect is where many of you learned it as well. . . . I want to make sure that public service is valued and respected because I want to encourage America's young people to pursue careers in government. There is nothing more fulfilling than to serve your country and fellow citizens and to do it well. That's what our system of self government depends on. And I have not known a finer group of people than those I have worked with in government. (Aberbach 1991, 236)

These kind and gentle words earned Bush nothing but scorn from the die-hard Reaganites. According to John Podhoretz, Bush declared himself "Chief Clerk of the United States" by this act. Calling the public service the highest and noblest calling, as he did, was to the Reaganites and Libertarians "the rhetorical equivalent of fingernails on a blackboard. Bush . . . used those words to declare his independence from the Republican majority and his intention to throw in his lot with his true fellows." They never forgave him for this and his other grievous sin, the tax increase, and so abandoned him to his fate in the 1992 election.

9. OPM statistics indicate 20 percent women and 14 percent minority PASs as of June 30, 1992.

10. PASs hired for reasons of competence rather than political connections were not reluctant to disclose that fact with some pride in the interviews. One told how he had been interviewed by the PPO and asked whom he knew in the White House, on whose campaign he had worked, or to which candidate he had contributed. The PPO official was incredulous that his answer to all three questions was negative and finally asked, "What the hell are *you* doing here?"

8. Intrabureaucratic Issues

1. The PASs' willingness to consult with careerists on policy making (72–74 percent) closely paralleled the 78 percent of the CSESs who reported in the GAO survey that their political boss allowed them to be involved in policy formulation.

2. Early in his administration Bill Clinton was advised to find a way to fire the political IGs, nearly all of whom had been appointed by Reagan or Bush. In the summer of 1993 the unlikely team of Republican Senator Jesse Helms and Democratic Senator Christopher Dodd came up with a way to do just that: They proposed a bill establishing terms of office for political IGs. It died a quiet death.

3. See Appendix 2, Question 39, for overall rates of satisfaction and dissatisfaction on these job-related factors.

4. Other examples of PAS levels and titles can be found in table 1 and with the names of the interviewees in Appendices 3, 4, and 5. See *The Plum Book* for the most accurate and easily accessible listing of PAS levels and titles (as well as Schedule C and SES noncareer and career positions). Even it, however, is not exhaustive. As noted above, a comparison of the 1988 and 1992 editions reveals that the former contains the PASs of the judicial branch, while the latter does not.

9. Interbureaucratic Issues

1. A case in point regarding agency overlap: eleven agencies are currently engaged in global change research (e.g., greenhouse gases and global warming) at a combined budget of $1.5 billion. This includes NASA, the Tennessee Valley Authority, the Smithsonian Institution, and the departments of Agriculture, Health and Human Services, and Defense. President Clinton announced his intention to create a National Science and Technology Council to oversee the implementation of his policies across the various agencies.

2. See Thompson 1992, Lardner 1988, and Stengel 1987.

3. It is unlikely that the Clinton administration's PASs felt any differently dealing with a Republican Congress.

4. With Republicans in control of the Congress after the 1994 elections, such document demands escalated, seemingly out of control in the case of the House Resources Committee and the Department of the Interior. The agenda of Don Young (R-Alaska), committee chair, was, according to columnist Jack Anderson, to conduct a witch hunt of and to neutralize Secretary Babbitt with demands for "tedious details . . . and dubious and voluminous requests for documents." For example, Young demanded photographs taken of the secretary during any trips from 1994 onward, to no conceivable end. As the secretary responded, "I can assure you that I have aged normally during that period . . . and if there were any truly titillating photos, we both know they would have been published long before this." Perhaps Young was inspired by a "how to gum up the works" manual circulated among Republicans in 1995 that was clearly reminiscent of the notorious Malek Manuel of the Nixon administration. It advised: "Demand documents, draft tough letters, and recall (Democrats) who forced Republican administrations to spend a lot of time on their requests." Its philosophy was blatantly stated: "The more time employees of the administration have (to take) to respond to legitimate congressional requests, the less time they have to carry out their agenda" (*Washington Post*, April 1, 1996).

5. The president can make a temporary appointment of no more than eighteen months when Congress is in recess.

6. This relates to White House review of an agency's regulations. The House Government Operations Committee and the Senate Government Affairs Committee felt OMB was doing this review in secret to undermine the agencies. This was holdover suspicion from Reagan, who had used administrative delay to slow promulgation of agency regulations. Bush used a variation of this tactic. He simply sent regulations back to the agencies for revisions if he did not like them, a somewhat more aboveboard procedure. The ongoing question is the degree of sunshine in the inner workings of the executive branch, as opposed to the rulemaking-as-lawmaking that agencies do. Vice President Quayle's Competitiveness Council, discussed above, was subject to this ongoing debate due to its unilateral power to block agency regulations.

7. In the case of one PAS, the cuts were "self-inflicted." Her story is illustrative: She headed a specialized agency and alienated the PPO by choosing her own staff and ignoring its candidates. She refused to have a White House liaison until they forced someone on her and then she ignored her. She wanted to get on the Domestic Council but when the White House rebuffed her, she appealed to her friends in Congress, neglecting to tell them she had already been turned down by the White House, and so alienated her Hill support when they discovered the truth. Eventually, she had no friends left. "If you alienate the PPO, they'll get you. It may take three years, but they'll get you," was Barreaux's ominous prediction.

8. It is difficult to imagine the team orientation of George Bush allowing the independence and "disloyalty" of a type shown to succeeding president, Bill Clinton: his secretary of Defense, Les Aspin, and his military chief of staff, Colin Powell, publicly and without presidential retaliation disagreed with the president's plan to open the military to self-affirming, out-of-the-closet lesbians and gay men. The independence shown by Attorney General Janet Reno, who bucked White House reorganization plans, and Surgeon General Joycelyn Elders, who suggested that legalization of drugs should be studied, was much-remarked upon by the press and, in the latter case, prompted calls for her resignation. Clinton's response was measured and calm. His spokeswoman, Dee Dee Myers, noted that the president knew in advance of calling these individuals that they would speak their minds and he expected that controversy would occasionally follow. (Although the Republican drumbeat of demands for Elders' ouster never did let up, he only threw his old friend overboard two years later after the disastrous midterm elections and for a mild comment about sex education.)

The personality of the president, perhaps as much as his or her party's number of years in the White House, determines the degree to which those who staff the White House and executive agencies toe the party line. It will be instructive to observe the degree to which this sufferance of dissent helps or hinders development of a sense of cohesion among Clinton's PASs.

10. Conclusion and Future Directions

1. The interviews took place in the summer and early fall of 1992 in the PASs' office and at a time when the outcome of the presidential contest was far from

clear (though some PASs did intimate that they did not expect their boss, George Bush, to be returned to office).

Appendix 1

1. See Appendix 2 for the complete Bush PAS Survey with composite response set.

2. In Washington-speak, *political hack* is a term generally applied to someone who has a political job for which she or he is not qualified. Primarily agenda-driven ideologues, political hacks are thought to have little experience in government and less commitment to it or to the best administration of their agency.

3. Clinton's secretary of state, Warren Christopher, pledged that 70 percent of all ambassadorships would go to career foreign service officers and that the political appointments would be merit-based. Even the normally caustic *Post* spoke approvingly of his choices: "most of the 'political' ambassadors named so far have substantial experience in foreign policy, either from prior administrations, from academia, or from the Hill" (*Washington Post,* June 25, 1993).

4. See Appendix 2, question 28.

5. GAO was particularly interested in questions of new-PAS orientation and accountability, which are given less attention in this study.

6. Though GAO's analytical approach relies less or sometimes not at all on collapsing response categories (e.g., combining "great" with "very great" for reporting purposes), GAO initially collapsed versions of the data but was then unwilling to make available that type of analysis for this study. Eventually, and after much lengthy high-level discussion, the collapsed results were run and are reflected in this book. As part of the contract with GAO the author agreed to make it clear that "collapsing of categories [in the manner requested] is not characteristic of GAO work," even though GAO had collapsed the categories on other surveys. This reference constitutes that disclaimer.

On occasion, the collapsed categories as given by the computer printouts and reported herein differ slightly from the uncollapsed version of the survey, which is found in Appendix 2. This is due to computer rounding.

Bibliography

Aberbach, Joel D. 1991. "The President and the Executive Branch." In Campbell and Rockman 1991, 223–47.

———. 1976. "Clashing Beliefs Within the Executive Branch: The Nixon Administration Bureaucracy." *American Political Science Review* 70, 2: 466–67.

Aberbach, Joel D., Robert D. Putnam, and Bert A. Rockman. 1981. *Bureaucrats and Politicians in Western Democracies.* Cambridge: Harvard University Press.

Aberbach, Joel D., and Bert A. Rockman. 1988. "Mandates or Mandarins? Control and Discretion in the Modern Administrative State." *Public Administration Review* 48, 2 (March/April): 606–12.

Ban, Carolyn, and Patricia Ingraham. 1990. "Short-Timers: Political Appointee Mobility and Its Impact on Political-Career Relations in the Reagan Administration." *Administration and Society* 22, 5 (May): 106–24.

Bonafede, Dom. 1987a. "The White House Personnel Office from Roosevelt to Reagan." In *The In-and-Outers: Presidential Appointees and Transient Government in Washington,* ed. G. Calvin Mackenzie, 30–59. Baltimore: Johns Hopkins University Press.

———. 1987b. "Presidential Appointees: The Human Dimension." In *The In-and-Outers: Presidential Appointees and Transient Government in Washington,* ed. G. Calvin Mackenzie, 120–40. Baltimore: Johns Hopkins University Press.

Brauer, Carl. 1987. "Tenure, Turnover, and Postgovernment Employment Trends of Presidential Employees." In *The In-and-Outers: Presidential Appointees and Transient Government in Washington,* ed. G. Calvin Mackenzie, 174–94. Baltimore: Johns Hopkins University Press.

Butler, Stuart M., Michael Sanera, and W. Bruce Weinrod, eds. 1984. *Mandate for Leadership II: Continuing the Conservative Revolution.* Washington, D.C.: The Heritage Foundation.

Campbell, Alan K. 1985. "No Permanent Damage." In *The Reagan Presidency and the Governing of America,* ed. Lester M. Salamon and Michael S. Lund, 410–13. Washington, D.C.: The Urban Institute.

Campbell, Colin. 1991. "The White House and Cabinet Under the 'Let's Deal' Presidency." In Campbell and Rockman 1991, 185–222.

Campbell, Colin, and Bert A. Rockman. 1991. *The Bush Presidency: First Ap-*

praisals. Chatham, N.J.: Chatham House Publishers, Inc.

Cigler, Beverly A. 1990. "Public Administration and the Paradox of Professionalism." *Public Administration Review* 50, 6 (November/December): 637–53.

Cole, Richard L., and David A. Caputo. 1979. "Presidential Control of the Senior Civil Service: Assessing the Strategies of the Nixon Years." *American Political Science Review* 73, 2: 399–413.

CRS (Congressional Research Service). July 27, 1992. *Presidential Nominations to Full-Time Positions on Regulatory and Other Collegial Boards and Commissions, 1991–1992.* Washington, D.C.

———. August 19, 1987. *The Senior Executive Service (SES) Morale and Staffing Problems—A Brief Overview.* Washington, D.C.

Durant, Robert F. 1991. "Whither Bureaucratic Influence?: A Cautionary Note." *Journal of Public Administration Research and Theory* 1, 4 (October): 461–76.

———. 1990. "Beyond Fear or Favor: Appointee-Careerist Relations in the Post-Reagan Era." *Public Administration Review* 50, 3 (May/June): 319–31.

Edwards, George C. III. 1991. "George Bush and the Public Presidenty: The Politics of Inclusion." In Campbell and Rockman 1991, 129–54.

GAO (United States General Accounting Office). 1992. *SES Members' Views of the Federal Work Environment.* Washington, D.C.

———. 1990. *The Public Service: Issues Affecting Its Quality, Effectiveness, Integrity, and Stewardship.* Washington, D.C.

———. 1988. *Senior Executive Service: Executives' Perspectives on Their Federal Service.* Washington, D.C.

———. 1987a. *Senior Executive Service: Reasons Why Career Members Left in Fiscal Year 1985.* Washington, D.C.

———. 1987b. *Federal Employees: Trends in Career and Noncareer Employee Appointments in the Executive Branch.* Washington, D.C.

———. 1985. *Evaluation of Proposals to Alter the Structure of the Senior Executive Service.* Washington, D.C.

Garnett, James L. 1987. "Operationalizing the Constitution Via Administrative Reorganization: Oilcans, Trends, and Proverbs." *Public Administration Review* 47, 1 (January/February): 35–42.

Goldenberg, Edie N. 1985. "The Permanent Government in An Era of Retrenchment and Redirection." In *The Reagan Presidency and the Governing of America,* ed. Lester M. Salamon and Michael S. Lund, 381–404. Washington, D.C.: The Urban Institute.

Grace Commission, The. *The President's Private Sector Survey on Cost Control.* 1983. Washington, D.C.: U.S. Government Printing Office.

Hart, John. 1995. *The Presidential Branch: From Washington to Clinton.* 2d ed. Chatham, N.J.: Chatham House Publishers, Inc.

Heatherly, Charles L., and Burton Yale Pines. 1989. *Mandate for Leadership III: Policy Strategies for the 1990s.* Washington, D.C.: The Heritage Foundation.

Heclo, Hugh. 1987. "The In-and-Outer System: A Critical Assessment." In *The In-and-Outers: Presidential Appointees and Transient Government in Wash-*

ington, ed. G. Calvin Mackenzie, 195–218. Baltimore: Johns Hopkins University Press.

———. 1986. "Reaganism and the Search for a Public Philosophy." In *Perspectives on the Reagan Years*, ed. John L. Palmer, 31–63. Washington, D.C.: The Urban Institute.

———. 1985. "An Executive's Success Can Have Costs." In *The Reagan Presidency and the Governing of America*, ed. Lester M. Salamon and Michael S. Lund, 371–74. Washington, D.C.: The Urban Institute.

———. 1984a. "In Search of a Role: America's Higher Civil Service." In *Bureaucrats and Policy Making*, ed. Ezra Suleiman, 8–34. New York: Holes and Meier Publishers, Ltd.

———. 1984b. "A Government of Enemies?" *The Bureaucrat* 13, 3 (Fall): 12–14.

———. 1977. *A Government of Strangers: Executive Politics in Washington.* Washington, D.C.: The Brookings Institution.

Hershey, Paul, and Kenneth H. Blanchard. 1988. *Management of Organizational Behavior.* 5th ed. Englewood Cliffs, N.J.: Prentice-Hall.

Hess, Stephen. 1988. *Organizing the Presidency.* 2d ed. Washington, D.C.: The Brookings Institution.

Huddleston, Mark W. 1987. *The Government's Managers: Report of the Twentieth Century Fund Task Force on the Senior Executive Service.* New York: Priority Press Publications.

Ingraham, Patricia W. 1991. "Political Direction and Policy Change in Three Federal Governments." In Pfiffner, 1991, 180–93.

———. 1987. "Building Bridges or Burning Them? The President, the Appointees, and the Bureaucracy." *Public Administration Review* 47, 5 (September/October): 425–35.

Ingraham, Patricia W., and Carolyn Ban. 1988. "Politics and Merit: Can They Meet in a Public Service Model?" *Review of Public Personnel Administration* 8, 2 (Spring): 7–19.

———. 1986. "Models of Public Management: Are They Useful to Federal Managers in the 1980s?" *Public Administration Review* 46, 2 (March/April): 152–59.

Joyce, Philip G. 1990a. "An Analysis of the Factors Affecting the Employment Tenure of Federal Political Executives." *Administration and Society* 22, 1 (May): 127–45.

———. 1990b. "An Empirical Analysis of Tenure Among Political Executives in the U.S. Federal Government." Draft paper for Joyce 1990a.

Kelman, Steven. 1982. "Reaganism and Managing the Government." *New Leader* 65 (April 5): 14–17.

King, Anthony, and Giles Alston. 1991. "Good Government and the Politics of High Exposure." In Campbell and Rockman 1991, 249–85.

Lardner, George Jr. 1988. Conduct Unbecoming an Administration." *Washington Post National Weekly Edition*, January 3, 31–32.

Levine, Charles H. 1986. "The Federal Government in the Year 2000: Administrative Legacies of the Reagan Years." *Public Administration Review* 46, 3 (May/June): 195–206.

Light, Paul C. 1995. *Thickening Government: Federal Hierarchy and the Diffu-sion of Accountability.* Washington, D.C.: The Brookings Institution.

———. 1987. "When Worlds Collide: The Political-Career Nexus." In *The In-and-Outers: Presidential Appointees and Transient Government in Washing-ton,* ed. G. Calvin Mackenzie, 156–73. Baltimore: Johns Hopkins Univer-sity Press.

Lorentzen, Paul. 1985. "Stress in Political-Career Relations." *Public Administra-tion Review* 45, 3 (May/June): 411–14.

———. 1984. "A Time for Action." *The Bureaucrat* 13, 3 (Fall): 5–11.

Lowi, Theodore J. 1985. "Ronald Reagan—Revolutionary?" In *The Reagan Presi-dency and the Governing of America,* ed. Lester M. Salamon and Michael S. Lund, 29–56. Washington, D.C.: The Urban Institute.

Lynch, Edward J. 1991. "No, We Don't Have Too Many Political Appointees." *Government Executive* 23, 4 (April): 54–55.

Lynn, Lawrence E., Jr. 1985. "The Reagan Administration and the Renitent Bu-reaucracy." In *The Reagan Presidency and the Governing of America,* ed. Lester M. Salamon and Michael S. Lund, 339–70. Washington, D.C.: The Urban Institute.

Mackenzie, G. Calvin, ed. 1987. *The In-and-Outers: Presidential Appointees and Transient Government in Washington.* Baltimore: Johns Hopkins Univer-sity Press.

———. 1981. *The Politics of Presidential Appointments.* New York: The Free Press.

Macy, John W., Bruce Adams, and J. Jackson Walter. 1983. *America's Unelected Government: Appointing the President's Team.* Cambridge, Mass.: Ballinger.

Maranto, Robert. 1993. "Still Clashing After All These Years: Ideological Conflict in the Reagan Executive." *American Journal of Political Science* 37, 3 (Au-gust): 681–98.

———. 1991. "Does Familiarity Breed Acceptance?: Trends in Career-Noncareer Relations in the Reagan Administration." *Administration and Society* 23, 2 (August): 247–66.

Marzotto, Toni, Carolyn Ban, and Edie N. Goldenberg. 1985. "The Senior Execu-tive Service and Political Control of the Bureaucracy." In *Public Personnel Policy: The Politics of Civil Service,* ed. David Rosenbloom, 111–29. Port Washington, N.Y.: Associated Faculty Press.

McFee, Thomas S. September 24, 1991. Robert W. Jones Lecture, The American University, Washington, D.C.

Moe, Terry M. 1991. "The Politicized Presidency." In Pfiffner 1991, 135–57.

Mosher, Frederick C. 1985. "Denigration of the Public Servant." In *The Reagan Presidency and the Governing of America,* ed. Lester M. Salamon and Michael S. Lund, 405–09. Washington, D.C.: The Urban Institute.

———. 1968. *Democracy in the Public Service.* New York: Oxford University Press.

Mosher, Frederick C., et al. 1974. *Watergate: Implications for Responsible Gov-ernment.* New York: Basic Books.

NAPA (National Academy of Public Administration). 1992. *Beyond Distrust: Building Bridges Between Congress and the Executive.* Washington, D.C.

———. 1988. *The Executive Presidency: Federal Management For the 1990s.* Washington, D.C.

———. 1985. *Leadership in Jeopardy: The Fraying of the Presidential Appointments System.* Washington, D.C.

———. 1980. *A Presidency for the Eighties.* Washington, D.C.

Nathan, Richard P. 1986. "Institutional Change Under Reagan." In *Perspectives on the Reagan Years,* ed. John L. Palmer, 121–45. Washington, D.C.: The Urban Institute.

———. 1985. "Political Administration Is Legitimate." In *The Reagan Presidency and the Governing of America,* ed. Lester M. Salamon and Michael S. Lund, 375–79. Washington, D.C.: The Urban Institute.

———. 1975. *The Plot That Failed: Nixon and the Administrative Presidency.* New York: Wiley and Sons, Inc.

Newland, Chester A. 1985. "Executive Office Policy Apparatus: Enforcing the Reagan Agenda." In *The Reagan Presidency and the Governing of America,* ed. Lester M. Salamon and Michael S. Lund, 135–68. Washington, D.C.: The Urban Institute.

———. 1983. "A Mid-Term Appraisal—the Reagan Presidency: Limited Government and Political Administration." *Public Administration Review* 43, 1 (January/February): 1–21.

O'Toole, Laurence J. 1987. "Doctrines and Developments: Separation of Powers, the Politics-Administration Dichotomy, and the Rise of the Administrative State." *Public Administration Review* 47, 1 (January/February): 17–23.

Palmer, John L., ed. 1986. *Perspectives on the Reagan Years.* Washington, D.C.: The Urban Institute.

PAR (Public Administration Review). 1991. "The Public Administration of James Q. Wilson: A Symposium on Bureaucracy." *Public Administration Review* 51, 3 (May/June): 193–201.

Patterson, Bradley H. 1988. *The Ring of Power: The White House Staff and Its Expanding Role in Government.* New York: Basic Books, Inc.

Pfiffner, James P. 1994. *The Modern Presidency.* New York: St. Martin's Press.

———. 1991. "Can the President Manage the Government? Should He?" In *The Managerial Presidency,* ed. Pfiffner, 1–16. Pacific Grove, Calif.: Brooks/Cole Publishing Co.

———. 1990. Establishing the Bush Presidency." *Public Administration Review* 50, 1 (January/February): 64–73.

———. 1988. *The Strategic Presidency: Hitting the Ground Running.* Chicago: Dorsey Press.

———. 1987a. "Nine Enemies and One Ingrate: Political Appointments During Presidential Transitions." In *The In-and-Outers: Presidential Appointees and Transient Government in Washington,* ed. G. Calvin Mackenzie, 60–76. Baltimore: Johns Hopkins University Press.

———. 1987b. "Strangers in a Strange Land: Orienting New Presidential Appointees." In *The In-and-Outers: Presidential Appointees and Transient*

Government in Washington, ed. G. Calvin Mackenzie, 141–55. Baltimore: Johns Hopkins University Press.

———. 1987c. "Political Appointees and Career Executives: The Democracy-Bureaucracy Nexus in the Third Century." *Public Administration Review* 47, 1 (January/February): 57–64.

———. 1985. "Political Public Administration." *Public Administration Review* 45, 2 (March/April): 352–56.

Rector, Robert, and Michael Sanera, eds. 1987. *Steering the Elephant: How Washington Works.* New York: Universe Books.

Rehfuss, John. 1973. *Public Administration as Political Process.* New York: Charles Scribner's Sons.

Riccucci, Norma M. 1995. "Execucrats, Politics, and Public Policy: What Are the Ingredients for Successful Performance in the Federal Government?" *Public Administration Review* 55, 3 (May/June): 219–30.

Richardson, Elliot L., and James P. Pfiffner. 1991. "Political Appointees: Fewer Is Better." *Government Executive* 23, 6 (June): 56–58.

Rockman, Bert A. "The Leadership Style of George Bush." In Campbell and Rockman 1991, 1–35.

Rosen, Bernard. 1989. "Revitalizing the Federal Civil Service." *Public Administration Review* 49, 5 (September/October): 501–06.

Rosenbloom, David. 1983. "Public Administration Theory and the Separation of Powers." *Public Administration Review* 43, 3 (May/June): 219–27.

Rourke, Francis E. 1991a. "American Bureaucracy in a Changing Political Setting." *Journal of Public Administration Research and Theory* 1, 2 (January): 111–29.

———. 1991b. "Presidentializing the Bureaucracy: From Kennedy to Reagan." In *The Managerial Presidency,* ed. James P. Pfiffner, 123–34. Pacific Grove, Calif.: Brooks/Cole Publishing Co.

———. 1981. "Grappling with the Bureaucracy." In Arnold J. Meltsner, *Politics and the Oval Office: Towards Presidential Governance,* 123–40. San Francisco: Institute for Contemporary Studies, 1981.

Salamon, Lester M., and Alan J. Abramson. 1984. "Governance: The Politics of Retrenchment." In *The Reagan Record: An Assessment of America's Changing Domestic Priorities.* Ed. John L. Palmer and Isabel Sawhill, 31–68. Washington, D.C.: The Urban Institute.

Salamon, Lester M., and Michael S. Lund. 1985. *The Reagan Presidency and the Governing of America.* Washington, D.C.: The Urban Institute.

Sanera, Michael. 1984. "Techniques for Managing Policy Change." In *Mandate for Leadership II: Continuing the Conservative Revolution,* ed. Stuart M. Butler et al., 511–45. Washington, D.C.: The Heritage Foundation.

Schott, Richard L., and Dagmar S. Hamilton. 1983. *People, Positions and Power: The Political Appointments of LBJ.* Chicago: University of Chicago Press.

Seidman, Harold, and Robert Gilmour. 1986. *Politics, Position and Power: From the Positive to the Regulatory State,* 4th ed. New York: Oxford University Press.

Smith, Hedrick. 1988. *The Power Game: How Washington Works.* New York: Random House.

Stengel, Richard. 1987. "Morality Among the Supply-Siders." *Time* magazine, May 25, 18–20.

Stillman, Richard J., II. 1987. "The Constitutional Bicentennial and the Centennial of the American Administrative State." *Public Administration Review* 47, 1 (January/February): 4–8.

Sundquist, James L. 1979. "Jimmy Carter as Public Administrator: An Appraisal at Midterm." *Public Administration Review* 39, 1 (January/February): 3–11.

Thompson, Dennis F. 1992. "Paradoxes of Government Ethics." *Public Administration Review* 52, 2 (May/June): 254–59.

Thoryn, Michael. 1983. "Staying the Course: Executive Turnover—a Major Problem in Other Administrations—Is Comparatively Minor in This One." *Nation's Business* 71, 2 (February): 78–79.

Trattner, John H. 1992. *The Prune Book: The 60 Toughest Science and Technology Jobs in Washington.* Washington, D.C.: The Center for Excellence in Government.

———. 1988. *The Prune Book: The 100 Toughest Management and Policy-Making Jobs in Washington.* Washington, D.C.: The Center for Excellence in Government.

TRB from Washington. 1985. "The Curse of the Giant Muffins." *New Republic* 192, 4 (January 28).

Twentieth Century Fund Task Force. See Huddleston, Mark. 1987.

United States Government Policy and Supporting Positions (The Plum Book). 1992. U.S. Congress, Senate, Committee on Governmental Affairs. Washington, D.C.

U.S. Congress. Senate. 1992. *The Report of the Task Force on Confirmation Delay.* (February 4). Washington, D.C.

USMSPB (U.S. Merit Systems Protection Board). 1990. *Why Are Employees Leaving the Federal Government?: Results of an Exit Survey.* Washington, D.C.

———. 1989. *The Senior Executive Service: Views of Former Federal Executives.* Washington, D.C.

———. 1984. *The Senior Executive Service.* Washington, D.C.

Ventriss, Curtis. 1991. "The Challenge of Public Service: Dilemmas, Prospects, and Options." *Public Administration Review* 51, 3 (May/June): 275–79.

Volcker, Paul. 1989. *Leadership for America: Rebuilding the Public Service.* The Report of the National Commission on the Public Service ("The Volcker Report"). Lexington, Mass.: D.C. Heath and Company.

Warren, Kenneth F. 1988. *Administrative Law in the Political System.* 2d ed. St. Paul, Minn.: West Publishing Company.

Waterman, Richard W. 1989. *Presidential Influence and the Administrative State.* Knoxville: University of Tennessee Press.

Zuck, Alfred M. 1984. "Education of Political Appointees." *The Bureaucrat* 13, 3 (Fall): 15–18.

Index

Potts, Steven D., 216, 266, 276
Presidency: bureaucratization of, 66–67, 80;
    centralization of power in, 10, 53, 56,
    59–61, 64–73, 77, 80. *See also* Executive
    Office of the President
President: appointment authority of, 78,
    100, 104; cooperation with career service
    by, 20, 55; efforts of to control bureau-
    cracy, 16–20, 53–59, 59–77, 170–83; ef-
    forts of to control PASs, 107–10; involve-
    ment of in appointment process, 19, 82,
    100–01, 121–23, 226; power of to per-
    suade, 18, 81; relations of with Congress,
    56, 85; relations of with appointees,
    107–08; and strategies to promote policy
    objectives, 16–20. *See also under specific
    presidents*
Presidential appointees: and Bush PASs' ad-
    vice to successors, 274–80; carrying out
    president's agenda by, 19–20; and condi-
    tions for success in job, 134–37; differ-
    ences between Reagan's and Bush's PASs,
    217–25, 253; dismissal of, 237, 271–72,
    332–33; divided loyalties among, 101,
    107–10, 123, 141, 177; evaluation of col-
    leagues by, 178–79, 212–17, 229–35; and
    evaluation of OPM by Bush's PASs, 248;
    filtration into career ranks by, 3–4,
    140–42, 144, 152, 172, 281; growth in
    numbers of, 3–4, 111–19, 154, 166, 184,
    194, 226, 244, 281, 284, 327; job satisfac-
    tion among, 238–54; and minority PASs,
    198, 224, 331; optimal number of,
    117–20, 152, 154, 244; orientation of,
    257–58; personal characteristics of,
    122–23; and post-PAS salary expecta-
    tions, 199–201; preparation for job
    among, 122–23, 127, 172, 201–02,
    210–12, 281–82; professional background
    and qualifications of, 121–23, 127,
    197–99, 201–02; recruitment of, 149,
    209–10; relations of with Congress,
    258–61, 275; relations of with GAO,
    259–60; relations of with interest groups,
    136, 138, 216, 251, 278–79; relations of
    with media, 136, 138, 211, 216, 251, 258,
    278; relations of with OMB, 266–68; rela-
    tions of with other political executives,
    7, 146–47, 255–56, 272, 281; relations of
    with White House, 265–69; revolving
    door/post-service employment of Bush's
    PASs, 131–33, 199–205; role of in choos-
    ing subordinates, 94, 98, 100, 249–50,
    270–71, 283; and salary issues, 127–31,
    199–201, 206–07; selection of, 79–120,
    282; tenure and turnover issues of,
    124–31, 139–40, 149, 152, 172, 205–10,

282, 316, 329; women PASs, 198, 201,
    224–25, 256, 331. *See also* Political-ca-
    reer relations; *specific presidents*
Presidential Personnel Office (PPO)/White
    House Personnel Office (WHPO), 65, 86,
    109, 266, 283: recommendations for im-
    proving performance of, 120, 211–12,
    225, 253, 258, 282; role of in selecting ap-
    pointees, 90–91, 95, 249, 263, 271
Privacy Act, 30, 66
Progressive Reform Movement, 111–12
Prune Book, 134, 225, 239, 251, 329
Putnam, Robert D., 191–92, 195

Quayle, Danforth, 43, 44, 49, 204
Quayle, Marilyn Taylor, 204

Reagan, Nancy, 51
Reagan, Ronald, 46, 58, 142, 204, 206, 223:
    career-political SES positions under,
    35–36; characteristics of appointees of, 4,
    32, 41, 142, 213, 327–28; and distrust of
    bureaucracy, 124, 128, 166–67; and Iran-
    Contra, 18, 41, 55–56, 67; criteria for
    choosing appointees by, 33–34, 94; efforts
    of to control PASs, 109–10, 177; growth
    of appointees under, 35–36, 117, 328–29;
    ideological commitment of appointees
    under, 32; illegal/unethical conduct of
    appointees under, 41–42, 257; judicial ap-
    pointments by, 31; PASs' evaluations of
    careerists under, 142; PASs' support for
    agenda of, 106–07; political-career rela-
    tions under, 7, 37–38, 124–25, 174, 190,
    233, 281; political control of bureaucracy
    by, 24, 30–42, 159–60, 164, 170–71, 175,
    177; political management under, 64, 72,
    159–60; relations of with cabinet, 63–64,
    102; relations of with Congress, 39, 44;
    relations of with inspectors general, 237;
    selection of appointees by, 31–32, 63, 69,
    75, 83–84, 93–96, 99, 104, 225, 270, 284;
    as the "Teflon President," 35, 42;
    tenure/turnover of appointees under, 125;
    use of administrative strategy/presidency
    by, 10, 20, 30–42; use of executive privi-
    lege by, 31; use of appointees to promote
    policy objectives by, 33–35, 37, 45; use of
    rulemaking, 12; use of Schedule C ap-
    pointments by, 37; use of SES by, 36, 164.
    See also Bureaucrat bashing
Rector, Robert and Michael Sanera, 185
Reform 88, 170
Regan, Don, 49, 61, 64, 67
Rehfuss, John, 144
Reilly, William, 45, 204
Religious right. *See* Radical right